T0353450

2D Computer Vision

Principles, Algorithms and Applications

2D Computer Vision

Principles, Algorithms and Applications

YU-JIN ZHANG

Tsinghua University, China

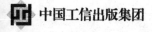中国工信出版集团

電子工業出版社·
PUBLISHING HOUSE OF ELECTRONICS INDUSTRY
http://www.phei.com.cn

World Scientific

Published by

World Scientific Publishing Co. Pte. Ltd.
5 Toh Tuck Link, Singapore 596224
USA office: 27 Warren Street, Suite 401-402, Hackensack, NJ 07601
UK office: 57 Shelton Street, Covent Garden, London WC2H 9HE

Library of Congress Cataloging-in-Publication Data
Names: Zhang, Yu-Jin, 1954– author.
Title: 2D computer vision : principles, algorithms and applications /
    Yu-Jin Zhang, Tsinghua University, China.
Other titles: Two dimensional computer vision
Description: Hackensack, NJ : World Scientific, 2022. |
    Includes bibliographical references and index.
Identifiers: LCCN 2021046188 | ISBN 9789811245084 (hardcover) |
    ISBN 9789811245091 (ebook for institutions) | ISBN 9789811245107 (ebook for individuals)
Subjects: LCSH: Computer vision.
Classification: LCC TA1634 .Z46 2022 | DDC 621.39/93--dc23
LC record available at https://lccn.loc.gov/2021046188

British Library Cataloguing-in-Publication Data
A catalogue record for this book is available from the British Library.

For any available supplementary material, please visit
https://www.worldscientific.com/worldscibooks/10.1142/12497#t=suppl

Desk Editors: Jayanthi Muthuswamy/Steven Patt

Typeset by Stallion Press
Email: enquiries@stallionpress.com

Printed in Singapore

Preface

This book is a special textbook that introduces the basic principles, typical methods, and practical techniques of 2D computer vision. It can serve as the first computer vision course material for undergraduates of related majors in university and higher-engineering colleges, and then they can study "3D Computer Vision: Principle, Algorithm, and Applications".

This book mainly covers the introductory content of computer vision from a selection of materials. This book is mainly for information majors but also useful for learners with different professional backgrounds. This book is self-contained in contents and also considers the needs of self-study readers. Readers can not only solve some specific problems in practical applications but also lay a foundation for further study and research on high-level computer vision technology.

This book pays more attention to practicality in writing. Considering that computer vision technology has been involved in many professional fields (but in which not all people are specialized in computer vision technology) in recent years, so this book does not emphasize the theoretical system too much, minimizes formula derivation, and focuses on commonly used methods. This book provides many examples through intuitive explanation to help readers understand abstract concepts. A subject index (marked in bold in the text) is given at the end of the book.

This book provides a large number of self-test questions (including hints and answers). In terms of purpose, on the one hand, it is convenient for self-study readers to judge whether they have mastered the

v

key content, and on the other hand, it is also convenient for teachers to carry out online teaching and strengthen teacher–student interaction during teaching. The types of questions are multiple-choice questions, which can be easily evaluated by a computer. In terms of content, many questions express the basic concepts in a different way and supplement the text so that learners can deepen their understanding. Some questions list descriptions that are similar but different or even opposite in meaning. Through dialectical thinking of pros and cons, learners can also deeply understand the essence. The hints have been provided for all self-test questions, allowing readers to obtain more information to further identify the meaning of the questions. At the same time, each question can be said to be divided into two levels in this way. Readers can complete the self-test after reading the hints to show that they basically understand it whereas to complete the self-test without looking at the hints indicates that they have an even better grasp.

From a structural point of view, this book has 13 chapters, two appendices, answers to self-test questions, and subject index. Under these 17 first-level headings, there are 109 second-level headings (sections) and 176 third-level headings (sub-sections). The book has a total of nearly 500,000 words (including figures, drawings, tables, formulas, etc.), a total of 278 numbered pictures, 30 numbered tables, and 497 numbered formulas. In order to facilitate teaching and understanding, this book gives a total of 121 examples of various types and 233 self-test questions (all with hints and answers). In addition, there are a catalog of more than 100 references and more than 600 terms used for indexing at the end of the book.

This book generally considers the following three aspects from the knowledge requirements of the prerequisite courses: (i) mathematics, including linear algebra and matrix theory, as well as basic knowledge of statistics, probability theory, and random modeling; (ii) computer science, including the mastery of computer software technology, understanding of computer structure system, and application of computer programming methods; (iii) electronics, including on the one hand, the characteristics and principles of electronic equipment, and on the other hand, circuit design and other content. In addition, it is best to study this book after finishing the course on signal processing.

Thanks to the editors of the publisher for carefully composing the manuscript, followed by serious review and attentive modifications.

Finally, the author thanks his wife Yun He and daughter Heming Zhang for their understanding and support in all aspects.

About the Author

 **Yu-Jin Zhang** received his Ph.D. degree in Applied Science from the State University of Liège, Liège, Belgium, in 1989. From 1989 to 1993, he was a post-doc fellow and research fellow at the Delft University of Technology, Delft, the Netherlands. In 1993, he joined the Department of Electronic Engineering, Tsinghua University, Beijing, China, where he was a professor (since 1997) and has been a tenured professor (since 2014) of Image Engineering.

He is active in the teaching and research of image engineering, has opened and taught more than 10 undergraduate and graduate courses, and published more than 550 research papers and more than 50 books. He has served as the program chair of a number of international conferences. He is a fellow and the honorary chairman of supervisors of China Society of Image and Graphics (CSIG). He is a fellow of International Society for Optical Engineering (SPIE) for achievements in image engineering.

Contents

Chapter 1

Computer Vision Fundamentals

Computer vision is an information discipline that uses computers to realize human visual functions. This book mainly introduces the basic content of computer vision, and hence can be used as an introductory textbook for learning computer vision. Some further in-depth content can be found in "3D Computer Vision: Principle, Algorithm, and Applications".

The **human visual** process can be regarded as a complex process from sensation (feeling the image obtained by 2D projection of the 3D world) to perception (cognition of the content and meaning of the 3D world from the 2D image). Computer vision refers to the realization of human visual functions with computers, hoping to make meaningful interpretations and judgments of actual targets and scenes based on the perceived images.

This chapter gives a general introduction to computer vision to lay some foundation for the study of the subsequent chapters. The sections of this chapter are arranged as follows:

Section 1.1 gives an overview of the basic concepts of human vision, the difference between visual sensation and visual perception, and the steps and processes of vision.

Section 1.2 summarizes the image foundation closely related to vision, including the representation of images and pixels, image storage and format, image display, and printing methods (including half-toning and dithering technology).

Section 1.3 discusses the relationship between computer vision system and image technology, the process of the vision system and

1

the hierarchical classification of related technologies, and introduces the connection among the three layers of image engineering technology and further classification of technical directions.

Section 1.4 introduces the structure of this book and provides a survey for each chapter. It also briefly describes the prerequisite knowledge and the suggestions for using this book.

1.1   Vision Basis

Computer vision is based on human vision and is closely related to human vision. Let us introduce and discuss human vision first.

1.1.1   Vision

Human vision is generally referred to as vision for short. **Vision** is the ability of humans to observe the world around them with their eyes and to perceive the world around them with their brains. The human visual system provides an important functional means to observe and recognize the world, and it is also the main source of information for humans from the outside world. According to statistics, about 75% of the information that humans obtain from the outside world comes from the visual system, which not only shows the huge amount of visual information but also shows that humans have a high utilization rate of visual information.

The following briefly introduces a few commonly used terms in vision:

Eye (human eye): A visual organ that responds to visible light. It mainly includes lens (eyeball), pupil, retina, and so on. The human eye is a photosensitive organ that receives incident light. In the eye-camera analogy, the lens, pupil, and retina of the human eye are usually corresponding to the lens, aperture, and imaging surface of the camera.

Retina: The last film on the peripheral wall of the human eye. It is the light-sensitive surface layer behind the eyes, containing photoreceptors and neural tissue networks. Photoreceptor cells are distributed on the retina, which convert incident light into nerve impulses and send them to the brain. The center of the retina is also called the **fovea**, where the photoreceptor cells are most concentrated, and which is the most sensitive region in the eye.

Brain (human brain): The functional unit of the human visual system that processes information. The brain uses nerve signals obtained from sensors on the retina and transmitted to the brain via the optic nerve to generate neural function patterns, which are perceived as images.

Visible light: Electromagnetic waves within a certain wavelength range that human eyes can feel. For normal people, the maximum range is between 380 and 780 nm, and the minimum range is between 400 and 700 nm. The colors felt are generally between bright blue and white to dark red.

Color: The human visual system has different perceptions of electromagnetic waves of different frequencies or different wavelengths. Color is a physical phenomenon as well as a psychological phenomenon.

Visual acuity: The spatial resolution ability of the visual organs (eyes). It is also the ability to finely distinguish the size and shape of objects. Sight is usually in units of the reciprocal of the distinguishable viewing angle (1/degree). The minimum discernible visual threshold of a normal person is about 0.5 second.

Field of view: The range of space that a person can see when his head and eyeballs are fixed, while watching the object directly in front of him. The maximum **visual field** of a normal person is about 200 degrees (width) × 135 degrees (height).

1.1.2 Visual sensation and visual perception

From a semantic point of view, it can be considered that "vision" includes two parts, "sensation" and "perception", so vision can be further divided into visual sensation and visual perception.

Human **visual feeling** mainly occurs in the process of imaging the scene on the retina. It mainly involves physics, chemistry, etc. It is to understand the basic properties of people's response to light (visible radiation) from a molecular perspective (such as brightness and color). The main concerns in visual sensation are as follows: (i) the physical properties of light, such as light quantum, light wave, and spectrum; (ii) the degree of light stimulation of visual receptors, involving photometry, eye structure, visual adaptation, visual intensity and sensitivity, and spatial-temporal characteristics of light; (iii) the sensations produced by the visual system after light acts on the retina, such as brightness and color tone.

Human **visual perception** is mainly related to how people transform an object image into a neural response after receiving a visual stimulus from the objective world, as well as the response manner and the result obtained (such as shrinking the pupil or even closing the eye when illuminated by strong light). It studies how to form people's representation of the external world space through vision (such as the size of the scene, and the smooth and rough surface), so it also has psychological factors. Visual perception is a group of activities carried out in the human brain nerve center. It organizes some scattered stimuli in the field of vision to form an entirety with a certain shape and structure. Based on this, the objective world can be understood (such as when observing a horse on the ground and a person on it, the observer could make the judgment that the person is riding a horse).

The objective matters that people perceived by using visual perception have many characteristics. After their light stimulation, the human visual system will produce different forms of response, so visual perception can be further categorized as brightness perception, color perception, shape perception, space perception, and motor perception.

From a cognitive perspective, humans not only need to obtain information from the outside world but also need to process the information to make judgments and decisions. Therefore, human visual function can also be divided into two levels: visual sensation and visual perception. Visual sensation is at a lower level, which mainly receives external stimuli. Visual perception is at a higher level, which converts external stimuli into meaningful content. Generally, visual sensation completely receives external stimuli without distinction, while visual perception must determine which parts of external stimuli should be combined into the "target" of concern, or analyze and make judgments on the nature of external stimuli, so as to understand the objective world.

1.1.3   Visual process

Vision is a complex process involving knowledge of geometry, optics, chemistry, physiology, psychology, etc. For example, referring to the

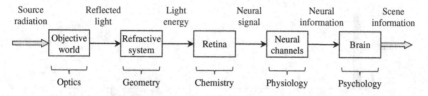

Figure 1.1. Schematic diagram of visual process and steps.

visual flow and step diagram in Figure 1.1, the process from the light source emitting radiation to the brain obtaining scene information involves a series of steps. First of all, the light source illuminates the scene in the objective world, then it is reflected (and may also be refracted and transmitted), and is entered in the human eye following certain optical laws; the radiation energy received by the human eye will pass through the refractive system inside the human eye (including the lens and pupil, as well as cornea, aqueous humor, and vitreous) according to the geometric law and is finally imaged on the retina; the photoreceptor cells on the retina are stimulated and respond, and the light energy is converted into the corresponding nerve signal according to the law of chemical reaction. The visual information contained in the stimulus is transformed into neural information; these neural signals are transmitted in the neural channels of the human body by the laws of physiology, and the information is sent to the brain under the processing of the brain's visual center, and combining with the laws of psychology. Only then can people finally obtain the cognition and interpretation of the properties of objects (such as the size, position, brightness, color, movement, trend, and situation) of the external scene.

The visual process is often broken down into three sequential steps/processes: optical process, chemical process, and neural processing process.

1. Optical process

The physical basis of the optical process is the human eye. From the imaging point of view, the eyes can be simply compared with the camera. The eye itself is a sphere with an average diameter of about 20 mm. There is a **lens** at the front of the sphere, which corresponds to the lens of the camera; the **pupil** in front of the lens corresponds to the aperture of the camera, which controls the light flux entering the human eye. There is a layer of **retina** on the inner wall of

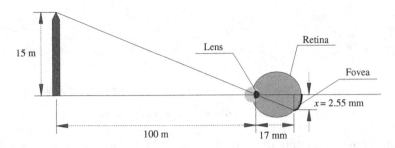

Figure 1.2.   Optical process determines image size.

the sphere, which is a thin film containing photoreceptors and neural tissue network, which corresponds to the photosensitive surface of the sensor in the camera (the film in the early camera). Outside light rays pass through the pupil and are focused on the retina by the lens to form the image. The optical process basically determines the size of the image, which can be introduced with the help of Figure 1.2.

In Figure 1.2, the light emitted from the scene first passes through the lens and then forms an image on the retina. When the refractive power of the lens changes from minimum to maximum, the distance between the focal center of the lens and the retina can change from about 17 mm to about 14 mm. For example, in Figure 1.2, the observer looks, from a distance of 100 m, at a columnar object with a height of 15 m. If x is used to represent the image size on the retina in mm, and according to the geometric relationship in the figure, $15/100 = x/17$, then $x = 2.55$ mm can be calculated.

2. Chemical process

Many light-receiving cells (light-sensitive cells) are distributed on the surface of the retina, which can receive the energy of light and form visual patterns. There are two types of light-receiving cells: **cone** cells and **rod** cells. There are about 6 million to 7 million cone cells in each eye. They are very sensitive to color. Cone cells can be divided into three types, which have different spectral response curves to incident radiation. Humans can use these cells to distinguish many details, because each cell is connected to its own nerve terminal. Cone cell vision is also called **photopic vision**, because cone cells only work in a brighter environment. The combined action of the three types of cone cells also makes people perceive color. The number of rod cells in each eye is much higher than that of cone cells, and there are approximately 75 million to 150 million rod cells on the surface of the retina. They have a large distribution region but low resolution because several rod cells are connected to the same nerve terminal. The rod cells only work in very dim light and are more sensitive to low illumination. The rod cells mainly provide the overall vision of the field of view, because there is only one type of rod cell, so there is no color perception. For example, brightly colored objects in daylight (as felt by cone cells) become colorless in moonlight because only rod cells are working in moonlight. This phenomenon is also called **scotopic vision**.

The density of cone cells is high in the fovea region. For the convenience of explanation, the fovea can be regarded as a 1.5 mm × 1.5 mm square sensor matrix. The density of cone cells in this region is about $150,000/\text{mm}^2$, so it is approximated that the number of cone cells in the fovea is about 337,000. The current electronic imaging sensor can already concentrate even higher density photoreceptive elements in its receiving array.

Both cone cells and rod cells are composed of pigment molecules, which contain light-absorbing **rhodopsin**. This substance decomposes through chemical reactions after absorbing light. Once the chemical reaction occurs, the molecules no longer absorb light. Conversely, if no further light passes through the retina, the chemical reaction proceeds in reverse direction and the molecules can work again (this conversion process often takes tens of minutes to complete). When the luminous flux increases, the number of retinal cells that are irradiated also increases, and the chemical reaction that decomposes rhodopsin increases, so that the generated neuronal signals become stronger. From this perspective, the retina can be regarded as a chemical laboratory that converts optical images into other forms of information through chemical reactions. The intensity of the signal generated everywhere in the retina reflects the light intensity of the corresponding position in the scene. It can be seen that the chemical process basically determines the brightness or color of the image.

3. Neuron processing

Neural processing is a process carried out in the nervous system in the center of the brain. With the help of **synapses**, each retinal receiving

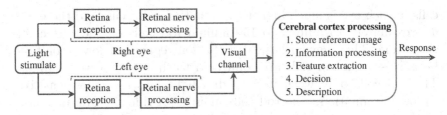

Figure 1.3.   Visual process flow diagram.

unit is connected to a neuron cell. Each neuron cell connects with other cells through other synapses to form an optical neural network. The optical neural network is further connected to the lateral regions of the brain and to the **striate cortex** in the brain. There, the sensory response to the light stimulus undergoes a series of processing to finally form the appearance of the scene, thereby transforming the sensation of light into the perceptual response to the scene. The processing of the cerebral cortex has to complete a series of tasks, from image storage to response and decision-making based on the image.

The above three processes constitute the entire visual process, and the overall flow diagram can be seen in Figure 1.3.

The visual process starts when the light source stimulates the human eye. The light is reflected by the scene and enters the left and right eyes when the visual receptors simultaneously act on the retina to cause visual sensation. The nerve impulse generated by light stimulation on the retina after neural processing is transmitted out of the eye along the optic nerve fiber, and is transmitted to the cerebral cortex through the visual channel for processing and finally causes visual perception, or the brain responds to light stimulation to form an image of the scene and provides explanation.

1.2   Vision and Image

A visual object is an image directly felt by the human eye, derived from an image obtained from a scene in the objective world, and is generally called a continuous image. Continuous here means that the image is densely valued in space and brightness. Continuous images are also called analog images, and the corresponding ones are digital images or discrete images. Discrete here means that the image is sampled intermittently in space and brightness. The processing and manipulation of digital images with computers are often collectively referred to as digital image technology. Because the objects that computers can operate are all digital, digital image technology is now directly called image technology, and digital images are also directly called images.

Computer vision needs to be realized by many image technologies. The objective world is three-dimensional (3D) in space, but most imaging devices project the 3D world onto a two-dimensional (2D) image plane, so the resulting image is 2D. 2D computer vision is basically based on various 2D image techniques.

In the following, let's first look at how to define and represent the image and its basic unit, pixel, and introduce image storage and image file format, as well as image display and printing methods. It will be combined with the introduction of the half-toning technique and dithering technique used in printing to further grasp the understanding of image space and amplitude (pixel gray level).

1.2.1 Images and digital images

An **image** can be defined as an entity that is obtained by observing the objective world in different forms and methods with various observation systems, and can directly or indirectly act on the human eye and thereby produce visual perception. For example, the human visual system is an observation system, and the image obtained through it is the image formed by the objective scene in the human mind. Visual information comes from images, where images are broad, such as photos, paintings, sketches, animations, and videos. The image contains a lot of information, seeing is better than hearing, a picture worth a thousand words, etc., illustrate this fact.

An image can generally be represented by a 2D function $f(x, y)$ or a 2D array in a computer, where x and y represent the position of a coordinate point in 2D space XY, and f represents the value of a certain property F of the image at point (x, y). For example, commonly used images are generally gray-level images; at this time, f represents the gray-level value. When imaging with visible light, the gray-level value corresponds to the observed brightness of the objective scene.

The concept of image has been expanded in recent years. Although generally speaking, images often refer to 2D images, 3D images, **stereo images**, color images, multi-spectral images, and multi-view images are also more and more common. Although generally speaking, an image often refers to a single still image, image sequences, moving images (such as TV and video), etc., have also been used more and more extensively. Although the image is usually displayed in the form of a gray dot matrix corresponding to the amount of radiation, the gray level of the image may also represent the distance or depth value in the objective world (depth image), texture change (texture image), material absorption value (computer tomography), etc. For example, with the advancement of science and technological development in recent years, imaging has expanded from visible light to other radiation bands, such as infrared, microwave, and radio waves at the low-frequency end and ultraviolet light, X-ray, γ rays, and cosmic rays at the high-frequency end. In these cases, the brightness value or gray value of the image can correspond to various radio-metrics.

Broadly speaking, an image can represent a spatial distribution of radiant energy. This distribution can be a vector function of five variables, denoted as $\boldsymbol{T}(x, y, z, t, \lambda)$, where x, y, z are space variables, t represents the time variable, λ is the spectral variable (wavelength), and for the same group of variables, the function value T can also be a vector (e.g., a color image includes three components, and a multi-spectral image may include hundreds or thousands of components). Since the actual image is limited in time and space, frequency spectrum, and energy, $\boldsymbol{T}(x, y, z, t, \lambda)$ is a 5D finite function.

Example 1.1 Image examples

Figure 1.4 shows two typical public images (Lena and Cameraman; they are also used as original images in many processing and analysis examples in this book). The coordinate system shown in Figure 1.4(a) is often used in screen display. Its origin O is at the upper left corner of the image, the vertical axis marks the image row, and the horizontal axis marks the image column. The coordinate system shown in Figure 1.4(b) is often used in image calculations. Its origin is at the lower left corner of the image, the horizontal axis is the X axis, and the vertical axis is the Y axis. In these two figures, $f(x, y)$ can

Figure 1.4.   Digital image and its display examples.

represent the entire image or the attribute value f of the image at coordinates (x, y). □

1.2.2   Pixel and image representation

An image can be broken down into many units. Each basic unit is called an image element. For 2D images, the image element is called **pixel** for short. To acquire an image for a spatial scene, the image resolution is proportional to the number of pixels contained. The more pixels, the higher the resolution of the image, that is, the details of the image would be more likely seen.

Example 1.2 Pixel examples

The image is composed of many pixels closely arranged, or a gray-level image is a collection of brightness points, which can be seen as long as the image is gradually enlarged. For example, select a small piece (32×32) from Figure 1.4(b) to enlarge, see Figure 1.5(a), and cover a 32×32 grid as shown in Figure 1.5(b) on it, then Figure 1.5(c) is obtained. Each small grid in Figure 1.5(c) corresponds to a pixel, and the gray level within the grid is consistent. Each small grid here corresponds to a pixel. □

To represent an image, it is necessary to represent each pixel in it. This can be achieved in multiple ways. The most commonly used representation method is to take a 2D array $f(x, y)$ to represent an image, where x and y represent the position of the pixel, and f represents the attribute value of the pixel. In this method, that

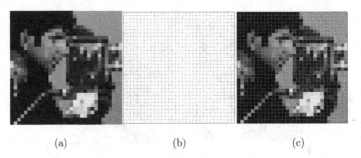

(a)   (b)   (c)

Figure 1.5.   Pixel examples.

is called raster representation, there is a one-to-one correspondence between image pixels and array elements.

An image can also be represented as a 2D $M \times N$ matrix $\boldsymbol{F}$ (where each element represents a pixel, and M and N are the number of rows and columns of the image, respectively):

$$\boldsymbol{F} = \begin{bmatrix} f_{11} & f_{12} & \cdots & f_{1N} \\ f_{21} & f_{22} & \cdots & f_{2N} \\ \vdots & \vdots & \ddots & \vdots \\ f_{M1} & f_{M2} & \cdots & f_{MN} \end{bmatrix} \tag{1.1}$$

The matrix representation method can be easily transformed into a more convenient vector representation method. The representation corresponding to Equation (1.1) is

$$\boldsymbol{F} = [\boldsymbol{f}_1 \quad \boldsymbol{f}_2 \quad \cdots \quad \boldsymbol{f}_N] \tag{1.2}$$

where

$$\boldsymbol{f}_i = \begin{bmatrix} f_{1i} & f_{2i} & \cdots & f_{Mi} \end{bmatrix}^{\mathrm{T}} \quad i = 1, 2, \ldots, N \tag{1.3}$$

The matrix representation and vector representation are equivalent, and they can be easily converted from each other.

1.2.3   Image storage and format

Images need to be represented by using a large amount of data in a computer, and they need to be stored in a specific format.

1. Image memory

Image storage requires a lot of space. In image processing and analysis systems, large capacity and fast image memory are essential. In a computer, the smallest unit of measurement for image data is bit. The storage capacity of the memory is commonly represented by Bytes (B, 1B = 8 bits), Kilobytes (10^3 bytes, KB), Megabytes (10^6 bytes, MB), Gigabytes (10^9 bytes, GB), Terabytes (10^{12} bytes, TB), and so on. For example, to store a 1024×1024 8-bit image requires 1 MB of memory. Digital storage used for image processing and analysis can be divided into three categories:

(1) Fast memory used in the procedure of processing and analysis;
(2) Online storage for faster recall;
(3) Infrequently used database (archive) storage.

Example 1.3 Memory examples

Computer memory is a kind of memory that provides fast storage functions. At present, the memory of a general microcomputer is often several GB. Another type of memory that provides fast storage is a special hardware card, also called frame buffer or video memory. It can often store multiple images and can be read at video speed (25 or 30 images per second). It can also allow real-time zoom in and zoom out of the image, as well as operations such as vertical flipping and horizontal flipping. At present, the commonly used frame buffer capacity can often reach dozens of GB. Flash memory, which has been widely used in recent years, has some similarities with computer memory in terms of its working principle and structure, but it can still retain the stored content after a power failure.

Disks are more general online storages. The commonly used Winchester disks can generally store several terabytes of data. In recent years, magneto-optical (MO) memory has also been commonly used, which can store gigabytes of data on a 51/4-inch optical chip. One feature of online storage is that data need to be read frequently and randomly, so sequential media such as tapes are generally not used. For greater storage requirements, a disc tower can be used. A disc tower can hold dozens to hundreds of optical discs, and uses mechanical devices to insert or extract optical discs from the optical disc drive.

A characteristic of the database memory is that it requires a very large capacity, but the data on it are read less frequently. Generally, tapes and CDs are commonly used as database storage. A 13-foot-long tape can store up to GB of data. However, the storage life of magnetic tapes is relatively short, only seven years in a well-controlled environment. The commonly used WORM (write-once read-many) disc can store 6 GB of data on a 12-inch disc and 10 GB of data on a 14-inch disc. In addition, WORM discs can be stored for more than 30 years under normal conditions. In applications that are mainly for reading, WORM discs can also be placed in the disc tower. A WORM disc tower with a storage capacity of terabytes can store millions of 1024×1024 8-bit images. □

2. Image file format

Image data are generally stored with various image file formats in online storage and database storage. In addition to the image data itself, the file generally needs to contain description information of the image to facilitate the extraction and use of the image data.

There are mainly two formats for image data files: one is the vector format and the other is raster format.

(1) In the vector format, the image is represented by a series of line segments or a combination of line segments. The gray level (or chromaticity) of the line segment can be uniform or variable. Different gray levels can also be used in each part of the line segment combination. A vector format file is generally like a program file, which contains a series of commands and data. By executing these commands, a pattern can be drawn based on the data. Vector files are mainly used for manually drawn graphics data files.

(2) The files that represent natural image data mainly use raster format, which is consistent with people's understanding of images (an image is a collection of many image points), and is more suitable for real images with complex color, shadow, or shape changes. Its main disadvantage is the lack of a structure that directly expresses the relationship between pixels and the limited resolution of the image. The latter brings about two problems. One is that if the image is enlarged to a certain extent, the

block effect will appear, and the other is that if the image is reduced and then restored to its original size, the image will become blurred.

Different system platforms and software often use different **image file formats**. The following briefly introduces five widely used formats:

(1) **Bitmap** (BMP): BMP format is a standard image format in the Windows environment, and its full name is Microsoft **Device Independent Bitmap** (DIP). The BMP image file is also called bitmap file, including three parts: (i) Bitmap file header (also called table header); (ii) Bitmap information (often called palette); and (iii) Bitmap array (image data). A bitmap file can only store one image.

The length of the bitmap file header is fixed at 54 bytes, and it provides information such as the type, size, print format, and starting position of the bitmap array of the image file. The bitmap information gives the length and width of the image, the number of bits per pixel (it can be 1, 4, 8, 24, corresponding to the case of monochrome, 16 colors, 256 colors, and true colors), compression method, the horizontal and vertical resolution of target device, and other information. The bitmap array gives the value of each pixel in the original image (e.g., every 3 bytes represent a pixel of a true color image, which is the value of red, green, and blue), and its storage format can be two kinds: compressed (only for 16-color and 256-color images) and uncompressed. The bitmap array data are arranged starting from the lower left corner of the image.

(2) **Graphics Interchange Format** (GIF): GIF format is a common image file format standard. It is an 8-bit file format (one byte per pixel), so it can only store images up to 256 colors, and does not support 24-bit true color images. The image data in the GIF file is compressed. The compression algorithm used is the improved LZW algorithm. The compression ratio provided is usually between 1:1 and 3:1. The effect is not good when there is random noise in the image.

The GIF file structure is more complex, generally including seven data units: file header, general palette, image data region, and four supplementary regions (if the user just uses the GIF format to store user image information, they may not be set). The header and image data regions are indispensable units.

A GIF file can store multiple images (this feature is very benefi-
cial for the realization of animation on the web), so the file header
will contain global data applicable to all images and local data only
belonging to the subsequent image. When there is only one image
in the file, the global data are consistent with the local data. When
multiple images are stored, each image is collected into one image
data block, and the first byte of each block is an identifier, which
indicates the type of data block (it can be an image block, extended
block, or end symbol of the file).

(3) **Joint Photographic Expert Group** (JPEG): JPEG format is an international compression standard for still gray-level or
color images, especially suitable for natural photos taken, so it has
been widely used in digital cameras. The JPEG format uses a lossy
encoding format (it also has a lossless encoding format, but it has
rarely been used), and the space it can save is generally quite large.
The JPEG image file format is more complicated than other image
file formats in terms of its content and encoding method, but it does
not need to use the detailed information of each data region when
using it.

The JPEG standard itself only defines a standardized coded data
stream, and does not specify the format of image data files. Cube
Microsystems company has defined a **JPEG file interchange format** (JFIF). JFIF image is a JPEG image that uses either gray-level
representation or color representation with Y, C_b, and C_r components. It contains a file header compatible with JPEG. A JFIF file
usually contains a single image. The image can be gray level and the
data part in it is a single component; it can also be color, and the
data part in it includes three components.

(4) **Portable Network Graphics** (PNG): PNG format is a
bitmap format with lossless compression. It uses a lossless data compression algorithm derived from LZ77, and is generally used in JAVA
programs, S60 programs, or web pages. The main reason is its high
compression ratio and small file size. The PNG format has three
forms: 8-bit, 24-bit, and 32-bit. The 8-bit PNG supports two different types of transparency (index transparency and alpha transparency). The 24-bit PNG does not support transparency (contains
only three color components R, G, and B). The 32-bit PNG adds an
8-bit transparency channel, or Alpha channel, on the basis of 24-bit,

so it can show 256 levels of transparency. It this case, one can specify the Alpha value of each pixel. When the Alpha value is 0, the pixel is completely transparent, and when the Alpha value is 255, the pixel is completely opaque. This allows the edges of the color image to blend smoothly with any background, thus completely eliminating jagged edges. This function is not available in GIF and JPEG.

Compared with the JPEG format, in case of saving text, lines, or similar images with clear edges and large areas of the same color, the compression effect of the PNG format would be much better than that of the JPEG, and the image that appears damaged in the high-contrast region, like JPEG, will not appear. However, JPEG adopts a specific encoding method for photo images, which is suitable for the characteristics of low-contrast, smooth color transition, more noise, and irregular structure. Therefore, if one uses PNG instead of JPEG at this time, the file size will increase a lot, while the improvement of image quality is limited.

(5) **Tagged Image Format File** (TIFF): TIFF format is a format independent of operating system and file system (e.g., it can be used on both the Windows environment and Macintosh environment), which is very convenient for image data exchange between software. A TIFF image file includes file header (table header), file directory (identification information region), and file directory entry (image data region). There is only one file header, and at the front end of the file. The file header gives the data storage order and the byte offset information of the file directory. The file directory gives information about the number of file directory entries, and has a set of identification information that gives the address of the image data region. The file directory is the basic unit for storing information, also called a domain. The domains are mainly divided into five categories: basic domain, information description domain, fax domain, document storage, and retrieval domain, as well as other domains that are no longer recommended.

The TIFF format has a strong descriptive ability and can develop personal identification information. The TIFF format supports images of any size, and files can be divided into five categories: binary images, gray-level images, palette color images, full-color RGB images, and YC_bC_r images. A TIFF file can store multiple images and multiple palette data.

1.2.4   Image display and printing

Image display refers to the display of image data in the form of graphs (in general, the spatial arrangement of the brightness mode, i.e., the brightness corresponding to f, is displayed in the space (x, y)). This is also an important content of computer graphics. For image processing, the results of the processing are mainly used for display to people. For image analysis, the analyzed data results can also be converted into images for intuitive display with the help of computer graphics technology. Therefore, image display is very important for image processing and analysis systems.

Example 1.4 Display device examples

There are many kinds of devices that can display images. The main display device used in common image processing and analysis systems is a TV monitor. The images input to the monitor can also be transferred to slides, photos, or transparencies via hard copy.

In addition to TV monitors, random access cathode ray tubes (CRTs) and various printing devices can also be used for image output and display.

In CRT, the horizontal and vertical positions of the electron gun beam can be controlled by a computer. At each deflection position, the intensity of the electron gun beam is modulated by voltage. The voltage of each point is proportional to the gray value corresponding to that point. In this way, the gray-level image is transformed into a pattern of spatial variation of light intensity, which is recorded and displayed on the screen of the CRT.

A printing device can also be regarded as a device that displays images, and it is generally used to output lower-resolution images. In the early days, an easy way to print gray-level images on paper was to take advantage of the repeatability of standard line printers. The gray value of any point on the output image can be controlled by the number and density of symbols or characters printed at that point. Various thermal, inkjet, and laser printers used in recent years have higher capabilities and can print images with higher resolution.   □

1. Half-toning

The original gray level of an image often has tens to hundreds or even thousands of levels, but some image output devices have only two gray levels, such as laser printers (either print and output black, or do not print and output white). In order to output multi-level gray-level images on these devices and maintain their original gray levels, a technique called **half-toning** is often used. The principle of half-toning is to use the integrated characteristics of the human eye by printing a black dot whose size is inversely proportional to the gray level of the pixel at each pixel position; that is, the dots printed in the bright image region are small, while the dots printed in the dark image region are large (the methods given in Example 1.5 have the same principles, but the implementation techniques are different). When the dot is small enough and the observation distance is far enough, it is not easy for the human eye to separate the small dots, and a relatively continuous and smooth gray-level image can be obtained. Generally, the resolution of pictures in newspapers is about 100 dots per inch (DPI), while the resolution of pictures in books or magazines is about 300 dots per inch.

Example 1.5 Half-toning method

A specific implementation technique for half-toning is to first subdivide the image region, and combine adjacent units to form the output region. In this way, each output region contains several units. As long as some units output black and others output white, different gray-level effects can be obtained. Generally, if a unit is black at a certain gray level, let it remain black in all outputs greater than this gray level (here, the greater the gray level, the darker the brightness). For example, dividing a region into 2×2 units can output five different gray levels according to the manner shown in Figure 1.6, and dividing a region into 3×3 units can output 10 different gray levels according to the manner shown in Figure 1.7.

Extending this manner, to output 256 gray levels, a region needs to be divided into 16×16 units. It should be noted that this manner

Figure 1.6. Dividing a region into 2×2 units to output five different gray levels.

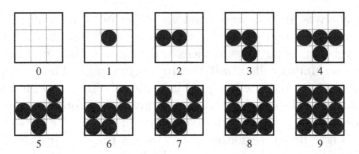

Figure 1.7. Dividing a region into 3×3 units to output 10 different gray levels.

increases the amplitude resolution of the image by reducing the spatial resolution of the image, so it may cause the image to be sampled too coarsely and affect the display quality of the image. □

2. Dithering technology

The half-toning method increases the amplitude resolution of the image by reducing the spatial resolution of the image, so the number of gray-level outputs is subject to certain restrictions. Displaying an image with a smaller number of gray levels may produce **false contours** and cause image quality degradation. At this time, **dithering** technology can be used to improve the display quality of the coarsely quantized image by changing the amplitude value of the image. The realization of dithering is generally to add a random small noise $d(x, y)$ to the original image $f(x, y)$, that is, to add these two values for image display. Because the values of $d(x, y)$ and $f(x, y)$ have a regular relationship, it can help eliminate false contours in the image caused by insufficient quantization (see also Example 2.11). For example, if b is the number of bits displayed in the image (generally, $b < 5$), first obtain the value of $d(x, y)$ with a uniform probability from the following five numbers: $-2^{(6-b)}$, $-2^{(5-b)}$, 0, $2^{(5-b)}$, $2^{(6-b)}$; then, add the b most significant bits of $d(x, y)$, which is equivalent to adding small random noise to $f(x, y)$, and finally the above sum is displayed as the value of the pixel.

Example 1.6 Dithering examples

Figure 1.8 shows a set of dithering examples. Figure 1.8(a) is an original image with 256 gray levels. Figure 1.8(b) shows the use of the

(a)　　　　　　　(b)　　　　　　　(c)　　　　　　　(d)

Figure 1.8.　Dithering example diagram.

half-toning technique in Example 1.5 with the output image obtained by using the units shown in Figure 1.7. Because there are only 10 gray levels now, there are obvious false contour phenomena in the regions where the gray-level transition is relatively slow, such as the face and shoulders (the original smooth surface has a step change now). Figure 1.8(c) is the result of using dithering technology to improve; the superimposed dithering values are -2, -1, 0, 1, 2, respectively. Figure 1.8(d) is also improved using dithering technology, but the superimposed dithering values are -4, -2, 0, 2, 4, respectively.

It can be seen from the above examples that the use of dithering technology can eliminate some false contours caused by using too few gray levels. The larger the superimposed dither value, the more obvious the effect. However, the superimposition of the dithering value also brings noise to the image, and the larger the dithering value, the greater the noise impact. □

1.3　Vision Systems and Image Techniques

The **vision system** is a system that obtains images by observing the world and then realizes the vision function. The human visual system includes organs such as eyes, neural networks, and cerebral cortex. With the advancement of science and technology, there are more and more artificial (man-made) vision systems composed of computers and electronic devices. They are trying to realize and improve the human vision system. Artificial vision systems mainly use digital images as input to the system.

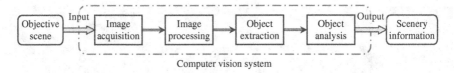

Figure 1.9.   2D vision system flowchart.

1.3.1   Vision system flowchart

From the perspective of function completion, the 2D vision system needs to be able to collect images of objective scenes, process the images (preprocess), improve image quality, and then extract the image objects corresponding to the scene of interest, as well as obtain useful information about the objective scene through the analysis of objects, as shown in Figure 1.9.

1.3.2   Three layers of image engineering

In order to complete the function of the vision system, a series of techniques are required. After years of development, computer vision technology has made great progress and there are many types of techniques. There are some classification methods for these techniques, but it seems that they are not stable and uniform. For example, different researchers divide computer vision technology into three layers, but they are not consistent. Someone divides it into low-level vision, middle-level vision, and 3D vision; someone divides it into early vision (which is further divided into two parts: only one image; multiple images), middle-level vision, and high-level vision (geometric method); and someone else divides it into early vision (which is divided into two portions: one image and multiple images), middle vision, and high-level vision (which is further divided into two parts: geometric methods; probability and inference methods).

Relatively speaking, a layered classification method for image technology has been more consistent in the past 26 years. This method combines various image technologies under the subject of **image engineering** (a new interdisciplinary subject that systematically studies various image theories, techniques, and applications). Image engineering can be divided into three layers: image processing, image analysis, and image understanding. As shown in Figure 1.10, each layer has its own characteristics.

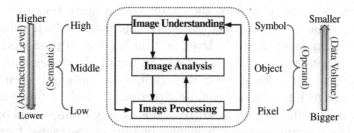

Figure 1.10.   Three layers of image engineering.

Image processing (IP) emphasizes the transformation between images. Although people often use image processing for referring to a wider range of image techniques, the more narrowly defined image processing mainly denotes various operations of images to improve the visual effect of the image and lays the foundation for automatic recognition, or compresses and encodes the image to reduce the necessary storage space and/or transmission time to meet the requirements of a given communication path.

Image analysis (IA) is focused on the detection and measurement of the objects of interest in the image to obtain their objective information for establishing a description of the image. If image processing is a process from image to image, then image analysis is a process from image to data. The data here can be the result of measuring the object feature, or the symbolic representation based on the measurement. They describe mainly the characteristics and properties of the object in the image.

The emphasis of **image understanding** (IU) is to further study the nature of the objects in the image and their interrelationships on the basis of image analysis, and to obtain an interpretation of the meaning of the image content and the understanding of the original objective scene. If image analysis is mainly based on the observer-centered study of the objective world (mostly studying observable things), then image understanding is, to a certain extent, centered on the objective world, and with the help of knowledge and experience to grasp and explain the whole real world (including things that are not directly observed).

As mentioned earlier, image processing, image analysis, and image understanding have their own characteristics in terms of abstraction level and data volume, and their operands and semantics are different. See Figure 1.10 for their interrelationships. Image processing corresponds to relatively low-level operations, which primarily treats the image at the pixel level, and the amount of processed data is very large. Image analysis enters the middle level; segmentation and feature extraction convert the original description of each pixel of the image into a more concise description of the object in the image. Image understanding corresponds largely to high-level operations. The operand is basically a concept symbol abstracted from the description. Its operating process and methods have many similarities with human thinking and reasoning. In addition, it can be seen from Figure 1.10 that the amount of data gradually decreases as the degree of abstraction increases. Specifically, the original image data are gradually transformed into a more organized and more abstract representation through a series of operations. In this process, semantics are continuously introduced, operating objects are changed, and the amount of data is compressed. On the other hand, high-level operations have a guiding role for low-level operations and can improve the efficiency of low-level operations.

Among the three levels of image engineering, image processing, and image analysis are the bases of image understanding. Their study is relatively mature compared to image understanding and they have been widely used in recent times. This book will mainly introduce the content of these two levels. For more in-depth and advanced content, see the book "3D Computer Vision: Principle, Algorithm, and Applications".

1.3.3   Categories of image technology

Among the three layers of image engineering, each layer includes several technical categories (currently there are 16 categories in total), as shown in Table 1.1.

In this book, the image processing technology mainly involves image acquisition, image enhancement/restoration, and image multiresolution processing; the image analysis technology mainly involves image segmentation and primitive detection, object representation, description and measurement, as well as object feature extraction and analysis, and object recognition. These categories are shown in bold letters in Table 1.1.

Table 1.1. Current image technology categories studied in the three layers of image engineering.

Three layers	Image technology categories and names
Image processing	**Image acquisition** (including various imaging methods, image capturing, representation and storage, and camera calibration)
	Image reconstruction (including image reconstruction from projection and indirect imaging)
	Image enhancement/image restoration (including transformation, filtering, restoration, repair, replacement, correction, and visual quality evaluation)
	Image/video coding and compression (including algorithm research, and implementation and improvement of related international standards)
	Image information security (including digital watermarking, information hiding, image authentication, and forensics)
	Image multi-resolution processing (including super-resolution reconstruction, image decomposition and interpolation, and resolution conversion)
Image analysis	**Image segmentation** and **primitive detection** (including edges, corners, control points, and points of interest)
	Object representation, object description, feature measurement (including binary image morphology analysis)
	Object feature extraction and analysis (including color, texture, shape, space, structure, motion, saliency, and attributes)
	Object detection and **object recognition** (including object 2D positioning, tracking, extraction, identification, and classification)
	Human body biological feature extraction and verification (including detection, positioning, and recognition of human body, face, and organs)
Image understanding	Image matching and fusion (including registration of sequence and stereo image, and mosaic)
	Scene restoration (including 3D scene representation, modeling, and reconstruction)
	Image perception and interpretation (including semantic description, scene model, machine learning, and cognitive reasoning)
	Content-based image/video retrieval (including corresponding labeling and classification)
	Spatial-temporal techniques (including high-dimensional motion analysis, object 3D posture detection, spatial-temporal tracking, behavior judgment, and behavior understanding)

1.4 Overview of the Structure and Content of This Book

As a basic textbook that introduces computer vision technology, how to choose appropriate content and how to use the chapters in it are also issues that need to be considered. They are discussed in the following.

1.4.1 Structural framework and main content

According to the 2D vision system flowchart in Figure 1.9, this book selects some related techniques for introduction. In image processing technology, it mainly discusses various techniques of image acquisition and image enhancement/restoration, which basically correspond to early vision or low-level vision. In image analysis technology, it mainly discusses typical techniques of image segmentation and primitive object detection, as well as some related techniques for object representation, description, feature extraction, analysis, and classification-related ones, which are mainly related to middle-level vision.

The structural framework and main content of this book are shown in Figure 1.11.

From the objective scene to the final extraction of scenery information, there are four modules (solid frame): image acquisition,

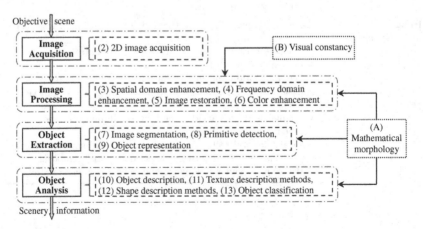

Figure 1.11.   The structure and main content of this book.

image (pre-)processing, extraction of the object, and analysis of the object. This book maps the techniques to be introduced to these four modules (dotted boxes), and the numbers in parentheses correspond to the numbers of chapters of the book. The mathematical morphology introduced in Appendix A can be applied to different techniques in different modules as a tool (as indicated by the arrows). The visual constancy introduced in Appendix B is mainly related to the image processing module (as shown by the arrow). The main content of this book can be divided into four units as shown in Figure 1.11 (as shown by the dotted line). The first unit includes Chapter 2, which mainly introduces the preliminary image acquisition and representation techniques; the second unit includes Chapters 3 to 6, which mainly introduces basic image processing techniques; the third unit includes Chapters 7 to 9, which mainly introduces the conversion techniques from image processing to image analysis; and the fourth unit includes Chapters 10 to 13, which mainly introduces extended image analysis techniques.

1.4.2 Overview of each chapter

The book has 13 chapters and two appendices.

Chapter 1 is for the introduction. It gives definitions of some basic terms, lists examples of various images, summarizes the overall situation of image technology, specifically introduces image representation and display methods, image storage and file formats, and makes some suggestions for the use of this book.

Chapter 2 introduces image acquisition methods, including geometric imaging models and brightness imaging models, sampling, and quantization for digitization, which are the keys to acquiring digital images. In addition, the relationship between pixels in the obtained image is also discussed.

Chapter 3 introduces spatial image enhancement methods. The content involved includes arithmetic and logical operations on images, gray-scale mapping technique, the use of histogram modification methods, and spatial filtering methods using pixel neighborhoods.

Chapter 4 introduces the frequency domain image enhancement method. Based on the summary of Fourier transform, it introduces a variety of low-pass, high-pass, band-stop, and band-pass filters, and analyses the principle of homomorphic filter combined with the brightness imaging model.

Chapter 5 introduces image restoration methods, analyses some examples of image degradation, discusses basic unconstrained restoration and constrained restoration techniques, presents methods to correct geometric distortions, and outlines image repair techniques.

Chapter 6 introduces color vision and color image enhancement methods. On the basis of discussing the fundamental color vision, physical-based and perceptual-based color models, some typical methods for false color enhancement and true color enhancement are given.

Chapter 7 introduces basic image segmentation methods. It first discusses segmentation definition and method classification, and then specifically introduces differential edge detection, active contour model, threshold segmentation, threshold selection based on transition region, and region growth technology.

Chapter 8 introduces primitive detection methods in images. Several detection methods of interest points are discussed. The idea of object detection is analyzed by taking ellipse as an example. The Hough transform that can detect multiple forms of primitives is also introduced and extended to the generalized Hough transform.

Chapter 9 introduces some basic methods for object representation, including the chain code representation of contours, projection signatures, and polygonal approximation, as well as the object's hierarchical representation, surrounding region, and skeleton representation.

Chapter 10 introduces the description techniques of the object. In addition to some basic contour description parameters and basic regional description parameters, it also discusses the Fourier description and wavelet description of the contour. In addition, the descriptions based on the region invariant moments and the description for the object relationship are also provided.

Chapter 11 introduces the analysis methods for the object surface texture, and discusses some typical techniques in the three types of texture research methods that are based on statistical theory, structural model and spectral function, respectively.

Chapter 12 introduces the analysis of object shape, and specifically discusses four types of shape characteristic descriptors, namely, shape compactness descriptors, shape complexity descriptors, discrete curvature-based descriptors, and topological structure descriptors.

Chapter 13 introduces the classification of object patterns. First, the cross ratio is taken as an example to present feature invariants, then several typical statistical pattern classifiers are discussed, and finally the principles and characteristics of support vector machines are analyzed.

Appendix A introduces binary mathematical morphology. Based on the review of basic set definitions, it introduces the essential operations of binary morphology, the combined operations of binary morphology, and the practical algorithms of binary morphology.

Appendix B introduces visual constancy, which is a type of perceptual constancy. Based on the overview of the theory of the retinal cortex, two applications of visual constancy in image enhancement are also described.

At the end of each chapter and appendix, there is a section "Key points and references for each section". On the one hand, it summarizes the central content of each section; and, on the other hand, it provides several references for in-depth study. Except the appendices, each chapter has a certain number of self-test questions (all including hints and answers).

1.4.3 Prerequisites

From the perspective of learning image processing and analysis techniques, three basic types of knowledge are more important.

(1) Mathematical knowledge: It is worth pointing out the linear algebra, because the image can be represented as a matrix; it is useful and efficient to use matrix expression to explain various processing operations. In addition, the knowledge of statistics and probability is also very helpful.

(2) Computer science knowledge: It is worth pointing out the computer software and hardware technology, because the image processing and analysis need to use a computer, through

programming with a certain algorithm to complete on a given platform.

(3) Knowledge of electronics: There are two branches worth pointing out. One is signal processing, because the image can be seen as an extension of 1D signal, and the processing of the image is an extension of the processing of the signal; the other is the circuit principle, because it is often necessary to finally realize the rapid processing of the image, by using certain electronic equipment and devices (including special hardware).

In order to use and study this book effectively, it is necessary to determine the required prerequisite foundation and understand the general content of each chapter in the book, so that the required chapters can be selected according to the student's foundation and class time.

This book is written in accordance with the introductory textbook for learning computer vision technology. The main goal is to introduce the basic concepts, typical methods, and practical techniques of 2D computer vision (corresponding to image processing and analysis). On the one hand, readers can solve practical problems accordingly in the application; on the other hand, it can lay the foundation for readers to further study and research the 3D computer vision (closer to image understanding) technology.

1.5   Key Points and References for Each Section

The following indicates the key points of each section and provides some targeted guidance for further references:

1. Vision basis

Human vision is closely related to computer vision, so this section first introduces some basic concepts and basic knowledge of human vision. People's sensation of light can be found in Ref. [1]. The relationship between human visual perception and psychological factors can be found in Ref. [2]. For further discussion of the human visual process, please refer Ref. [3]. There are many specialized books on computer vision, for example, see Refs. [4,5].

2. Vision and image

Image is the object of vision and the object of computer vision research. The representation, display, and storage of images are the foundation of computer vision technology. The basic concepts of images and pixels are introduced in all image processing books, such as Refs. [6–9].

Many image storage formats use a variety of image compression methods (such as more than 10 kinds in the TIFF format). To understand these methods, please refer Ref. [10].

3. Vision systems and image techniques

Computer vision technology is closely related to image technology, and computer vision systems need to rely on many image techniques to build. The objective world is three-dimensional (3D) in space, but most imaging devices project the 3D world to two-dimensional (2D). This book mainly discusses 2D computer vision technology or 2D image technology. A comprehensive introduction to computer vision can be found in Refs. [6,11,12]. A complete introduction to image engineering technology can be found in Refs. [13–15]. The three layers of image engineering and the related technical application, as well as their developments in the last years, can be found in Refs. [16–42]. They have constituted a 26-year-long literature survey series.

4. Overview of the structure and content of this book

The main content of this book is in four units, which can be studied sequentially. This book mainly introduces the principles and techniques of computer vision, while their specific implementation of various algorithms can be achieved with different programming languages. For example, if MATLAB is to be used, please refer Refs. [43,44]. For more detailed analysis and answers to various problems in learning, please refer Ref. [45].

Self-Test Questions

The following questions include both single- and multiple-choice questions, so each option should be individually judged.

1.1 Vision Basis

1.1.1 Which of the following statement(s) is/are incorrect? ( )

(A) The perception of brightness is only related to the brightness of the scene;

(B) The chemical process in the visual process affects the perception of color;

(C) The optical process in the visual process affects the perception of brightness;

(D) The neural processing in the visual process is related to the perception of brightness.

[Hint] Analyze the function of each step in the visual process carefully.

1.1.2 The international image compression standard JPEG2000 uses the region of interest (ROI) technology which in turn uses different compression multiples for different regions of an image. Which of the following factor(s) is/are considered here? ( )

(A) The field of view of the human visual system;

(B) The structural characteristics of the retina;

(C) The size and shape of the pupil of the eye;

(D) The brightness perceived by the human visual system.

[Hint] The spatial resolution of the central region of the retina (fovea) and the surrounding region are different.

1.1.3 Which of the following is/are the result(s) of visual sensation? ( )

(A) There is a book on the table;

(B) There is a changing of the guard;

(C) The eyes shine through the tunnel;

(D) A shooting star crosses the sky.

[Hint] The visual sensation mainly occurs during the process of imaging the scene on the retina and does not involve the activities of the nerve center of the human brain.

1.2 Vision and Image

1.2.1 A digital image is ( )

(A) An element in a 2D array;

(B) A scene in a 3D space;

(C) An observation system;

(D) An entity composed of many arranged pixels.

[Hint] Consider the definitions of image and digital image.

1.2.2 $f(x, y)$ can be used to represent ( )

(A) A 2D digital image;

(B) A projection of an objective scene in 3D space;

(C) The position of a coordinate point in 2D space XY;

(D) The value of a certain property F at the coordinate point (x, y).

[Hint] Pay attention to the meaning of the three symbols.

1.2.3 Consider f in digital image $f(x, y)$. ( )

(A) It can correspond to the intensity of X-ray;

(B) It can correspond to the radiance of objects in a scene;

(C) It can represent the position of a coordinate point in the 2D space XY;

(D) It can indicate the brightness of a photo.

[Hint] The image is the projection of a scene, and f corresponds to a certain property at the scene point.

1.2.4 Which of the following device(s) has/have image-storage function? ( ).

(A) Scanner;

(B) Digital camera;

(C) TV monitor;

(D) Laser printer.

[Hint] An image-storage device can be understood as a device that can save image data files.

1.2.5 In the image data file using raster format, ( )

(A) The resolution of the image is proportional to the size of the data file;

(B) There are not only data but also commands;

(C) The geometric figure is represented by a collection of spatially distributed pixels;

(D) If the image in the file is displayed, there will be a block effect.

[Hint] Consider the characteristics of transforming data into images with vector form.

1.2.6 Among the BMP, GIF, JPEG, and TIFF formats, ( ).

(A) To represent the same image, the BMP format uses the most data;
(B) The GIF format is independent of the operating system;
(C) One JPEG format data file can store multiple images;
(D) The header of TIFF format file is the most complicated.

[Hint] Consider the characteristics of these four formats separately.

1.2.7 Which of the following device(s) is a / are digital-image display device(s)? ( )

(A) Slide projector;
(B) Printer;
(C) Plotter;
(D) Film projector.

[Hint] The input of digital-image display device is data and the output is image.

1.2.8 The half-toning technique can ( )

(A) Improve the amplitude resolution of the image;
(B) Improve the spatial resolution of the image;
(C) Eliminate false contour phenomenon;
(D) Use dither technology to achieve.

[Hint] The half-toning technique sacrifices spatial resolution to improve amplitude resolution.

1.2.9 If each position of a 2×2 half-toning template can represent four kinds of gray, then the total number of kinds of gray that can be represented by this template is ( )

(A) 5;
(B) 9;
(C) 13;
(D) 17.

[Hint] The minimum gray scale is 0 for each position, whereas the maximum is 3 for each position.

1.2.10 Dithering technique can ( )

(A) Improve the amplitude resolution of the image;
(B) Improve the spatial resolution of the image;
(C) Eliminate false contour phenomenon;
(D) Use half-toning technique to achieve.

[Hint] The dithering technique increases the number of amplitude output values of the image by adding random noise.

1.3 Vision Systems and Image Techniques

1.3.1 Which of the following image technique(s) is an/are image-processing technique(s)? ( )

(A) Image enhancement;
(B) Image segmentation;
(C) Image restoration;
(D) Image matching.

[Hint] Under the narrow meaning of image-processing technique, the input and output are both images.

1.3.2 Which of the following image technique(s) is an/are image-analysis technique(s)? ( )

(A) Image synthesis;
(B) Object description;
(C) Image enhancement;
(D) Image segmentation.

[Hint] Image analysis starts from the image and obtains the object data.

1.3.3 The composition of a basic image processing and analysis system can be shown as in Figure 1.3.3, where ( )

(A) A—image display, B—image storage, C—image communication, D—image acquisition;
(B) A—image communication, B—image acquisition, C—image display, D—image storage;
(C) A—image storage, B—image communication, C—image acquisition, D—image display;

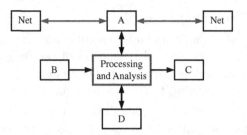

Figure 1.3.3.

(D) A—image acquisition, B—image display, C—image storage, D—image communication.

[Hint] The direction of the arrows represents the flow of data.

1.4 Overview of the Structure and Content of This Book

1.4.1 The following techniques correspond to the four modules of this book: ( )

(A) 2D image acquisition, spatial enhancement, image segmentation, and object representation;

(B) 2D image acquisition, color enhancement, object description, and shape analysis;

(C) 2D image acquisition, image restoration, primitive extraction, and texture analysis;

(D) 2D image acquisition, frequency domain enhancement, object representation, and object classification.

[Hint] Refer to Figure 1.11.

1.4.2 Which of the following statement(s) is/are correct? ( )

(A) A band-pass filter can be used for spatial image enhancement;

(B) A homomorphic filter can be used for frequency domain image enhancement;

(C) Hough transformation and surrounding region can be used for object representation;

(D) Both contour description parameters and skeleton representation can be used for primitive detection.

[Hint] Refer to the introduction in the overview of each chapter.

1.4.3 Which of the following statement(s) is/are incorrect? ( )

(A) Image restoration is a special case of image repair;
(B) The threshold selected based on the transition region can be used for image segmentation;
(C) Region-growing technique is a kind of regional description parameter;
(D) The generalized Hough transform can be used for object pattern classification.

[Hint] Pay attention to the definition of each concept and the relationship between the concepts.

References

[1] Hao, B. Y., Zhang, H. C., and Chen, S. Y. *Experimental Psychology*. China, Beijing: Beijing University Press, 1983.
[2] Guo, X. Y. and Yang, Z. L. *Basic Experimental Psychology*. China, Beijing: Higher Education Press, 2005.
[3] Kong, B. Comparison between human vision and computer vision. *Chinese Journal of Nature*, 2002, 24(1): 51–55.
[4] Shapiro, L. and Stockman, G. *Computer Vision*. USA, New Jersey: Prentice Hall, 2001.
[5] Forsyth, D. and Ponce, J. *Computer Vision: A Modern Approach*. USA, New Jersey: Prentice Hall, 2003.
[6] Sonka, M., Hlavac, V., and Boyle, R. *Image Processing, Analysis, and Machine Vision*, 4th Edn. Singapore: Cengage Learning, 2014.
[7] Russ, J. C. and Neal, F. B. *The Image Processing Handbook*, 7th Edn. UK, London: CRC Press, 2016.
[8] Gonzalez, R. C. and Woods, R. E. *Digital Image Processing*, 4th Edn. UK, London: Prentice Hall, 2018.
[9] Zhang, Y.-J. *Image Engineering: Processing, Analysis, and Understanding*. Singapore: Cengage Learning, 2009.
[10] Salomon, D. *Data Compression: The Complete Reference*, 2nd Edn. Germany, Berlin: Springer-Verlag, 2000.
[11] Davies, E. R. *Computer and Machine Vision: Theory, Algorithms, Practicalities*, 4th Edn. The Netherlands, Amsterdam: Elsevier, 2012.
[12] Forsyth, D. and Ponce, J. *Computer Vision: A Modern Approach*, 2nd Edn. USA, New Jersey: Prentice Hall, 2012.
[13] Zhang, Y.-J. *Image Engineering, Vol. 1: Image Processing*. Germany, Berlin: De Gruyter, 2017.

[14] Zhang, Y.-J. *Image Engineering, Vol. 2: Image Analysis.* Germany, Berlin: De Gruyter, 2017.

[15] Zhang, Y.-J. *Image Engineering, Vol. 3: Image Understanding.* Germany, Berlin: De Gruyter, 2017.

[16] Zhang, Y.-J. Image engineering in China: 1995. *Journal of Image and Graphics*, 1996, 1(1): 78–83.

[17] Zhang, Y.-J. Image engineering in China: 1995 (Complement). *Journal of Image and Graphics*, 1996, 1(2): 170–174.

[18] Zhang, Y.-J. Image engineering in China: 1996. *Journal of Image and Graphics*, 1997, 2(5): 336–344.

[19] Zhang, Y.-J. Image engineering in China: 1997. *Journal of Image and Graphics*, 1998, 3(5): 404–414.

[20] Zhang, Y.-J. Image engineering in China: 1998. *Journal of Image and Graphics*, 1999, 4A(5): 427–438.

[21] Zhang, Y.-J. Image engineering in China: 1999. *Journal of Image and Graphics*, 2000, 5A(5): 359–373.

[22] Zhang, Y.-J. Image engineering in China: 2000. *Journal of Image and Graphics*, 2001, 6A(5): 409–424.

[23] Zhang, Y.-J. Image engineering in China: 2001. *Journal of Image and Graphics*, 2002, 7A(5): 417–433.

[24] Zhang, Y.-J. Image engineering in China: 2002. *Journal of Image and Graphics*, 2003, 8A(5): 481–498.

[25] Zhang, Y.-J. Image engineering in China: 2003. *Journal of Image and Graphics*, 2004, 9A(5): 513–531.

[26] Zhang, Y.-J. Image engineering in China: 2004. *Journal of Image and Graphics*, 2005, 10A(5): 537–560.

[27] Zhang, Y.-J. Image engineering in China: 2005. *Journal of Image and Graphics*, 2006, 11(5): 601–623.

[28] Zhang, Y.-J. Image engineering in China: 2006. *Journal of Image and Graphics*, 2007, 12(5): 753–775.

[29] Zhang, Y.-J. Image engineering in China: 2007. *Journal of Image and Graphics*, 2008, 13(5): 825–852.

[30] Zhang, Y.-J. Image engineering in China: 2008. *Journal of Image and Graphics*, 2009, 14(5): 809–837.

[31] Zhang, Y.-J. Image engineering in China: 2009. *Journal of Image and Graphics*, 2010, 15(5): 689–722.

[32] Zhang, Y.-J. Image engineering in China: 2010. *Journal of Image and Graphics*, 2011, 16(5): 693–702.

[33] Zhang, Y.-J. Image engineering in China: 2011. *Journal of Image and Graphics*, 2012, 17(5): 603–612.

[34] Zhang, Y.-J. Image engineering in China: 2012. *Journal of Image and Graphics*, 2013, 18(5): 483–492.

[35] Zhang, Y.-J. Image engineering in China: 2013. *Journal of Image and Graphics*, 2014, 19(5): 649–658.

[36] Zhang, Y.-J. Image engineering in China: 2014. *Journal of Image and Graphics*, 2015, 20(5): 585–598.

[37] Zhang, Y.-J. Image engineering in China: 2015. *Journal of Image and Graphics*, 2016, 21(5): 533–543.

[38] Zhang, Y.-J. Image engineering in China: 2016. *Journal of Image and Graphics*, 2017, 22(5): 563–574.

[39] Zhang, Y.-J. Image engineering in China: 2017. *Journal of Image and Graphics*, 2018, 23(5): 617–629.

[40] Zhang, Y.-J. Image engineering in China: 2018. *Journal of Image and Graphics*, 2019, 24(5): 665–676.

[41] Zhang, Y.-J. Image engineering in China: 2019. *Journal of Image and Graphics*, 2020, 25(5): 864–878.

[42] Zhang, Y.-J. Image engineering in China: 2020. *Journal of Image and Graphics*, 2021, 26(5): 978–990.

[43] Marques, O. *Practical Image and Video Processing Using MATLAB*. USA, New Jersey: Wiley Publishing, Inc. 2013.

[44] Peters, J. F. *Foundations of Computer Vision*. Germany, Berlin: Springer, 2017.

[45] Zhang, Y.-J. *Problem Analysis in Image Engineering*. China, Beijing: Tsinghua University Press, 2018.

Chapter 2

2D Image Acquisition

Image acquisition refers to the technology and process of collecting images. As pointed out in Chapter 1, artificial vision systems mainly use digital images as input to the system. Therefore, image acquisition is the operational foundation of various computer vision technologies.

Image acquisition is an important means to obtain information from the objective world. Taking a gray-level image $f(x, y)$ as an example, $f(x, y)$ also represents the gray-scale value f at the image space (x, y). Image acquisition is to determine the f and (x, y) of the objective world scene after projection. Corresponding to the two parts expressed by the image $f(x, y)$, image acquisition involves two aspects whose models need to be established separately:

(1) **Photometry** (*more generally* **radiometry**): To solve the problems of how "bright" the object in the image is and what the relationship between this brightness and the optical properties of the object and imaging system is. It determines the f at (x, y).

(2) **Geometry**: To solve the problem of where in the scene the object will be projected to the position (x, y) in the image.

Taking into account the use of computers to process and analyze images, the images obtained from the original analog or continuous objective world are to be finally converted into digital images. Corresponding to the two parts expressed by the image $f(x, y)$, when acquiring a digital image that can be processed by a computer,

41

the former is related to **sampling** and the latter is related to **quantization**. Sampling and quantization determine the results obtained when an image is captured with an imaging device and represented by a digital matrix.

The acquired image is composed of many pixels. There are many connections between pixels in an image, including spatial adjacency or contact relationships, and similar or identical relationships in gray levels (attributes). On this basis, the composition of the connected set of pixels and the distance between pixels can also be considered. Many image processing and analysis techniques take advantage of these connections and relationships.

The sections of this chapter are arranged as follows:

Section 2.1 summarizes the typical image acquisition devices and the performance indicators of their concern, and also gives the acquisition flow process.

Section 2.2 discusses the image brightness imaging model, which is mainly related to f. On the basis of introducing the basic concepts of photometry, how to obtain uniform illuminance is analyzed, and a simple brightness imaging model is given.

Section 2.3 discusses the image space imaging model, which is mainly related to (x, y). According to the projection imaging geometry, the basic and general imaging models are introduced.

Section 2.4 introduces the relationship between the sampling and quantization of analog images with the spatial and amplitude resolutions of digital images, and further discusses the relationship between image quality and its data volume.

Section 2.5 introduces the various relationships between pixels: neighborhood, adjacency, connection, connectivity, etc. and also discusses the calculation of the distance between pixels.

2.1   Acquisition Device and Performance Index

In order to acquire digital images, special image acquisition equipment are required. What such image acquisition equipment have in common is that they receive external excitations and generate (continuous analog) responses, and then convert the analog responses into digital signals, which can be used by computers. Therefore, the image acquisition equipment need to include two kinds of devices. One is a physical device that is sensitive to a certain electromagnetic energy spectrum band (such as X-ray, ultraviolet, visible light, and infrared). It can receive radiation and generate (analog) electrical signals proportional to the received electromagnetic radiation energy. The physical devices sensitive to electromagnetic waves used in recent years are mainly charge-coupled devices (CCDs) and complementary metal oxide semiconductors (CMOS). A solid-state planar sensor array formed by them has a remarkable feature, that is, it has a very high shutter speed (up to 10^{-4} s), so it can freeze motion significantly. The other is a digital device which can convert the input (analog) electrical signal into a digital (discrete) form (analog-to-digital conversion) for input into the computer.

2.1.1 CCD sensor

A **charge-coupled device** is a typical solid-state array component composed of discrete silicon imaging elements called photosites. Such a photosensitive element can generate an output voltage proportional to the received input light intensity. A CCD sensor refers to a sensor composed of CCD as the core, which can be divided into two types according to geometric organization: line scan sensor and plane scan sensor. The line scan sensor includes a line of photosensitive primitives, which rely on the relative scanning movement between the scene and the detector to obtain a 2D image. The planar scanning sensor is composed of photosensitive elements arranged in a square array, which can directly obtain 2D images.

Example 2.1 Line scan sensor

Figure 2.1 shows a schematic diagram of a line scan CCD sensor. This sensor is composed of a line of photosites, two transmission gates that periodically transmit the contents of the photosites to the transfer (shift) registers, and an output gate that periodically transmits the contents of the transfer register to the amplifier. The intensity of the voltage signal output by the amplifier is proportional to the signal intensity of the photosites. □

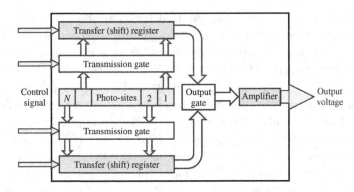

Figure 2.1.   Line scan sensor.

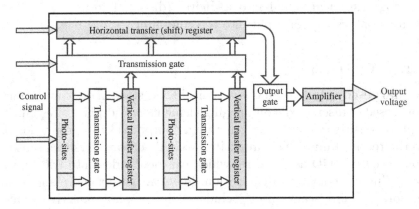

Figure 2.2.   Planar scan sensor.

Example 2.2 Planar scan sensor

The planar scan sensor has a charge-coupled planar array whose working principle is similar to that of a linear array, but here the photosites are arranged in an array (as shown in multiple columns in Figure 2.2). Each column of photosites is separated by transmission gates and transfer registers. During operation, the contents of the odd-numbered photosites are sequentially sent to the vertical transfer register, and then to the horizontal transfer register. Then, the contents of the horizontal transfer register are sent to the amplifier to get one interlaced frame of the video signal. If the above process is repeated for even-numbered columns of photosites, another interlaced frame of the video signal can be obtained. Combine these two frames to get one field (f) of the interlaced TV. The scanning speed of National Television Standards Committee (NTSC) system is 30 f/s, and the scanning speed of Phase Alteration Line (PAL) system is 25 f/s. □

2.1.2 CMOS sensor

Complementary Metal Oxide Semiconductor is also a typical solid-state array element. The imaging sensor formed by it mainly includes the sensor core, analog-to-digital converter, output register, control register, gain amplifier, etc. There are three types of photosensitive pixel circuits in the sensor core:

(1) Photodiode-type passive pixel structure: The passive pixel structure consists of a reverse-biased photodiode and a switch tube. When the switch tube is turned on, the photodiode is connected to the vertical column line, and the amplifier at the end of the column line reads the column line voltage. When the signal stored by the photodiode is read, the voltage is reset. At this time, the amplifier will communicate with the input light. The signal proportional to the charge is converted into a voltage output.
(2) Photodiode-type active pixel structure: The active pixel structure adds an active amplifier to the pixel unit.
(3) Grating active pixel structure: The signal charge is integrated under the grating. Before output, the diffusion point is reset, then the grating pulse is changed, and the signal charge under the grating is collected and transferred to the diffusion point. The difference between the reset and signal voltage levels is the output signal.

Compared with the traditional CCD camera device, the CMOS camera device integrates the entire system on a chip, which reduces power consumption, size, and overall cost.

2.1.3 Common performance indicators

For various image acquisition equipment, the main performance indicators that are often considered in use are:

(1) Linear response: refers to whether there is a linear relationship between the strength of the input physical signal and the strength of the output response signal.

(2) Sensitivity: Absolute sensitivity can be expressed by the minimum number of photons that can be detected, and relative sensitivity can be expressed by the number of photons required to make a single-level change in the output signal intensity.

(3) Signal-to-noise ratio: refers to the (energy or intensity) ratio of useful signal to unnecessary interference in the acquired image.

(4) Shading (unevenness): refers to the phenomenon that the input physical signal is constant but the output digital form is not constant.

(5) Shutter speed: the shooting/exposure time required to acquire an image.

(6) Reading rate: refers to the rate at which signal data is read (transmitted) from the photosensitive unit.

If one looks at the acquired image, its **spatial resolution** (that is, the number of digitized spatial sampling points) and **amplitude resolution/magnitude resolution** (that is, the quantization level of the sampling point value, for example, for gray-scale images refers to the number of gray level, and for depth images refers to the number of depth values) are also very important measures (see Section 2.4 for a more detailed discussion).

2.1.4 Image acquisition process

The commonly used image acquisition flowchart is shown in Figure 2.3. The light source radiates to the objective scene, and the reflected light from the scene enters the imaging sensor. The sensor performs photoelectric conversion to obtain analog signals related to the spatial relationship and surface properties of the objective scene. The analog signal is sampled and quantized to be converted into a digital signal output that can be used by a computer to obtain a scene image.

In practice, not only the reflected light of the objective scene but also the refracted and transmitted light of the objective scene can

Figure 2.3.   Image acquisition process.

be imaged. In addition, the spatial resolution of the image is mainly determined by the size and arrangement of the photoelectric sensing unit in the image acquisition matrix in the camera (equivalent to the sampling step moved forward), while the amplitude resolution of the image is mainly determined by the number of stages used for quantifying the intensity of electrical signals.

2.2 Image Brightness Imaging Model

The purpose of constructing the brightness imaging model is to determine the f of the image. This involves knowledge of photometry (including brightness and illuminance) as well as imaging models.

2.2.1 Fundamentals of photometry

Photometry is the discipline studying the light radiation intensity. The more general **radiometry** is the discipline studying the electromagnetic radiation intensity. The **brightness** of the scene itself is related to the intensity of light radiation in the scene. For a luminous scene (light source), the brightness of the scene is proportional to its own radiated power or the amount of light radiation. In photometry, **luminous flux** is used to express the power or amount of light radiation, and its unit is lm (lumens). The brightness of a light source along a certain direction is measured by its unit projected area in that direction and the luminous flux emitted by unit **solid angle** (its unit is ste-radian, sr), and its unit is cd/m^2 (candela per square meters), where cd is the unit of luminous intensity, $1\,cd = 1\,lm/sr$. For scenes that do not emit light, the **illuminance** from other light sources is considered. The illuminance obtained by the scene needs to be measured by the illuminance on the surface illuminated by the light, that is, the luminous flux illuminating on a unit area; the unit is lx (also lux), $1\,lx = 1\,lm/m^2$. After the non-luminous scene is illuminated by the light source, it reflects the incident light, which is equivalent to a luminous scene for imaging.

Example 2.3 Illustration of common light source brightness

Table 2.1 gives the brightness values of some common light sources and scenes, as well as the visual divisions (zones) they belong to, to

Table 2.1.   Brightness of some light sources and scenery seen daily (in cd/m^2).

Brightness	Zone	Example
10^{10}	Dangerous vision zone	The Sun seen through the atmosphere
10^9		Electric arc light
10^8		—
10^7	Transition zone	—
10^6	**Photopical zone**	Tungsten filament incandescent lamp filament
10^5		Cinema screen
10^4		White paper under the sun
10^3		Moonlight/Candle flame
10^2		Readable printing paper
10	Transition zone	—
1		—
10^{-1}		—
10^{-2}	**Scotopical zone**	White paper in the moonlight
10^{-3}		—
10^{-4}		Moonless night sky
10^{-5}		—
10^{-6}		Absolute perception threshold

help establish some numerical concepts. Here, the dangerous vision zone means that the brightness value in it will be harmful to the human eye. At the brightness corresponding to the **photopical zone**, the cone cells in the human eye respond to light radiation, enabling us to perceive various colors. Under the brightness corresponding to the **scotopical zone**, only the rod cells in the human eye respond to the light radiation, and the person does not have color perception.   □

Example 2.4 Some illuminance instances of actual scene

In order to establish some numerical concepts, Table 2.2 gives some actual values for scene illuminance.

Brightness and illuminance are not only related to a certain degree but also have obvious differences. **Illuminance** is a measure of the

Table 2.2.   Illuminances in some practical situations.

Actual situation	Illumination (in lx)
Moonless sky shining on the ground	Approximately 3×10^{-4}
Full moon approaching the zenith shining on the ground	Approximately 0.2
Illumination necessary for office work	Approximately $20 \sim 100$
Sunny summer day in a well-lit indoor	Approximately $100 \sim 500$
On the open ground where the sun does not directly shine in summer	Approximately $10^3 \sim 10^4$

amount of radiation that a light source with a certain intensity illuminates a scene, and **brightness** is a measure of the light intensity felt by the observer based on the illuminance. The illuminance value is affected by the distance from the light source to the surface of the object, while the brightness value has nothing to do with the distance from the surface of the object to the observer. □

2.2.2   Uniform illuminance

To image the scene, it is necessary to consider the illumination of the scene. The illuminance of the scene is not only related to the radiation intensity of the light source but also related to the relative positions of the light source and scene. The actual scenes are all of a certain size. Even if a light source at a fixed position is used to illuminate, the illuminance of different positions on the scene may be different. In order to obtain uniform illuminance, the number and position of light sources need to be designed.

Consider first the use of a single point light source. In Figure 2.4, the scene is placed at the coordinate origin O, the light source S is at the height h over the object, the horizontal offset is a, the actual distance from the object is d, and the incident angle θ is the angle between the surface normal direction n and the incident ray direction of light source s.

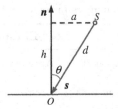

Figure 2.4.   Single point light source lighting geometry.

Considering that the radiation attenuates with the square of the distance, the illuminance of a point on the scene is (k is a constant factor)

$$E = k\frac{\cos\theta}{d^2} = \frac{kh}{d^3}. \tag{2.1}$$

Obviously, the illumination of a single point light source will cause non-uniform illuminance regions at different positions on the surface of the scene (corresponding to different incident angles). If two point light sources are arranged symmetrically, when one angle of incidence decreases and the other angle of incidence increases, then it is possible to obtain a more uniform illuminance along the connection line of the two point light sources.

Example 2.5 Illuminance with two point light sources

Consider placing two point-light sources symmetrically as shown in Figure 2.5(a). The solid line in Figure 2.5(b) represents the intensity curves generated by the two light sources, and the dotted line represents the intensity value obtained by combining these two intensities. Figure 2.5(c) represents the intensity curve obtained by slightly extending the two light sources apart. Here, Figure 2.5(b) corresponds to the elimination of second-order terms, leaving only fourth- or higher-order terms. Figure 2.5(c) represents the situation in which the distance between the two light sources is appropriately increased to make the intensity fluctuations still within the allowable range, while the available (relatively uniform) illuminance range is as large as possible.   □

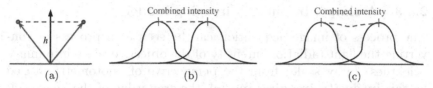

Figure 2.5. Geometry of two point light sources symmetrically arranged.

Example 2.6 Illuminance with strip light source

If the point light source in Figure 2.5 is replaced with a strip light source (the strip is parallel to the paper surface), the region of uniform illuminance obtained is a slender rectangle, as shown in Figure 2.6(a). If an illuminance region with an aspect ratio of 1 is required in practice, instead of a slender illuminance region, an arrangement of four strip light sources in parallel and orthogonal to each other, as shown in Figure 2.6(b), can be used. The resulting uniform illuminance region is a square. Figure 2.6(c) shows the circular uniform illuminance region obtained with a circular ring light source.

When imaging, the brightness of the scene after it is illuminated should be considered. For non-luminous scenes, the radiant brightness depends not only on the luminous flux illuminating the surface (illuminance) of the scene (related to the normal direction of the scene surface as well as the intensity and direction of the incident light source) but also on the luminous flux received by the observer when the incident light is reflected on the scene surface, which is related to the position and distance of the observer with respect to the scene as well as the reflection characteristics of the scene surface. □

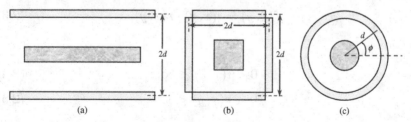

Figure 2.6. Several light source distributions to obtain a uniform illuminance region.

2.2.3   A simple brightness imaging model

The process of image acquisition can be seen as a process of converting the light radiation intensity of the objective scene into image brightness (gray scale) from the perspective of photometry. Based on this **intensity imaging model**, the gray value of the image collected from the scene is determined by two factors: one is the brightness (radiation intensity) of the scene itself, and the other is how to convert the scene brightness into image brightness (gray level) during imaging.

A simple brightness imaging model is introduced in the following. The image here is represented by a 2D brightness function $f(x, y)$; $f(x, y)$ also represents the brightness of the image at a specific coordinate point (x, y) in space. Because brightness f is actually a measure of energy, $f(x, y)$ must not be 0 and should be a finite value, namely:

$$0 < f(x, y) < \infty. \tag{2.2}$$

Generally, the image brightness is obtained by measuring the reflected light from objects in the scene. So, $f(x, y)$ is basically determined by the following two factors: (i) light intensity incident on the visible scene; (ii) ratio of the incident light reflection from the surface of the object in the scene. They can be represented by the illuminance function $i(x, y)$ and the reflection function $r(x, y)$, respectively, which are also called the **illumination component** and **reflection component**, respectively. Some typical $r(x, y)$ values are: 0.01 for black velvet, 0.65 for stainless steel, 0.80 for whitewashed wall planes, 0.90 for silver-plated utensils, and 0.93 for snow. Because $f(x, y)$ is proportional to $i(x, y)$ and $r(x, y)$, it can be considered that $f(x, y)$ is obtained by multiplying $i(x, y)$ and $r(x, y)$:

$$f(x, y) = i(x, y) \cdot r(x, y), \tag{2.3}$$

where

$$0 < i(x, y) < \infty, \tag{2.4}$$

$$0 < r(x, y) < 1. \tag{2.5}$$

Equation (2.4) shows that the incident quantity is always greater than 0 (only the incident case is considered), but it is not infinite (because it should be physically possible). Equation (2.5) shows that the reflectivity is between 0 (total absorption) and 1 (total reflection). The values given in both equations are theoretical limits. It should be noted that the value of $i(x, y)$ is determined by the lighting source and the value of $r(x, y)$ is determined by the surface characteristics of the objects in the scene.

Generally, the brightness value of the monochrome image $f(\cdot)$ at the coordinates (x, y) is called the **gray value** of the image at that point (it can be represented by g). According to Equations (2.3)–(2.5), g will take values in the following range:

$$G_{\max} \leq g \leq G_{\min}. \tag{2.6}$$

In theory, the only restriction on $G_{\min}$ is that it should be positive (that is, there is incidence, but it is generally taken as 0), and the only restriction on $G_{\max}$ is that it should be limited. In practical applications, the interval $[G_{\min}, G_{\max}]$ is called the **gray-scale range**. Generally, this interval is digitally moved to the interval $[0, G)$ (G is a positive integer). If $g = 0$, it is regarded as black; if $g = G - 1$, it is regarded as white; all intermediate values represent the gray value from black to white in turn.

2.3 Image Space Imaging Model

The space imaging model is to determine the (x, y) of the image, that is, the 2D spatial position of the 3D objective scene projected onto the image.

2.3.1 Projection imaging geometry

Projection imaging involves conversion between different coordinate systems. These transformations can be linearized using homogeneous coordinates.

1. Coordinate systems

The image acquisition process can be regarded as a process of projecting and transforming the scene of the objective world. This projection can be described by imaging transformation (also called geometric perspective transformation). Imaging transformation involves the transformation between different coordinate systems, including:

(1) *World coordinate system*: also called the real-world coordinate system XYZ, which is the absolute coordinates of the objective world (so, it is also called the objective coordinate system). Generally, 3D scenes are represented by this coordinate system.

(2) *Camera coordinate system*: The coordinate system xyz formulated with the camera as the center generally takes the optical axis of the camera as the z axis.

(3) *Image coordinate system*: also called the image plane coordinate system, which is the plane coordinate system $x'y'$ where the image is formed in the camera.

In practice, the image plane is often taken to be parallel to the xy plane of the camera coordinate system, the x and x' axes as well as the y and y' axes are coincident, respectively, so that the origin of the image plane is on the optical axis of the camera.

The process of image acquisition is to first convert the objective scene in the world coordinate system to the camera coordinate system, and then to the image coordinate system. According to the different interrelationships of the above several coordinate systems, different types of imaging models can be obtained. These imaging models are also called camera models, and they are models describing the relationship between the three coordinate systems.

2. Homogeneous coordinates

When discussing the conversion between different coordinate systems, if the coordinate system can be represented in the form of homogeneous coordinates, the conversion between these coordinate systems can be represented in the form of a linear matrix.

Example 2.7 Homogeneous representation of lines and points

A straight line on the plane can be represented by the straight line equation $ax + by + c = 0$. Different a, b, c can represent different straight lines, so a straight line can also be represented by the vector

$l = [a, b, c]^{\mathrm{T}}$. Because the straight line $ax + by + c = 0$ and the straight line $(ka)x + (kb)y + kc = 0$ are the same when k is not 0, so when k is not 0, the vectors $[a, b, c]^{\mathrm{T}}$ and $k[a, b, c]^{\mathrm{T}}$ represent the same straight line. In fact, these vectors that differ by only one scale can be considered equivalent. The vector set that satisfies this equivalent relationship is called a **homogeneous vector**, and any specific vector $[a, b, c]^{\mathrm{T}}$ is a representative vector of the vector set.

For a straight line $l = [a, b, c]^{\mathrm{T}}$, if and only if $ax + by + c = 0$, the point $\boldsymbol{x} = [x, y]^{\mathrm{T}}$ is on this straight line. This can be represented by the inner product of the vector $[x, y, 1]$ of the corresponding point and the vector $[a, b, c]^{\mathrm{T}}$ of the corresponding line, that is, $[x, y, 1] \cdot [a, b, c]^{\mathrm{T}} = [x, y, 1] \cdot l = 0$. Here, the point vector $[x, y]^{\mathrm{T}}$ is represented by a 3D vector with a value of 1 added as the last item. Note that for any non-zero constant k and any straight line l, if and only if $[x, y, 1] \cdot l = 0$, there is $[kx, ky, k] \cdot l = 0$. Therefore, all vectors $[kx, ky, k]^{\mathrm{T}}$ (obtained by the change of k) can be considered as the representation of the point $[x, y]^{\mathrm{T}}$. In this way, like a straight line, a point can also be represented by a homogeneous vector. □

In general, the Cartesian coordinate XYZ corresponding to a point in space is defined as (kX, kY, kZ, k), where k is an arbitrary non-zero constant. Obviously, to transform from homogeneous coordinates back to Cartesian coordinates, the first three coordinates should be divided by the fourth coordinate. In this way, a point in a Cartesian world coordinate system can be represented in vector form as

$$\boldsymbol{W} = [X \ Y \ Z]^{\mathrm{T}}. \tag{2.7}$$

Its corresponding homogeneous coordinates can be represented as (using h to indicate homogeneous)

$$\boldsymbol{W}_{\mathrm{h}} = [kX \ kY \ kZ \ k]^{\mathrm{T}}. \tag{2.8}$$

2.3.2 Basic imaging model

Let's first look at the basic **projection imaging model**. Figure 2.7 shows a schematic diagram of the basic geometric model of a projection imaging process (projecting a 3D objective scene onto a 2D image plane). As shown in Figure 2.7, suppose that the world coordinate system coincides with the camera coordinate system, and the

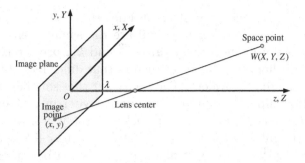

Figure 2.7.   Schematic diagram of projection imaging.

image plane coordinate system $x'y'$ coincides with the xy plane of the camera coordinate system (the x and x' axes as well as the y and y' axes respectively coincide, so xy is used here to represent $x'y'$); in addition, the optical axis (through the center of the lens) is along the z axis. In this way, the center of the image plane is at the origin (on the optical axis of the camera), the coordinates of the lens center are $(0, 0, \lambda)$, where λ is the focal length of the lens (a lens may contain multiple lenses, and λ represents the total integrated focal length on this case).

1. Projection and projection matrix

Let (X, Y, Z) be the world coordinates of any point W in 3D space. In the following discussion, it is assumed that all the points of interest in the objective scene are in front of the lens, and $Z > \lambda$. With the help of similar triangle relations, the following two equations are established:

$$\frac{x}{\lambda} = \frac{-X}{Z - \lambda} = \frac{X}{\lambda - Z},\tag{2.9}$$

$$\frac{y}{\lambda} = \frac{-Y}{Z - \lambda} = \frac{Y}{\lambda - Z}.\tag{2.10}$$

The negative sign before X and Y in Equations (2.9) and (2.10) represents the opposite signs of the image and W points. From Equations (2.9) and (2.10), the image plane coordinates of a 3D point in space after projection can be

$$x = \frac{\lambda X}{\lambda - Z}\tag{2.11}$$

and

$$y = \frac{\lambda Y}{\lambda - Z}. \tag{2.12}$$

Note that both Equations (2.11) and (2.12) are nonlinear because they contain the variable Z in the denominator. They can be represented in the form of a linear matrix with the help of homogeneous coordinates.

The homogeneous coordinates of the Cartesian coordinates XYZ of a point in space are defined as (kX, kY, kZ, k), where k is an arbitrary non-zero constant. Obviously, changing the homogeneous coordinates back to Cartesian coordinates can be achieved by dividing the first three coordinate values by the fourth coordinate value. The points in a Cartesian world coordinate system can be represented in vector form as

$$\boldsymbol{W} = [X\ Y\ Z]^{\mathrm{T}}. \tag{2.13}$$

Its corresponding homogeneous coordinates can be represented as

$$\boldsymbol{W}_{\mathrm{h}} = [kX\ kY\ kZ\ k]^{\mathrm{T}}. \tag{2.14}$$

If the **projection matrix** for perspective projection imaging is defined as

$$\boldsymbol{P} = \begin{bmatrix} 1 & 0 & 0 & 0 \\ 0 & 1 & 0 & 0 \\ 0 & 0 & 1 & 0 \\ 0 & 0 & -1/\lambda & 1 \end{bmatrix}, \tag{2.15}$$

the product $\boldsymbol{P}\boldsymbol{W}_{\mathrm{h}}$ of the matrix $\boldsymbol{P}$ in Equation (2.15) and $\boldsymbol{W}_{\mathrm{h}}$ gives a vector denoted by $\boldsymbol{C}_{\mathrm{h}}$:

$$\boldsymbol{C}_{\mathrm{h}} = \boldsymbol{P}\boldsymbol{W}_{\mathrm{h}} = \begin{bmatrix} 1 & 0 & 0 & 0 \\ 0 & 1 & 0 & 0 \\ 0 & 0 & 1 & 0 \\ 0 & 0 & -1/\lambda & 1 \end{bmatrix} \begin{bmatrix} kX \\ kY \\ kZ \\ k \end{bmatrix} = \begin{bmatrix} kX \\ kY \\ kZ \\ -kZ/\lambda + k \end{bmatrix}. \tag{2.16}$$

Here, the elements of $\boldsymbol{C}_{\mathrm{h}}$ are camera coordinates in homogeneous form. These coordinates can be converted into Cartesian form by dividing the first three items by the fourth item of C_h. Therefore, the Cartesian coordinates of any point in the camera coordinate system can be represented in vector form:

$$c = [x\ y\ z]^T = \left[\dfrac{\lambda X}{\lambda - Z}\quad \dfrac{\lambda Y}{\lambda - Z}\quad \dfrac{\lambda Z}{\lambda - Z} \right]^T. \tag{2.17}$$

2. Inverse projection and inverse projection matrix

Inverse projection is the projection from the 2D plane to the 3D space. According to the inverse projection matrix, the 2D image coordinates can be used to determine the coordinates of the imaging 3D objective scene, or the inverse projection matrix can be used to map a 2D image point back to the 3D space. Using matrix operation rules, from Equation (2.16), we can get

$$W_h = P^{-1}c_h, \tag{2.18}$$

where the **inverse projection matrix** P^{-1} is

$$P^{-1} = \begin{bmatrix} 1 & 0 & 0 & 0 \\ 0 & 1 & 0 & 0 \\ 0 & 0 & 1 & 0 \\ 0 & 0 & 1/\lambda & 1 \end{bmatrix}. \tag{2.19}$$

Can the coordinates of the corresponding 3D objective scene points be determined from the 2D image coordinate points using the previously mentioned inverse projection matrix? Suppose the coordinates of an image point are $(x, y, 0)$, where 0 at the z position only means that the image plane is at $z = 0$. This point can be represented as a homogeneous vector:

$$c_h = [kx\ ky\ 0\ k]^T. \tag{2.20}$$

Substituting it into Equation (2.18), the world coordinate vector in homogeneous form is obtained:

$$W_h = [kx\ ky\ 0\ k]^T. \tag{2.21}$$

The world coordinate vector in the corresponding Cartesian coordinate system is

$$W = [X\ Y\ Z]^T = [x\ y\ 0]^T. \tag{2.22}$$

Equation (2.22) shows that the Z coordinate of a 3D point cannot be uniquely determined by the image point (x, y) because it gives $Z = 0$ for any 3D point. The problem here is caused by the many-to-one transformation of the 3D objective scene mapped to the image plane. The image point (x, y) now corresponds to the set of all collinear 3D points on the straight line passing $(x, y, 0)$ and $(0, 0, \lambda)$, that is, the line connecting the image and space points in Figure 2.7. The equation of this straight line can be represented by Equations (2.11) and (2.12) in the world coordinate system, from which X and Y are inversely solved:

$$X = \frac{x}{\lambda}(\lambda - Z), \tag{2.23}$$

$$Y = \frac{y}{\lambda}(\lambda - Z). \tag{2.24}$$

Equations (2.23) and (2.24) indicate that unless there is some prior knowledge about the 3D space point projected to the image point (such as knowing its Z coordinate), it is impossible to fully recover the coordinates of a 3D point from its image. In fact, the spatial scene loses part of the information after projection, and it is impossible to recover this information only by inverse projection. To recover a 3D space point from the projection point on the image by inverse projection, at least one world coordinate of the space point needs to be known.

2.3.3　General imaging model

The following considers a more general situation when the camera coordinate system is separated from the world coordinate system, but the image plane system coincides with the camera coordinate system. Figure 2.8 shows a schematic diagram of the geometric model of the imaging process for this case. The position deviation between the center of the image plane (origin) and the world coordinate system is recorded as a vector $\boldsymbol{D}$, and its components are D_x, D_y, and D_z. Here, it is assumed that the camera pans at an angle γ (γ is the angle between x and X axes) and tilts at an angle α (α is the angle between z and Z axes). To put it vividly, if the XY plane is taken as the equatorial plane of the earth and the Z axis points to the north

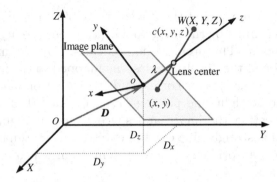

Figure 2.8.   Schematic diagram of projection imaging when the world coordinate system and the camera coordinate system do not coincide.

pole of the earth, the pan angle corresponds to the longitude and the tilt angle corresponds to the latitude.

The above model can be converted into the camera model such that the world coordinate system and the camera coordinate system coincide, as shown in Figure 2.7, through the following series of steps:

(1) move the origin of the image plane out of the origin of the world coordinate system by vector D;
(2) pan the x axis (around the z axis) at a certain γ angle;
(3) tilt the z axis (rotate around the x axis) at a certain α angle.

The movement of the camera relative to the world coordinate system is also equivalent to the inverse movement of the world coordinate system relative to the camera. Specifically, each point in the world coordinate system can be subjected to the three steps of the above geometric relationship conversion. Translating the origin of the world coordinate system to the origin of the image plane can be accomplished with the following **translation matrix**:

$$
T = \begin{bmatrix} 1 & 0 & 0 & -D_x \\ 0 & 1 & 0 & -D_y \\ 0 & 0 & 1 & -D_z \\ 0 & 0 & 0 & 1 \end{bmatrix}. \tag{2.25}
$$

In other words, the homogeneous coordinate point D_h with coordinates (D_x, D_y, D_z) is located at the origin of the new coordinate system after transformation $T D_h$.

Further, consider how to overlap the coordinate axes. The pan angle γ is the angle between the x and X axes. These two axes are parallel in the normal (nominal) position. In order to scan the x axis at the required γ angle, one only needs to rotate the camera counterclockwise (defined by looking at the origin from the positive direction of the rotation axis) around the z axis by γ angle, namely:

$$\boldsymbol{R_\gamma} = \begin{bmatrix} \cos\gamma & \sin\gamma & 0 & 0 \\ -\sin\gamma & \cos\gamma & 0 & 0 \\ 0 & 0 & 1 & 0 \\ 0 & 0 & 0 & 1 \end{bmatrix}. \tag{2.26}$$

In the case of no rotation ($\gamma = 0°$), the x and X axes are parallel. Similarly, the tilt angle α is the angle between the z and Z axes. The camera can be rotated counterclockwise around the x axis to achieve the effect of tilting the camera α angle, that is,

$$\boldsymbol{R_\alpha} = \begin{bmatrix} 1 & 0 & 0 & 0 \\ 0 & \cos\alpha & \sin\alpha & 0 \\ 0 & -\sin\alpha & \cos\alpha & 0 \\ 0 & 0 & 0 & 1 \end{bmatrix}. \tag{2.27}$$

In the case of no tilt ($\alpha = 0°$), the z and Z axes are parallel.

The two transformation matrices that complete the above two rotations can be cascaded to form a single **rotation matrix**:

$$\boldsymbol{R} = \boldsymbol{R_\alpha}\boldsymbol{R_\gamma} = \begin{bmatrix} \cos\gamma & \sin\gamma & 0 & 0 \\ -\sin\gamma\cos\alpha & \cos\alpha\cos\gamma & \sin\alpha & 0 \\ \sin\alpha\sin\gamma & -\sin\alpha\cos\gamma & \cos\alpha & 0 \\ 0 & 0 & 0 & 1 \end{bmatrix}. \tag{2.28}$$

Here, $\boldsymbol{R}$ represents the effect of the camera's rotation in space.

If the previously mentioned series of transformations $\boldsymbol{RTW}_\mathrm{h}$ is performed on the homogeneous coordinate $\boldsymbol{W}_\mathrm{h}$ of the space point, the world and camera coordinate systems can be superimposed. A homogeneous world coordinate point observed by a camera that satisfies the geometric relationship shown in Figure 2.8 has the following homogeneous representation in the camera coordinate system (where P is the projection matrix):

$$C_h = PRTW_h. \tag{2.29}$$

When the first and second items of C_h are divided by the fourth item of C_h, the Cartesian coordinates (x, y) of the world coordinate point after imaging can be obtained. Expanding Equation (2.29) and converting it to Cartesian coordinates will give

$$x = \lambda \frac{(X - D_x)\cos\gamma + (Y - D_y)\sin\gamma}{(X - D_x)\sin\alpha\sin\gamma + (Y - D_y)\sin\alpha\cos\gamma - (Z - D_z)\cos\alpha + \lambda} \tag{2.30}$$

and

$$y = \lambda \frac{-(X - D_x)\sin\gamma\cos\alpha + (Y - D_y)\cos\alpha\cos\gamma + (Z - D_z)\sin\alpha}{-(X - D_x)\sin\alpha\sin\gamma + (Y - D_y)\sin\alpha\cos\gamma - (Z - D_z)\cos\alpha + \lambda}. \tag{2.31}$$

These give the coordinates of the world point $W(X, Y, Z)$ in the image plane coordinate system.

Example 2.8 Image plane coordinate calculation in general imaging model

Suppose a camera is placed as shown in Figure 2.9 to observe the scene. Suppose the center position of the camera is $(0, 0, 1)$, focal

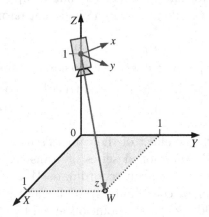

Figure 2.9.   Schematic diagram of camera observing 3D scene.

length of the camera is 0.05 m, pan angle is 135°, and tilt angle is 135°. Now, it is necessary to determine the image plane coordinates of the space point $W(1, 1, 0)$ in the figure at this time.

To this end, consider the steps required to move the camera from the normal position and orientation shown in Figure 2.10(a) to the position and orientation shown in Figure 2.9:

(1) Move out of the origin, and the result is shown in Figure 2.10(b). Note that after this step, the world coordinate system is only used as an angle reference, that is, all rotations are performed around the new (i.e., camera) coordinate axis.

(2) Rotate and pan around the z axis, which means that the observation surface panned along the z axis of the camera is shown in Figure 2.10(c), where the direction of the z axis is out of the paper. Note that the rotation of the camera around the z-axis is counterclockwise, so γ is positive.

(3) Rotate and tilt around the x-axis, which means that the camera rotates around the x-axis and tilts the observation surface relative to the z-axis as shown in Figure 2.10(d), where the x-axis points out of the paper. The rotation of the camera around the x axis is also counterclockwise, so α is positive.

In Figures 2.10(c) and (d), the world coordinate axes YZ and XY are represented by dashed lines to emphasize that they are only used to help establish the original reference for angles α and γ.

Substituting the parameter values given in the question into Equations (2.30) and (2.31), the image coordinates of point $W(1, 1, 0)$ can be calculated as $x = 0$ m and $y = -0.008837488$ m. □

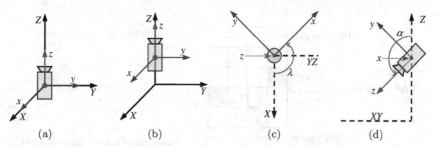

Figure 2.10. Translate and rotate the camera to determine the image plane coordinates.

For more introduction to the space imaging model, see "3D Computer Vision".

2.4   Sampling and Quantization

The objective world is an analog world, so the images acquired from the scene must be discretized in space and gray level before they can be processed by the computer. The discretization of spatial coordinates is called spatial **sampling**, and the discretization of gray values is called gray **quantization**.

2.4.1   Spatial and amplitude resolutions

The brightness imaging model discussed above determines the amplitude range of the image, while the spatial imaging model determines the spatial field of view corresponding to the image. From the acquired images, the precision in the spatial field of view corresponds to its **spatial resolution**, and the precision in the amplitude range corresponds to its **amplitude resolution** or **magnitude resolution**. Sampling determines the spatial resolution of the image, and quantization determines the amplitude resolution of the image. Spatial resolution and amplitude resolution are both important performance indicators of image acquisition devices (see Section 2.1).

When acquiring images, the spatial resolution is mainly determined by the size and arrangement of the photoelectric sensing units in the image acquisition matrix of the camera, and the amplitude

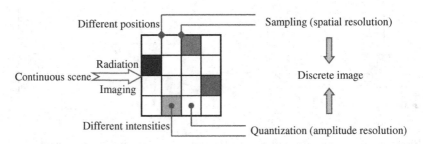

Figure 2.11.   Spatial resolution and amplitude resolution.

resolution is mainly determined by the number of levels used to quantify the intensity of the electrical signal. As shown in Figure 2.11, the signal radiated to the photoreceptive unit in the image acquisition matrix is sampled in space and quantized in intensity.

Let G, X, and Y be sets of real integers. The sampling process can be seen as dividing the image plane into regular grids. The position of the center point of each grid is determined by a pair of Cartesian coordinates (x, y), where x belongs to X and y belongs to Y. Let $f(\cdot)$ be the function of assigning the amplitude value (f belongs to G) to the coordinate pair (x, y) of the point, then $f(x, y)$ is a digital image, and this assignment process is the quantization process.

If the size of an image (corresponding to the spatial resolution) is $M \times N$, it means that MN samples were taken during imaging, or the image contains MN pixels. If each pixel is assigned with one of the G amplitude values, it means that it is quantized into G amplitude levels (corresponding to amplitude resolution, for gray-scale images, it is **gray-level resolution**) during imaging.

Example 2.9 Spatial resolution of some image display formats

The spatial resolutions of some common image display formats are shown in Table 2.3. □

Table 2.3.   The spatial resolutions of some image display formats.

Display formats	Spatial resolution/pixel
Source input format (SIF-525, NTSC)	352×240
Source input format (SIF-625, PAL)	352×288
Common intermediate format (CIF)	352×288
1/4 Common intermediate format (QCIF)	176×144
NTSC Standard interface format (NTSC-SIF)	352×240
PAL Standard interface format (PAL-SIF)	352×288
NTSC system CCIR/ITU-R 601	720×480
PAL system CCIR/ITU-R 601	720×576
Video graphics array (VGA)	640×480
High-definition television (HDTV)	$1440 \times 1152, 1920 \times 1152$

2.4.2   Image data volume and quality

For a continuous image, the corresponding digital image $f(x, y)$ can be approximated by an $M \times N$ array or matrix, namely:

$$f(x, y) = \begin{bmatrix} f(0,0) & f(0,1) & \cdots & f(0, M-1) \\ f(1,0) & f(1,1) & \cdots & f(1, M-1) \\ \vdots & \vdots & \ddots & \vdots \\ f(N-1,0) & f(N-1,1) & \cdots & f(N-1, M-1) \end{bmatrix}.$$

$$(2.32)$$

The spatial resolution of the image is $M \times N$, and the amplitude resolution is the discrete amplitude level G (the number of different gray values) that each $f(\cdot)$ can take. In order to facilitate computer processing, these quantities are generally taken as an integer power of 2, namely:

$$M = 2^m, \quad (2.33)$$

$$N = 2^n, \quad (2.34)$$

$$G = 2^k. \quad (2.35)$$

It is assumed here that these discrete amplitude levels are uniformly distributed. From Equations (2.33)–(2.35), the number of bits b (unit is bit) required to store a digital image can be calculated by

$$b = MNk. \quad (2.36)$$

If $N = M$ (i.e., a square image), then

$$b = N^2 k. \quad (2.37)$$

The number of bits required to represent or store a digital image is often very large. For example, for a 512×512, 256-gray-level image, 2097152 bits are required, while for a 1-second PAL system 512×512 color video, 157286400 bits are required.

Because Equation (2.32) is an approximation of continuous images, a question often arises: How many samples and gray levels are needed to achieve a better approximation? In theory, the larger the two parameters, the closer the discrete array is to the original continuous image. However, starting from the actual situation, Equation

(2.37) clearly indicates that the storage and processing requirements will increase rapidly with the increase of N and k, so the sampling numbers and number of gray levels cannot be too large.

Let's take a look at how the **visual quality** of digital images degrades as the spatial resolution and gray-scale quantization levels (corresponding to amplitude resolution) decrease (see Examples 2.10–2.12) to give some relationship information between **image quality** and **data volume**.

For an image having many details with 512×512, 256 gray levels, if one keeps the number of gray levels unchanged and only reduce its spatial resolution (by pixel copy) to 256×256, a square checkerboard pattern may be seen at the boundaries between regions, and the pixel particles become thicker in the whole picture, which has a great influence on the texture regions in the picture. This effect is generally more noticeable in a picture of 128×128, and it is quite obvious in pictures of 64×64 and 32×32.

Example 2.10 Effect produced by the change of image spatial resolution

Figure 2.12 gives a set of examples showing the change effect of image spatial resolutions. The spatial resolutions, number of gray levels, and amount of data of each image are listed in the columns of Table 2.4. The ratios of the amount of data between two adjacent images are also given between the corresponding two columns. Here, each image keeps the number of gray levels unchanged, and the spatial resolution of the previous image is successively halved in both horizontal and vertical directions. In these images, the phenomenon described above can be seen. For example, in Figure 2.12(b), the brim of the hat has been jagged; in Figure 2.12(c), this phenomenon is more obvious, and one has a feeling that the hair becomes thickened and unclear; in Figure 2.12(d), the hair is no longer in the form of strips; in Figure 2.12(e), it is almost impossible to distinguish the person's face, and on looking at Figure 2.12(f) alone, it is almost impossible to see what is in it. □

Now, the previously mentioned 512×512, 256-level gray-scale image is used to consider the effect of reducing the image amplitude resolution (i.e., the number of gray levels). If the spatial resolution is maintained and only the number of gray levels is reduced to 128

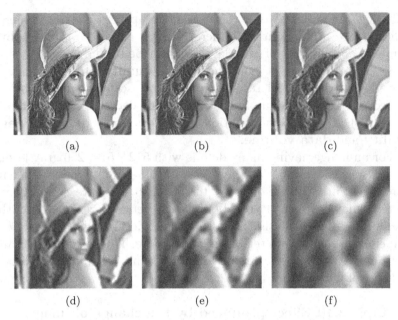

Figure 2.12.   Change effect of image spatial resolutions.

Table 2.4.   Set of images with varying spatial resolutions.

Figure 2.12	(a)	(b)	(c)	(d)	(e)	(f)
Spatial resolution	512×512	256×256	128×128	64×64	32×32	16×16
Number of gray levels	256	256	256	256	256	256
Amount of data/bit	67108864	16777216	4194304	1048576	262144	65536
Ratio of data volume		4::1	4::1	4::1	4::1	4::1

or 64, one cannot generally find any difference. If the number of gray levels is further reduced to 32, some very fine ridge-like structures that are almost invisible will often appear in the regions of slow gray-scale changes. This effect is called **false contour**, and it is caused by the insufficient number of gray levels used in the smooth region of the digital image. It is generally more obvious in the images with 16 levels or less than 16 levels.

Example 2.11 Effect produced by the change of image spatial resolutions

Figure 2.13 gives a set of examples showing the change effect of image gray levels. The spatial resolutions, number of gray levels, and amount of data of each image are listed in the columns of Table 2.5. The ratios of the amount of data between two adjacent images are also given between the corresponding two columns. Here, the spatial

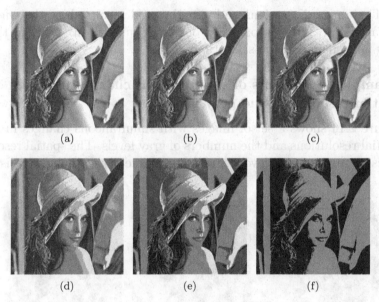

(a)   (b)   (c)

(d)   (e)   (f)

Figure 2.13. Change effect of image amplitude resolutions.

Table 2.5. Set of images with varying numbers of gray level.

Figure 2.13	(a)	(b)	(c)	(d)	(e)	(f)
Spatial resolution	512×512	512×512	512×512	512×512	512×512	512×512
Number of gray levels	256	64	16	8	4	2
Amount of data/bit	67108864	16777216	4194304	2097152	1048576	524288
Ratio of data volume		4::1	4::1	2::1	2::1	2::1

resolution of each image is unchanged, and the gray level of the previous image is reduced in turn (in the first two times, it is reduced to 1/4, and in the last three times, it is reduced to 1/2). In these images, the phenomenon discussed above can be seen. For example, Figure 2.13(b) is basically similar to Figure 2.13(a), and some false contours can be seen from Figure 2.13(c). In Figure 2.13(d), the false contours are very obvious, and in Figure 2.13(e), this can be seen everywhere. Finally, Figure 2.13(f) has a woodcut effect.   □

The above discussions and experimental results show the effects of varying N and k, separately, on image quality. In addition, they may also change at the same time.

Example 2.12 Effects of simultaneous changes in image spatial resolutions and gray levels

Figure 2.14 shows a set of images with simultaneous changes in the spatial resolutions and the numbers of gray levels. The spatial resolutions, number of gray levels, and data volume of each image are listed

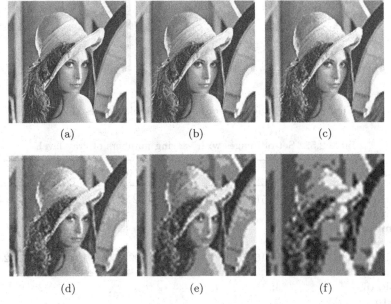

(a)   (b)   (c)

(d)   (e)   (f)

Figure 2.14.   Effect of simultaneous changes in image spatial resolutions and gray levels.

Table 2.6.   Set of images with changes both in spatial resolutions and gray levels.

Figure 2.14	(a)	(b)	(c)	(d)	(e)	(f)
Spatial resolution	256×256	181×181	128×128	90×90	64×64	45×45
Number of gray levels	256	64	32	16	8	4
Amount of data/bit	16777216	2096704	524288	129600	32768	8100
Ratio of data volume		8::1	4::1	4::1	4::1	4::1

in the columns of Table 2.6. The ratios of the amount of data between two adjacent images are also given between the corresponding two columns.

Since the spatial resolution and amplitude resolution of the image decrease at the same time, the image quality decreases faster here.   □

2.5   Relationship Between Pixels

The pixels in the actual image are arranged in space according to a certain law, and there are certain connections between them. When processing and analyzing images, the relationship between pixels should be considered.

2.5.1   Pixel neighborhood and connectivity

The relationship between pixels is related to each pixel's **neighborhood** composed of its neighboring pixels. For a pixel p with coordinates (x, y), it can have four horizontal and vertical neighbor pixels. Their coordinates are $(x + 1, y)$, $(x - 1, y)$, $(x, y + 1)$, and $(x, y - 1)$. These pixels (all denoted by r) form the **4-neighborhood** of p, denoted as $N_4(p)$, as shown in Figure 2.15(a). It should be pointed out that if the pixel p itself is at the edge of the image, several pixels in its $N_4(p)$ will fall outside the image.

The coordinates of the four diagonal neighboring pixels (indicated by s) of pixel p are $(x + 1, y + 1)$, $(x + 1, y - 1)$, $(x - 1, y + 1)$, and

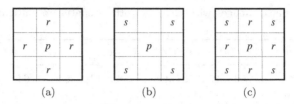

Figure 2.15.   Three types of neighborhood of pixels.

$(x-1, y-1)$. They are denoted as $N_D(p)$, as shown in Figure 2.15(b). The four pixels in 4-neighborhood of pixel p plus the four diagonal neighboring pixels together form the **8-neighborhood** of p, denoted as $N_8(p)$, as shown in Figure 2.15(c). It should be pointed out that if the pixel p itself is at the edge of the image, several pixels in its $N_D(p)$ and $N_8(p)$ will fall outside the image.

For two pixels p and q, if q is in the neighborhood of p (can be 4-neighborhood, 8-neighborhood, or diagonal neighborhood), then p and q are called **adjacent** (4-adjacent, 8-adjacent, or diagonally adjacent), or they are said to be in **adjacency**. If pixels p and q are adjacent, and their gray values meet a certain similarity criterion (such as their gray values are equal or in the same gray value range), then p and q are said to be in connection to each other. It can be seen that the **connectivity** is more demanding than the adjacency; not only the spatial relationship (adjacent) must be considered but also the gray-level relationship (similar) must be considered.

If pixels p and q are not (directly) adjacent, but they are both in the same neighborhood (can be 4-neighborhood, 8-neighborhood, or diagonal neighborhood) of another pixel, and if the gray values of these three pixels all meet a certain similarity criterion (such as their gray values are equal or in the same gray value set), then p and q are called **connected** (can be 4-connected or 8-connected). Further, as long as there is a series of sequentially connected pixels between these two pixels p and q, they are connected. This series of sequentially connected pixels constitutes a **path** between pixels p and q. A path from a pixel p with coordinates (x, y) to a pixel q with coordinates (s, t) consists of a series of independent pixels with coordinates (x_0, y_0), $(x_1, y_1), \ldots, (x_n, y_n)$. Here, $(x_0, y_0) = (x, y)$, $(x_n, y_n) = (s, t)$, and (x_i, y_i) is adjacent to (x_{i-1}, y_{i-1}), where $1 \leq i \leq n$, n is the path length.

2.5.2 Distance between pixels

An important concept of the relationship between pixels is the **distance** between pixels. Given three pixels p, q, r, the coordinates are (x, y), (s, t), (u, v), if the following conditions are met, the function D is called a distance metric function:

(1) $D(p, q) \geq 0 (D(p, q) = 0$ if and only if $p = q)$;
(2) $D(p, q) = D(q, p)$;
(3) $D(p, r) \leq D(p, q) + D(q, r)$.

Among the above three conditions, the first condition indicates that the distance between two pixels is always positive (when the spatial positions of two pixels are the same, the distance between them is zero); the second condition indicates that the distance between two pixels is irrelevant with the choice of start and end points; the third condition indicates that the shortest distance between two pixels is along a straight line.

In digital images, there are different ways of measuring distance. The **Euclidean distance** D_E between pixels p and q (also the distance with norm 2) is defined as

$$D_E(p, q) = [(x - s)^2 + (y - t)^2]^{1/2}. \qquad (2.38)$$

According to this distance metric, pixels whose distance from (x, y) is less than or equal to a certain value d are included in a circle with (x, y) as the center and d as the radius. In digital images, the circle can only be approximated. For example, pixels whose D_E distance from (x, y) is less than or equal to 3 form the region shown in Figure 2.16(a), in which the distance values in the figure have been rounded.

The D_4 distance between points p and q (also the distance with norm 1), also called the **city-block distance**, is defined as

$$D_4(p, q) = |x - s| + |y - t|. \qquad (2.39)$$

According to this distance metric, pixels whose D_4 distance from (x, y) is less than or equal to a certain value d form a diamond with (x, y) as the center. For example, pixels whose D_4 distance from (x, y) is less than or equal to three form the region shown in Figure 2.16(b). The pixel with $D_4 = 1$ is the 4-neighbor pixel of (x, y).

```
              3                      3              3 3 3 3 3 3 3
    2.8 2.2 2 2.2 2.8            3  2  3           3 2 2 2 2 2 3
    2.2 1.4 1 1.4 2.2        3  2  1  2  3         3 2 1 1 1 2 3
3   2   1  0  1  2   3    3  2  1  0  1  2  3      3 2 1 0 1 2 3
    2.2 1.4 1 1.4 2.2        3  2  1  2  3         3 2 1 1 1 2 3
    2.8 2.2 2 2.2 2.8            3  2  3           3 2 2 2 2 2 3
              3                      3              3 3 3 3 3 3 3

          (a)                      (b)                  (c)
```

Figure 2.16.   Example of equidistant contour.

The D_8 distance between points p and q (also the distance with norm ∞), also called the **chessboard distance**, is defined as

$$D_8(p, q) = \max(|x - s|, |y - t|). \qquad (2.40)$$

According to this distance metric, pixels whose D_8 distance from (x, y) is less than or equal to a certain value d form a square with (x, y) as the center. For example, pixels whose D_8 distance from (x, y) is less than or equal to three form the region shown in Figure 2.16(c). The pixel with $D_8 = 1$ is the 8-neighbor pixel of (x, y).

The result provided by Euclidean distance is accurate, but because the calculation requires square and square-root operations, the amount of calculation is large and the result is often not an integer. Both the city-block distance and chessboard distance are non-Euclidean distances, and the calculation amount is small, but there are certain errors (not very accurate). Note that the calculation of distance only considers the (relative) positions of the two pixels in the image without considering the gray values of these two pixels.

Example 2.13 Illustration of distance calculation

According to the above three distance definitions, different values are obtained when calculating the distance between the same two pixels in the image. As shown in Figure 2.17, the D_E distance between two pixels p and q is 5, as shown in Figure 2.17(a); the D_4 distance is 7, as shown in Figure 2.17(b); the D_8 distance is 4, as shown in Figure 2.17(c).   □

The distance between pixels can also be used to define the neighborhood of pixels. For example, the pixels with $D_4 = 1$ form the

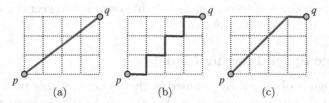

Figure 2.17. Calculating the distance between pixels.

4-neighborhood of pixel (x, y). In other words, the 4-neighboring pixels of p can also be defined as

$$N_4(p) = \{r | D_4(p, r) = 1\}. \tag{2.41}$$

The pixels with $D_8 = 1$ form the 8-neighborhood of pixel (x, y). Similarly, the 8-neighboring pixels of p can also be defined as

$$N_8(p) = \{r | D_8(p, r) = 1\}. \tag{2.42}$$

2.6 Key Points and References for Each Section

The following indicates the key points of each section and provides some targeted guidance for further references.

1. Acquisition Device and Performance Index

Image acquisition is the first step in computer vision. Acquisition equipment and devices need to receive external stimuli and digitize the response. In addition to charge-coupled devices (CCD) and complementary metal oxide semiconductors (CMOS), solid-state acquisition devices also include charge-injection devices (CID), see Ref. [1]. The discussion of the performance indicators of the acquisition device can be found in Ref. [2].

2. Image Brightness Imaging Model

The attribute values of the image are determined by the brightness imaging model. This section gives an overview of some photometry (including brightness and illuminance) knowledge and also introduces a basic brightness imaging model. Table 2.1 refers to Ref. [3] for the brightness values of some common light sources and sceneries as well as the visual zones they are in.

3. Image Space Imaging Model

The image is obtained by projecting the scene, and this provides the spatial distribution information of the scene. In this imaging process, multiple spatial coordinate systems are involved. These coordinate systems can have different spatial (position and orientation) relationships, and these changes constitute different imaging models. A more comprehensive discussion of space imaging models can be found in Ref. [4].

4. Sampling and Quantization

Sampling and quantization are important means in image digitization, and they are also key factors in determining the quality of the acquired image. The relevant basic content is described in detail in books on signal processing. The subjective and objective evaluation of image quality can also be found in Ref. [1].

5. Relationship between Pixels

There are many relationships between pixels in an image. For the connection and transformation among pixel adjacency, connection, path, and connectivity, please refer to Ref. [1]. The distance between pixels is used in image enhancement (Section 3.5) and other processing and analysis techniques.

Self-Test Questions

The following questions include both single- and multiple-choice questions, so each option should be individually judged.

2.1 Acquisition Device and Performance Index

2.1.1 The image acquisition equipment should include ( )

   (A) Devices capable of emitting infrared light;

(B) Devices that can absorb infrared light;

(C) Devices capable of analog-to-digital conversion;

(D) Devices capable of digital-to-analog conversion.

[Hint] Consider the function of the image acquisition equipment.

2.1.2 Using a line scan CCD with 1024 pixels to acquire an image of 64 × 64 pixels, one needs to scan ( )

(A) 4 lines;

(B) 64 lines;

(C) 1024 lines;

(D) 64 × 64 lines.

[Hint] The width of this line scan CCD is one pixel.

2.1.3 For an image acquisition equipment, which of the following performance indicator(s) should be considered? ( )

(A) Shutter speed, gray level;

(B) Illumination conditions, image size;

(C) Sensitivity, signal-to-noise ratio;

(D) Reading speed and storage capacity.

[Hint] What to consider is the performance indicators of the image acquisition equipment itself.

2.2 Image Brightness Imaging Model

2.2.1 Which of the following statement(s) is/are correct? ( )

(A) The brightness of a light source along a certain direction is only related to the surface area of the light source;

(B) The illuminance obtained by a non-luminous scene is not only related to the surface area of the scene;

(C) For a light source, the intensity of its radiation can be expressed by luminous flux;

(D) For a non-luminous scene, the light intensity obtained can be expressed by luminous flux.

[Hint] Compare the definition of brightness and the definition of illuminance.

2.2.2 Which of the following statement(s) is/are incorrect? ( )

    (A) A single light source will cause a uniform illuminance area at the adjacent position on the surface of the scene;

    (B) A single light source will cause a non-uniform illuminance area adjacent to the surface of the scene;

    (C) A single light source may obtain the same illuminance at multiple locations on the surface of the scene;

    (D) It is impossible for a single light source to obtain the same illuminance at multiple locations on the surface of the scene.

[Hint] Consider the distribution of illuminance in space.

2.2.3 Which of the following statement(s) is/are incorrect? ( )

    (A) The image brightness (gray scale) is proportional to the light source radiation intensity;

    (B) The image brightness (gray scale) is directly proportional to the light reflection ratio of the surface in the scene;

    (C) In brightness imaging, the illuminance component can be zero;

    (D) In brightness imaging, the reflection component can be zero.

[Hint] Analyze the meaning of the illuminance component and reflection component in the brightness imaging model.

2.3 Image Space Imaging Model

2.3.1 According to projection imaging transformation, ( )

    (A) The position of a point in the scene on the image plane after imaging can be determined;

    (B) The gray level on the image plane after a point in the scene is imaged can be determined;

    (C) The position of a point on the image plane in the scene can be determined;

    (D) The distance between a point on the optical axis and the image plane can be determined.

[Hint] The imaging transformation is a projection transformation in space.

2.3.2 Compare Cartesian coordinates and homogeneous coordinates. ( )

   (A) The vector dimensions of a space point for Cartesian coordinates and for homogeneous coordinates are the same;
   (B) The vector dimensions of an image plane point for Cartesian coordinates and for homogeneous coordinates are the same;
   (C) One can convert the Cartesian coordinates of a point into homogeneous coordinates;
   (D) One can convert the homogeneous coordinate of a point into Cartesian coordinates.

   [Hint] Pay attention to the representation form of homogeneous coordinates.

2.3.3 When the human eye observes an object beyond 3 m, it is equivalent to a lens with a focal length of 17 mm. When viewing a columnar object with a height of 5 m and at a distance of 50 m, the image size on the retina is about ( )

   (A) 1.1 mm;
   (B) 1.7 mm;
   (C) 3.0 mm;
   (D) 5.0 mm.

   [Hint] Calculate according to the formula of space imaging.

2.3.4 The camera coordinates of the space points $(-1, -2, 3)$ through the perspective lens of $\lambda = 0.5$ are ( )

   (A) $(0.1, 0.2, -0.3)$;
   (B) $(0.1, 0.3, -0.5)$;
   (C) $(0.2, 0.3, -0.4)$;
   (D) $(0.2, 0.4, -0.6)$;

   [Hint] Calculate according to the formula of space imaging.

2.4 Sampling and Quantization

2.4.1 For a 512×512 image, if the number of gray levels is 64, the number of bits required to store it is ( )

   (A) 0.5 M;

(B) 1 M;
(C) 1.5 M;
(D) 2 M.

[Hint] The number of bits required to represent an image is the multiplication of the number of bits corresponding to the length of the image, width of the image, and number of bits for gray levels.

2.4.2 The appearance of false contours in the image is essentially caused by ( )

(A) The image having too many gray levels;
(B) The spatial resolution of the image being too high;
(C) The image not having enough gray levels;
(D) The spatial resolution of the image not being high enough;

[Hint] The false contour in the image is most likely to be produced in the smooth region.

2.4.3 When changing the spatial resolution of an image, the most affected part in the image is ( )

(A) The region with smooth gray levels;
(B) The region with gradient gray levels;
(C) The object boundary region;
(D) The texture region (the region with many repeating units).

[Hint] The reduction of spatial resolution will merge the spatially adjacent pixels.

2.4.4 The appearance of digital image woodcut effect is due to the following reasons: ( )

(A) The image spatial resolution is too small;
(B) The image amplitude resolution is too small;
(C) The image spatial resolution is too large;
(D) The image amplitude resolution is too large.

[Hint] The woodcut effect in the image means that there are too few gray levels in the image.

2.4.5 When changing the amplitude resolution of the image, the most affected part in the image is ( )

(A) The region with smooth gray levels;
(B) The region with gradient gray levels;

(C) The object boundary region;

(D) The texture region (the region with many repeating units).

[Hint] The reduction of the amplitude resolution will merge the pixels that are close in gray level and adjacent in space.

2.5 Relationship between Pixels

2.5.1 Which of the following statement(s) is/are correct in the various neighborhoods of pixels? ( )

(A) 4-neighborhood is a special case of 8-neighborhood;

(B) One 8-neighborhood can be decomposed into two 4-neighborhoods;

(C) We only need to rotate the 4-neighborhood to get the diagonal neighborhood;

(D) The diagonal neighborhood is a special case of the 8-neighborhood.

[Hint] Consider the distribution of neighboring pixels in the three neighborhoods.

2.5.2 Given the two pixels p and q in Figure 2.5.2, which of the following statement(s) is/are correct? ( )

Figure 2.5.2.

(A) The D_4 distance between the two pixels p and q is five;

(B) The D_8 distance between the two pixels p and q is five;

(C) The D_E distance between the two pixels p and q is five;

(D) The D_E distance between the two pixels p and q is shorter than the D_4 distance and D_8 distance between them.

[Hint] It can be calculated separately according to the definition of three distances.

2.5.3 Because the number of neighboring pixels in the 8-neighborhood is twice the number of neighboring pixels in the 4-neighborhood, so ( )

(A) The number of pixels whose D_8 distance from a certain pixel is less than or equal to one is equal to the number of pixels whose D_4 distance from the pixel is less than or equal to two;

(B) The number of pixels whose D_8 distance from a certain pixel is less than or equal to one is less than the number of pixels whose D_4 distance from the pixel is less than or equal to two;

(C) The number of pixels whose D_8 distance from a certain pixel is less than or equal to one is more than the number of pixels whose D_4 distance from the pixel is less than or equal to two;

(D) The number of pixels whose D_8 distance from a certain pixel is less than or equal to two is equal to the number of pixels whose D_4 distance from the pixel is less than or equal to three.

[Hint] Calculate according to the definition of the neighborhood and distance involved.

References

[1] Zhang, Y.-J. *Image Engineering, Vol. 1: Image Processing.* Germany, Berlin: De Gruyter, 2017.

[2] Young, I. T., Errands, J., and Viet, L. J. *Fundamental of Image Processing.* Delft University of Technology, The Netherlands, 1995.

[3] Aumont, J. *The Image. Translation: Pajackowska C.* UK, London: British Film Institute, 1994.

[4] Zhang, Y.-J. *Image Engineering, Vol. 3: Image Understanding.* Germany, Berlin: De Gruyter, 2017.

Chapter 3

Spatial Domain Enhancement

Image enhancement technology is a basic and typical image processing technology. The goal of image enhancement is to obtain, via various processing of images, a "good" visual effect or a more "useful" image. Due to different applications and specific requirements, the meanings of "good" and "useful" here are also different. Because the means and methods of image acquisition are developing with each passing day, there are many types of images with different visual quality, and the actual application requirements are different, so there are many kinds of techniques for image enhancement.

In image enhancement, the image processing can be performed directly in the image domain (spatial domain), that is, the position or gray scale of each pixel is directly changed to obtain the enhanced effect. In image enhancement, the processing of the image can also be performed in the transform domain indirectly, that is, indirectly changing some of the overall characteristics of the image to obtain an enhanced effect. Some common methods of image enhancement in transform domain will be introduced in Chapter 4.

The sections of this chapter are arranged as follows.

Section 3.1 introduces the principle and method of image enhancement by performing arithmetic and logical operations on the entire image.

Section 3.2 discusses the basic ideas and some typical techniques for image enhancement by mapping the pixel gray levels from one value to another. The mapping here can be realized with the help of some analytic functions; the key point is these functions are designed according to the enhancement requirements.

83

Section 3.3 introduces the image histogram equalization method, which modifies and adjusts the image's histogram (a statistical form) to make the distribution of pixel gray levels in the image as uniform as possible.

Section 3.4 further introduces the histogram specification method, in which the desired image histogram for selective enhancement is designed. In addition, the single mapping law and the group mapping law are analyzed and compared.

Section 3.5 discusses how to use the neighborhood properties of pixels to perform convolution operations for image enhancement. Different designs of masks are used to achieve the purpose of smoothing or sharpening the image.

3.1   Operation Between Images

Combining different images may change the visual effect of the image. Some image enhancement technologies are realized by performing operations between images on multiple images. The basic operations between images include arithmetic and logical operations.

3.1.1   Arithmetic operations

Arithmetic operations are generally used for gray-scale images, and the arithmetic operations on the entire image are carried out pixel by pixel. For the two images involved in the operation, the two pixels at their corresponding positions are taken to perform the calculation. The arithmetic operations between two pixels p and q include:

(1) addition: denoted as $p + q$;
(2) subtraction: denoted as $p - q$;
(3) multiplication: denoted as $p \times q$ (can also be written as pq and $p * q$);
(4) division: denoted as $p \div q$.

The arithmetic operation only involves one pixel position at a time, so it can be completed "in-place", that is, the result of an arithmetic operation at the position (x, y) of the image can be stored in the corresponding position of one of the images because that position will not be used anymore.

1. Image addition

One application form of image addition is to reduce the noise in image acquisition through image averaging. Suppose that the image $g(x, y)$ mixed with noise during acquisition is the super-position of the original image $f(x, y)$ and the noise image $e(x, y)$, namely:

$$g(x, y) = f(x, y) + e(x, y). \tag{3.1}$$

It is assumed here that the noises at each point of the image are uncorrelated and have a zero mean value. In this case, the noise can be eliminated by adding a series of images $\{g_1(x, y)g_2(x, y) \ldots g_M(x, y)\}$. Suppose that M images are added and averaged to obtain a new image, namely:

$$\bar{g}(x, y) = \frac{1}{M} \sum_{i=1}^{M} g_i(x, y). \tag{3.2}$$

Then, it can be proved that the expected value of the image is

$$E\{\bar{g}(x, y)\} = f(x, y). \tag{3.3}$$

If one considers the relationship between the mean square error between the addition result image and the noise image, then

$$\sigma_{\bar{g}(x,y)} = \sqrt{\frac{1}{M}} \times \sigma_{e(x,y)}. \tag{3.4}$$

It can be seen that as the number of images participating in the summation M increases, the influence of noise at each pixel position (x, y) gradually decreases.

Example 3.1 Removal of random noise with image average

Figure 3.1 shows an example of using image addition to average and eliminate random noise. Figure 3.1(a) is an 8-bit gray-scale image superimposed with zero mean Gaussian random noise ($\sigma = 32$). Figures 3.1(b), (c), and (d) are the results of adding and averaging 4, 8, and 16 similar images (different samples with the same noise mean and variance), respectively. It can be seen from these figures

(a)   (b)   (c)   (d)

Figure 3.1.   Remove random noise with image average.

that as the number of averaging images increases, the influence of noise gradually decreases.   □

2. Image subtraction

Image subtraction can also be used for image enhancement. Given images $f(x, y)$ and $h(x, y)$, their difference is

$$g(x, y) = f(x, y) - h(x, y). \tag{3.5}$$

The result of image subtraction can highlight the difference between the two images. For example, in medical imaging, image subtraction can be used to remove fixed background information and more clearly highlight the foreground information of interest. In addition, image subtraction is also useful in motion detection. In the sequence of images, the difference between the two images before and after can be directly obtained by comparing pixel by pixel. Assuming that the lighting conditions basically do not change among multiple frames of images, the non-zero region in the difference image indicates that the pixel at that position has moved. In other words, the difference between two adjacent images in time can highlight the changes in the position and shape of the moving object in the image.

Example 3.2 Use of image subtraction to detect the object motion information in the image

In Figure 3.2, Figures 3.2(a) to (c) are three consecutive frames in a video sequence, Figure 3.2(d) shows the difference between the first and second frames, Figure 3.2(e) shows the difference between the second and third frames, and Figure 3.2(f) shows the difference

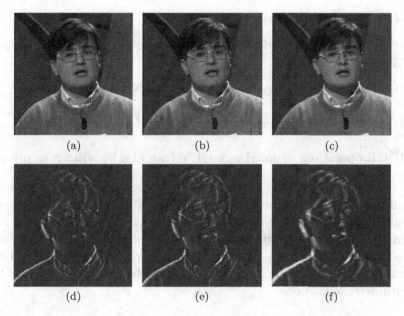

(a) (b) (c)

(d) (e) (f)

Figure 3.2. Use of image subtraction for motion detection.

between the first and third frames. From the bright edges in Figures 3.2(d) and (e), one can see the position and shape of the moving object in the figure, and the object basically moves from the left to the right. It can be seen from Figure 3.2(f) that as the time difference increases, the distance of movement also increases. Therefore, if the object moves slowly, one can use the method of increasing the frame difference (the time difference is larger) to detect enough motion information.   □

3. Image multiplication and image division

A typical application of image multiplication is in mask operations (see Section 3.5). In this case, the mask can be regarded as a small image, and it can be (partially) multiplied with the image to be processed to obtain the effect of changing the pixel gray value. Image division can be used to eliminate the sensitive effects of spatially variable quantization. In addition, image multiplication and image division can also be used to correct image gray shading caused by illumination or sensor non-uniformity.

3.1.2 Logical operation

The three basic **logic operations** commonly used in image processing are:

(1) COMPLEMENT operation: denoted as NOT q (can also be written as $\bar{q}$);
(2) AND operation: denoted as p AND q (can also be written as $p \cdot q$);
(3) OR operation: denoted as p OR q (can also be written as $p + q$).

The functions of the above basic logic operations are complete, and they can be combined to further form all other logic operations. Unlike arithmetic operations, logical operations are only used for binary images. The logic operation of the whole image is also carried out pixel by pixel. Because logical operations only involve one pixel position at a time, they can be completed "in-place" similar to arithmetic operations.

Example 3.3 Logic operations of binary image

Figure 3.3 shows some examples of binary image logic operations. In the figure, black represents 1 and white represents 0. Figures 3.3(a) and (b) are two binary images. Figures 3.3(c), (d), and (e) correspond to the results of using three basic logical operations, respectively; Figures 3.3(f) and (g) are examples of logical operation combinations.

Only when the two binary variables are both 1, the result of their AND operation is 1, so only when the corresponding pixels in the two input images are both 1, it is possible to make the result in the corresponding position of the AND image to be 1. For the XOR (exclusive OR) operation, when one of the two pixels (not same time) is 1, the result is 1, and the result is 0 in all other cases. This operation

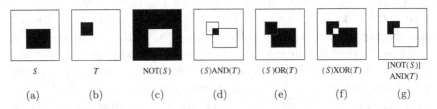

Figure 3.3. Logical operation of binary image.

is different from the OR operation, which is 1 when one of the two pixels is 1 or when they are 1 at the same time. □

3.2 Image Gray-scale Mapping

Changing the gray level of each pixel in the gray-scale image (according to a certain rule) is a common method of enhancement. Specifically, assuming that the gray level of the original image at (x, y) is f and the gray level of the changed image at (x, y) is g, the enhancement of the image can be expressed as the operation of mapping the gray level f to the gray level g at position (x, y). In many cases, the value ranges of f and g are the same. In the following, suppose the value ranges of f and g all in $[0, L - 1]$, where L is the number of gray levels in the image. Different gray levels f can be mapped to g according to different rules. These mapping rules can only be written as analytic formulas sometimes and are often expressed by function curves (called transformation curves). Three commonly used mapping rules are introduced in the following.

3.2.1 Image negation

Image negation is to reverse the gray values of the original image. Simply put, it turns black to white and white to black. The mapping rule of image negation can be expressed as

$$g(x, y) = (L - 1) - f(x, y). \tag{3.6}$$

The corresponding transformation curve can be seen in Figure 3.4(b). The original pixels with a larger gray level close to $L - 1$ will have a gray level close to 0 after transformation, while the original darker pixels will become brighter pixels after transformation. This is the relationship between early black and white negatives and photos.

Example 3.4 Image negation example

In Figure 3.4, Figure 3.4(a) shows a gray-scale image, Figure 3.4(b) shows the transformation curve for image negation, and Figure 3.4(c) shows the result of the image negation. Comparing the two images

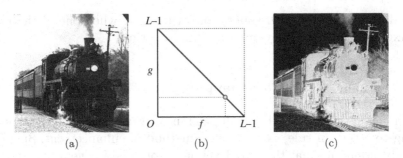

Figure 3.4. Image negation example.

in Figures 3.4(a) and (c), it is easy to see the relationship between the negative and the photo.   □

3.2.2 Contrast stretching

Contrast stretching makes enhancement by increasing the contrast (gray-level difference) between parts of the image. In specific operations, when the value ranges of f and g are the same, it is often achieved by increasing the dynamic range between two gray values in the original image. A typical contrast stretching curve (here, it is a broken line) is shown in Figure 3.5(b), which can be expressed as

$$g(x,y) = \begin{cases} g_1/f_1 & 0 < f(x,y) \le f_1 \\ (g_2 - g_1)/(f_2 - f_1) & f_1 < f(x,y) \le f_2 \\ (L - 1 - g_2)/(L - 1 - f_2) & f_2 < f(x,y) \le L - 1. \end{cases} \quad (3.7)$$

It can be seen that through such a transformation, the dynamic ranges of gray values between 0 to f_1 and f_2 to $L - 1$ in the original image are reduced, while the dynamic range of gray values between f_1 and f_2 in the original image is increased. So, the contrast in this range is enhanced. In practice, f_1, f_2, g_1, and g_2 can be combined with different values to obtain different effects.

Example 3.5 Contrast stretching example

Figure 3.5(a) is an underexposed image, Figure 3.5(b) is the transformation curve for contrast stretching, and Figure 3.5(c) is the enhancement result. Comparing the two images in Figures 3.5(a) and (c), it can be seen that the Great Wall becomes more prominent

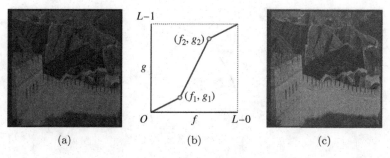

Figure 3.5. Example of contrast stretching.

through contrast stretching and the mountains in the distance are also clearer. □

3.2.3 Dynamic range compression

The goal of **dynamic range compression** is the opposite of contrast stretching. Sometimes, the dynamic range of the original image is too large and exceeds the allowed range of some display devices. At this time, if the original image is directly displayed in gray scale, some details may be lost. The solution is to perform dynamic range compression on the original image. A commonly used method is to use logarithmic transformation, as shown in the curve in Figure 3.6(b), which can be expressed as

$$g(x, y) = k \log[1 + f(x, y)]. \qquad (3.8)$$

According to the characteristics of the logarithmic function, darker gray values will be separated, and too high gray values will be pulled down. Most of the f values will be mapped to the gray range close to $L - 1$. If only this part of gray value is displayed, the purpose of compressing the dynamic range is achieved.

Example 3.6 Dynamic range compression example

Figure 3.6(a) shows the spectrogram (frequency image) obtained by directly performing Fourier transform on a 2D gate function image, where the 2D gate function image is shown in Figure 4.1(a). Since the center pixel value is very large (reflected in the image, it is very bright), the surrounding pixels will be very dark, or even invisible,

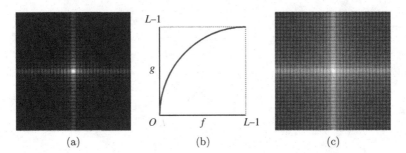

(a)   (b)   (c)

Figure 3.6. Example of dynamic range compression.

when the image is displayed in 256 gray levels. Figure 3.6(b) shows
the logarithmic transformation curve for dynamic range compression.
Figure 3.6(c) shows the image obtained by dynamic range compression of Figure 3.6(a). The brightness of the details other than the
center cross increases and is closer to the center pixel value, which
looks clearer.   □

3.3 Histogram Equalization

Histogram equalization is a method of enhancing the image with
the help of transforming the image histogram to perform gray-scale
mapping.

3.3.1 Image histogram

The gray-scale statistical **histogram** of an image is a discrete function of one dimension:

$$p_f(f_k) = \frac{n_k}{n} \quad k = 0, 1, \ldots, L - 1 \tag{3.9}$$

In the above equation, f_k is the kth gray-scale value of the image
$f(x, y)$, n_k is the number of pixels with gray-scale value f_k in the
image $f(x, y)$, and n is the total number of pixels in the image.
According to the above definition, an array with L elements can be
set, and the histogram of the image can be obtained by counting the
number of pixels with different gray values. Because $p_f(f_k)$ gives an
estimate of the probability of each f_k, the histogram provides the
gray-value distribution of the original image. It can also be said that

it gives an overall description of the gray values of all pixels in an image.

Example 3.7 Different images and corresponding histograms

Figure 3.7 shows several different images obtained from the same scene and their corresponding histograms.

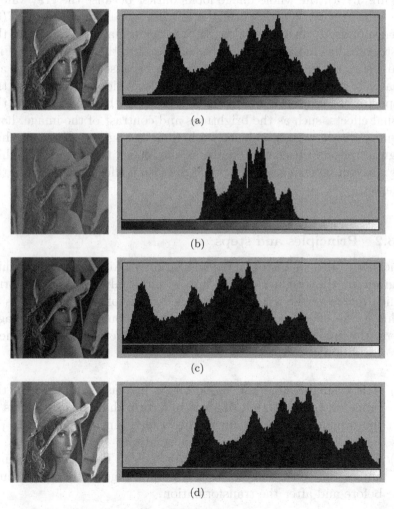

(a)

(b)

(c)

(d)

Figure 3.7. Examples of different types of images and their histograms.

Figure 3.7(a) corresponds to a normal image, and its histogram basically spans the entire gray-scale range, and the whole image has many distinct gray levels; Figure 3.7(b) corresponds to an image with small dynamic gray-scale range, the values of the histogram are concentrated in the middle of the gray-scale range, the whole image looks dim due to the small contrast in the image; Figure 3.7(c) corresponds to an image with larger dynamic gray-scale range, but the histogram has moved to the left compared to the histogram of Figure 3.7(a), the whole image looks darker because the gray values are relatively concentrated on the low gray-level side; Figure 3.7(d) corresponds to an image also with larger dynamic range, but the histogram has moved to the right compared to the histogram of Figure 3.7(a), the whole image looks brighter because the gray values are relatively concentrated on the high gray-level side, which is just the opposite of Figure 3.7(c). It can be seen from these figures that the visual effects, such as the brightness and contrast of the image, have a more direct correspondence with their histogram. Since the histogram reflects the characteristics of the image, the shape of the histogram can be changed to improve the visual effect and enhance the image.   □

3.3.2   Principles and steps

The basic idea of histogram equalization is to transform the histogram of the original image into a uniformly distributed form, which increases the dynamic gray-scale range of the pixel values to achieve the effect of enhancing the overall contrast of the image. Here, the enhancement function (mapping function) needs to meet two conditions:

(1) It is a single value and monotonous increasing function in the range of $0 \leq f \leq L - 1$. This is to ensure that the gray levels of the original image remain in the order from black to white (or from white to black) after transformation.
(2) For $0 \leq f \leq L - 1$, there is $0 \leq g \leq L - 1$. This condition guarantees the consistency of the dynamic range of the gray values before and after the transformation.

It can be proved that the **cumulative distribution function** (CDF) satisfies the above two conditions and can transform the distribution of f into a uniform distribution of g. In fact, the CDF of the image $f(x, y)$ is the **cumulative histogram** of $f(x, y)$, which is defined as

$$g_k = \sum_{i=0}^{k} \frac{n_i}{n} = \sum_{i=0}^{k} p_f(f_i) \quad \begin{array}{l} 0 \le f_k \le 1 \\ k = 0, 1, \ldots, L - 1. \end{array} \tag{3.10}$$

It can be seen from Equation (3.10) that the gray value of each pixel after the histogram equalization can be directly computed according to the histogram of the original image. Of course, the g_k value calculated in this way must be rounded to meet the requirements of digital images.

Example 3.8 Histogram equalization calculation example

Consider a 64×64, 8-bit gray-level image, and its histogram is shown in Figure 3.8(a). The transformation function (i.e., cumulative histogram) used for the histogram equalization is shown in

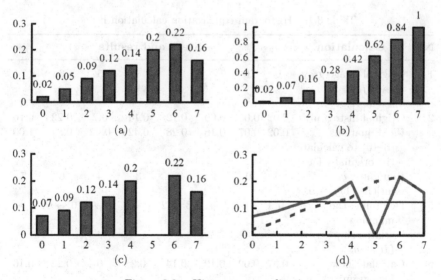

Figure 3.8.   Histogram equalization.

Figure 3.8(b), and the histogram obtained after equalization is shown in Figure 3.8(c). It should be noted that since it is impossible (or there is no reason) to transform each pixel belonging to the same gray value to different gray levels (the pixels in a histogram bin are always in the same histogram bin), the result of digital image histogram equalization in general is only an approximate equalized histogram. Here, one can try to compare the thick broken line (actual equalization result) in Figure 3.8(d) with the horizontal straight line (ideal equalization result). The dotted line in the figure is the original histogram envelope.

Table 3.1 lists the calculation steps and results of the above histogram equalization (the rounding in step 4 means taking the integer part of the real number in square brackets, and the symbol "→" represents the mapping).

It can be seen from Table 3.1 that some different gray values of the original histogram may be mapped to the same gray levels of the equalized histogram (histogram bins), so the number of gray levels in the equalized histogram (actually used) may be smaller than that in the original histogram. □

Table 3.1.　Histogram equalization calculation list.

No.	Calculation	Steps and results							
1	Original image gray level f_k, $k = 0, 1, \ldots, 7$	0	1	2	3	4	5	6	7
2	Original histogram	0.02	0.05	0.09	0.12	0.14	0.2	0.22	0.16
3	Use Equations (3–10) to calculate the original CDF	0.02	0.07	0.16	0.28	0.42	0.62	0.84	1.00
4	Rounding: $g_k =$ int$[(L-1)g_k + 0.5]$	0	0	1	2	3	4	6	7
5	Determine the mapping relationship $(f_k \to g_k)$	$0,1 \to 0$	$2 \to 1$	$3 \to 2$	$4 \to 3$	$5 \to 4$	$6 \to 6$	$7 \to 7$	
6	Calculate new histogram	0.07	0.09	0.12	0.14	0.2	0	0.22	0.16

    (a)   (b)   (c)   (d)

Figure 3.9.　Example of histogram equalization.

Example 3.9 An example of histogram equalization effects

Figure 3.9 shows an example of histogram equalization.

Figures 3.9(a) and (b) are an original image of 8-bit gray scale and its histogram, respectively. Here, the original image is darker and the dynamic range is small, which is reflected in the histogram that the gray-value range of the histogram is relatively narrow and concentrated on the side of the low gray values. Figures 3.9(c) and (d) are the results of the histogram equalization of the original image and its corresponding histogram. Now, the histogram occupies the entire allowable range of the gray value of the image. Because the histogram equalization increases the dynamic range of the gray levels of the image, it also increases the contrast of the image. It is reflected in the image that the image has now a larger contrast, and many details can be seen more clearly.　□

3.4　Histogram Specification

Histogram specification is also a method to enhance the image by means of histogram transformation. It obtains a predetermined enhancement effect by converting the histogram of the original image into a desired histogram.

3.4.1　Principles and steps

The advantage of histogram equalization is that it can automatically enhance the contrast of the entire image, but its specific enhancement effect is not easy to control, and the result of the processing is always a globally equalized histogram. In practice, sometimes it is necessary to transform the histogram into a certain shape to selectively enhance the contrast in a certain gray-value range. For such cases, a more flexible histogram specification method can be used. Generally, by suitably selecting the predetermined histogram (enhancement function), it is possible to obtain a more satisfactory effect than the histogram equalization. The histogram specification method mainly has three steps (here, M and N are the gray levels in the original and specified images, respectively, and only the case of $N \leq M$ is considered):

(1) As in the equalization method, perform gray-level equalization on the histogram of the original image:

$$g_k = \sum_{i=0}^{k} p_f(f_i) \quad k = 0, 1, \ldots, M - 1. \tag{3.11}$$

(2) Specify the required histogram, and calculate the transformation that can equalize the specified histogram:

$$v_l = \sum_{j=0}^{l} p_u(u_j) \quad l = 0, 1, \ldots, N - 1. \tag{3.12}$$

(3) Invert the transformation obtained in step (2) and apply it to the result of step (1), that is, map the statistical values of each gray level in the original histogram to the specified histogram, that is, map all $p_f(f_i)$ to $p_u(u_j)$.

Let's use a specific example for illustration. Suppose the histogram of an original image is shown in Figure 3.10(a), and the required histogram is shown in Figure 3.10(b). Their corresponding cumulative histograms can be represented by Equations (3.11) and (3.12), respectively, and separately shown in Figures 3.10(c) and (d).

To achieve the specified mapping, the original cumulative histogram is transformed into a shape as close as possible to the specified cumulative histogram in step (3). This conversion can take different strategies, which will be discussed in the next section.

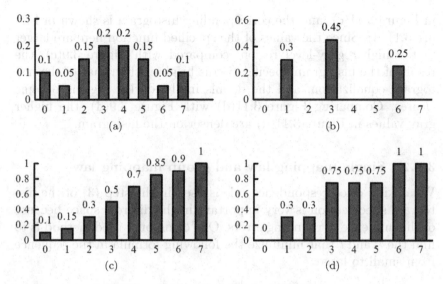

Figure 3.10.   Histogram specification.

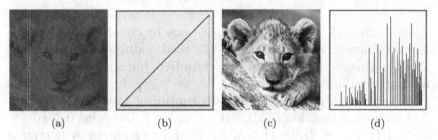

(a)   (b)   (c)   (d)

Figure 3.11.   Example of histogram specification.

Example 3.10 An example of histogram specification effects

Figure 3.11 shows an example of using histogram specification.

The original image used here is Figure 3.11(a), which is the same as Figure 3.10(a) in Example 3.9. The result obtained by using histogram equalization method, as in Example 3.9, is Figure 3.9(c), which is mainly an increase in the contrast of the whole image, but some details are still not clear in darker regions. In this example, the specified function, as shown in Figure 3.11(b), is used to perform a histogram specification on the original image. The result is shown in Figure 3.11(c), and the corresponding histogram is shown in Figure 3.11(d). Since the values of the specified function here are larger in the higher gray-level region, compared with Figure 3.9(c), the result of the histogram specification is brighter than that of the histogram equalization, and the details in the darker regions become clearer. Comparing Figure 3.11(d) with Figure 3.9(d), the higher gray values in Figure 3.11(d) are denser on the histogram.   □

3.4.2 Single mapping law and group mapping law

What kind of correspondence rule is used in the step (3) of the histogram specification is very important in the discrete space because of the influence of rounding errors. One commonly used method is to find the k and l that minimize the following formula in the sequence from small to large:

$$\left| \sum_{i=0}^{k} p_f(f_i) - \sum_{j=0}^{l} p_u(u_j) \right| \quad \begin{array}{l} k = 0, 1, \ldots, M - 1 \\ l = 0, 1, \ldots, N - 1. \end{array} \quad (3.13)$$

Then, each $p_f(f_i)$ is mapped to $p_u(u_j)$ one by one. Since each $p_f(f_i)$ here is mapped separately, it can be called a **single mapping law** (SML). This method is simple and intuitive, but sometimes there is a large rounding error.

A better method is to use **group mapping law** (GML). Set up first an integer function $I(l)$, $l = 0, 1, \ldots, N-1$, satisfying $0 \leq I(0) \leq \cdots \leq I(l) \leq \cdots \leq I(N-1) \leq M-1$. Now, it is required to determine the function $I(l)$ that can minimize the following equation:

$$\left| \sum_{i=0}^{I(l)} p_f(f_i) - \sum_{j=0}^{l} p_u(u_j) \right| \quad l = 0, 1, \ldots, N - 1. \quad (3.14)$$

If $l = 0$, the $p_f(f_i)$ of i from 0 to $I(0)$ is mapped to $p_u(u_0)$; if $l \geq 1$, then the $p_f(f_i)$ of i from $I(l-1)+1$ to $I(l)$ is mapped to $p_u(u_j)$.

Example 3.11 Illustration of single mapping law and group mapping law

The SML and GML can be explained with the help of graphic illustration. The cumulative histogram can be converted into a bar, where

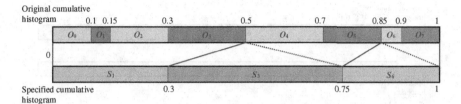

Figure 3.12. Illustration of single mapping law.

each segment corresponds to a bin in the statistical histogram, and the entire bar represents the whole cumulative histogram. The data in Figure 3.10 are still used here. Consider the SML first, and the graphic illustration is shown in Figure 3.12, where the upper bar is for the original cumulative histogram (with O_i indicating a bin) and the lower bar is for the specified cumulative histogram (with S_i indicating a bin). Single mapping is performed in the direction from the original cumulative histogram to the specified cumulative histogram, so if one wants to map some original cumulative histogram bins to the specified cumulative histogram bins, it is required to select the shortest distance (take the line as vertical as possible). According to this rule and starting from 0, the original three bins O_0, O_1, and O_2 are all mapped to the specified bin S_1. Note that the original bin O_3 is also mapped to the specified bin S_1 (see thick line) according to Equation (3.13) while not to the specified bin S_3 (see dotted line). Next, the original bin O_4 is mapped to the specified bin S_3, and the original bin O_5 is also mapped to the specified bin of S_3 (see thick line) instead of the specified bin S_6 (see dotted line); finally, both the original bins of O_6 and O_7 are mapped to the specified bin of S_6.

The GML used in the histogram specification is the mapping in the direction from the specified cumulative histogram to the original cumulative histogram, as shown in Figure 3.13 (still using the data in Figure 3.10). To determine which specified cumulative histogram bin needs to establish a mapping relationship with the original cumulative histogram bins, one needs to select the shortest distance (take the line as vertical as possible). According to Equation (3.14), the specified cumulative histogram bin S_1 should include three original cumulative histogram bins O_0, O_1, and O_2 (see thick line), excluding O_2 or including O_3 increases the distance (see dotted lines); similarly, the specified cumulative histogram bin S_3 should include two

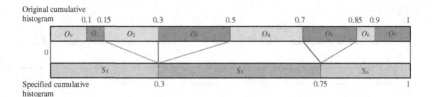

Figure 3.13.   Illustration of group mapping law.

Table 3.2.   Histogram specification calculation list.

No.	Calculation	Steps and results							
1	Original image gray level f_k, $k = 0, 1, \ldots, 7$	0	1	2	3	4	5	6	7
2	Original histogram	0.1	0.05	0.15	0.2	0.2	0.15	0.05	0.1
3	Use Equations (3–10) to calculate the original CDF	0.1	0.15	0.3	0.5	0.7	0.85	0.9	1.00
4	Specified histogram	0	0.3	0	0.45	0	0.	0.25	0
5	Use Equations (3–10) to calculate the specified CDF	0	0.3	0.3	0.75	0.75	0.75	1.0	1.0
6S	SML mapping	1	1	1	1	3	3	6	6
7S	Determine the mapping relationship $(f_k \to g_k)$		$0, 1, 2, 3 \to 1$			$4, 5 \to 3$		$6, 7 \to 6$	
8S	Histogram after mapping	0	0.5	0	0.35	0	0	0.15	0
6G	GML mapping	1	1	1	3	3	6	6	6
7G	Determine the mapping relationship $(f_k \to g_k)$		$0, 1, 2 \to 1$		$3, 4 \to 3$		$5, 6, 7 \to 6$		
8G	Histogram after mapping	0	0.3	0	0.4	0	0	0.3	0

Note: Steps 6S to 8S in the table correspond to the SML mapping process, and steps 6G to 8G correspond to the GML mapping process.

original cumulative histogram bins O_3 and O_4 (see thick line), including O_5 increases the distance (see dotted line); finally, the specified cumulative histogram bin S_6 should include the last three original cumulative histogram bins O_5, O_6, and O_7. Intuitively, the mapping lines obtained by the GML are relatively more vertical, which indicates that the specified cumulative histogram is more consistent with the original cumulative histogram.

The calculation steps and results of the above two methods are summarized in Table 3.2 (the symbol "$\to$" represents the mapping). $\qquad\square$

Example 3.12 Comparison of single mapping law and group mapping law

Compare the histograms after mapping in the two cases in Example 3.11; see Figure 3.14. Among them, Figure 3.14(a) is the result obtained with the SML, which is quite different from the specified histogram in Figure 3.10(b); Figure 3.14(b) is the result obtained with the GML, which is more consistent with the specified histogram in Figure 3.10(b).

Finally, the possible errors that may occur when using the two mapping laws are discussed. The error generated by the mapping can be represented by the sum of the difference values (absolute value) between the specified histogram bins and the obtained histogram bins after mapping. Generally, the smaller the value of this sum, the better the mapping effect. Under ideal conditions, this sum is zero. Both laws can give precise specified results in the continuous case, but the degrees of precision are often different in the discrete case. When a certain $p_f(f_i)$ is mapped to $p_u(u_j)$, the maximum error that may be generated by the SML is $p_u(u_j)/2$, and the maximum error that may be generated by the GML is $p_f(f_i)/2$. Because $N \leq M$, there must be $p_f(f_i)/2 \leq p_u(u_j)/2$, which means that the expected error of the GML will not be greater than the expected error of the SML. In addition, it can be seen from Figures 3.12 and 3.13 that the SML is a biased mapping law because some corresponding gray levels will be biased toward gray levels near the starting of the calculation, and the GML is statistically unbiased. The actual situation is that the GML will always get a result closer to the specified histogram than the SML, and in many cases the error produced by the GML is much smaller than the error produced by the SML. Still taking the

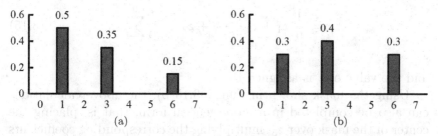

Figure 3.14. Comparison of the results of histogram specification.

above data (as in Figure 3.10) as an example, for SML, this sum is: $|0.5 - 0.3| + |0.35 - 0.45| + |0.15 - 0.25| = 0.4$; for GML, this sum is: $|0.3 - 0.3| + |0.4 - 0.45| + |0.3 - 0.25| = 0.1$. Comparing the two sums, the advantages and disadvantages of the two mapping laws are obvious.   □

3.5   Spatial Domain Convolution Enhancement

In the image space, in addition to the pixel-by-pixel processing of the entire image, the combination of pixels in a region of the image can also be considered. Depending on the various combination methods, different enhancement effects can be obtained.

3.5.1   Mask convolution

The pixels in a region of an image are often represented as a collection of a central pixel and its neighboring pixels. Processing in the neighborhood is mainly implemented in the form of mask operations (template, windows, and filters are also commonly used to represent masks). The idea of **mask operation** is to assign the value of a certain pixel as a function of its own gray value and the gray values of pixels in its neighborhood in image processing. When designing the mask, the spatial occupancy array can be used to represent the image, and different calculation purposes can be achieved by taking different values of the array elements. For example, consider the sub-image region shown in Figure 3.15(a) and replace the value of z_5 with the average value of the pixels in the 3×3 region centered on z_5, then the following arithmetic operations are required:

$$z = \frac{1}{9}(z_1 + z_2 + \cdots + z_9) = \frac{1}{9}\sum_{i=1}^{9} z_i, \tag{3.15}$$

and the value of z is assigned to z_5.

Using the mask shown in Figure 3.15(b), the above calculations can also be completed in a more general form, that is, placing the center of the mask over z_5, multiplying the corresponding coefficients on the mask with the pixel values under the mask, and accumulating

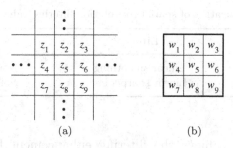

(a)   (b)

Figure 3.15.   Template calculation example.

the result:

$$z = w_1 z_1 + w_2 z_2 + \cdots + w_9 z_9 = \sum_{i=1}^{9} w_i z_i. \qquad (3.16)$$

If $w_i = 1/9$ and $i = 1, 2, \ldots, 9$, this operation gives the same result as the aforementioned averaging process.

Equation (3.16) is widely used in image processing, and the operation is actually a correlation operation. Appropriate selection of the coefficients of the mask and the use of the mask to perform operations at each pixel position of the image can result in a series of useful image processing operations, such as noise elimination, region thinning, and edge extraction.

3.5.2   Spatial filtering

When the mask is spatially symmetrical about the center pixel, the aforementioned multiplication and addition operation is equivalent to a convolution operation. **Spatial filtering** is done by convolution in the image space with the help of masks. Different filtering techniques can generally be divided into linear and nonlinear based on their characteristics. In addition, various spatial filters according to their functions are mainly divided into two categories: smooth filters (used to remove noise or to blur images in order to remove too small details before extracting larger objects or connect small discontinuities in the object) and sharpening filters (enhance the edge details in the image). Combining these two classification methods, spatial filtering enhancement methods can be divided into four categories, as shown in Table 3.3.

Table 3.3.   Classification of spatial convolution filtering enhancement methods.

Function	Linear	Nonlinear
Smoothing	Linear smoothing	Nonlinear smoothing
Sharpening	Linear sharpening	Nonlinear sharpening

The way to achieve the filtering enhancement function in the spatial domain is to use mask convolution. By selecting different mask coefficients, the four enhancement effects in Table 3.3 can be achieved.

1. Linear smoothing filtering

All coefficients in the mask for **linear smoothing filtering** are positive. For the 3×3 mask, the simplest way is to take all coefficients as one. In order to ensure that the output image is still in the original gray value range, after the result is calculated, it must be divided by nine and then assigned, as in Equation (3.15). This method is also often called **neighborhood averaging**, which is equivalent to an integral operation.

Example 3.13 Blurring and de-noising effect of spatial smoothing filter

Looking at Figure 3.16, Figure 3.16(a) is an original 8-bit gray-scale image, Figure 3.16(b) is the image after adding uniformly distributed random noise, Figures 3.16(c) to (f) are in sequence the results of filtering with $5 \times 5, 7 \times 7, 9 \times 9$, and 11×11 masks of smoothing filter to Figure 3.16(b). It can be seen that when the size of the smoothing mask increases, the effect of eliminating noise is enhanced. However, the resulting image becomes more blurred and the details gradually decrease at the same time.   □

2. Nonlinear smoothing filtering

The aforementioned smoothing filters will blur certain details in the image while eliminating noise. If one wants to eliminate noise and maintain the details of the image, one can use **median filtering**. It

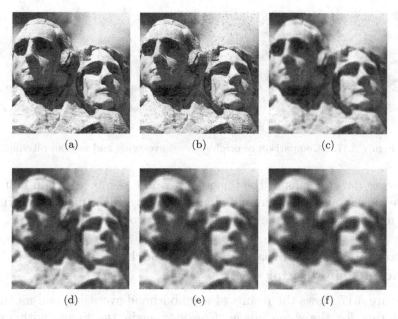

(a)   (b)   (c)

(d)   (e)   (f)

Figure 3.16. Blurring effect of spatial smoothing filter.

implements a nonlinear smooth filtering, and its working steps are as follows:

(1) Scan the image with the mask, and overlap the center of the mask with a certain pixel position in the image.
(2) Read the gray values of all corresponding pixels under the mask.
(3) Arrange these gray values in a row from small to large.
(4) Find the middle position (in sequence) among these gray values.
(5) Assign this median value to the pixel at the center of the corresponding mask.

It can be seen from the above steps that the main function of the median filter is to change the pixels with a larger difference in the gray value relative to that of the surrounding pixels to a value close to the value of the surrounding pixels, thereby eliminating isolated noise points. If a mask with a size of $M \times M$ (M is an odd number) is used, set the pixels read from the image to be arranged according to the gray value from small to large $\{f_1, f_2, \ldots, f_M, f_{M+1}, \ldots, f_{M \times M}\}$, the output value is equal to $f_{(M \times M+1)/2}$. Generally, the over-bright

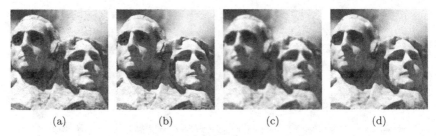

(a)　　　　　　(b)　　　　　　(c)　　　　　　(d)

Figure 3.17.　Comparison of neighborhood averaging and median filtering.

or over-dark regions in the image and whose size is less than half of the mask size will be eliminated after filtering. Since median filtering is not simply taking the average value, it produces less blur.

Example 3.14 Comparison of neighborhood averaging and median filtering

Figure 3.17 shows the results of neighborhood averaging and median filtering for the same image. Consider again the image with uniformly distributed random noise superimposed in Figure 3.16(b). Here, Figures 3.17(a) and (c) show the results of neighborhood averaging with the 3 × 3 mask and 5 × 5 mask, respectively; Figures 3.17(b) and (d) are the results of median filtering with 3 × 3 and 5 × 5 masks, respectively. Comparison of the two sets of images shows that the visual effect of median filtering is better than that of neighborhood averaging. The main feature of median filtering is that the contours of each region in the image after filtering are still relatively clear.

In addition, it is necessary to select a mask of a suitable size according to the application requirements in practice, by taking into account the calculation time and the noise reduction effect.　　□

3. Linear sharpening filtering

The center coefficient in the mask for **linear sharpening filtering** should be positive and the surrounding coefficients should be negative. When using a 3 × 3 mask, the typical value for the center coefficient is $w_5 = 8$ in Figure 3.15(b), and the remaining coefficients are -1, so that the sum of all coefficients is 0. When such a mask is placed in a region in the image, where the gray values are constant or changing slightly, the convolution output will be zero or very small. Note that this filter will remove the zero frequency component in the original image, that is, the average gray value of the output image will become zero, so that the gray value of some pixels in the output image will be less than zero. Generally, only positive gray values are considered in image processing, so the gray value range of the output image needs to be transformed back to the range of $[0, G_{max}]$.

The effect of the sharpening filtering can also be obtained by subtracting the smoothed image $L(x, y)$ from the original image $f(x, y)$. Furthermore, if the original image is multiplied by an amplification factor A and then the smoothed image is subtracted, the **high-frequency boost filtering** can be realized:

$$H_b(x, y) = A \times f(x, y) - L(x, y) = (A - 1) \times f(x, y) + H(x, y).$$

(3.17)

In the above equation, when $A = 1$, it is a normal sharpening filtering. When $A > 1$, a part of the original image is added to the sharpened image obtained with $H(x, y)$ filtering, which restores the low-frequency components lost during sharpening filtering; this can make the final result closer to the original image. Because smooth filtering often results in **image blur**, it is generally called (unsharpened) masking if the blur image is subtracted from the original image. In this case, for the 3×3 mask shown in Figure 3.15(b), the value of the center coefficient should be $w_5 = 9A - 1$.

Example 3.15 Comparison of linear sharpening filtering and high-frequency boost filtering

Figure 3.18 shows a comparison example of linear sharpening filtering and high-frequency boost filtering. Figure 3.18(a) is an experimental image with a certain blur; Figure 3.18(b) is the result of linear sharpening filtering of Figure 3.18(a); Figure 3.18(c) is the result of high-frequency boost filtering ($A = 2$) of Figure 3.18(a); Figure 3.18(d) is the final result of expanding the gray value range (using histogram equalization) of Figure 3.18(c). It can be seen from the final result that the enhancement effect of eliminating blur is still very obvious. □

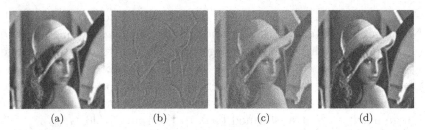

(a)   (b)   (c)   (d)

Figure 3.18.   Comparison of linear sharpening filtering and high-frequency boost filtering.

4. Nonlinear sharpening filtering

The linear sharpening filter calculates the gray value difference between adjacent pixels, which is equivalent to a differential operation. It can be seen that the image can be sharpened by using the differential operation. The most commonly used differentiation method in image processing is to use gradients. For a continuous function $f(x, y)$, its gradient is a vector which consists of (using two masks) the results of separately calculating the differential along the x and y directions:

$$\nabla f(x, y) = \left[\frac{\partial f}{\partial x} \frac{\partial f}{\partial y} \right]^{\mathrm{T}}. \tag{3.18}$$

The magnitude of the gradient can be calculated using the norm 2 (corresponding to the **Euclidean distance**), namely:

$$|\nabla f_{(2)}| = \mathrm{mag}(\nabla f) = \left[\left(\frac{\partial f}{\partial x} \right)^2 + \left(\frac{\partial f}{\partial y} \right)^2 \right]^{1/2}. \tag{3.19}$$

In order to simplify the calculation in practice, other methods can also be used to combine the differential results along the two directions. A simple method is to use the **city-block distance** (using the norm 1), namely:

$$|\nabla f_{(1)}| = \left| \frac{\partial f}{\partial x} \right| + \left| \frac{\partial f}{\partial y} \right|. \tag{3.20}$$

Another simple method is to use the **chessboard distance** (using the norm ∞), namely:

$$|\nabla f_{(\infty)}| = \max \left\{ \left| \frac{\partial f}{\partial x} \right|, \left| \frac{\partial f}{\partial y} \right| \right\}. \tag{3.21}$$

Since the methods for calculating gradient amplitudes using various norms are nonlinear, they are also nonlinear filtering methods. For further discussion on using these different distances to calculate the gradient magnitude, see Section 7.2.

3.6 Key Points and References for Each Section

The following indicates the key points of each section and provides some targeted guidance for further references.

1. Operation between images

Operations between images mainly include arithmetic operations and logical operations. Arithmetic operation is to use the corresponding pixels of two images as the operands to perform four arithmetic operations, and logical operation is to use the corresponding pixels of the two images as the operands to perform AND, OR, complement (NOT), and their combination operations. More combination examples are available, for example, in Ref. [1]. There are many application examples of arithmetic operations between images, which are also functions of many image processing software. Some related discussions can be found in Ref. [2].

2. Image gray-scale mapping

Gray-scale mapping is a typical method for image enhancement in image space. By converting pixels with different gray levels in the image one by one according to the determined mapping rules (functions), the image can have the required visual effects. The design of the mapping rules is a key step. Different mapping rules may provide completely different enhancement effects. This section only introduces a few mapping rules as examples. For more gray-scale mapping examples, please refer to various image processing and analysis books [1–5].

3. Histogram equalization

The histogram of a gray-scale image is a 1D statistics of the gray scale of each pixel in the image, reflecting the occurrence probability of different gray scales in the image. The shape of the histogram is closely related to the visual effect of the image, and the image can be enhanced by changing the shape of the histogram. Histogram equalization uses the cumulative histogram of the image as a gray-scale mapping function to transform the original image to obtain an enhanced effect. Its principles and methods are introduced in various books on image processing [1,4,5].

4. Histogram specification

Histogram specification techniques map the pixel gray level according to the desired histogram shape, and the method is more flexible. For example, see book [5]. Histogram equalization can be regarded as a special case of histogram specification, and the discussion of the relationship between the two methods can be found in Ref. [6]. When performing gray-scale mapping in histogram specification, an SML can be used to proceed from the original histogram to a specified histogram, or a group mapping rule can be used to proceed from the specified histogram to the original histogram. The GML is better than the SML in terms of the consistency of the mapping between the resultant histogram and the specified histogram as well as the expected error. For the discussion and comparison of SML and GML, please refer to Ref. [7]. The explanations of the SML and GML using the graph illustration method can also be extended to the calculation of histogram equalization; see Ref. [1].

5. Spatial domain convolution enhancement

Spatial filtering is an enhancement method implemented directly in the image space with the help of mask convolution. According to different mask designs, spatial filtering can not only achieve the function of smoothing the image but also the function of sharpening the image. For the spatial filtering, the results of mask operations can be united linearly, and the results of mask operations can also be used nonlinearly. These two methods can also be combined, for example, see Ref. [8]. A discussion on the different size masks for median filtering can also be found in Ref. [1]. An analysis example of combining masks to obtain different results can be found in Ref. [9].

Self-Test Questions

The following questions include both single- and multiple-choice questions, so each option should be individually judged.

3.1 Operation Between Images

3.1.1 It is assumed that the image of a work piece in industrial inspection is affected by zero-mean uncorrelated noise. If the work-piece acquisition device can acquire 25 images per second and the image averaging method is used to reduce the variance of noise to 1/10 of a single image, how long should the work piece remain fixed in front of the acquisition device? ( )

(A) 1 s;
(B) 2 s;
(C) 4 s;
(D) 5 s.

[Hint] Consider the relationship between the mean square error of the new image and the original noise image after image averaging.

3.1.2 Consider the arithmetic operations between images. ( )

(A) The addition operation and the subtraction operation are the inverse operations of each other, so the functions realized by the addition operation can also be realized by the subtraction operation;
(B) The arithmetic operation can be "completed in situ" because each operation only involves one spatial position;
(C) Similar to logical operations, arithmetic operations can also be used for binary images;
(D) Similar to logical operations, arithmetic operations can be performed on one image or on two images.

[Hint] Compare the operands and characteristics of arithmetic operations and logical operations.

3.1.3 There are two binary images with a circle centered on the center of the image, but their radii are different. To obtain a binary image with a ring object, one can use ( )

(A) AND operation;
(B) Complementary operation;
(C) OR operation;
(D) Exclusive OR operation.

[Hint] Consider the effects according to the definitions of these operations.

3.2 Image Gray-scale Mapping

3.2.1 The transformation curve $g = T(f)$ shown in Figure 3.2.1 can ( )

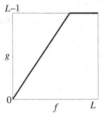

Figure 3.2.1.

(A) Reduce the brightness of the low gray-scale regions of the image;
(B) Enlarge the contrast of the low gray-scale regions of the image;
(C) Decrease the brightness of the high gray-scale regions of the image;
(D) Increase the contrast in the high gray-scale regions of the image.

[Hint] Pay attention to the part of the transformation curve, whose slope is greater than one, corresponds to the gray-scale regions of the image.

3.2.2 The purpose of compressing the dynamic range of image gray scale can be achieved with the help of logarithmic transformation curve; this is because ( )

(A) The ranges of gray value before and after transformation are different;
(B) The gray value range before transformation is larger than the that after transformation;

(C) Only part of the gray value range is taken after transformation;

(D) The logarithmic transformation curve is a single increasing curve.

[Hint] Analyze against the transformation curve in logarithmic form.

3.2.3 The following gray-scale transformation functions can be used to obtain the effect of enhancing image contrast ( )

(A) Linear function: $g = f$;

(B) Quadratic function: $g = f^2$;

(C) Logarithmic function: $g = \log(1 + f)$;

(D) Exponential function: $g = \exp(f)$.

[Hint] Analyze the curve of each transformation and compare it with the linear transformation $t = s$.

3.3 Histogram Equalization

3.3.1 Suppose the histogram of a gray-scale image as shown in Figure 3.3.1(a), and now use the envelope in Figure 3.3.1(b) as the gray-level transformation curve for gray-level mapping, then the effect achieved is to

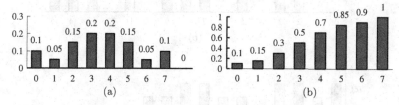

Figure 3.3.1.

(A) Enlarge the contrast of high gray-scale region;

(B) Enlarge the contrast in the low gray-scale region;

(C) Enlarge the overall contrast;

(D) Enlarge the contrast in the high gray-scale region and reduce the contrast in the low gray-scale region.

[Hint] Analyze Figure 3.3.1(b) and notice that it is the cumulative histogram of the image corresponding to Figure 3.3.1(a).

3.3.2 Figure 3.3.2.1 is the statistical histogram of a gray-scale image.

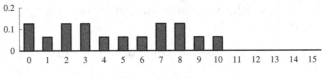

Figure 3.3.2.1.

After histogram equalization, which of the following form(s) is/are the new histogram(s)? ( )

(A) Figure 3.3.2.2(a);
(B) Figure 3.3.2.2(b);
(C) Figure 3.3.2.2(c);
(D) Figure 3.3.2.2(d).

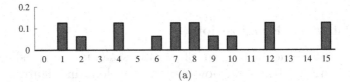

(a)

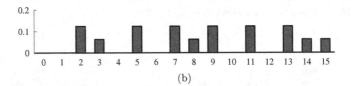

(b)

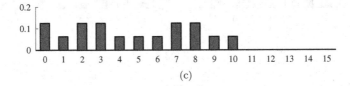

(c)

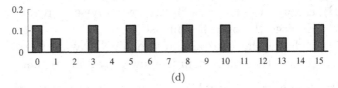

(d)

Figure 3.3.2.2.

[Hint] Histogram equalization will increase the dynamic range of the pixel gray value to achieve the effect of enhancing the overall contrast of the image.

3.3.3 For an image, if the gray levels of pixels corresponding to the even-numbered histogram bins are replaced by the gray levels of pixels corresponding to the odd-numbered histogram bins, the resulting image will have ( )

(A) Increased contrast;
(B) Decreased contrast;
(C) Increased brightness;
(D) Decreased brightness.

[Hint] Note that each even-numbered histogram bin is one less than the corresponding odd-numbered histogram bin, and a large gray value corresponds to high brightness.

3.4 Histogram Specification

3.4.1 Which of the four specified histogram(s) in Figure 3.4.1 can make the contrast between light and dark pixels in the image more obvious? ( )

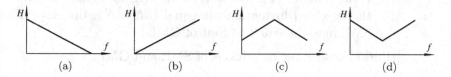

Figure 3.4.1.

(A) Figure 3.4.1(a);
(B) Figure 3.4.1(b);
(C) Figure 3.4.1(c);
(D) Figure 3.4.1(d).

[Hint] Pay attention to the changes of low gray value and high gray value after the histogram specification.

3.4.2 According to the calculation list (GML mapping) for histogram specification in Table 3.4.2, point out the group mapping integer function $I(r)$ used, where $r = 0, 1, 2$. ( )

Table 3.4.2.

Original gray level s_i	0	1	2	3	4	5	6	7
Original CDH	0.19	0.44	0.65	0.81	0.89	0.95	0.98	1.00
Specified CDF	0	0	0	0.2	0.2	0.8	0.8	1.0
GML mapping result	3	5	5	5	7	7	7	7

(A) $I(0) = 0$, $I(1) = 3$, $I(2) = 5$;
(B) $I(0) = 0$, $I(1) = 3$, $I(2) = 7$;
(C) $I(0) = 1$, $I(1) = 4$, $I(2) = 7$;
(D) $I(0) = 0$, $I(1) = 5$, $I(2) = 7$.

[Hint] Consider the calculation of GML in Equation (3.14).

3.4.3 Which of the following description(s) of the two mapping methods (SML and GML) for histogram specification is/are correct? ( )

(A) The error of SML must be greater than that of GML;
(B) SML and GML are both statistically unbiased;
(C) If $N < M$, the error of SML must be greater than that of GML;
(D) If the number of gray levels in the original histogram and the specified histogram are equal $(M = N)$, the error of SML must be equal to that of GML.

[Hint] Consider the definitions of SML and GML.

3.5 Spatial Domain Convolution Enhancement

3.5.1 When performing neighborhood operations in the image, ( )

(A) The size of the mask used is always 3×3;
(B) The calculation effect is only determined by the size of the mask used;
(C) The operations can be either arithmetic operations or logical operations;
(D) The operation can be either linear or nonlinear.

[Hint] Consider the principles and characteristics of neighborhood operations.

3.5.2 The smoothing filter can be used for low-pass filtering the image to eliminate noise, but at the same time, it blurs the details. Which of the following measure(s) cannot reduce the blur of the image? ( )

(A) Use median filtering method;

(B) Use neighborhood average processing;

(C) Add the threshold processing to the output of the smoothing filter (that is, only keep the output greater than the threshold);

(D) Properly reduce the neighborhood operation mask of the smoothing filter.

[Hint] The smoothing filter is divided into linear filter and non-linear filter; its processing effect is related to the size of the mask and the way the pixel is processed by the mask.

3.5.3 When using the median filter, ( )

(A) The average value of the mask is assigned to the pixel corresponding to the center of mask;

(B) The geometric center value of the mask is assigned to the pixel corresponding to the center of mask;

(C) The value of the middle rank in all values of the mask after sorting is assigned to the pixel corresponding to the center of mask;

(D) The value ranked at 50% of the value range in the mask is assigned to the pixel corresponding to the center of mask.

[Hint] Carefully understand the definition of the filter median.

3.5.4 The median filter can ( )

(A) Detect the edge;

(B) Eliminate isolated noise;

(C) Blur image details;

(D) Smooth isolated noise.

[Hint] Consider the definition and characteristics of median filter.

3.5.5 Figure 3.5.5 gives four kinds of masks (* represents a value that is not zero). Which shape of the mask used for median filtering has less impact on the object (that is, the mask will eliminate noise while causing relatively smaller error)? ( )

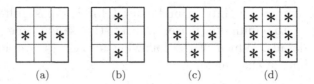

Figure 3.5.5.

(A) Figure 3.5.5(a);
(B) Figure 3.5.5(b);
(C) Figure 3.5.5(c);
(D) Figure 3.5.5(d).

[Hint] It can be judged according to the error characteristics of the direction and size of each mask.

3.5.6 Which of the following filter(s) is/are similar to the effect of histogram equalization on the image? ( )

(A) Linear smoothing filter;
(B) Nonlinear smoothing filter;
(C) Linear sharpening filter;
(D) Nonlinear sharpening filter.

[Hint] The gray-scale transformation function used for histogram equalization is a cumulative histogram, which can enhance the overall contrast of the image.

3.5.7 To eliminate isolated noise points in the image, which filter(s) cannot get the desired effect? ( )

(A) High frequency boost filter;
(B) Linear sharpening filter;
(C) Median filter;
(D) Neighborhood average filter.

[Hint] Pay attention to which filter(s) has/have smoothing function.

3.5.8 Let $f(x, y)$ be a gray-scale image, given the following four transformations:

(1) $g(x,y) = |f(x,y)-f(x+1,y)|+|f(x+1,y+1)-f(x,y+1)|$;
(2) $g(x,y) = |f(x,y)-f(x+1,y+1)|+|f(x+1,y)-f(x,y+1)|$;
(3) $g(x,y) = |\partial f/\partial x| + |\partial f/\partial y|$;

(4) $g(x, y) = \max\{|\partial f/\partial x|, |\partial f/\partial y|\}$.

Among the above transformations, those belonging to the sharpening filter are ( )

(A) (1) and (2);
(B) (3) and (4);
(C) (1), (3), and (4);
(D) (1), (2), (3), and (4).

[Hint] Pay attention to the various approximation forms of differential operators.

3.5.9 Let $f(x, y)$ be a gray-scale image; using $G[f(x, y)] = |f(x, y) - f(x + 1, y + 1)| + |f(x + 1, y) - f(x, y + 1)|$ to process can obtain the edge of the object for further enhancement. If one only cares about the position of the contour of the object but does not care about the other content, which of the following method(s) is/are the best ($L_{\max}$ is the maximum gray level, $L_{\min}$ is the minimum gray level)? ( )

(A) $g(x, y) = \begin{cases} L_{\max} & G[f(x, y)] \geq T \\ f(x, y) & \text{Otherwise} \end{cases}$;

(B) $g(x, y) = \begin{cases} L_{\max} & G[f(x, y)] \geq T \\ L_{\min} & \text{Otherwise} \end{cases}$;

(C) $g(x, y) = \begin{cases} G[f(x, y)] & G[f(x, y)] \geq T \\ L_{\min} & \text{Otherwise} \end{cases}$;

(D) $g(x, y) = \begin{cases} G[f(x, y)] & G[f(x, y)] \geq T \\ f(x, y) & \text{Otherwise} \end{cases}$.

[Hint] Adding the threshold value for judgment can separately process the object and background.

References

[1] Zhang, Y.-J. *Image Engineering, Vol. 1: Image Processing*. Germany, Berlin: De Gruyter, 2017.
[2] Sonka, M., Hlavac, V., and Boyle R. *Image Processing, Analysis, and Machine Vision*, 4th Edn. Singapore: Cengage Learning, 2014.
[3] Pratt, W. K. *Digital Image Processing: PIKS Scientific Inside*, 4th Edn. USA, Hoboken: Wiley Interscience, 2007.

[4] Russ, J. C. and Neal, F. B. *The Image Processing Handbook*, 7th Edn. USA, New York: CRC Press, 2016.

[5] Gonzalez, R. C. and Woods, R. E. *Digital Image Processing*, 4th Edn. UK, London: Prentice Hall, 2018.

[6] Zhang, Y.-J. Mapping laws for histogram processing of digital images, Comments on "A binary mapping law (BML) for histogram processing of digital image". *Journal of Image and Graphics*, 2004, 9A(10): 1265–1268.

[7] Zhang, Y.-J. Improving the accuracy of direct histogram specification. *IEE Electronics Letters*, 1992, 28(3): 213–214.

[8] Li, R. and Zhang, Y.-J. A hybrid filter for the cancellation of mixed Gaussian noise and impulse noise. *Proc. 4th IEEE PCM*, 2003, 1: 508–512.

[9] Zhang, Y.-J. Quantitative study of 3-D gradient operators. *IVC*, 1993, 11: 611–622.

Chapter 4

Frequency Domain Enhancement

The enhancement techniques introduced in Chapter 3 are carried out in the image space, and they directly operate on the image pixels. If the image is transformed first, the image enhancement can also be carried out in the transform domain. In other words, in addition to directly operating in the image space, the image enhancement can also be achieved by first transforming the image into the transform domain and then making the enhancement in the transform domain.

The most commonly used transform domain is the frequency domain (frequency domain is the result of Fourier transform). **Frequency domain enhancement** also has intuitive physical meaning. For example, image blur is the result of insufficient high-frequency components in the image. If one increases the high-frequency component or reduces the low-frequency component in the frequency domain, one can eliminate some blur and make the image clear. Another example is that images are sometimes affected by recurring regular periodic noise. This noise is often caused by electrical interference when images are acquired, and the specific impact varies with spatial location. Since periodic noise has a specific frequency, frequency domain filtering can often be used to filter out the frequency of the corresponding noise so as to eliminate periodic noise.

The sections of this chapter are arranged as follows.

Section 4.1 first introduces the 2D Fourier transform and its related characteristics, and also introduces the overall process of frequency domain filtering.

123

Section 4.2 discusses frequency domain low-pass filters. First, the principle and characteristics of frequency domain low-pass filtering are introduced with the help of ideal low-pass filters, and then the Butterworth low-pass filters that can be used in practice are introduced.

Section 4.3 discusses frequency domain high-pass filters. First, with the help of ideal high-pass filter, the principle and characteristics of frequency domain high-pass filtering are introduced, and then the Butterworth high-pass filter and high-frequency emphasis filter that can be used in practice are introduced.

Section 4.4 further introduces band-pass and band-stop filters, which can be regarded as extensions of the low-pass or high-pass filters. In addition, the relationship between the band-pass and band-stop filters is also discussed. Considering the characteristics of 2D images, a more general notch filter is also presented. Finally, an application example of the notch filter for interactive elimination of periodic noise is provided.

Section 4.5 introduces a special filter, the homomorphic filter. It uses the simple imaging model introduced in Section 2.2, which can simultaneously compress the image brightness range and enhance the image contrast, and can also be used to eliminate multiplicative noise in the image.

4.1   Fourier Transform and Frequency Domain Enhancement

Fourier transform is a transformation that connects image space and frequency space.

4.1.1   Fourier transform

This book mainly discusses 2D images, and the 2D Fourier transform is directly considered here. For a 2D image $f(x, y)$, its 2D Fourier transform $F(u, v)$ is

$$F(u, v) = \frac{1}{N} \sum_{y=0}^{N-1} \sum_{x=0}^{N-1} f(x, y) \exp[-j2\pi(ux + vy)/N]$$

$$u, v = 0, 1, \ldots, N - 1 \tag{4.1}$$

and the inverse Fourier transform of $F(u, v)$ is $f(x, y)$ is

$$f(x, y) = \frac{1}{N} \sum_{v=0}^{N-1} \sum_{u=0}^{N-1} F(u, v) \exp[j2\pi(xu + yv)/N]$$

$$x, y = 0, 1, \ldots, N - 1. \tag{4.2}$$

Generally, $f(x, y)$ is a real function, but the corresponding $F(u, v)$ is often a complex function, which can be written as

$$F(u, v) = R(u, v) + jI(u, v), \tag{4.3}$$

where $R(u, v)$ and $I(u, v)$ are the real and imaginary parts of $F(u, v)$, respectively. Further, the spectrum, phase angle, and power spectrum of the 2D Fourier transform can be defined as follows:

$$|F(u, v)| = \sqrt{[R^2(u, v) + I^2(u, v)]}, \tag{4.4}$$

$$\phi(u, v) = \arctan[I(u, v)/R(u, v)], \tag{4.5}$$

$$P(u, v) = |F(u, v)|^2 = R^2(u, v) + I^2(u, v). \tag{4.6}$$

Example 4.1 Display of image function and Fourier spectrum

Figure 4.1(a) shows a perspective view of a simple 2D image function, where $Z = f(x, y)$. This function is a positive constant in a square centered at the origin and zero elsewhere. Figure 4.1(b) shows the gray-scale image (here, binary image) of the function in Figure 4.1(a). Figure 4.1(c) shows the gray-scale display of the Fourier spectrum amplitude of this 2D image function. □

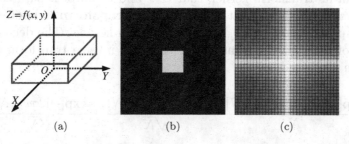

(a)　　　　(b)　　　　(c)

Figure 4.1.　A simple 2D image function and its Fourier spectrum display.

(a)   (b)   (c)   (d)

Figure 4.2.   Actual image and Fourier spectrum.

Example 4.2 Actual image and Fourier spectrum

The two actual images and their corresponding Fourier spectrums are shown in Figure 4.2. The image in Figure 4.2(a) has a small contrast and is a mild image, which are reflected in the Fourier spectrum with more low-frequency components and a larger center value of the spectrum (the center is the frequency domain origin). In the image in Figure 4.2(b), there are some relatively regular linear objects, which are reflected in the Fourier spectrum with some relatively obvious ray-like bands.   □

4.1.2   Fourier transform properties

In Equations (4.1) and (4.2), $\exp[-j2\pi(ux + vy)/N]/N$ and $\exp[j2\pi(ux + vy)/N]/N$ are the kernel of Fourier transform and the kernel inverse Fourier transform, respectively. The Fourier transform has many properties that are determined by its kernel.

When performing 2D Fourier transform, the properties of separability and symmetry can be used to simplify the calculation. The separability of 2D Fourier transform means that the two pairs of variables in its transform kernel, that is, x and u can be separated from y and v. This shows that a 2D **Fourier transform kernel** can be decomposed into two 1D Fourier transform kernels. The decompositions of the forward transform kernel and inverse transform kernel can be expressed as

$$\frac{\exp[-j2\pi(ux + vy)/N]}{N} = \frac{\exp[-j2\pi ux/N]}{\sqrt{N}} + \frac{\exp[-j2\pi vy/N]}{\sqrt{N}}$$

(4.7)

and

$$\frac{\exp[j2\pi(xu+yv)/N]}{N} = \frac{\exp[j2\pi xu/N]}{\sqrt{N}} + \frac{\exp[j2\pi yv/N]}{\sqrt{N}}, \quad (4.8)$$

respectively.

The symmetry of the 2D Fourier transform means that the two parts of the Fourier transform kernel and the inverse Fourier transform kernel have the same forms after separation. This can also be easily seen from Equations (4.7) and (4.8). Because both the forward and inverse transform kernels of the 2D Fourier transform are separable and symmetrical, the Fourier transform is a separable and symmetrical transform.

The 2D transform with separable transform kernel can be calculated in two steps, and each step uses a 1D transform. Take the 2D Fourier transform as an example here; see Figure 4.3.

First, substitute Equation (4.7) into Equation (4.1), and perform 1D transformation along each column of $f(x,y)$ to get

$$G(x,y) = \frac{1}{N} \sum_{y=0}^{N-1} f(x,y) \exp[-j2\pi vy/N] \quad x,v = 0,1,\ldots,N-1.$$

$$(4.9)$$

Then, perform 1D transformation along each row of $G(x,v)$ to get

$$F(u,v) = \frac{1}{N} \sum_{x=0}^{N-1} G(x,v) \exp[-j2\pi ux/N] \quad u,v = 0,1,\ldots,N-1.$$

$$(4.10)$$

In this way, in order to calculate a 2D Fourier transform, it is only necessary to calculate the 1D Fourier transform twice. Because

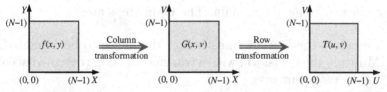

Figure 4.3. Calculation of 2D transformation from the two-step 1D transformation.

directly performing an $N \times N$ 2D Fourier transform requires N^4 complex multiplication operations and $N^2(N^2 - 1)$ complex addition operations, while performing a 1D Fourier transform of length N only requires N^2 complex multiplication operations and $N(N - 1)$ complex addition operations, so converting one 2D Fourier transform into two 1D Fourier transforms can greatly save computation cost.

4.1.3   Frequency domain enhancement

Fourier transform has an important theorem, **convolution theorem**, which is the basis of **frequency domain enhancement**. Suppose that the convolution result of the function $f(x, y)$ and the linear shift invariant operator $h(x, y)$ is $g(x, y)$, that is, $g(x, y) = h(x, y) \otimes f(x, y)$, then according to the convolution theorem in the frequency domain:

$$G(u, v) = H(u, v)F(u, v), \qquad (4.11)$$

where $G(u, v)$, $H(u, v)$, $F(u, v)$ are the Fourier transforms of $g(x, y)$, $h(x, y)$, $f(x, y)$, respectively. In terms of linear system theory, $H(u, v)$ is the **transfer function**. It can be seen that selecting different $H(u, v)$ is equivalent to selecting different masks in the spatial domain, and filtering enhancement can also be achieved through multiplication in the frequency domain.

In specific enhancement applications, $f(x, y)$ is given (so, $F(u, v)$ can be obtained by Fourier transform) and what needs to be determined is $H(u, v)$, so that $g(x, y)$ can be calculated by Equation (4.11) to compute $G(u, v)$ and obtain through the inverse Fourier transform:

$$g(x, y) = \mathcal{F}^{-1}[G(u, v)] = \mathcal{F}^{-1}[H(u, v)F(u, v)]. \qquad (4.12)$$

Based on the above discussion, it is quite intuitive to enhance the image in the frequency domain. The main steps are:

(1) Calculate the Fourier transform of the image to be enhanced.
(2) Multiply the transform with a transfer function (designed according to requirements).
(3) Inverse Fourier transform is performed on the result to obtain an enhanced image.

The basic principle of frequency domain enhancement is to suppress the components of the image in a certain frequency range while leaving other components unaffected, thereby changing the frequency distribution of the output image to achieve the purpose of enhancement. For example, the edges and noise in the image correspond to the high-frequency components in the spectrum after the Fourier transform of the image, so according to Equation (4.11), a suitable $H(u,v)$ needs to be selected to reduce the high-frequency components of $F(u,v)$ in $G(u,v)$. As another example, the blurred part of the image corresponds to the low-frequency component in the spectrum after the Fourier transform of the image; so, according to Equation (4.11), a suitable $H(u,v)$ needs to be selected to reduce the low-frequency components of $F(u,v)$ in $G(u,v)$.

4.2 Frequency Domain Low-Pass Filter

The function of the low-pass filter is to attenuate or eliminate high-frequency components while retaining low-frequency components.

4.2.1 Ideal low-pass filter

The transfer function of a 2D **ideal low-pass filter** satisfies the following conditions:

$$H(u,v) = \begin{cases} 1 & \text{if } D(u,v) \leq D_0 \\ 0 & \text{if } D(u,v) > D_0, \end{cases} \tag{4.13}$$

where D_0 is a non-negative integer. $D(u,v)$ is the distance from the point (u,v) to the origin of the frequency plane, $D(u,v) = (u^2 + v^2)^{1/2}$. Figure 4.4(a) shows a cross-sectional view of H (suppose D is symmetric about the origin), and Figure 4.4(b) shows a perspective view of H. Here, ideal means that frequencies less than D_0 can pass the filter completely unaffected, while frequencies greater than D_0 cannot pass. Therefore, D_0 is also called the **cutoff frequency**. Although the ideal low-pass filter is clearly defined mathematically and can be realized in computer simulation, the ideal low-pass filter that goes straight up and down at the cutoff frequency cannot be realized with actual electronic devices.

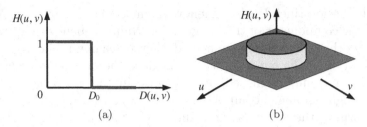

Figure 4.4.   Sectional view of the transfer function of ideal low-pass filter.

Example 4.3 Frequency domain low-pass filtering and image energy

Most of the energy in the image is concentrated in the low-frequency components. Figure 4.5(a) is the Fourier spectrum of the image in Figure 1.5(a), and the radii of the four circles superimposed on it are 5, 11, 45, and 68, respectively. These circles respectively contain 90%, 95%, 99%, and 99.5% of the energy in the original image. If R is the radius of the circle, and B is the percentage of image energy in the circle (retained after filtering), then:

$$B = 100\% \times \left[\sum_{u \in R} \sum_{v \in R} P(u,v) \middle/ \sum_{u=0}^{N-1} \sum_{v=0}^{N-1} P(u,v) \right], \qquad (4.14)$$

where $P(u,v)$ is the power spectrum of the Fourier spectrum of $f(x,y)$. Figures 4.5(b) to (e) are the results obtained by using the ideal low-pass filter with the cutoff frequency determined by the radius of each circle above.

It can be seen from Figure 4.5(b) that although only 10% of the (high-frequency) energy is filtered out, most of the details in the image have been lost. In fact, this image has no practical use. It can be seen from Figure 4.5(c) that when only 5% of the (high-frequency) energy is filtered out, there is still a significant **ringing effect** in the image. It can be seen from Figure 4.5(d) that if only 1% of the (high-frequency) energy is filtered out, the image will have a certain degree of blur but the visual effect is acceptable. Finally, it can be seen from Figure 4.5(e) that the filtering result obtained after filtering

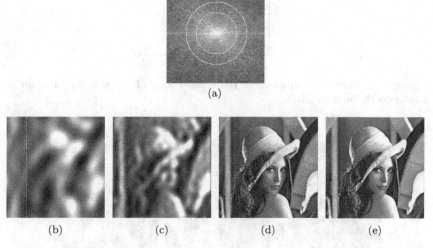

Figure 4.5. Blur produced by low-pass filtering in the frequency domain.

out 0.5% (high-frequency) energy is almost the same as the original image. □

4.2.2 Butterworth low-pass filter

A low-pass filter that can be physically realized is the **Butterworth low-pass filter**. The transfer function of a Butterworth low-pass filter with an order of n and a cutoff frequency of D_0 is

$$H(u,v) = \frac{1}{1 + [D(u,v)/D_0]^{2n}}. \tag{4.15}$$

The schematic diagram of the cross-section of the Butterworth low-pass filter of order 1 is shown in Figure 4.15. It can be seen from the figure that its transition between high and low frequencies is relatively smooth, so not only can it be physically realized, but also the resulting output image has no obvious ringing effect.

In general, the cutoff frequency is often taken as the frequency at which the maximum value of H drops to a certain percentage. In Equation (4.15), when $D(u,v) = D_0$, then $H(u,v) = 0.5$ (that is,

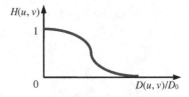

Figure 4.6.   Schematic diagram of the cross-section of the transfer function of Butterworth low-pass filter.

| (a) | (b) | (c) |

Figure 4.7.   Frequency domain low-pass filtering to eliminate false contours.

down to 50%). Another commonly used cutoff frequency value is the frequency at which H drops to the $1/\sqrt{2}$ of its maximum value.

Example 4.4 Frequency domain low-pass filtering to eliminate false contours

When images have **false contours** due to insufficient quantization, low-pass filtering can often be used to smooth them to improve the image quality. Figure 4.7 shows an example of eliminating false contours. Figure 4.7(a) is an image uniformly quantized from 256 gray levels to 12 gray levels. There are different degrees of false contour phenomena in hats and shoulders. Figures 4.7(b) and (c) are the results of smoothing with an ideal low-pass filter and a Butterworth low-pass filter with an order of one, respectively. The radii corresponding to the cutoff frequencies of the two filters used are both 30. Comparing the two filtering result images, the result image obtained with the ideal low-pass filter has obvious ringing phenomenon, while the result image obtained with the Butterworth filter has a better effect. □

4.3 Frequency Domain High-Pass Filter

The function of the high-pass filter is to attenuate or eliminate low-frequency components while retaining high-frequency components.

4.3.1 Ideal high-pass filter

The transfer function of a 2D **ideal high-pass filter** satisfies the following conditions (the meaning of each parameter is the same as in Equation (4.13)):

$$H(u,v) = \begin{cases} 0 & \text{if } D(u,v) \leq D_0 \\ 1 & \text{if } D(u,v) > D_0, \end{cases} \qquad (4.16)$$

Figure 4.8(a) shows a schematic cross-sectional view of H (assuming D is symmetric about the origin), and Figure 4.8(b) shows a perspective view of H. They are exactly the opposites of the cross-sectional shape of the ideal low-pass filter described earlier, but like the ideal low-pass filter, this ideal high-pass filter cannot be realized with actual electronic devices and the ringing effect will also be more obvious.

4.3.2 Butterworth high-pass filter

The transfer function of a Butterworth high-pass filter with order n and cutoff frequency D_0 is

$$H(u,v) = \frac{1}{1 + [D_0/D(u,v)]^{2n}}. \qquad (4.17)$$

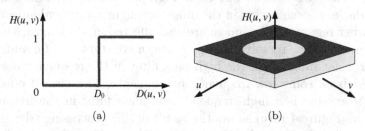

(a)   (b)

Figure 4.8. Schematic diagram of the cross-section of the transfer function of an ideal high-pass filter.

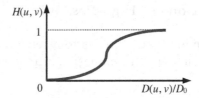

Figure 4.9.　Sectional view of the transfer function of Butterworth high-pass filter.

The cross-sectional view of a Butterworth high-pass filter of order one is shown in Figure 4.9. Comparing it with Figure 4.6, it can be seen that, similar to the Butterworth low-pass filter, the high-pass Butterworth filter has no discontinuous border between the passed and filtered frequencies. Since the transition between high and low frequencies is relatively smooth, the ringing effect of the output image obtained by the Butterworth filter is not noticeable.

In general, as for the Butterworth low-pass filter, the frequency at which the maximum value of $H(u, v)$ is reduced to a certain percentage is also taken as the cutoff frequency of the Butterworth high-pass filter.

Example 4.5 Frequency domain high-pass filter enhancement example

Figure 4.10 shows an example of high-pass filter enhancement in the frequency domain. Figure 4.10(a) shows a relatively blurred image, and Figure 4.10(b) shows the result of processing with a Butterworth high-pass filter of order one. Because most of the low-frequency components are filtered out after high-pass filtering, although the boundaries of each region in the image are significantly enhanced, the smoother regions in the image are also affected, and the entire image becomes darker. To solve this problem, a constant can be added to the transfer function of the high-pass filter in the frequency domain to add back some low-frequency components. The overall effect of this processing is a high-frequency emphasis filter in the frequency domain. Figure 4.10(c) shows the result of this processing (the added constant is 0.5). Not only the edges are enhanced but the entire image is also richer in level.　　□

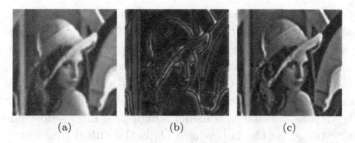

(a)   (b)   (c)

Figure 4.10.   Frequency domain high-pass filter.

The effect of the previously mentioned **high-frequency emphasis filtering** in the frequency domain can also be proved as follows: Set the Fourier transform of the degradation image to $F(u, v)$ and the transfer function to $H(u, v)$, then the Fourier transform of the output image is $G(u, v) = H(u, v)F(u, v)$, according to Equation (4.11). Now, add a constant c to the transfer function to obtain the high-frequency emphasis transfer function $H_e(u, v) = H(u, v) + c$, where c is the constant between $[0, 1]$. In this way, the Fourier transform of the high-frequency emphasis output image is $G_e(u, v) = G(u, v) + c \times F(u, v)$, that is, a certain amount of low-frequency information $c \times F(u, v)$ is retained after high-pass filtering. If the high-frequency emphasis output image is transformed back by the inverse Fourier transform, the following result can be obtained from Equation (4.12):

$$g_e(x, y) = g(x, y) + c \times f(x, y). \tag{4.18}$$

This result is similar to the **high-frequency boost filter** of Equation (3.17), which shows that it has a similar enhancement effect with the spatial method.

4.4   Band-Pass Filter and Band-Stop Filter

Band-pass and band-stop filters are two closely related and complementary filters.

4.4.1   Band-pass filter

As the name implies, a **band-pass filter** is a filter that allows signals in a certain frequency range to pass and prevents signals in other frequency ranges from passing. The band-pass filter can be seen as an extension of the low-pass or high-pass filter. Consider a low-pass filter whose allowable frequency range is $[0, D_0]$, where D_0 is the cutoff frequency. If the lower limit of the previously mentioned frequency range is increased from 0 to D_1 which is less than D_0, the filter becomes a band-pass filter that allows signals in the frequency range $[D_1, D_0]$ to pass. Similarly, consider a high-pass filter whose allowable frequency range is $[D_0, \infty]$, where D_0 is the cutoff frequency. If the upper limit of the above frequency range is lowered from ∞ to D_2, which is greater than D_0, the filter becomes a band-pass filter that allows signals in the frequency range $[D_0, D_2]$ to pass.

In practice, the band-pass filter that allows signals in the surrounding ring zone, with the origin of the frequency domain as the center, to pass through is **radially symmetric**. The transfer function of a radially symmetrical ideal band-pass filter is

$$H(u,v) = \begin{cases} 0 & D(u,v) < D_0 - W/2 \\ 1 & D_0 - W/2 \leq D(u,v) \leq D_0 + W/2 \\ 0 & D(u,v) > D_0 + W/2, \end{cases} \tag{4.19}$$

where W is the width of the ring zone and D_0 is the frequency of the center of the ring zone.

Example 4.6 Schematic diagram of a radially symmetrical band-pass filter

Figure 4.11 is a perspective schematic diagram of a radially symmetrical band-pass filter $H(u,v)$. The meaning of each letter in the figure is shown in Equation (4.19). □

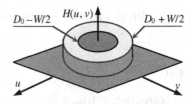

Figure 4.11.   Perspective view of radially symmetrical band-pass filter.

The transfer function of an nth order radially symmetrical Butterworth band-pass filter is

$$H(u, v) = \frac{[D(u, v)W]^{2n}}{[D^2(u, v) - D_0^2]^{2n} + [D(u, v)W]^{2n}}. \tag{4.20}$$

The W and D_0 in Equation (4.20) are the same as in Equation (4.19).

4.4.2 Band-stop filter

The **band-stop filter** (also called **band-reject filter**), as its name implies, is a filter that prevents signals in a certain frequency range from passing and allows signals in other frequency ranges to pass. The band-stop filter can also be seen as an extension of the low-pass or high-pass filter. Consider a low-pass filter whose allowable frequency range is $[0, D_0]$, where D_0 is the cutoff frequency. If the signal from the frequency D_1 exceeding D_0 to ∞ is allowed to pass, the filter becomes a band-stop filter that prevents the signal in the frequency range $[D_0, D_1]$ from passing. Similarly, consider a high-pass filter whose allowable frequency range is $[D_0, \infty]$, where D_0 is the cutoff frequency. If the signal from 0 to the frequency D_2 that is less than D_0 is allowed to pass, the filter becomes a band-stop filter that prevents signals in the frequency range $[D_2, D_0]$ from passing.

In practice, the band-stop filter that prevents the signal in the surrounding ring zone with the origin of the frequency domain as the center from passing through is **radially symmetric**. The transfer function of a radially symmetrical ideal band-stop filter is

$$H(u, v) = \begin{cases} 1 & D(u, v) < D_0 - W/2 \\ 0 & D_0 - W/2 \leq D(u, v) \leq D_0 + W/2 \\ 1 & D(u, v) > D_0 + W/2, \end{cases} \tag{4.21}$$

where W is the width of the ring zone and D_0 is the frequency of the center of the ring zone.

Example 4.7 Perspective schematic diagram of a radially symmetrical band-stop filter

Figure 4.12 is a perspective schematic diagram of a radially symmetrical band-stop filter $H(u, v)$. The meaning of each letter in the figure is shown in Equation (4.21). □

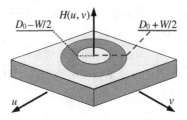

Figure 4.12.   Perspective view of radially symmetrical band-stop filter.

The transfer function of an nth order radially symmetrical Butterworth band-stop filter is

$$H(u,v) = \frac{[D^2(u,v) - D_0^2]^{2n}}{[D^2(u,v) - D_0]^2 + [D(u,v)W]^{2n}}. \qquad (4.22)$$

The W and D_0 in Equation (4.22) are the same as in Equation (4.21).

4.4.3   Relation between band-pass filter and band-stop filter

The band-pass filter and the band-stop filter are complementary to each other. So, if $H_R(u,v)$ is the transfer function of the band-stop filter, then the corresponding band-pass filter $H_P(u,v)$ can be obtained by just flipping $H_R(u,v)$:

$$H_P(u,v) = -[H_R(u,v) - 1] = 1 - H_R(u,v). \qquad (4.23)$$

Further analysis can be performed by comparing Equation (4.19) with Equation (4.21) and Equation (4.20) with Equation (4.22).

It can be seen from Equation (4.23) that if a band-pass filter is used to extract the frequency components in a certain band and then subtract the result from the image, it is also possible to achieve the effect of eliminating or reducing the components in a certain frequency range in the image.

Example 4.8 Comparison of the effects of various filters

Figure 4.13 shows a set of examples for comparing various filtering effects. Figure 4.13(a) is the original image. Figure (b) is a schematic

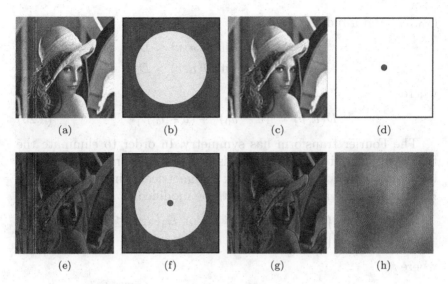

Figure 4.13. Examples of the effects of various filters.

diagram of the low-pass filter; the central low-frequency part (white) can pass, and the surrounding high-frequency part (gray) cannot pass. Figure 4.13(c) is the result of low-pass filtering. Figure 4.13(d) is a schematic diagram of the high-pass filter; the central low-frequency part cannot pass, and the surrounding high-frequency parts can pass. Figure 4.13(e) is the result of high-pass filtering. Figure 4.13(f) is a schematic diagram of a band-pass filter; the low-frequency part in the center cannot pass and the intermediate frequency part of a certain range around can pass, but the higher-frequency part further away cannot pass. Figure 4.13(g) is the result of band-pass filtering. Figure 4.13(h) is the result of band-stop filtering, and the band-stop filter used is just complementary to that of Figure 4.13(f). □

4.4.4 Notch filter

A **notch filter** can stop or pass the frequencies in the neighborhood centered on a given frequency, so it is still a band-stop filter or band-pass filter in essence, and can be called band-stop notch filter and band-pass notch filter, respectively.

In a 2D image, the transfer function of an **ideal band-stop notch filter** used to eliminate all frequencies in a region centered on

(u_0, v_0) and a radius of D_0 is

$$H(u, v) = \begin{cases} 0 & \text{if } D(u, v) \le D_0 \\ 1 & \text{if } D(u, v) > D_0, \end{cases} \tag{4.24}$$

where

$$D(u, v) = [(u - u_0)^2 + (v - v_0)^2]^{1/2}. \tag{4.25}$$

The Fourier transform has symmetry. In order to eliminate the frequency in a given region that is not centered on the origin, the band-stop notch filter must work symmetrically in pairs, that is, Equations (4.24) and (4.25) need to be modified to

$$H(u, v) = \begin{cases} 0 & \text{if } D_1(u, v) \le D_0 \text{ or } D_2(u, v) \le D_0 \\ 1 & \text{otherwise}, \end{cases} \tag{4.26}$$

where

$$D_1(u, v) = [(u - u_0)^2 + (v - v_0)^2]^{1/2} \tag{4.27}$$

and

$$D_2(u, v) = [(u + u_0)^2 + (v + v_0)^2]^{1/2} \tag{4.28}$$

Example 4.9 Perspective schematic diagram of an ideal band-stop notch filter

Figure 4.14 shows a perspective schematic diagram of a typical ideal band-stop notch filter $H(u, v)$.

Similar to the complementary relationship between the band-pass filter and the band-stop filter, the band-pass notch filter and the band-stop notch filter are also complementary each other. The **ideal band-pass notch filter** can be obtained from the ideal band-stop notch filter. □

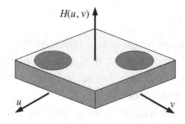

Figure 4.14.   Perspective view of an ideal band-stop notch filter.

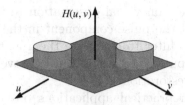

Figure 4.15. Perspective view of an ideal band-pass notch filter.

Example 4.10 Perspective schematic diagram of an ideal band-pass notch filter

Figure 4.15 shows a perspective schematic diagram of a typical ideal band-pass notch filter $H(u, v)$.

The transfer function of an nth order **Butterworth band-stop notch filter** is

$$H(u, v) = \frac{1}{1 + \left[\frac{D_0^2}{D_1(u,v)D_2(u,v)}\right]^n}. \tag{4.29}$$

The transfer function of a **Gaussian band-stop notch filter** is

$$H(u, v) = 1 - \exp\left\{\frac{1}{2}\left[\frac{D_1(u, v)D_2(u, v)}{D_0^2}\right]\right\}. \tag{4.30}$$

Both the Butterworth and Gaussian band-stop notch filters become high-pass filters if $u_0 = v_0 = 0$. Taking into account the complementary relationship between the band-pass filter and the band-stop filter, with $u_0 = v_0 = 0$, various band-pass notch filters become low-pass filters. □

4.4.5   Interactively eliminate periodic noise

With the help of a notch filter, **periodic noise** can be eliminated, but this requires prior knowledge of the frequency of the noise. If you know the frequency of periodic noise in advance, you can design a corresponding filter to automatically eliminate this noise. If the frequency of periodic noise is not known in advance, the spectral amplitude graph $G(u, v)$ of the degraded image can be displayed. Because the noise of a single frequency will produce two bright spots far away from the origin of the coordinate on the spectrum amplitude map, it is easy to rely on visual observation to interactively determine the position of the pulse component in the frequency domain and use a band-stop filter to eliminate them at that position. This kind of human–computer interaction can improve the flexibility and efficiency of image restoration.

Periodic noise in practical applications often has multiple frequency components, for which the main frequency needs to be extracted. This requires placing a band-pass filter $H(u, v)$ at the position corresponding to each bright spot in the frequency domain. If one can construct a $H(u, v)$ that allows only components related to the interference pattern to pass, then the Fourier transform of this structural pattern is

$$P(u, v) = H(u, v)G(u, v). \tag{4.31}$$

To construct such a $H(u, v)$, many judgments are needed to determine whether each bright spot is an interference bright spot. So, this work often needs to be done interactively by observing the spectrum display of $G(u, v)$. When a filter is determined, the periodic noise can be obtained by the following:

$$p(x, y) = \mathcal{F}^{-1}\{H(u, v)G(u, v)\}. \tag{4.32}$$

If $p(x, y)$ can be completely determined, then subtract $p(x, y)$ from $g(x, y)$ to get $f(x, y)$. Only a certain approximation of this pattern can be obtained in practical applications. In order to reduce the influence of the components that are not considered in the estimation of $p(x, y)$, the weighted $p(x, y)$ can be subtracted from $g(x, y)$ to obtain the approximate $f_e(x, y)$ of $f(x, y)$, which is

$$f_e(x, y) = g(x, y) - w(x, y)p(x, y). \tag{4.33}$$

In the above equation, $w(x, y)$ is called the weight function, and the optimal result in a certain sense can be obtained by changing it.

Example 4.11 Interactive recovery example

Figure 4.16 shows an example of using **interactive restoration** to eliminate sinusoidal interference mode (a type of periodic noise). Figure 4.16(a) is an image covered by a sinusoidal interference pattern.

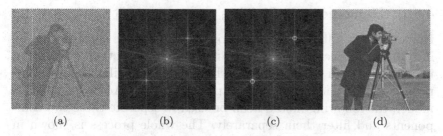

(a) (b) (c) (d)

Figure 4.16. Interactive recovery example.

Figure 4.16(b) is its amplitude image of Fourier spectrum, on which there is a pair of more obvious (pulse) white dots (the intersection of bright lines). This is because if the amplitude of the sinusoidal interference pattern $s(x, y)$ is A and the frequency component is (u_0, v_0), that is, $s(x, y) = A \sin(u_0 x + v_0 y)$, then its Fourier transform is

$$S(u, v) = \frac{-\mathrm{j}A}{2} \left[\delta \left(u - \frac{u_0}{2\pi}, v - \frac{v_0}{2\pi} \right) - \delta \left(u + \frac{u_0}{2\pi}, v + \frac{v_0}{2\pi} \right) \right].$$

(4.34)

The above equation has only imaginary components, which represents a pair of pulses that have coordinates located on the frequency plane $(u_0/2\pi, v_0/2\pi)$ and $(-u_0/2\pi, -v_0/2\pi)$ and with the intensities $-A/2$ and $A/2$, respectively.

To filter out such pairs of pulses, two band-stop filters can be placed at the two white points in the frequency plane in an interactive manner, as shown in Figure 4.16(c). The cutoff frequency of these two band-stop filters (the radii of circle) should be as small as possible to avoid filtering out too much original image content. After removing the noise, one can take the inverse Fourier transform, and finally one can get the recovery result shown in Figure 4.16(d). □

4.5 Homomorphic Filter

Homomorphic filtering is a method that simultaneously compresses the image brightness range and enhances the image contrast in the frequency domain. Homomorphic filtering can also be used to eliminate multiplicative noise in images.

4.5.1   Homomorphic filtering process

Homomorphic filtering is based on the luminance imaging model introduced in Section 2.2. It was mentioned in Section 2.2 that an image $f(x, y)$ can be expressed as the product of its illuminance component $i(x, y)$ and reflection component $r(x, y)$. According to this model, the following method can be used to separate these two components and filter them separately. The whole process is shown in Figure 4.17. The main steps are as follows:

(1) First, take the logarithm of both sides of Equation (2.3), namely:

$$\ln f(x, y) = \ln i(x, y) + \ln r(x, y). \tag{4.35}$$

(2) Perform Fourier transform on both sides of Equation (4.35) and get

$$F(u, v) = I(u, v) + R(u, v). \tag{4.36}$$

(3) Suppose a frequency domain enhancement function $H(u, v)$ is used to process $F(u, v)$:

$$H(u, v)F(u, v) = H(u, v)I(u, v) + H(u, v)R(u, v). \tag{4.37}$$

(4) Inversely transform the processing result back to the space domain to get

$$h_f(x, y) = h_i(x, y) + h_r(x, y). \tag{4.38}$$

It can be seen that the enhanced image is made up of the superposition of two parts corresponding to the illuminance component and the reflection component.

(5) Take the exponents on both sides of the inverse transformation results to obtain

$$g(x, y) = \exp|h_f(x, y)| = \exp|h_i(x, y)| \bullet \exp|h_r(x, y)|. \tag{4.39}$$

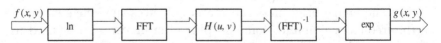

Figure 4.17.   Flowchart of homomorphic filtering.

Here, $H(u, v)$ is called a **homomorphic filtering function,** which can separately act on the illuminance component and reflection component. Because in general the illuminance component changes slowly in space, and the reflection component (determined by the surface properties of the scene) changes sharply at the junction of different objects, the low-frequency part, after the Fourier transform of the logarithm image, mainly corresponds to the illuminance component, while the high-frequency part mainly corresponds to the reflection component. The above characteristics show that it is possible to design a filter function $H(u, v)$ that has different effects on the high-frequency and low-frequency components of the Fourier transform result. Figure 4.18 shows a cross-sectional view of such a function. It is rotated 360° around the vertical axis to get the complete 2D $H(u, v)$. If one chooses $H_L < 1$, $H_H > 1$, then $H(u, v)$ reduces the low-frequency components in the image on the one hand and increase the high-frequency components in the image on the other hand. The final result is that the overall dynamic range of the image is compressed (low-frequency components are weakened) and the contrast between adjacent parts of the image is increased (high-frequency components are strengthened).

By looking at Figure 4.18, it can be found that the homomorphic filter function has a similar shape to the transfer function of the high-pass filter in Section 4.3. In fact, the transfer function of the high-pass filter can be used to approximate the homomorphic filter function as long as the transfer function of the high-pass filter originally defined in $[0, 1]$ is mapped to the interval $[H_L, H_H]$, and then H_L is added. If the transfer function of the high-pass filter is represented by $H_{\text{high}}(u, v)$ and the homomorphic filter function is represented by

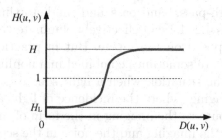

Figure 4.18.   Sectional view of the homomorphic filter function.

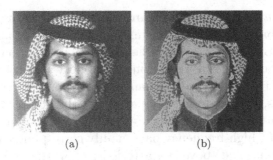

(a)   (b)

Figure 4.19.   Homomorphic filtering enhancement effect.

$H_{\text{homo}}(u, v)$, the mapping from $H_{\text{high}}(u, v)$ to $H_{\text{homo}}(u, v)$ is

$$H_{\text{homo}}(u, v) = [H_{\text{H}} - H_{\text{L}}]H_{\text{high}}(u, v) + H_{\text{L}}. \qquad (4.40)$$

Example 4.12 Enhancement effect of homomorphic filtering

Figure 4.19 shows an example of the effect of homomorphic filtering.

Figure 4.19(a) shows an image of a human face. Due to a single side-light illumination, the human face has a shadow on the right side of the image, and the hairline of the hair is very unclear. Figure 4.19(b) shows the enhancement result obtained by homomorphic filtering with $H_{\text{L}} = 0.5$ and $H_{\text{H}} = 2.0$. After the image is enhanced, the face and hair are clearly separated, and the collar is also visible. In this example, homomorphic filtering simultaneously compresses the dynamic range (such as the eyes) and increases the contrast (such as the junction of the face and hair).   □

4.5.2   Homomorphic filter denoising

The low-pass, high-pass, band-pass, and band-stop linear filters introduced in Sections 4.2–4.4 can effectively eliminate the additive noise linearly superimposed on the image. But in practical applications, noise and images are sometimes combined in a nonlinear way. A typical example is the situation when a light source is used for illumination in the imaging, where the incidence of light and reflection of the scene contribute to the imaging in the form of multiplication, so that the noise in the imaging and the noise in the scene are also multiplicative. This is exactly the brightness imaging model used in the homomorphic filtering principle introduced in this section. In homomorphic filtering and denoising, first use nonlinear logarithmic transformation to convert multiplicative noise into additive noise, then use linear filter to eliminate the additive noise, and finally perform nonlinear inverse exponential transformation to obtain the original "noise-free" image.

Homomorphic filter denoising can be analyzed as follows. Consider the image obtained with noise $g(x,y)$ as

$$g(x,y) = f(x,y)[1 + n(x,y)]. \tag{4.41}$$

In this equation, $f(x,y)$ is a noiseless image and $n(x,y)$ represents noise and satisfies $|n(x,y)| \ll 1$. Take the logarithm of both sides to get

$$\ln g(x,y) = \ln f(x,y) + \ln[1 + n(x,y)] \approx \ln f(x,y) + n(x,y). \tag{4.42}$$

If $n(x,y)$ can be completely eliminated from $\ln[g(x,y)]$, then a more accurate approximation to $f(x,y)$ can be obtained.

The principle of homomorphic filtering can work when any noise model can be transformed into the following formula:

$$g(x,y) = H^{-1}\{H[f(x,y)] + N(u,v)\}, \tag{4.43}$$

where $g(x,y)$ is the collected image, H represents the nonlinear reversible transform, and $N(u,v)$ is the corresponding noise spectrum.

4.6 Key Points and References for Each Section

The following indicates the key points of each section and provides some targeted guidance for further references.

1. Fourier Transform and Frequency Domain Enhancement

Fourier transform is a kind of complex transform, which transforms the image from image space to frequency space, and the introduction of its many useful properties can be found in Ref. [1]. According to the convolution theorem of Fourier transform, the convolution of two functions in the spatial domain corresponds to the multiplication of their Fourier transforms in the frequency domain. Conversely, the multiplication of two functions in the spatial domain corresponds to the convolution of their Fourier transforms in the frequency domain. This is the basis of frequency domain filtering. The required enhancement effect can be obtained by transforming the image into the frequency domain for processing and then by inversely transforming the result back to the spatial domain.

2. Frequency Domain Low-Pass Filter

The frequency domain low-pass filter maintains low-frequency components while suppressing high-frequency components, which can eliminate noise but blur the image. An ideal low-pass filter that is not realizable in practice can cause ringing effects. The practical ones are Butterworth low-pass filters, ladder-shaped low-pass filters, exponential low-pass filters, etc.; see Ref. [1]. For more information, see other books on image processing and analysis (such as [2–5]).

3. Frequency Domain High-Pass Filter

The frequency domain high-pass filter is the opposite of the frequency domain low-pass filter. It can maintain high-frequency components while suppressing low-frequency components and can enhance the edges in the image to make the contours of the regions in the image obvious. Similar to the ideal low-pass filter, the ideal high-pass filter cannot be realized physically. The actually used filters include Butterworth high-pass filter, ladder-shaped high-pass filter, exponential high-pass filter, etc.; please refer to Ref. [1]. If a constant is added to the transfer function of the high-pass filter to maintain some low-frequency components, a high-frequency emphasis filter can be formed; see Ref. [1].

4. Band-Pass Filter and Band-Stop Filter

The common feature of the frequency domain band-pass filter and band-stop filter is to allow signals in a certain frequency range to pass while preventing signals in other frequency ranges from passing. They can both be regarded as the extensions of low-pass and high-pass filters. As long as the cutoff frequency of the band-pass or band-stop filter is adjusted, the effects of the low-pass and high-pass filters can be obtained; see Ref. [1]. Taking into account the symmetry of the Fourier transform, band-pass or band-stop filters must work symmetrically to preserve or eliminate frequencies in a given region that is not centered at the origin. This is also called a notch filter. For more details, please refer to Refs. [1,5].

5. Homomorphic Filter

The homomorphic filter is a special frequency domain enhancement filter. It is based on the image brightness imaging model, introduced in Section 2.2, and is helped by a combination of linear and nonlinear techniques. Homomorphic filtering can also eliminate multiplicative noise. The specific method is to first use nonlinear logarithmic transformation to convert multiplicative noise into additive noise and then use linear filter to eliminate noise and finally perform nonlinear inverse exponential transformation to obtain the original "noise-free" image; please refer to Ref. [6].

Self-Test Questions

The following questions include both single- and multiple-choice questions, so each option should be individually judged.

4.1 Fourier Transform and Frequency Domain Enhancement

4.1.1 The Fourier spectrum of a point source function is grid-like. When the size of the point source decreases, ( )

   (A) The grid of its Fourier spectrum becomes sparser;
   (B) The grid of its Fourier spectrum becomes denser;
   (C) The grid of its Fourier spectrum becomes darker;
   (D) The grid of its Fourier spectrum becomes brighter.

   [Hint] Consider the scaling property of Fourier transform.

4.1.2 When a 2D Fourier transform is implemented with two consecutive 1D Fourier transforms, if $f(x, y)$ is transformed along each column but then not multiplied by N, the magnitude of the resulting $F(x, v)$ will ( )

(A) Become zero;
(B) Reduce to $1/N$;
(C) Be unchanged;
(D) Be increased by N times.

[Hint] Try to decompose the formula of 2D Fourier transform.

4.1.3 When performing frequency domain enhancement, it is required to ( )

(A) Perform Fourier transform on the original image;
(B) Perform Fourier transform on the transfer function;
(C) Convolve the original image with the transfer function;
(D) Calculate the Fourier transform and the inverse Fourier transform, successively.

[Hint] Analyze the three steps of frequency domain enhancement in detail.

4.1.4 Image enhancement method based on frequency domain is ( )

(A) The linear transformation of the image gray level;
(B) An image enhancement method based on pixel neighborhood;
(C) Able to obtain the same image enhancement effect as that of the spatial domain image enhancement method;
(D) Always more computationally complex than methods based on image domain, since Fourier transform and inverse Fourier transform are commonly used.

[Hint] Consider the definition and specific methods of various enhancement methods.

4.2 Frequency Domain Low-Pass Filter

4.2.1 For the first-order Butterworth low-pass filter, select the frequency when H drops to $1/2$ of the maximum value as the cutoff frequency D_0 and select the frequency when H drops to $1/\sqrt{2}$ of the maximum value as the cutoff frequency D_1. For the second-order Butterworth low-pass filter, select the cutoff frequency D_2 as the frequency when H drops to $1/\sqrt{2}$ of the maximum value. In these cases, then ( )

(A) $D_0 < D_1$;
(B) $D_0 > D_1$;
(C) $D_1 < D_2$;
(D) $D_1 > D_2$.

[Hint] The transfer function of Butterworth low-pass filter is a monotone decreasing curve.

4.2.2 In the frequency domain low-pass filtering, the three filters in Figure 4.2.2 are commonly used: Figure 4.2.2(a) is a Butterworth filter; Figure 4.2.2(b) is an exponential filter; Figure 4.2.2(c) is a ladder-shaped filter. Which of the following statement(s) is/are correct? ( )

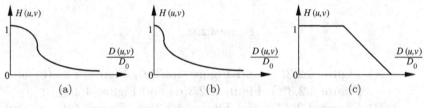

Figure 4.2.2.

(A) The attenuation of noise by the exponential filter is greater than that of the Butterworth filter;
(B) The processing effect of these three filters is clearer than that of the ideal low-pass filter;
(C) The ringing effect produced by these three filters is more pronounced than that of the ideal low-pass filter;
(D) These three filters improve the blur phenomenon of the ideal low-pass filter.

[Hint] Consider the shape of the low-pass filter curve and pay attention to the tail extension on its influence to the filter effect.

4.2.3 Figure 4.2.3(a) is a noisy image. The images obtained after three types of low-pass filter processing are shown in Figures 4.2.3(b)–(d). Now, it is known that the frequency domain curves of these three low-pass filters are shown in Figures 4.2.3(e)–(g). Please indicate the corresponding relationship between the filtered image and the filter. ( )

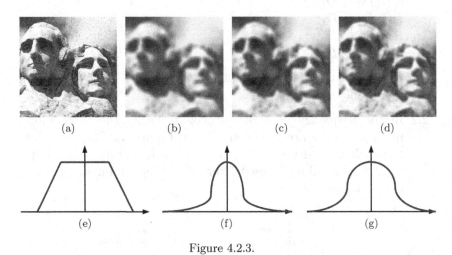

Figure 4.2.3.

(A) Figure 4.2.3(b) and Figure 4.2.3(e), Figure 4.2.3(c) and Figure 4.2.3(f), Figure 4.2.3(d) and Figure 4.2.3(g);

(B) Figure 4.2.3(b) and Figure 4.2.3(g), Figure 4.2.3(c) and Figure 4.2.3(e), Figure 4.2.3(d) and Figure 4.2.3(f);

(C) Figure 4.2.3(b) and Figure 4.2.3(f), Figure 4.2.3(c) and Figure 4.2.3(g), Figure 4.2.3(d) and Figure 4.2.3(e);

(D) Figure 4.2.3(b) and Figure 4.2.3(f), Figure 4.2.3(c) and Figure 4.2.3(e), Figure 4.2.3(d) and Figure 4.2.3(f).

[Hint] The narrower the frequency domain curve of the low-pass filter, the more the high-frequency components are filtered out and the more blurred the resulting image is.

4.3 Frequency Domain High-Pass Filter

4.3.1 The incorrect description for the low-pass and high-pass Butterworth filters is/are ( )

(A) They can all reduce the ringing effect than ideal low-pass and high-pass processing do;

(B) They all have the same cutoff frequency;

(C) They can all be used to eliminate false contours;

(D) The transition between the foreground and background after they are processed is smoother than that of the ideal low-pass and high-pass processed.

[Hint] It is necessary to distinguish the similarities and differences between low-pass and high-pass filters as well as to consider the characteristics of Butterworth filters.

4.3.2 High-frequency emphasis filter relatively weakens low-frequency components, so the filtered image is often darker and poorer in contrast. Therefore, it is often necessary, after filtering, to perform ( )

(A) Median filtering;

(B) Low-frequency enhancement;

(C) Histogram equalization;

(D) Evenly brighten the image.

[Hint] Note that the original dynamic range needs to be restored after filtering.

4.3.3 In the frequency domain, the high-pass filtering result is compared with the high-frequency emphasis filtering result. ( )

(A) There are more low-frequency components in the high-pass filtering result than in the high-frequency emphasis filtering result;

(B) There are more high-frequency components in the high-pass filtering result than in the high-frequency emphasis filtering result;

(C) The result of high-pass filtering is brighter than that of high-frequency emphasis filtering;

(D) The result of high-frequency emphasis filtering is brighter than that of high-pass filtering.

[Hint] The transfer function of the high-frequency enhancement filter is the transfer function of the high-pass filter plus a constant.

4.4 Band-Pass Filter and Band-Stop Filter

4.4.1 To preserve the components in a certain frequency range in the image, one can use ( )

(A) Band-stop filter;
(B) Band-pass filter;
(C) Low-pass filter;
(D) High-pass filter.

[Hint] A certain frequency range should have upper and lower limits.

4.4.2 To preserve the components in a certain frequency range in the image, one can combine to use ( )

(A) Linear smoothing filter and nonlinear smoothing filter;
(B) Linear sharpening filter and nonlinear sharpening filter;
(C) Nonlinear smoothing filter and linear sharpening filter;
(D) Nonlinear sharpening filter and linear smoothing filter.

[Hint] Consider the filtering characteristics of the smoothing filters and sharpening filters for different frequency components; smoothing corresponds to low-pass and sharpening corresponds to high-pass.

4.4.3 To get the effect of band-pass filtering, one can combine to use ( )

(A) A low-pass filter and a high-pass filter;
(B) Two low-pass filters with different cutoff frequencies;
(C) Two low-pass filters with the same cutoff frequency;
(D) Two high-pass filters with different cutoff frequencies.

[Hint] Considering both low-pass and high-pass filters can filter out certain frequency components.

4.4.4 Examine the frequency domain diagrams (white pass, gray stop) of the four filters in Figure 4.4.4. Which one(s) is/are band-stop filters? ( )

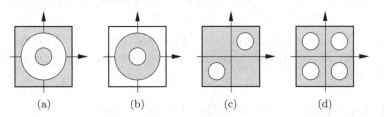

(a)   (b)   (c)   (d)

Figure 4.4.4.

(A) Figure 4.4.4(a);

(B) Figure 4.4.4(b);

(C) Figure 4.4.4(c);

(D) Figure 4.4.4(d).

[Hint] Analyze the frequency domain structure of the band-stop filter.

4.4.5 Consider the frequency domain diagram of the four filters in Figure 4.4.5. If one wants to filter out sinusoidal interference $n = A\sin(ax + by)$, which type of filter(s) should be used? ( )

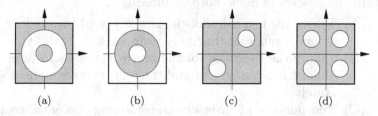

(a)　　　　　(b)　　　　　(c)　　　　　(d)

Figure 4.4.5.

(A) Figure 4.4.5(a);

(B) Figure 4.4.5(b);

(C) Figure 4.4.5(c);

(D) Figure 4.4.5(d).

[Hint] Analyze the frequency domain structure of sinusoidal interference with the help of Fourier transform.

4.4.6 To remove the components in a certain frequency range in the image, in addition to the band-stop filter, one can also use ( )

(A) Low-pass filter;

(B) High-pass filter;

(C) Band-pass filter;

(D) Low-pass filter and high-pass filter.

[Hint] The band-stop filtering is to remove the intermediate frequencies (a certain frequency bands between the lowest and the highest).

4.4.7 Notch filter is ( )

(A) Unrealizable physically;

(B) Always prevent a certain frequency component from passing;

(C) A combination of low-pass filter and high-pass filter;

(D) Similar in function to band-pass filter or band-stop filter.

[Hint] The notch filter can stop or pass frequencies in the neighborhood centered on a certain frequency.

4.5 Homomorphic Filter

4.5.1 In the process of homomorphic filtering, ( )

(A) Taking the logarithm of the image $f(x, y)$ is to reduce the dynamic range of the image gray level;

(B) Taking the logarithm of the image $f(x, y)$ is to filter the illuminance component and the reflection component separately;

(C) The purpose of inversely transforming the enhancement result into the spatial domain and then taking the exponent is to expand the dynamic range of the illuminance component and the reflection component;

(D) The purpose of inversely transforming the enhancement result into the spatial domain and then taking the exponent is to combine the illuminance component and the reflection component.

[Hint] Analyze the changes in the relationship between the illuminance component and the reflection component during the filtering process.

4.5.2 The homomorphic filter function adopts different strategies/countermeasures for the illuminance component and the reflection component because ( )

(A) The illuminance component corresponds to the low-frequency part and changes rapidly in space;

(B) The illuminance component corresponds to the high-frequency part and changes slowly in space;

(C) The illuminance component corresponds to the low-frequency part and changes slowly in space;

(D) The illuminance component corresponds to the high-frequency part and changes rapidly in space.

[Hint] Analyze the causes/reasons for the spatial variation of the illuminance component.

4.5.3 The homomorphic filter function adopts different strategies/countermeasures for the illuminance component and the reflected component because ( )

(A) The reflection component corresponds to the low-frequency part and changes rapidly in space;

(B) The reflection component corresponds to the high-frequency part and changes slowly in space;

(C) The reflection component corresponds to the low-frequency part and changes slowly in space;

(D) The reflection component corresponds to the high-frequency part and changes rapidly in space.

[Hint] Analyze the causes/reasons for the spatial variation of the illuminance component.

4.5.4 Homomorphic filtering ( )

(A) Can eliminate multiplicative noise;

(B) Is unable to eliminate multiplicative noise;

(C) Can eliminate additive noise;

(D) Is unable to eliminate additive noise.

[Hint] Analyze the characteristics of homomorphic filtering and the principle of noise elimination.

References

[1] Zhang, Y.-J. *Image Engineering, Vol. 1: Image Processing.* Germany, Berlin: De Gruyter, 2017.

[2] Pratt. W. K. *Digital Image Processing: PIKS Scientific Inside*, 4th Edn. USA, Hoboken: Wiley Interscience, 2007.

[3] Sonka, M., Hlavac, V., and Boyle, R. *Image Processing, Analysis, and Machine Vision*, 4th Edn. Singapore: Cengage Learning, 2014.

[4] Russ, J. C. and Neal, F. B. *The Image Processing Handbook*, 7th Edn. USA, New York: CRC Press, 2016.

[5] Gonzalez, R. C. and Woods, R. E. *Digital Image Processing*, 4th Edn. UK, London: Prentice Hall, 2018.

[6] Dougherty, E. R. and Astola, J. *An Introduction to Nonlinear Image Processing*, USA, Bellingham: SPIE Optical Engineering Press, 1994.

Chapter 5

Image Restoration

Image restoration refers to a large class of technologies in image processing.

Image restoration is closely related to **image enhancement**. Image restoration and image enhancement are the same in that they both want to obtain an improved output image in a certain sense (compared to the original input image) or both hope to improve the visual quality of the input image. The difference between image restoration and image enhancement is that image enhancement technology generally takes advantage of the characteristics of the human visual system to obtain better-looking visual results, while image restoration considers that the image (quality) is originally high but is degraded or deteriorated (image quality is reduced, distorted) in certain situations/conditions, and now it is necessary to reconstruct or restore the original (high-quality) image based on the corresponding degradation model and knowledge. In other words, the image restoration technology is to model the process of image degradation and take the opposite process accordingly to recover the original image. It can be seen that image restoration should be carried out according to a certain image degradation model.

The sections of this chapter are arranged as follows.

Section 5.1 discusses first the image degradation models and some degradation examples, then analyzes some related properties of the image degradation model, and gives both the spatial domain and frequency domain expressions of the linear degradation model.

159

Section 5.2 introduces the unconstrained restoration model and one of the typical recovery techniques under this model: inverse filtering.

Section 5.3 introduces the constrained restoration model and one of the typical recovery techniques under this model: Wiener filtering.

Section 5.4 introduces the correction method for image geometric distortion. Geometric distortion correction requires spatial transformation to restore the spatial relationship of the pixel positions in the distorted image and gray-level interpolation to restore the gray-scale value of the pixels in the distorted image.

Section 5.5 discusses the principles and techniques of repairing image defect information. Here, image repair is divided into image inpainting and image completion, and the principles and characteristics of corresponding techniques are presented.

5.1   Image Degradation and Model

Image degradation means that the image obtained from the scene does not fully reflect the real content of the scene, causing problems such as distortion and contamination. There are many ways to acquire and collect images, and there are many reasons that can cause image degradation, such as lens chromatic aberration and image blur caused by inaccurate focus (out of focus).

In practical applications, the most common degradations include blur and noise.

Many degradations produced in the image acquisition process are often called **blur**, and blur has a band-limiting effect on the object's spectral width. Blur is the process of suppressing or eliminating high-frequency components in the language of frequency analysis. Generally, blur is a determinacy process. In most cases, we have a sufficiently accurate mathematical model to describe it.

The degradation produced in the image recording process is often called **noise**, and noise can come from measurement errors, counting errors, etc. Noise is a random process, so the effect of noise on a particular image is uncertain. In many cases, we can at best have some knowledge of the statistical properties of this process. For example, the probability density function of common Gaussian noise conforms to the Gaussian distribution; the probability density function of uniform noise conforms to the uniform distribution; the probability density function of salt-and-pepper noise has two pulses, where the negative pulse corresponds to pepper noise and the positive pulse corresponds to salt noise. Their amplitudes can reach the gray-level limits of the image.

5.1.1 Image degradation model

Figure 5.1 shows a simple and general **image degradation model**. In this model, the image degradation process is modeled as a degenerate system H acting on the input image $f(x, y)$. Its combined effect with an additive random noise $n(x, y)$ leads to a degraded image $g(x, y)$. Restoring an image according to this model is a process of obtaining a certain approximation to $f(x, y)$ based on a given $g(x, y)$ with H representing the degradation. It is assumed that the statistical properties of $n(x, y)$ are known.

Example 5.1 Degradation example

Specific models can be established for specific degradation processes. Figure 5.2 shows four examples of degradation. The upper figure shows the situation when there is no degradation, and the figure below shows the situation when there is degradation.

Figure 5.1. A simple and general image degradation model.

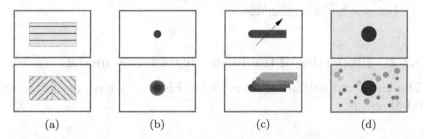

Figure 5.2. Four common specific degradation models.

(1) Figure 5.2(a) shows that the nonlinear degradation causes the original pattern with smooth brightness or regular shape to become irregular. For example, the development process of photographic film can be represented by this model. The photosensitive characteristic of photographic film is expressed according to the density of silver left on the film as a logarithmic function of the exposure. The photosensitive characteristic curve is basically linear in the middle and both side ends are bending. In this way, the originally linearly changing brightness becomes nonlinearly changing. The human eye's response to external brightness stimuli is similar to this situation.

(2) Figure 5.2(b) shows a degradation caused by blur. For many practical optical imaging systems, the degradation due to aperture diffraction can be represented by this model. Its main feature is that the original relatively clear pattern becomes larger and the edges are blurred.

(3) Figure 5.2(c) shows the blur degradation caused by the (fast) movement of the object in the scene (this degradation also occurs if the camera vibrates during the shooting process). The pattern of the object is elongated along the direction of movement and becomes overlapping. During shooting, if the object moves beyond the distance of more than one pixel on the image plane, the blur will be produced. Systems using telescopic lenses (with a narrow field of view) are very sensitive to this type of image degradation.

(4) Figure 5.2(d) shows the degradation caused by the superposition of random noise, which can also be regarded as a kind of random degradation. The original image with obvious objects is superimposed with many random bright and dark spots, so that the objects and background in the image are affected and the objects become indistinguishable.   □

5.1.2   Properties of the image degradation model

The input and output in the model of Figure 5.1 have the following relationship:

$$g(x,y) = H[f(x,y)] + n(x,y). \tag{5.1}$$

For the degenerate system H, whether H has the following four properties can be discussed (at first, $n(x, y)$ is not considered for simplicity):

(1) Linearity: If k_1 and k_2 are constants and $f_1(x, y)$ and $f_2(x, y)$ are two input images, then the linear system H satisfies

$$H[k_1 f_1(x, y) + k_2 f_2(x, y)] = k_1 H[f_1(x, y)] + k_2 H[f_2(x, y)]. \quad (5.2)$$

(2) Additivity: If $k_1 = k_2 = 1$ in Equation (5.2), then it becomes

$$H[f_1(x, y) + f_2(x, y)] = H[f_1(x, y)] + H[f_2(x, y)]. \quad (5.3)$$

Equation (5.3) indicates that the linear system's response to the sum of two input images is equal to the sum of its responses to the two input images.

(3) Consistency: If $f_2(x, y) = 0$ in Equation (5.2), then it becomes

$$H[k_1 f_1(x, y) = k_1 H[f_1(x, y)]. \quad (5.4)$$

Equation (5.4) indicates that the response of a linear system to the product of a constant and any input is equal to the response of the product of a constant and the input.

(4) Position (space) invariance: If for any $f(x, y)$ as well as a and b, we have

$$H[f(x - a, y - b)] = g(x - a, y - b). \quad (5.5)$$

Equation (5.5) points out that the response of the linear system at any position of the image is only related to the input value at that position and has nothing to do with the position itself.

If the degenerate system H satisfies the above four properties, then Equation (5.1) can be written as

$$g(x, y) = h(x, y) \otimes f(x, y) + n(x, y), \quad (5.6)$$

where $h(x, y)$ is the impulse response of the degenerate system. With the help of matrix representation, Equation (5.6) can be written as

$$\boldsymbol{g} = \boldsymbol{H}\boldsymbol{f} + \boldsymbol{n}. \quad (5.7)$$

According to the convolution theorem, we have

$$G(u, v) = H(u, v)F(u, v) + N(u, v). \tag{5.8}$$

Among the four common specific degradation models given in Figure 5.2, the models shown in Figure 5.2(a)–(c) are all spatially invariant and the models shown in Figure 5.2(b)–(d) can all be linear.

5.2   Inverse Filtering

Inverse filtering is a simple and direct **unconstrained restoration** method.

5.2.1   Unconstrained restoration

The characteristic of the unconstrained restoration method is that the image is only regarded as a digital matrix, and the restoration process is performed from a mathematical point of view without considering the physical constraints of the restored image.

From Equation (5.7), one can get

$$n = g - Hf. \tag{5.9}$$

Without any prior knowledge of n, image restoration can be described as looking for an estimate f_e of the original image f such that Hf_e is closest to the degraded image g in the sense of minimum mean square error, that is, to make the **norm** (2) of n minimum:

$$\|n\|^2 = n^{\mathrm{T}}n = \|g - Hf_e\|^2 = (g - Hf_e)^{\mathrm{T}}(g - Hf_e). \tag{5.10}$$

According to Equation (5.10), the image restoration problem can be regarded as to minimize the value of Equation (5.11) for f_e:

$$L(f_e) = \|g - Hf_e\|^2. \tag{5.11}$$

Here, we only need to differentiate L to f_e and set the result to zero. In addition, suppose the existence of H^{-1}, then the unconstrained restoration equation can be obtained:

$$f_e = (H^{\mathrm{T}}H)^{-1}H^{\mathrm{T}}g = H^{-1}(H^{\mathrm{T}})^{-1}H^{\mathrm{T}}g = H^{-1}g. \tag{5.12}$$

Equation (5.12) shows that the estimated f_e of the original image f can be obtained by multiplying the degraded image with the inverse matrix of the degradation system.

5.2.2 Inverse filtering model

Consider turning the problem into the frequency domain for discussion. Regardless of noise, according to Equation (5.8), if the Fourier transform of the degraded image is divided by the degenerate function, then an estimate of the Fourier transform of the original image can be obtained:

$$F_{\mathrm{e}}(u, v) = \frac{G(u, v)}{H(u, v)}. \tag{5.13}$$

The above equation is often called **inverse filtering**. If $H(u, v)$ is regarded as a filter function, then the product of this function and $F(u, v)$ is the Fourier transform of the degraded image $g(x, y)$. In this way, dividing $G(u, v)$ by $H(u, v)$ is an inverse filtering process. Taking the inverse Fourier transform of the result of Equation (5.13) can produce the restored image:

$$f_{\mathrm{e}}(x, y) = \mathcal{F}^{-1}[F_{\mathrm{e}}(u, v)] = \mathcal{F}^{-1}\left[\frac{G(u, v)}{H(u, v)}\right]. \tag{5.14}$$

In reality, noise is inevitable. The inverse filtering form with the consideration of noise is

$$F_{\mathrm{e}}(u, v) = F(u, v) + \frac{N(u, v)}{H(u, v)}. \tag{5.15}$$

Two problems can be seen in Equation (5.15). First of all, because $N(u, v)$ is random, even if the degradation function is known, the original image cannot be restored accurately. Second, if $H(u, v)$ takes zero or a very small value on the UV plane, $N(u, v)/H(u, v)$ will make the restoration result far from the expected result. In practice, $H(u, v)$ generally decreases fast with respect to the increasing distance between u, v, and the origin, while the noise $N(u, v)$ changes relatively slowly. In this case, the restoration of the image can only be done in a range close to the origin (center of the frequency domain). In other words, in general, the inverse filter is not exactly $1/H(u, v)$

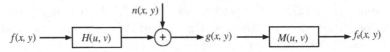

Figure 5.3.   Image degradation and restoration model.

but a function of u and v, which can be denoted as $M(u,v)$. $M(u,v)$ is often called the **restoration transfer function**, so the image degradation and restoration model can be represented in Figure 5.3.

A common method is to take $M(u,v)$ as the following function:

$$M(u,v) = \begin{cases} 1/H(u,v) & \text{if } u^2 + v^2 \leq w_0^2 \\ 1 & \text{if } u^2 + v^2 > w_0^2, \end{cases} \qquad (5.16)$$

where the selection principle of w_0 is to remove the point where $H(u,v)$ is zero. The disadvantage of this method is that the **ringing effect** of the restoration result is quite obvious. An improved method is to take $M(u,v)$ as

$$M(u,v) = \begin{cases} k & \text{if } H(u,v) \leq d \\ 1/H(u,v) & \text{otherwise,} \end{cases} \qquad (5.17)$$

where k and d are both constants less than 1, and it is better to choose a smaller d.

Example 5.2 Blur point source to obtain transfer function for image restoration

The transfer function $H(u,v)$ of the degraded system can be approximated by the Fourier transform of the degraded image. An image can be regarded as a collection of multiple point source images. If the point source image is regarded as an approximation of the unit pulse function $(F[\delta(x,y)] = 1)$, then $G(u,v) = H(u,v)F(u,v) \approx H(u,v)$.

Figure 5.4 shows an example of image restoration. Figure 5.4(a) is a simulated degraded image that is obtained by blurring an ideal image with a low-pass filter. The Fourier transform of the low-pass filter used is shown in Figure 5.4(b). According to Equations (5.16) and (5.17), the restoration results obtained by inverse filtering are shown in Figures 5.4(c) and (d), respectively. Comparing these two images, the ringing effect in Figure 5.4(d) is relatively small.   □

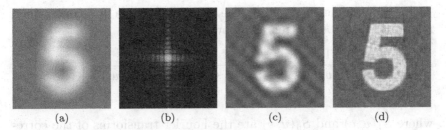

(a)   (b)   (c)   (d)

Figure 5.4.   Image restoration example with inverse filtering.

5.3   Wiener Filtering

Wiener filtering is a basic **constrained restoration** method.

5.3.1   Constrained restoration

The constrained restoration methods are different from the uncon-strained restoration methods such as inverse filtering. It not only considers from the mathematical point of view but also considers if the restored image should be subject to certain physical constraints, such as being relatively smooth in space and its gray value being positive.

Also starting from Equation (5.7), the constrained restoration considers selecting a linear operator Q (transformation matrix) of f_e to minimize $\|Qf_e\|^2$. This problem can be solved by Lagrangian multiplier method. Let l be the Lagrangian multiplier, and we try to find f_e that minimizes the following criterion function:

$$L(f_e) = \|Qf_e\|^2 + l(\|g - Hf_e\|^2 - \|n\|^2). \qquad (5.18)$$

Similar to the solution of Equation (5.11), by differentiating L to f_e and setting the result to zero, the constrained restoration equation can be obtained (let $s = 1/l$):

$$f_e[[H^{T}H + sQ^{T}Q]^{-1}H^{T}g. \qquad (5.19)$$

5.3.2   Wiener filter

The **Wiener filter** is a minimum mean square error filter. It can be derived from Equation (5.19).

In the frequency domain, the general formula for constrained restoration can be written as follows:

$$F_e(u, v) = \left[\frac{1}{H(u, v)} \times \frac{|H(u, v)|^2}{|H(u, v)|^2 + s[S_n(u, v)/S_f(u, v)]} \right] G(u, v),$$

(5.20)

where $S_f(u, v)$ and $S_n(u, v)$ are the Fourier transforms of the correlation matrix elements of the original image and noise, respectively.

Let's discuss several situations of Equation (5.20) as follows:

(1) If $s = 1$, the item in the square brackets is the Wiener filter.
(2) If s is a variable, it is called a parametric Wiener filter.
(3) If there is no noise, $S_n(u, v) = 0$ and the Wiener filter degenerates into the inverse filter of Section 5.2.

Because s must be adjusted to satisfy Equation (5.19), if $s = 1$, using Equation (5.20) cannot get the optimal solution that satisfies Equation (5.18), but it is optimal in the sense of minimization of $E\{[f(x, y) - f_e(x, y)]^2\}$. Here, both $f(\cdot)$ and $f_e(\cdot)$ are regarded as random variables to obtain a statistical criterion.

If $S_n(u, v)$ and $S_f(u, v)$ are both unknown (it is often the case in practice), Equation (5.20) can be approximated by the following equation (where K is a predetermined constant):

$$F_e(u, v) \approx \left[\frac{1}{H(u, v)} \times \frac{|H(u, v)|^2}{|H(u, v)|^2 + K} \right] G(u, v).$$

(5.21)

Example 5.3 Comparison of inverse filter restoration and Wiener filter restoration

Figure 5.5(a) shows a column of images that first convolves a normal image with a smoothing function $h(x, y) = \exp[\sqrt{(x^2 + y^2)}/240]$ to produce blur and then superimposes Gaussian random noise with zero mean and variance of 8, 16, and 32 (from top to bottom), respectively. Thus, the obtained images are used for restoration. Figure 5.5(b) shows a column of the images obtained by using the inverse filter restoration method. Figure 5.5(c) shows a column of images obtained by using the Wiener filter restoration method. From Figures 5.5(b) and (c), it can be seen that the Wiener filtering provides a better restoration result than the inverse filtering if the image

Figure 5.5. Comparison of inverse filtering and Wiener filtering.

is affected by noise, and the stronger the noise, the more obvious this
advantage. □

5.4 Geometric Distortion Correction

In many actual image acquisition processes, the spatial relationship
between different parts of the original scene and the spatial relationship between the corresponding pixels in the image may change, that
is, distortion may occur. In order to restore their original corresponding relationship, **geometric distortion correction** (also a kind of
image restoration work) is required, that is, the position of each
pixel in the distorted image is corrected by geometric transformation
to regain the original spatial relationship in the scene. For gray-scale

images, in addition to considering the spatial relationship, the gray-level relationship among pixels must also be considered, that is, the gray-scale correction is required to restore the original pixel gray-level values while performing geometric distortion correction. In this way, the geometric distortion correction of the image mainly includes the following two steps: (i) spatial transformation; (ii) gray-level interpolation.

5.4.1　Spatial transformation

Spatial transformation is to adjust the pixel position on the image plane to restore the original spatial relationship between pixels. Suppose the original image is $f(x, y)$, and it becomes a distorted image $g(x', y')$ affected by geometric deformation. Here, (x', y') represents the coordinates of the pixels whose original coordinates are (x, y) in the distorted image, which can generally be written as

$$x' = S(x, y), \tag{5.22}$$

$$y' = T(x, y), \tag{5.23}$$

where $S(x, y)$ and $T(x, y)$ represent two spatial transformation functions that produce geometrically distorted images.

The simplest case is linear distortion, which is given by

$$S(x, y) = k_1 x + k_2 y + k_3, \tag{5.24}$$

$$T(x, y) = k_4 x + k_5 y + k_6. \tag{5.25}$$

For a general (nonlinear) second-order distortion, we have

$$S(x, y) = k_1 + k_2 x + k_3 y + k_4 x^2 + k_5 xy + k_6 y^2, \tag{5.26}$$

$$T(x, y) = k_7 + k_8 x + k_9 y + k_{10} x^2 + k_{11} xy + k_{12} y^2. \tag{5.27}$$

If the analytical representations of $S(x, y)$ and $T(x, y)$ are known, one can restore the image by inverse transformation. In practice, the analytical representation of the distortion is usually not known. For this reason, it is necessary to find some points whose positions are exactly known (called constraint corresponding points) on the input image (distorted image) and output image (corrected image) of the restoration process. These points are then used to calculate

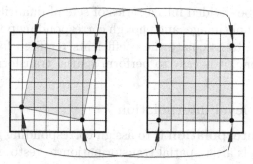

Figure 5.6.   Constraint corresponding points on distorted image and corrected image.

the coefficients in the distortion function according to the equations of the distortion model, so as to establish the correspondence (in the spatial position) between other pixels in these two images.

Now, look at Figure 5.6 which shows a quadrilateral region on the distorted image (left side) and the corresponding quadrilateral region on the corrected image (right side). The vertices of these two quadrilateral regions can be used as the constraint corresponding points.

The geometric distortion process in the quadrilateral region can be represented by a pair of bilinear equations (a special case of general nonlinear second-order distortion), namely

$$S(x, y) = k_1 x + k_2 y + k_3 xy + k_4, \qquad (5.28)$$

$$T(x, y) = k_5 x + k_6 y + k_7 xy + k_8. \qquad (5.29)$$

Substituting the above two equations into Equations (5.22) and (5.23), the relationship between the coordinates of the two images before and after the distortion can be obtained:

$$x' = k_1 x + k_2 y + k_3 xy + k_4, \qquad (5.30)$$

$$y' = k_5 x + k_6 y + k_7 xy + k_8. \qquad (5.31)$$

From Figure 5.6, it can be seen that there are four pairs of known corresponding (8) points in the two quadrilateral regions, so the eight coefficients k_i ($i = 1, 2, \ldots$) in Equations (5.30) and (5.31) can all be solved. From these coefficients, an equation for spatial mapping of all points in the quadrilateral region can be established. Generally, an image can be divided into a series of sets of quadrilateral regions covering the whole image, and enough corresponding points are found for each region to calculate the coefficients required for mapping. If this can be done, it is easy to perform spatial transformations.

5.4.2   Gray-level interpolation

Gray-level interpolation is to assign corresponding gray-level values to the pixels after spatial transformation to restore the gray values that should be in the original position.

Although (x, y) in the actual digital image is always an integer, the value of (x', y') calculated by Equations (5.22) and (5.23) is generally not an integer. The distorted image $g(x', y')$ is a digital image, and the pixel value is only defined where the coordinate is an integer, and the value of the pixel at a non-integer position must be calculated with the help of the pixel values at some integers around it, which is called gray-level interpolation, and can be explained with the help of Figure 5.7.

In Figure 5.7, the left part is the original undistorted image (also the expected result of geometric correction) and the right part is the distorted image actually acquired. The goal of geometric correction is to restore the distorted image to obtain the original image. Due to the distortion, the original integer coordinate point (x, y) will be mapped to the non-integer coordinate point (x', y') in the distorted image, and g is not defined at this point. The spatial transformation discussed above can transform the point (x', y') that should be at (x, y) back to the point (x, y) of the original image. What one needs to do now is to estimate the gray value of the point (x', y') to assign to the pixel at (x, y) in the original image.

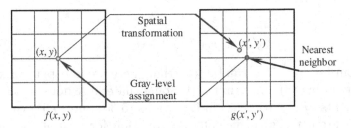

Figure 5.7.   Schematic diagram of gray-level interpolation.

Gray-level interpolation often adopts the following scheme to map the gray level from the original undistorted image to the pixels of the distorted image actually acquired. As shown in Figure 5.8, the left part is the distorted image actually acquired and the right part is the ideal original undistorted image. If the pixel position in the undistorted image corresponds to the place among four pixels (a non-integer point) of the actual acquired distortion image, one first calculates the gray value at that position (left image) according to the interpolation algorithm, and then one can map this value to the corresponding pixels in undistorted image (right image).

There are many ways to calculate the interpolation gray value. The simplest is **nearest neighbor interpolation**, also called zero-order interpolation. Nearest neighbor interpolation is to assign the gray value of the pixel closest to (x', y') as the gray value of the point (x', y') to the pixel at (x, y) in the original image (see Figure 5.7). This method has a small amount of calculation, but its disadvantage is that it is sometimes not precise enough.

To improve the precision, **bi-linear interpolation** can be applied. It uses the gray values of the four nearest neighbor pixels of (x', y') to calculate the gray value at point (x', y'). Refer to Figure 5.9. Let the four nearest neighbor pixels of point (x', y') be

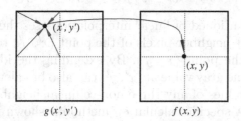

Figure 5.8. Schematic diagram of gray-level mapping.

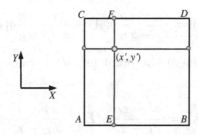

Figure 5.9. Schematic diagram of bi-linear interpolation.

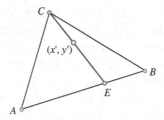

Figure 5.10.   Bi-linear interpolation with three neighboring pixels.

A, B, C, D, and their coordinates are (i, j), $(i + 1, j)$, $(i, j + 1)$, $(i + 1, j + 1)$, respectively. Their gray values are noted as $g(A)$, $g(B), g(C), g(D)$, respectively. First use the proportional relationship (linear interpolation) to calculate the gray values $g(E)$ and $g(F)$ of the two points E and F:

$$g(E) = (x' - i)[g(B) - g(A)] + g(A), \qquad (5.32)$$

$$g(F) = (x' - i)[g(D) - g(C)] + g(C). \qquad (5.33)$$

Then, starting from $g(E)$ and $g(F)$, the gray value of point (x', y') is obtained similarly:

$$g(x', y') = (y' - j)[g(F) - g(E)] + g(E). \qquad (5.34)$$

The aforementioned bi-linear interpolation uses the gray values of the four nearest neighbor pixels of the point (x', y') to calculate the gray value at the point (x', y'). By extending the idea of bi-linear interpolation, the gray value at (x', y') can also be calculated by using only the gray values of any three non-collinear neighboring pixels of point (x', y'). A specific calculation method is shown in Figure 5.10. First, the gray value $g(E)$ of point E is calculated according to $g(A)$ and $g(B)$:

$$g(E) = \frac{x_E - x_B}{x_A - x_B} g(A) + \frac{x_A - x_E}{x_A - x_B} g(B). \qquad (5.35)$$

Then, the gray value at the point (x', y') is calculated according to $g(C)$ and $g(E)$:

$$g(x', y') = \frac{x' - x_C}{x_E - x_C} g(E) + \frac{x_E - x'}{x_E - x_C} g(C). \qquad (5.36)$$

5.5 Image Repairing

In image acquisition, transmission, and processing, sometimes certain regions of the image are defective or missing, and the gray levels of adjacent pixels change sharply. Some example are:

(1) part of the content is missing when collecting an occluded scene image or scanning an old picture with damage (tear or scratch);
(2) the blank left after removing a specific region (irrelevant scene) in image processing;
(3) changes caused by the overlay of text on the image;
(4) loss of part of the information caused by the lossy compression of the image;
(5) pixel loss caused by network failure when transmitting data (on the network).

To solve these problems, the image needs to be repaired. **Image repairing** is based on the incomplete image and prior knowledge of the original image, through the use of corresponding methods to correct the aforementioned regional defects, in order to achieve the purpose of restoring the original image. Therefore, image repairing technology is also a kind of distinctive image restoration technology. Refer to Section 5.4 for the discussion of image geometric distortion correction; both position information and gray-scale information need to be considered in image repairing.

Image repairing can be further divided into **image inpainting** and **image completion**. The former represented the interpolation of oil paintings in the restoration of museum artworks in the early days. The latter is also often referred to as **region filling** and is directly referred to as filling hereinafter. Generally, repairing the region with smaller scale is called inpainting, and repairing the region with larger scale is called filling. Both repair and complete the missing information in the image, but there is no strict boundary on the scale between them. However, qualitative changes can cause quantitative changes. Judging from the currently used technologies, the two technologies have their own characteristics. Inpainting uses the local structure information of the image instead of the texture information of the region. Filling often needs to consider the entire image and rely on texture information. In terms of function, the former is mostly used for image recovery and the latter is mostly used for scene removal.

5.5.1 Principle of image repairing

Image repairing is the restoration of defective images. **Image defect** can be regarded as a special case of image degradation, but it has its own characteristics. Generally, after the image is affected by the defect, some parts of the image may be completely lost, while other parts may not be changed at all. In actual application, it is necessary to establish a certain model for repairing the image.

For an original image $f(x, y)$, let the spatial region of its distribution be denoted by F; if the missing part or the part to be repaired is $d(x, y)$, its spatial region is denoted by D; then, the image to be repaired is $g(x, y)$, and the spatial region of its distribution is also F, but some parts of them (F) remain intact and some parts of them (D) are completely missing. The so-called image repairing is to use the original spatial region, that is, the information in $F - D$ is used to estimate and restore the missing information in D.

Refer to Figure 5.11; Figure 5.11(a) is the original image $f(x, y)$ and Figure 5.11(b) is the image $g(x, y)$ to be repaired, where the region D represents the part to be repaired (the original information is completely lost), the region $F - D$ represents the part of the original image that can be used to repair the region D, also called the **source region**, while the region D is also called the **target region**.

With reference to the degradation model of Equation (5.1), the image repair model can be expressed as

$$[g(x,y)]_{F-D} = \{H[f(x,y)] + n(x,y)\}_{F-D}. \qquad (5.37)$$

The left side of Equation (5.37) is the part of the degraded image that has not been degraded. The goal of image repairing is to estimate

(a)   (b)

Figure 5.11.   Schematic diagram of various regions in image repairing.

and restore $\{f(x,y)\}_D$ with the help of Equation (5.37). From the perspective of the repair effect, on the one hand, the gray scale, color, and texture in the region D after the repair should correspond to or be consistent with the gray scale, color, and texture around D; on the other hand, the structural information around D should be extended to the inside of D (such as the broken edge and contour line should be connected).

5.5.2 Image repair examples

Image defects may be small in scale or large in scale, and their repair techniques used often have their own characteristics. When the scale is small, the techniques employed mainly uses the local structure information of the image; when the scale is large, it is often necessary to fully consider the entire image and use the texture information of the region. Of course, both techniques are used to repair and complete the missing information in the image, so there is no strict limit on the scale.

1. Small-scale image inpainting

From an application point of view, the technique of inpainting small-scale defects is often used to remove scratches or target regions of small size (including a small size in just one dimension, for example, the line or curved regions such as strokes, ropes, text, etc.) on the image. The methods commonly used here are mostly based on partial differential equations or variational models, and these two methods can be derived equivalently with the help of variational principles. This type of image inpainting method achieves the purpose of repairing image by diffusing the target region pixel by pixel (diffusing the information around the missing region to the interior of missing region). A typical method is to extend and diffuse from the source region to the target region along the line of equal intensity (line of equal gray value), which helps to maintain the structural character-istics of the image itself. For specific diffusion, the **total variation** (TV) model can be used to restore the missing information in the image.

The total variation model is a basic and typical image inpainting model. The algorithm based on this model is a non-isotropic diffusion algorithm that can be used to denoise while maintaining the continuity and sharpness of the edges.

Define the cost function of diffusion as

$$R[f] = \iint\limits_{F} |\nabla f(x, y)| dx\, dy. \qquad (5.38)$$

In Equation (5.38), ∇f is the gradient of f. Considering the case of Gaussian noise, in order to remove noise, Equation (5.38) is also subject to the following constraints:

$$\frac{1}{\|F - D\|} \iint\limits_{F-D} |f - g|^2 dx\, dy = \sigma^2. \qquad (5.39)$$

In Equation (5.39), $\|F - D\|$ is the area of region $F - D$, and σ is the mean square error of noise. The goal of Equation (5.38) is to make the region and its boundary part to be repaired as smooth as possible, while the function of Equation (5.39) is to make the repair process more robust to noise.

With the help of Lagrangian factor λ, the constrained problem formed by combining Equations (5.38) and (5.39) can be transformed into an unconstrained problem:

$$E[f] = \iint\limits_{F} |\nabla f(x, y)| dx\, dy + \frac{\lambda}{2} \iint\limits_{F-D} |f - g|^2 dx\, dy. \qquad (5.40)$$

If the extended Lagrangian factor λ_D is introduced:

$$\lambda_D(r) = \begin{cases} 0 & r \in D \\ \lambda & r \in (F - D). \end{cases} \qquad (5.41)$$

Then, Equation (5.40) becomes

$$J[f] = \iint\limits_{F} |\nabla f(x, y)|\, dx\, dy + \frac{\lambda_D}{2} \iint\limits_{F} |f - g|^2\, dx\, dy. \qquad (5.42)$$

According to the principle of variation, the corresponding energy gradient descent equation is

$$\frac{\partial f}{\partial t} = \nabla \cdot \left[\frac{\nabla f}{|\nabla f|} \right] + \lambda_D(f - g). \qquad (5.43)$$

In Equation (5.43), $\nabla\cdot$ represents divergence.

Equation (5.43) is a nonlinear reaction diffusion equation, where the diffusion coefficient is $1/|\nabla f|$. If λ_D is zero in the region to be repaired, Equation (5.43) degenerates into a pure diffusion equation; around the region to be repaired, the second term of Equation (5.43) makes the solution of the equation tend to the original image. The original image can be obtained by solving the partial differential equation in Equation (5.43).

Example 5.4 Small-scale image inpainting example

In some cases, the image surface is covered with various text. Relatively speaking, the text strokes are thinner and the structural information on both sides of the strokes still maintains a certain continuity. The set of images in Figure 5.12 shows an example of image inpainting to remove the overlaid text. Figure 5.12(a) is the original image; Figure 5.12(b) is the image to be repaired (with text superimposed on it); Figure 5.12(c) is the resulting image; Figure 5.12(d) is the difference image between the original image and the result image (after histogram equalization for clear display) and is used to show the inpainting effect. □

2. Large-scale image completion

The method of small-scale image inpainting will have some problems when facing larger-scale regions. On the one hand, small-scale inpainting is to diffuse the information around the missing region into the missing region, but for the missing region with a larger scale, diffusion will cause a certain blur, and the degree of blur increases with the increase in the size of the missing region. On the other hand, small-scale inpainting does not consider the texture characteristics

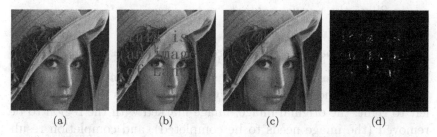

(a)　　　　　　(b)　　　　　　(c)　　　　　　(d)

Figure 5.12.　Example of small-scale image inpainting: removing text.

inside the missing region and directly moves the texture characteristics around the missing region into the missing region. Due to the
large-scale of missing region, the internal and external texture characteristics may be quite different, and direct copying often leads to
unsatisfactory repair results.

The basic ideas to solve the above problems include the following
two:

(1) Decompose the image into structural and textured parts. The
    structural parts can still be copied and filled with the diffusion
    method for small-scale inpainting, while the part with obvious
    texture should be filled with the help of texture synthesis tech-
    nology. Since natural images are mostly composed of texture and
    structure, this hybrid method using diffusion and texture synthe-
    sis could comprehensively utilize the structure information and
    texture information of the image. However, there will still be
    a certain amount of risk and difficulty to fully rely on texture
    synthesis for filling a large-scale target region.
(2) Select some sample blocks in the un-degraded part of the image;
    use these sample blocks to replace the image blocks at the bound-
    ary of the regions to be filled (the un-degraded parts of these
    blocks have similar characteristics to the selected sample blocks),
    gradually filling these regions in progression. This type of method
    directly uses the information in the source region to fill the target
    region and is often called a sample-based image filling method.
    This idea is inspired by texture filling. For the image blocks in
    the target region, they are filled with the direct replacement by
    finding the most similar image blocks in the source region. When
    the scale of the target region is relatively large, the sample-based
    method can often achieve better results than texture synthesis
    in filling the texture content.

Example 5.5 Large-scale image completion example

The set of images in Figure 5.13 shows an example of image completion that removes (unnecessary) regions (parts of scene). From
left to right, the original image, image marked with the region to be
removed (the image needs to be completed), and completion result
are given in sequence. The scale of the region here is relatively large

(a)　　　　　　　　　(b)　　　　　　　　　(c)

Figure 5.13.　An example of large-scale image completion: removing region.

(compared to the text stroke, it has bigger "depth"), but the visual effect of the completion is still relatively satisfactory.　　　□

By the way, if the noise points in the image are regarded as the target region, the problem of image denoising can also be treated as an image repair problem, that is, pixels not affected by noise are used to restore the gray scale of pixels affected by noise. If the inpainting of the image affected by text superimposition or scratches is regarded as the repair of the curved target region, and the completion of the removed scene image is regarded as the repair of the planar target region, then the image affected by the noise can also be regarded as the repair of the point-shaped target region. The above discussion mainly focuses on impulse noise, because the intensity of impulse noise is very high, the superimposition of this noise on the image will make the gray levels of the affected pixels attending to the limit value, and the original pixel information is completely covered by the noise. If it is Gaussian noise, the pixels superimposed with noise often still contain some original gray-scale information, while the pixels in the target region of the image completion generally no longer contain the original image information (the information is removed).

5.6　Key Points and References for Each Section

The following indicates the key points of each section and provides some targeted guidance for further references.

1. Image degradation and model

This section introduced a simple and general image degradation model and some common properties of the degradation system.

Related content is introduced in many image processing books (e.g., see Refs. [1,2]). There are many types of image degradation, including image noise, blur, geometric distortion, and various interferences. They all lead to a decline in image quality. More examples can be found in Ref. [3]. For a comparative discussion of noise and blur, please refer to Ref. [4].

2. Inverse filtering

Inverse filtering is a basic unconstrained image restoration method. The inverse filtering technique can be used to recover the blurred image due to the uniform motion of the camera during image acquisition (see Refs. [1,2]). The fast calculation of inverse filtering can be found in Ref. [2].

3. Wiener filtering

Wiener filtering is a typical constrained image restoration method. The Wiener filter is a statistical-based minimum mean square error filter. The optimal criterion it uses is based on the respective correlation matrices of the image and noise, so the result obtained is only optimal in the average sense, see Ref. [1]. The discussion and derivation of some other constrained image restoration methods can be found in Ref. [2].

4. Geometric distortion correction

The correction of geometric distortion in the image is a typical image restoration work. According to the image representation $f(x, y)$, the correction includes two steps: spatial transformation to correct the position of the pixel and gray-level interpolation to correct the intensity of the pixel. Spatial transformation can essentially be carried out by means of image coordinate transformation, see Ref. [2]. In this section, only the backward mapping method is introduced in the gray-level interpolation, and the comparison between it and forward mapping can be found in Ref. [2]. In addition, the cubic linear interpolation method with higher accuracy than bi-linear interpolation (but also more computationally expensive) can also be found in Ref. [2].

5. Image repairing

Image repairing is a general term for image inpainting and image completion. A comprehensive overview of image restoration can be found in Ref. [5]. A typical method is to extend and diffuse from the source region to the target region along the line of equal intensity (line of equal gray value); see Ref. [6]. For further introduction of total variation model and mixed model, please refer to Ref. [2]. A detailed discussion of image inpainting can also be found in Ref. [7]. Image completion focuses more on the region filling of the image after a region has been removed, damaged, undergone breakage, or missed. The use of sample-based methods and sparse representation (see Ref. [8]) methods for image completion can be found in Ref. [2]. In addition, with the help of filling technology, on the basis of the (automatic) segmentation of the foreground in the image (see Chapter 7), the replacement of background can be achieved.

Self-Test Questions

The following questions include both single- and multiple-choice questions, so each option should be individually judged.

5.1 Image Degradation and Model

5.1.1 The reasons for image degradation can be ( )

    (A) Up and down shooting;

    (B) Camera noise;

    (C) Changes of ambient light;

    (D) The rapid movement of the target in the scene.

[Hint] Image degradation means that the image obtained from the scene does not fully reflect the real content of the scene, resulting in distortion.

5.1.2 Image degradation caused by blur ( )

    (A) Will cause the target pattern size to become larger;

    (B) Will cause the target pattern to produce overlapping shadows;

    (C) Will cause the pattern with regular shape becoming irregular;

(D) Will make the image superimposed with many random bright and dark spots.

[Hint] Blurring will cause the spatial resolution of the image to decrease.

5.1.3 Noise in the image ( )

(A) Contains only high frequency components;
(B) Has always a certain degree of randomness;
(C) Can always cover the entire frequency spectrum;
(D) Has always the same energy in the frequency interval of equal width.

[Hint] There are many types of noise, and the characteristics and similarities of different noises need to be considered.

5.1.4 Which of the following statement(s) could be correct? ( )

(A) The linear degenerate system must have additive property;
(B) Degenerate systems with additive properties are also consistent;
(C) The degenerate system with position (space) invariance is linear;
(D) A degenerate system with consistency also has position (space) invariance.

[Hint] Pay attention to the sufficiency and necessity of the mutual establishment of the four properties.

5.2 Inverse Filtering

5.2.1 If the degenerate system in Figure 5.1 is linear, the power spectrum of $g(x, y)$ is ( )

(A) $|G(u,v)|^2 = |H(u,v)|^2 \cdot |F(u,v)|^2 + |N(u,v)|^2$;
(B) $|G(u,v)|^2 = (|H(u,v)| \cdot |F(u,v)| + |N(u,v)|)^2$;
(C) $|G(u,v)|^2 = (|H(u,v)| \cdot |F(u,v)|)^2 + |N(u,v)|^2$;
(D) $|G(u,v)|^2 = |H(u,v)|^2 \cdot |F(u,v)|^2 + 2|H(u,v)| \cdot |F(u,v)| \cdot |N(u,v)| + |N(u,v)|^2$.

[Hint] Note that (A) and (C) are the same, (B) and (D) are the same.

5.2.2 In inverse filtering method, ( )

    (A) The filter used is a function of the frequencies u and v;

    (B) No consideration is given to the physical constraints that the image should be subjected to;

    (C) The image affected by noise cannot be completely restored;

    (D) The effect becomes worse as the distance from the origin of the spectrum increases.

[Hint] Note that the restoration effect is better when the value of $H(u, v)$ is larger.

5.2.3 Given an image degradation system with constant linear displacement (its impulse response can be written as $h(x - s, y - t) = \exp\{-[(x - s)^2 + (y - t)^2]\}$). Input an infinitely long thin straight line signal at $x = a$ (modeled with $f(x, y) = \delta(x - a)$), the output of the system is proportional to ( )

    (A) $\exp\{-[(x - s)^2]\}$;

    (B) $\exp\{-[(x - a)^2]\}$;

    (C) $\exp\{-[\delta(x - a)^2]\}$;

    (D) $\exp\{-[(x - a)^2 + (y - a)^2]\}$.

[Hint] Convolve the input signal with the impulse response of the degradation system.

5.3 Wiener Filtering

5.3.1 Wiener filter ( )

    (A) Takes the ideal inverse filter as a special case;

    (B) Needs to use the respective correlation matrices of image and noise;

    (C) Can obtain the optimal restoration effect for every image;

    (D) Considers the physical constraints that the image should be subjected to after restoration.

[Hint] The Wiener filter is a statistical minimum mean square error filter, and the results obtained are only optimal in the average sense.

5.3.2 If the transfer function of a blur degraded system can be represented by $H(u, v) = \exp[-(u^2 + v^2)/2\sigma^2]$, when the noise is negligible, the equation of Wiener filter for restoring this kind of blur should be ( )

(A) $\exp[(u^2 + v^2)/2\sigma^2]$;

(B) $\exp[-(u^2 + v^2)/2\sigma^2]$;

(C) $1/\exp[(u^2 + v^2)/2\sigma^2]$;

(D) $1/\exp[-(u^2 + v^2)/2\sigma^2]$.

[Hint] When the noise is negligible, the Wiener filter degenerates into an ideal inverse filter.

5.3.3 Suppose the restoration filter $R(u, v)$ satisfies $|F_e(u, v)|^2 = |R(u, v)|^2 \cdot |G(u, v)|^2 = |F(u, v)|^2$, then the $F_e(u, v)$ written by a form similar to Equation (5.20) should be ( )

(A) $F_e(u, v) = \dfrac{1}{|H(u,v)|+|N(u,v)||F(u,v)|}G(u, v)$;

(B) $F_e(u, v) = \sqrt{\dfrac{1}{|H(u,v)|^2+|N(u,v)|^2|F(u,v)|^2}}G(u, v)$;

(C) $F_e(u, v) = \sqrt{\dfrac{1}{|H(u,v)|^2+|N(u,v)|^2/|F(u,v)|^2}}G(u, v)$;

(D) $F_e(u, v) = \dfrac{1}{|H(u,v)|^2+|N(u,v)|^2/|F(u,v)|^2}G(u, v)$.

[Hint] First, find $R(u, v)$ according to $|F(u, v)|^2$, $|H(u, v)|^2$, and $|N(u, v)|^2$.

5.4 Geometric Distortion Correction

5.4.1 In Figure 5.6, if the bottom=left corner of the image is set as the origin of the coordinate system, the distorted image and the quadrilateral in the corrected image are related by linear distortion. According to Equations (5.24) and (5.25), we get ( )

(A) $k_1 = 1/6$, $k_2 = 5/6$, $k_3 = 0$, $k_4 = -5/6$, $k_5 = 1/6$, $k_6 = 8/6$;

(B) $k_1 = 5/6$, $k_2 = 1/6$, $k_3 = 0$, $k_4 = -1/6$, $k_5 = 5/6$, $k_6 = 8/6$;

(C) $k_1 = -1/6$, $k_2 = 1/6$, $k_3 = 0$, $k_4 = 1/6$, $k_5 = 1/6$, $k_6 = 8/6$;

(D) $k_1 = 5/6$, $k_2 = -1/6$, $k_3 = 0$, $k_4 = 1/6$, $k_5 = 5/6$, $k_6 = 2/6$.

[Hint] Select one point to calculate specifically.

5.4.2 In Figure 5.6, if the bottom-left corner of the image is the origin of the coordinate system, it is known that $f(1,1) = 1$, $f(7,1) = 7$, $f(1,7) = 7$, $f(7,7) = 13$, then ( )

(A) $f(2,4) = 3$;

(B) $f(2,4) = 4$;

(C) $f(2,4) = 5$;

(D) $f(2,4) = 6$.

[Hint] This can be calculated according to interpolation formula.

5.4.3 Bilinear interpolation ( )

(A) Has the calculation amount larger than the nearest neighbor interpolation;

(B) Needs to use four nearest neighbor pixels to calculate;

(C) Has the interpolation result on the plane determined by the gray values of the four nearest neighbor pixels;

(D) Has the linear interpolations in both the horizontal and vertical directions.

[Hint] Refer to Figure 5.9.

5.5 Image Repairing

5.5.1 Image repair is divided into image inpainting and image completion because ( )

(A) The functions of these two processes are different;

(B) The repair scales of these two processes are different;

(C) The image information used by these two processes are different;

(D) The image repair models used by these two processes are different.

[Hint] The difference between these two processes is mainly qualitative.

5.5.2 In the repair of an image, ( )

(A) If the area to be repaired is small, image inpainting should be used;
(B) If the scale of the part to be repaired is small, image inpainting should be used;
(C) If the area to be repaired is large, image completion should be used;
(D) If the scale of the part to be repaired is large, image completion should be used.

[Hint] The area and scale of a region may not be proportional.

5.5.3 Image repair technology can repair the defect region; when it is used for noise elimination, ( )

(A) It is suitable for eliminating Gaussian noise;
(B) It is suitable for eliminating uniform noise;
(C) It is suitable for eliminating pepper noise;
(D) It is suitable for eliminating salt noise.

[Hint] Analyze the influence of noise on the image.

References

[1] Gonzalez, R. C. *Woods R E. Digital Image Processing*, 4th Edn. UK, London: Prentice Hall, 2018.
[2] Zhang, Y.-J. *Image Engineering, Vol. 1: Image Processing*. Germany, Berlin: De Gruyter, 2017.
[3] Jähne, B. *Digital Image Processing — Concepts, Algorithms and Scientific Applications*. Germany, Berlin: Springer, 1997.
[4] Bertero, M. and Boccacci, P. *Introduction to Inverse Problems in Imaging*. UK, London: IOP Publishing Ltd., 1998.
[5] Zhang, Y.-J. Image inpainting as an evolving topic in image engineering. *Encyclopedia of Information Science and Technology*, 3rd Edn. 2015, Chapter 122 (1283–1293).
[6] Bertalmio, M., Bertozzi, A. L. and Sapiro, G. Navier–strokes, fluid dynamics, and image and video inpainting. *Proc. CVPR*, 417–424, 2001.
[7] Chan, T. F. and Shen, J. *Image Processing and Analysis — Variational, PDE, Wavelet, and Stochastic Methods*. USA, Philadelphia: Siam, 2005.
[8] Donoho, D. L. Compressed Sensing. http://www.stat.stanford.edu/-donoho/Reports/2004.

Chapter 6

Color Enhancement

With the advancement of technology and crafts, **color images** have been used more and more widely, and color image processing and analysis technologies have also received more and more attention, which has also promoted the research on the human visual system. The purpose of many image technologies is to improve the visual quality of images, which often requires the use of the characteristics of the human visual system.

Color images contain more information than gray-scale images. In order to effectively represent and process color information, it is necessary to establish a corresponding color representation model, and it is also necessary to study the corresponding color image processing technology. Among them, color image enhancement technologies can be divided into two categories. On the one hand, because people have stronger color-resolving ability and sensitivity than gray scale, the image enhancement can be achieved by converting gray-scale images into color images. These technologies are often called false-color enhancement technologies. On the other hand, modern image acquisition equipment directly obtains color images, so it is also necessary to directly enhance these images to obtain the required effects. The related technologies are true-color enhancement technologies.

The sections of this chapter are arranged as follows:

Section 6.1 first introduces some basic concepts and characteristics of human vision, and discusses the representation methods based on three primary colors.

Section 6.2 discusses basic color models, including red, green, blue (RGB) models for hardware devices and hue, saturation, intensity (HSI) models for color processing. It also introduces the mutual conversion between these two models.

Section 6.3 introduces the false-color enhancement technology, including both typical spatial methods and basic frequency domain methods.

Section 6.4 introduces the true-color enhancement technology. On the one hand, it discusses the method of enhancing each color component separately; on the other hand, it also discusses the method of combining each component to directly enhance the whole.

6.1   Color Vision

Human color vision is a complicated process. In addition to the stimulation of the light source to the eyes, the human brain also needs to explain the stimulation. The color of an object perceived by a person mainly depends on the characteristics of the reflected light. If the object reflects various spectra in a balanced manner, the object appears to be white. If the object reflects more of certain spectra, the object will appear to show the corresponding colors.

6.1.1   Three primary colors and color representation

According to the structure of the human eye, all colors can be regarded as different combinations of three basic colors, namely **red** (R), **green** (G), and **blue** (B). These three basic colors are also called **three primary colors**. In order to establish standards, the International Committee on Illumination (CIE), as early as in 1931, stipulated that the wavelengths of the three primary colors were R: 700 nm, G: 546.1 nm, and B: 435.8 nm. The different super-positions of the three primary colors can produce **three complementary colors** of light: **magenta** (M, that is red and blue), **cyan** (C, that is green and blue), and **yellow** (Y, that is red and green). Mixing the three primary colors in a certain ratio or mixing a complementary color with the opposite primary color can produce white.

When looking at a surface of an object from a color perspective, it can be achromatic or chromatic. Achromatic refers to white, black, and various shades of gray. The surface that can absorb all wavelengths of light equally looks gray. If the reflected light is more, it will be light gray. If the reflected light is less, it will be dark gray. If the reflected light is less than 10% of the incident light, it generally looks black. When taking white at one end, passing through a series of various grays arranged from light to dark, and reaching the black at the other end, these grays can form a black-and-white series. Color, in a strict sense, refers to various colors other than this black-and-white series.

When the three colors of red, green, and blue are mixed, white and various colors can be obtained by changing the respective intensity ratios of the three:

$$C \equiv rR + gG + bB, \tag{6.1}$$

where C represents a specific color, "$\equiv$" represents matching, R, G, and B respectively represent three primary colors, and r, g, and b represent proportional coefficients. Here,

$$r + g + b = 1. \tag{6.2}$$

In fact, if the three stimuli required to form a certain color C are represented by X, Y, and Z, respectively, then the three stimuli have the following relationship with the R, G, and B of CIE:

$$X = 0.4902R + 0.3099G + 0.1999B, \tag{6.3}$$

$$Y = 0.1770R + 0.8123G + 0.0107B, \tag{6.4}$$

$$Z = 0.0000R + 0.0101G + 0.9899B. \tag{6.5}$$

Conversely, according to the three stimulus values of X, Y, and Z, the three primary colors can also be obtained:

$$R = 2.3635X - 0.8958Y - 0.4677Z, \tag{6.6}$$

$$G = -0.5151X + 1.4264Y + 0.0887Z, \tag{6.7}$$

$$B = 0.0052X - 0.0145Y + 0.0887Z. \tag{6.8}$$

For white light, $X = 1$, $Y = 1$, and $Z = 1$. If the proportional coefficient of each stimulus is x, y, and z, then $C = xX + yY + zZ$.

The scale factors x, y, and z are also called the color coefficients:

$$x = \frac{X}{X + Y + Z}, \tag{6.9}$$

$$y = \frac{Y}{X + Y + Z}, \tag{6.10}$$

$$z = \frac{Z}{X + Y + Z}. \tag{6.11}$$

From Equations (6.9)–(6.11), the relation between color coefficients can be obtained as

$$x + y + z = 1. \tag{6.12}$$

6.1.2   Chromaticity diagram

People often use three basic characteristic quantities when analyzing or distinguishing colors: **intensity**, **hue**, and **saturation**. The intensity is directly proportional to the reflectivity of the object. If there is no color, there is only one degree of freedom change in intensity. For colored light, the more white the color it mixes, the higher the intensity, and the more black it mixes, the lower the intensity. Hue is related to the dominant light wavelength in the mixed spectrum. Saturation is related to the purity of a certain hue. Pure spectral colors are completely saturated, and the saturation gradually decreases with the addition of white light.

Hue and saturation are collectively called **chroma**. Color can be represented by both intensity and chroma. In 1931, CIE developed a tongue-shaped **chromaticity diagram**. Figure 6.1 gives a schematic diagram (the value surrounding the tongue in the diagram represents the wavelength of light in nm) which uses the ratio of the three primary colors that make up a certain color to specify this color. In the diagram, the horizontal axis corresponds to the red color coefficient r, and the vertical axis corresponds to the green color coefficient g. The blue color coefficient can be obtained by Equation (6.2), which is in the direction perpendicular to the paper surface. Each point in the diagram gives the chromaticity coordinates of a corresponding color in the spectrum. Red is in the lower right of the diagram, green is in the upper left of the diagram, and blue-purple is in the lower left

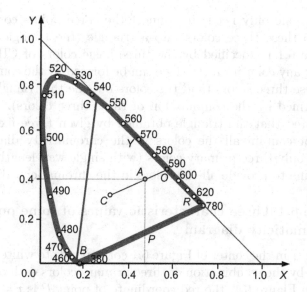

Figure 6.1. Schematic diagram of chromaticity diagram.

of the diagram. The straight line connecting 400 nm and 700 nm corresponds a series from purple to red that is not on the spectrum.

Through observation and analysis of Figure 6.1, the following can be seen:

(1) Each point in the chromaticity diagram corresponds to a visible color, and any visible color occupies a certain position in the chromaticity diagram. The points inside the triangle whose vertices are (0, 0), (0, 1), and (1, 0) and outside the tongue-shaped form of the chromaticity diagram correspond to invisible colors.

(2) The points on the tongue-shaped border of the chromaticity diagram represent pure colors, and moving to the center indicates that the mixed white light increases and the purity decreases. The energies of the various spectra at the center point C are equal, and this point appears white, where the purity is zero. The purity of a certain color is generally called the saturation of the color, and the saturation of a pure color is one.

(3) Each point on the straight line connecting any two end points in the chromaticity diagram represents a color formed by adding the colors represented by these two end points. Based on this, to determine the color range that can be combined by three given

colors, one only needs to connect the three points corresponding to these three colors into a triangle (the triangle given in Figure 6.1 is specified by the three basic colors of CIE as vertices); any color in the triangle can be formed by the combination of these three colors (and the colors outside the triangle cannot be formed by the combination of these three colors). It should be noted that the triangle obtained by given three fixed colors cannot contain all the colors in the chromaticity diagram, so using only three primary colors (with single wavelength) cannot combine to provide all the colors in the chromaticity diagram.

Example 6.1 Three characteristic values of some points in the chromaticity diagram

The point C in the center of Figure 6.1 corresponds to white, which is produced by the combination of three primary colors each occupying a third. In Figure 6.1, the red coordinate of point P is $r = 0.48$ and the green coordinate of point P is $g = 0.40$. Draw a straight line from C through P to point Q on the boundary (corresponding to about 590 nm). The dominant wavelength of the color of point P is 590 nm, where the color of the spectrum is the hue of point Q (orange). In Figure 6.1, point P is located at 66% from C to the pure orange point, so its color purity (saturation) is 66%. □

Example 6.2 PAL and NTSC chromaticity triangle

For various color display reproduction systems, it is necessary to select appropriate R, G, and B as the basic colors. For example, the chromaticity triangles used by the PAL and NTSC television systems are shown by the two triangles in Figure 6.2. The main factors considered here for choosing R, G, B are as follows:

(1) It is technically difficult to produce highly saturated colors, so these basic colors are not fully saturated colors.
(2) The triangle should be larger to include a bigger area, that is, to include more various colors.
(3) Saturated blue and green are not commonly used, so the red vertex of the triangle is closest to the spectral saturation locus, while both the blue and green vertices are at a greater distance from full saturation (the NTSC system is more blue than the PAL system). □

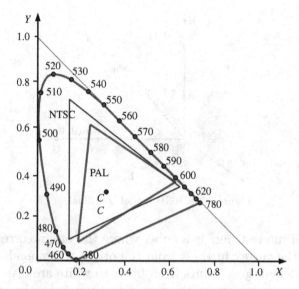

Figure 6.2.   PAL and NTSC chromaticity triangle.

6.2   Color Model

In order to represent and use colors correctly, an appropriate color model needs to be established. As mentioned earlier, a color can be described by three basic quantities, so to establish a color model is to establish a 3D coordinate system, in which each spatial point represents a certain color.

Currently, the commonly used color models can be divided into two categories. One is for hardware devices, such as color monitors or printers. The other is oriented to applications aimed at color processing. The most commonly used color model for hardware devices is the RGB model, and the most commonly used color model for color processing is the HSI model. These two color models are also the most common models in image technology, which are discussed separately as follows.

6.2.1   RGB model

The **RGB model** is a rectangular space structure model, which can be represented by a Cartesian rectangular coordinate system with three axes representing R, G, and B, as shown in Figure 6.3.

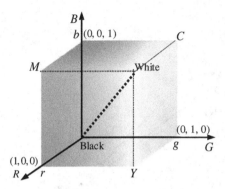

Figure 6.3.   RGB model coordinates.

The part of interest here is a cube, where the origin corresponds to black and the vertex furthest from the origin corresponds to white. In this model, all gray values from black to white are distributed on the line from the origin to the vertex furthest from the origin, and the remaining points in the cube correspond to different colors. For convenience, the cube can be normalized to a unit cube, so that all the values of R, G, and B are in the interval $[0, 1]$.

According to this model, each color image includes three independent primary color planes, or it can be decomposed into three planes.

The two-by-two super-position of three primary colors can produce three complementary colors of light: **cyan** (C, namely green and blue), **magenta** (M, red and blue), and **yellow** (Y, red and green). If the three primary colors are mixed in a certain ratio or a complementary color light is mixed with the opposite primary color light, white light can be produced. It should be pointed out that in addition to the three primary colors of light, there are also the three primary colors of pigments. The primary color in the pigment refers to the color that absorbs one primary color light and allows the other two primary color lights to reflect, so the three primary colors of the pigment are exactly the three complementary colors of light, and they form the CMY model:

$$\begin{bmatrix} C \\ M \\ Y \end{bmatrix} = \begin{bmatrix} 1 \\ 1 \\ 1 \end{bmatrix} - \begin{bmatrix} R \\ G \\ B \end{bmatrix}. \tag{6.13}$$

The **CMY model** is mainly used for color printing. In theory, CMY is the complementary model of RGB, and their super-position should output black. But in reality, their super-position only outputs a turbid dark color. Therefore, the publishing industry adds a black color (indicated by K), and uses the so-called **CMYK model** for **four-color printing**.

6.2.2 HSI model

In the **HSI model**, H represents hue, S represents saturation, and I represents intensity (corresponding to imaging brightness and image gray scale). This model has two characteristics, or it is based on two important facts: First, the I component has nothing to do with the color information of the image; second, the H and S components are closely connected with the way people perceive colors. These characteristics make the HSI model very suitable for image processing algorithms that use the human visual system to perceive color characteristics. Each component in the HSI model can be defined in a double pyramid, as shown in Figure 6.4(a), where each cross section is shown in Figure 6.4(b). For any one of the color points P, the value of H corresponds to the angle between the vector pointing to that point and the R axis. The S of this point is proportional to

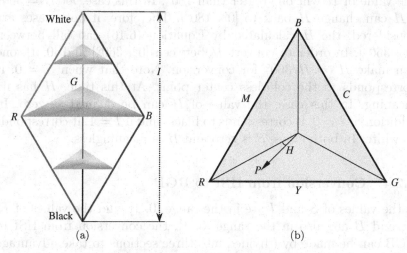

Figure 6.4. HSI model coordinates.

the length of the vector pointing to the point; the longer it is, the more saturated it is. In this model, the value of I is measured along a straight line that passes through the center of the triangle and is perpendicular to the plane of the triangle. The more it comes out of the paper, the whiter it gets, and the more it goes into the paper, the blacker it gets.

6.2.3   Conversion from RGB to HSI

For any three R, G, B values in the range of $[0, 1]$, the corresponding I, S, and H components in the HSI model can be calculated using the equations given in the following:

$$I = \frac{1}{3}(R + G + B), \tag{6.14}$$

$$S = 1 - \frac{3}{(R + G + B)}[\min(R, G, B)], \tag{6.15}$$

$$H = \arccos\left\{\frac{[(R - G) + (R - B)]/2}{[(R - G)^2 + (R - B)(G - B)]^{1/2}}\right\}. \tag{6.16}$$

The H value directly calculated from Equation (6.16) is in the range $[0°, 180°]$, corresponding to the case of $G \geq B$. If $G < B$, the value of H will be greater than $180°$. In this case, let $H = 360°$ $-H$ can change H back to $[0°, 180°]$. Therefore, if both cases are considered, the H calculated by Equation (6.16) can fall between $[0°, 360°]$. In order to convert H between $[0°, 360°]$ and $[0, 1]$, one can make $H' = H/360°$ for conversion. Note that when $S = 0$, it corresponds to the colorless center point. At this time, H has no meaning. In this case, the value of H can be defined as zero. In addition, if $I = 0$, it corresponds to black, and if $I = 1$, it corresponds to white. In both cases, S is zero and H is meaningless.

6.2.4   Conversion from HSI to RGB

If the values of S and I are in the range $[0, 1]$, and the values of R, G, and B are also in the range $[0, 1]$, the conversion from HSI to RGB can be made by (divided into three sections to take advantage of symmetry):

(1) If H is in the range $[0°, 120°]$,

$$B = I(1 - S), \tag{6.17}$$

$$R = I\left[1 + \frac{S \cos H}{\cos(60° - H)}\right], \tag{6.18}$$

$$G = 3I - (B + R). \tag{6.19}$$

(2) If H is in the range $[120°, 240°]$,

$$R = I(1 - S), \tag{6.20}$$

$$G = I\left[1 + \frac{S \cos(H - 120°)}{\cos(180° - H)}\right], \tag{6.21}$$

$$B = 3I - (R + G). \tag{6.22}$$

(3) If H is in the range $[240°, 360°]$,

$$G = I(1 - S), \tag{6.23}$$

$$B = I\left[1 + \frac{S \cos(H - 240°)}{\cos(300° - H)}\right], \tag{6.24}$$

$$R = 3I - (G + B). \tag{6.25}$$

Example 6.3 R, G, B and H, S, I components of a color image

Each component in a color image can also be represented in the form of a gray-scale image. For example, a light color (lighter gray) indicates a larger component value and a dark color (darker gray) indicates a smaller component value. However, this representation only shows the amplitude value of each component, and the frequency or wavelength they represent cannot be reflected here. Figure 6.5 shows an example of a set of color images represented in gray-scale format.

In Figure 6.5, Figures 6.5(a) to (c) are the R, G, B components of a color image (each component uses eight bits of representation), respectively and Figures 6.5(d) to (f) are the H, S, I components of this color image (each component is also represented by eight bits). Combining the three components of the first three pictures or the last three pictures will give the same color image. Note that the

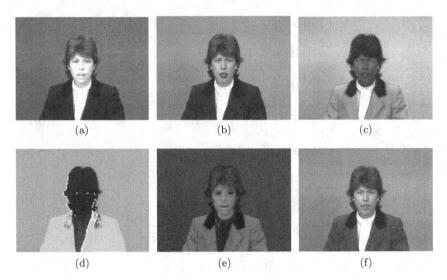

Figure 6.5.   R, G, B and H, S, I components of a color image.

H component picture and S component picture look very different from the I component picture. The difference between the three components of H, S, and I is greater than the difference between the three components of R, G, and B, which shows that the correlation between H, S, and I is smaller than the correlation between R, G, and B.   □

6.3   Pseudo-Color Enhancement

Although the human eye can only distinguish dozens of different shades of gray levels, it can distinguish thousands of different colors. Therefore, in image processing, colors can often be used in image processing to obtain enhanced visual effects for the human eye. The commonly used color enhancement methods can be divided into pseudo-color enhancement methods and true-color enhancement methods. Although there is only one word of difference, they are based on very different principles. This section introduces pseudo-color enhancement methods, and the next section introduces true-color enhancement methods.

The pseudo-color enhancement method distinguishes regions with different gray values in the original gray-scale image by assigning them different colors. Because there is no color in the original image, the artificial color is often called **pseudocolor**. This assigning process is actually a coloring process. The following discusses three simple methods to assign pseudo-colors based on the characteristics of the gray scale of the image.

6.3.1 Intensity slicing

A gray-scale image can be regarded as a 2D intensity function (that is, a function with two independent variables). A plane parallel to the image coordinate plane can be used to cut the image intensity function, thereby dividing the intensity function into two gray value intervals, which is called **intensity slicing**. Figure 6.6 shows a schematic diagram of a slicing section (the horizontal axis is the coordinate axis (representing the coordinate plane) and the vertical axis is the gray-value axis).

According to Figure 6.6, for each input gray value, if it is above the slicing gray value lm (it is the section of the slicing plane), a certain color will be assigned, and if it is below lm, another color will be assigned. Through this transformation (from continuous gray values to two colors), the original image with multiple gray values is transformed into an image with only two colors. By moving the slicing plane up and down, one can get different display results.

This method can be generalized and summarized as follows: Suppose that M planes are defined at gray levels $l_1, l_2, \ldots, l_m$; let l_0 represent black ($f(x, y) = 0$) and l_L represent white ($f(x, y) = L$), then under the condition of $0 < M < L$, M planes will divide the image gray value into $M + 1$ intervals, and each pixel in the gray

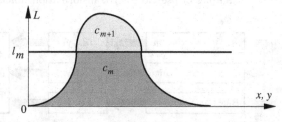

Figure 6.6.   Schematic diagram of intensity slicing.

value interval can be assigned one color, namely:

$$f(x, y) = c_m \quad \text{if} \quad \begin{aligned} f(x, y) &\in R_m \\ m &= 0, 1, \ldots, M, \end{aligned} \tag{6.26}$$

where R_m is the gray value interval defined by the slicing plane and c_m is the assigned color.

6.3.2 Conversion from gray scale to color

In the **grayscale-to-color conversion** method, the gray value of each pixel in the original image can be processed by three independent transformations. An example is shown in Figure 6.7. Here, the gray value of each pixel in the original image is processed by three independent continuous transformations, so that each gray level is mapped to a different color. According to the transformation function in Figure 6.7, pixels with small gray values will mainly appear blue, pixels with large gray values will mainly appear red, and pixels with intermediate gray values will appear greenish and have lower saturation.

If the results of the three transformations are input into the three electron guns of a color TV screen, one can get a mixed image whose color content is modulated by three transformation functions, as

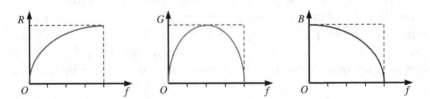

Figure 6.7.   Examples of pseudo-color transformation functions.

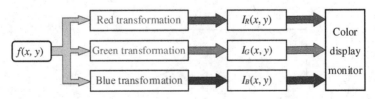

Figure 6.8.   Schematic diagram of pseudo-color conversion process.

shown in Figure 6.8. What is modulated here is the gray value of the image rather than the position of the pixel.

The intensity slicing method discussed in the previous section can be regarded as a piecewise linear function to achieve the transformation from gray to color, so it can be regarded as a special case of the gray-to-color conversion method. But this method can also use smooth, nonlinear transformation functions, so it is more flexible. In practice, the transformation function usually takes the absolute value of sine function, which is characterized by relatively flat peaks and sharper troughs. By changing the phase and frequency of each sine wave, the color corresponding to the related gray value can be changed. For example, if the three transformations have the same phase and frequency, the output image is still a gray image. If there is a small difference in the phase between the three transformations, the pixel whose gray value is around the peak of the sine function will be affected little (especially when the frequency is relatively low and the peak is relatively wide), but the pixel whose gray value is around the valleys of the sine function are more affected. Especially where the three sine functions are at the troughs, the phase change leads to greater amplitude changes. In other words, where the value of the three sine functions changes drastically, the gray value of the pixel is more obviously affected by the color change. In this way, pixels with different gray-value ranges get different pseudo-color enhancement effects.

6.3.3 Frequency domain filtering

Color enhancement can also be performed in the frequency domain with various filters. A basic block diagram is shown in Figure 6.9. The Fourier transform (FT) of the input image is divided into different frequency components through three different filters (commonly using band-pass or band-stop filters). The frequency components in

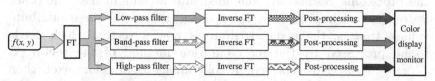

Figure 6.9. Block diagram of frequency domain filtering for pseudo-color enhancement.

each range are subjected to inverse Fourier transform first, and the results can be further processed (such as histogram equalization or specification). The enhanced image can be obtained by inputting the images of each channel into the red, green, and blue input ports of the color display monitor.

The basic idea here is to assign distinctive colors to different regions according to the various frequency content of each region in the image. To obtain different frequency components, low-pass, band-pass (or band-stop), and high-pass filters can be used as the three filters in Figure 6.9.

6.4   True-Color Enhancement

In **true-color enhancement** or **full-color enhancement**, the image to be enhanced is originally in color and the enhanced image is also in color. Normally, a true-color RGB image can be represented by 24 bits, in which each R, G, and B component has eight bits, that is, each pixel takes 256 values in each of the R, G, and B component of images. One can also normalize R, G, and B to the range of $[0, 1]$, so that the difference between adjacent values is $1/255$. A true-color RGB image can also be represented by three component images of eight bits for each of H, S, and I. The difference here is that the pixel values in the hue (H) image are measured in angles. If represented by eight bits, 256 values are distributed between $[0°, 360°]$, so the difference between adjacent values is $(360/255)°$, or the 256 values corresponds to $n(360/255)°$, where $n = 0, 1, \ldots, 255$, but the degree corresponding to the H may not be an integer.

There are two types of processing strategies for true-color images. One is to treat a color image as a combination of three component images. In the process of processing, each image is processed separately (following the gray-scale image processing method), and then the processing results are combined into a color image. The other is to treat each pixel in a color image as having three attribute values, that is, the pixel attribute is now a vector, which needs to be processed by the representation method of the vector. If $C(x, y)$ is used to represent a color image or a color pixel, then $C(x, y) = [R(x, y)G(x, y)B(x, y)]^T$. Here, it is needed to extend the gray-scale image processing method to the processing of color images, or to extend the processing of a scalar attribute to the processing of a vector attribute, so there are certain requirements for the processing methods and the objects to be processed. First of all, the processing method used should be applicable to both scalar and vector. Second, the processing of each component in a vector must be independent of other components. A simple neighborhood averaging of an image is an example satisfying these two conditions. For a gray-scale image, the specific operation of neighborhood averaging is to add up the pixel values in a mask centered around one pixel and divide the result by the number of pixels in the mask. For a color image, the neighborhood averaging can be performed on whole attribute vector (vector operation) or on each single component of attribute vector separately (like scalar operation for gray-scale images) and then combined. This can be expressed as

$$\sum_{(x,y)\in N} \mathbf{C}(x,y) = \sum_{(x,y)\in N} [R(x,y) + G(x,y) + B(x,y)]$$

$$= \left\{ \sum_{(x,y)\in N} R(x,y) + \sum_{(x,y)\in N} G(x,y) + \sum_{(x,y)\in N} B(x,y) \right\}. \quad (6.27)$$

It should be noted that not every processing operation satisfies the above conditions, and only for linear processing operations, the two results are equivalent.

6.4.1 Single-component true-color enhancement

In true-color enhancement, although the direct use of the gray-scale image enhancement method for the R, G, and B components can increase the intensity or contrast of the visible details in the image, the hue in the enhanced image may be completely meaningless or impractical. This is because the three components of R, G, and B corresponding to the same pixel in the enhanced image have been changed, and their relative values are different from the original, which leads to a large change in the color of the original image. In addition, this change is difficult to control.

If the RGB image is converted to the HSI image, the luminance component and chrominance components are separated, and the enhancement method of the gray image can be used for one of them to obtain the expected effect. The basic steps of a simple and commonly used true-color enhancement method with this idea are as follows:

(1) Convert the R, G, B components of the original color image into H, S, I components of an image.
(2) Use the method of enhancing the gray image to enhance one of H, S, I component images.
(3) Convert the above results into R, G, and B component images for display on a color monitor.

The HSI image contains three component images, so the enhancement of the second step above can be divided into three cases:

(1) The image to be enhanced is the I-component image, which does not change the color content of the original image, but the enhanced image may still look somewhat different in color. This is because although the hue and saturation have not changed, the intensity component has been changed, which will have a certain impact on the color perception of the entire image.
(2) The image enhanced is the S-component image, and the change of saturation is related to the enhancement mode. If the saturation component of each pixel in the image is multiplied by a constant greater than one, the colors in the image could be more vivid, while if it is multiplied by a constant smaller than one, the color perception of the image will be reduced.

Example 6.4 Saturation enhancement examples

Figure 6.10 shows a set of example images with saturation enhancements. Figure 6.10(a) is an original color image; Figure 6.10(b) is the result of only increasing the saturation component, in which the image color is more saturated and with increased contrast and clearer edges; Figure 6.10(c) is the result of reducing the saturation. The original low-saturation part becomes gray, and the entire image is relatively flat. ☐

(3) The image to be enhanced is the H-component image, which produces some special feelings in the image. According to the representation method of the HSI model, the hue corresponds to

Figure 6.10. Effects of saturation enhancement.

Figure 6.11. A set of images with changing hues.

an angle and is cyclic. If one adds a constant (angle value) to the hue value of each pixel, the color of the corresponding object will move on the color spectrum. If this constant is relatively small, it will generally make the hue of the color image "warm" or "cold"; if the constant is relatively large, the perception of the color image may change drastically.

Example 6.5 Hue enhancement examples

The group of images in Figure 6.11 gives the change effects of hue. Figure 6.11(a) is an original image; Figure 6.11(b) is the result of subtracting a smaller value from the H-component. Some of the red color turns to purple color, and some of the blue color turns to green color. Figure 6.11(c) is the result of adding a larger value to the hue component. Here, the image is basically inverted, similar to image negation. □

6.4.2   Full-color enhancement

The advantage of single-component enhancement is that it is easier to perform enhancement transformation operations due to the decomposition of intensity, saturation, and hue; but the disadvantage is that there will always be changes in overall color perception (especially visual perception hue), and the change effect is not easy to control. Therefore, in some enhancements, all color components need to be considered. Two methods are described in the following.

1. Color slicing for enhancement

In color space, a color always occupies a position in the space. For the pixels corresponding to the same object or part of the object in the natural image, their colors should be clustered together in the color space. The color space is a 3D space. For the RGB space, the three coordinate axes are R, G, and B; for the HSI space, the three coordinate axes are H, S, and I. Consider the region W corresponding to an object in the image. If the corresponding cluster can be determined in the color space, then it is possible to assign a color to the pixels corresponding to this cluster, and let other parts of the image take other colors (can be even white or black). In this way, the object can be distinguished or highlighted from other objects, and the purpose of enhancement can be achieved. This method is similar to the intensity slicing method introduced in pseudo-color enhancement in Section 6.3, so it can be called **color slicing for enhancement**.

The following takes the use of RGB color space as an example to introduce the method in detail, and the methods of using other color spaces should be similar. The three color components corresponding to the region W are $R_W(x, y)$, $G_W(x, y)$, and $B_W(x, y)$. First, their respective averages (that is, the coordinates of the cluster centers in the color space) are calculated:

$$m_R = \frac{1}{\#W} \sum_{(x,y)\in W} R_W(x, y), \qquad (6.28)$$

$$m_G = \frac{1}{\#W} \sum_{(x,y)\in W} G_W(x, y), \qquad (6.29)$$

$$m_B = \frac{1}{\#W} \sum_{(x,y)\in W} B_W(x,y). \tag{6.30}$$

In Equations (6.28)–(6.30), $\#W$ represents the number of pixels in the region W. Then, the distribution width of each color component, d_R, d_G, d_B, is determined. According to the average value and distribution width, the color enclosing rectangle $\{m_R - d_R/2 : m_R + d_R/2; m_G - d_G/2 : m_G + d_G/2; m_B - d_B/2 : m_B + d_B/2\}$ in the color space for the corresponding region W can be fixed. In practice, the average value and distribution width often need to be obtained through human–computer interaction.

2. Color filtering for enhancement

The color-slicing enhancement operation is based on the point operation, and the mask operation can also be used to enhance the color image, which can also be called **color filtering for enhancement**. In order to ensure there is no color cast, each component needs to be processed at the same time.

Taking the neighborhood averaging as an example, let the neighborhood of the color pixel $C(x, y)$ be W, and the result of convolving the color image with the mask covering this neighborhood is

$$C_{\text{avc}} = \frac{1}{\#W} \sum_{(x,y)\in W} C(x,y) = \frac{1}{\#W} \begin{bmatrix} \sum_{(x,y)\in W} R(x,y) \\ \sum_{(x,y)\in W} G(x,y) \\ \sum_{(x,y)\in W} B(x,y) \end{bmatrix}. \tag{6.31}$$

It can be seen that the result of averaging the vector can be obtained by averaging its components using the same method and then combining them. In other words, one color image can be decomposed into three gray-scale images, and the three gray-scale images can be averaged and combined with the same mask. The above method is also applicable to weighted average. In fact, this can be done for various linear filtering methods, but it becomes very complicated for different nonlinear filtering methods.

6.5   Key Points and References for Each Section

The following indicates the key points of each section and provides some targeted guidance for further references.

1. Color vision

According to the structure of the human eye, the three basic colors, red, green, and blue, can be combined to form various colors. This is a basic theory about color vision, and other theories can also be found in Ref. [1]. The chromaticity diagram is used to quantitatively describe various combinations of colors, and a supplementary discussion of the chromaticity diagram can also be found in the Refs. [2,3]. In addition, the theory of three primary colors is also the basis of television broadcasting. It can be found in books on television principles [4]. A comprehensive discussion of color and color image technology can be found in [5].

2. Color model

The RGB model and the HSI model are representative of two types of models for hardware devices, such as color monitors or printers, and for color processing applications, respectively. Other models of these two types can often be derived from the RGB model or the HSI model. In addition, there are some other types of color models; see Refs. [1,5]. The proof of the conversion formula from RGB to HSI can be found in Ref. [2].

3. Pseudo-color enhancement

Pseudo-color enhancement can be regarded as the process of coloring the gray-scale images, that is, giving different colors to regions with different gray-scale values in the original gray-scale image to distinguish them more clearly. The input of pseudo-color enhancement is a gray-scale image, and the output is a color image. For further discussion of pseudo-color image enhancement technology, please refer to Ref. [5]. The false color has very similar literal meaning with pseudo-color, but its actual meaning is very different from pseudo-color. False-color enhancement is actually a kind of true-color enhancement. The specific contents of false-color enhancement can be found in Ref. [6] and also in Ref. [3].

4. True-color enhancement

True-color enhancement changes the visual effect of the original color image by separately mapping different components of the color image. Both the input and output of true-color enhancement are color images (vector images). In true-color enhancement, RGB images are often converted into HSI images to separate the luminance and chrominance components, and then these components are enhanced separately. When enhancing a true-color image, one can also consider its three components at the same time and use the point operation technique. For more discussion of true color image enhancement technology, please refer to Refs. [6,7].

Self-Test Questions

The following questions include both single- and multiple-choice questions, so each option should be individually judged.

6.1 Color Vision

6.1.1 The three complementary colors of light can be generated by the super-position of the three primary colors of light, including ( )

   (A) Yellow;
   (B) Purple;
   (C) Orange;
   (D) Magenta.

   [Hint] The three basic colors of light are red, green, and blue, and the three complementary colors of light are their pairwise combinations.

6.1.2 Which of the following method(s) can be used to obtain the three primary colors in a pigment? ( )

   (A) Blue + red, green + yellow, red + green;
   (B) Red + blue, green + blue, magenta + green;
   (C) Blue + red, green + blue, red + green;
   (D) Red + blue, green + red, blue + green.

   [Hint] The three primary colors in the pigment correspond to the three complementary colors of light.

6.1.3 Which of the following statement(s) on the chromaticity diagram is/are correct? ( )

(A) Any visible color in the chromaticity diagram occupies a certain position;

(B) The intensity of the point on the boundary of the chromaticity diagram is lower than the intensity of the center point;

(C) The point with zero purity in the chromaticity diagram corresponds to the point with the least saturation;

(D) The chromaticity diagram shows that any visible color can be composed of three primary colors.

[Hint] Analyze the meaning of each point in the chromaticity diagram.

6.1.4 Consider the marked points in Figure 6.1.4 (chromaticity diagram).

The correct one in the following statements is ( )

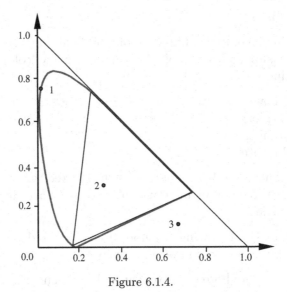

Figure 6.1.4.

(A) Points 1 and 2 are in the visible color region (inside the tongue shaped region) and Point 3 is in the invisible color region;

(B) Point 1 is in the region of visible color, Point 2 is in the color region composed of three primary colors of red, green, and blue, and Point 3 is in the region of invisible color;

(C) Points 1 and 2 are in the color region composed of three primary colors of red, green, and blue, and Point 3 is not in this color region;

(D) Point 2 is in the visible color region and Points 1 and 3 are in the invisible color region.

[Hint] The tongue-shaped part of the chromaticity diagram is the visible color region, and the triangle takes the three primary color coordinates as the vertex.

6.2 Color Model

6.2.1 A "3D histogram" can be created for a color image, this is because ( )

(A) The image itself is 3D;

(B) The color space used is 3D;

(C) The image can be represented by a 3D array;

(D) The histogram can be represented by a 3D array.

[Hint] A color image can be decomposed into three component images, and each image must be represented by three variables.

6.2.2 When $R = 0$, $G = 0$, $B = 1$, ( )

(A) $H = 120°$, $S = 0$;

(B) $H = 120°$, $S = 1$;

(C) $H = 240°$, $S = 0$;

(D) $H = 240°$, $S = 1$.

[Hint] Draw a cross-sectional view of the HSI model to help the judgement.

6.2.3 The color points with a saturation of one are all in the following plane of RGB color cube of Figure 6.3: ( )

(A) RG plane;

(B) RB plane;

(C) BG plane;

(D) RG plane, RB plane, and BG plane.

[Hint] If the saturation is one, one of R, G, B must be zero.

6.2.4 Given two points a and b of the RGB color cube, add their corresponding coordinates to get a new point, set as c. If the H, S, I values of these three points in the HSI coordinate system are represented by the point labels as subscripts, then we have ( )

(A) $I_c = I_a + I_b$;
(B) $S_c = S_a + S_b$;
(C) $S_c = S_a = S_b$;
(D) $H_c = H_a + H_b$.

[Hint] The transformation between two spaces is nonlinear.

6.2.5 The H, S, and I values of the points r and Y in the RGB color cube of Figure 6.3 are respectively ( )

(A) r: $H = 0°$, $S = 1$, $I = 1/3$; Y: $H = 60°$, $S = 1$, $I = 1/3$;
(B) r: $H = 0°$, $S = 1$, $I = 1/3$; Y: $H = 45°$, $S = 1$, $I = 1/3$;
(C) r: $H = 0°$, $S = 1$, $I = 1/3$; Y: $H = 60°$, $S = 1$, $I = 2/3$;
(D) r: $H = 0°$, $S = 1$, $I = 1/3$; Y: $H = 45°$, $S = 1$, $I = 2/3$.

[Hint] The H angle of Point Y is defined in HSI space.

6.2.6 Which of the following color model(s) is/are closest to the characteristics of the human visual system? ( )

(A) RGB model;
(B) CMY model;
(C) HSI model;
(D) CMYK model.

[Hint] The components of CMY model and CMYK model are all obtained by linear combination of the components of RGB model.

6.3 Pseudo-Color Enhancement

6.3.1 The transformation from gray to color can process the gray value of each pixel in the original image with three independent transformations. It is now known that the three transformation functions of red, green, and blue and the statistical histogram of the original image are as follows, as shown in the diagrams in Figure 6.3.1, which color component(s) is/are most in the converted color image? ( )

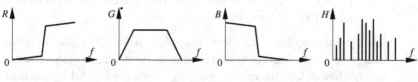

Figure 6.3.1.

(A) Unable to judge;
(B) Red;
(C) Green;
(D) Blue.

[Hint] Consider the output magnitude of the histogram after three color transformations.

6.3.2 The reasons why HSI model is suitable for image enhancement are ( )

(A) When using this model, the original image can be kept unchanged;
(B) When using this model, the intensity of visible details in the image can increased;
(C) When using this model, the luminance component and chrominance component can be separated for enhancement;
(D) When using this model, the hue component and the saturation component can be separated for enhancement.

[Hint] Consider the meaning of the three components in the HSI model.

6.3.3 Pseudo-color processing and false color processing are two different color enhancement processing methods. From the following various functions, please point out those that belong to pseudo-color enhancement processing: ( )

(A) Reproduce multi-spectral scenes with natural colors;
(B) Change the blue sky in the scene to red and the green grass to blue;

(C) Send the red, green, and blue color signals to the blue, red, and green display control channels, respectively;

(D) Send the signal of the gray-scale image through the frequency domain high-pass/low-pass filters to the red/blue color display control channel.

[Hint] False color considers mapping a single color original image or a set of multi-spectral images depicting the same scene to another color space; the original image processed by pseudo-color processing is not a color image, which is artificially colored to distinguish gray levels.

6.4 True-Color Enhancement

6.4.1 The output of true color image enhancement can be seen as a ( )

(A) Vector image;

(B) Gray image;

(C) Pseudo-color image;

(D) True color image.

[Hint] The pseudo-color image is also a color image.

6.4.2 For a color image, which of the following operation(s) can be performed directly on its attribute vector; it can also be performed on each attribute component separately and then combined? ( )

(A) Median filtering;

(B) Weighted neighborhood averaging;

(C) Linear sharpening filtering;

(D) Nonlinear sharpening filtering.

[Hint] Only linear operation can meet the conditions.

6.4.3 In single-component transformation enhancement, the most likely operation to make people feel that the image content has changed is ( )

(A) Enhancement of intensity;

(B) Enhancement of hue;

(C) Increased saturation;

(D) Not necessarily which kind of enhancement.

[Hint] The change in color hue has a relatively large impact on visual perception.

6.4.4 The gray-scale noise is superimposed on each component of an RGB color image and then the result is converted into three component images of H, S, and I. Here, ( )

(A) The noise in the H-component image is reduced compared to the original RGB color image;
(B) The noise in the S-component image is reduced compared to the original RGB color image;
(C) The noise in the I-component image is reduced compared to the original RGB color image;
(D) It is not necessarily that the noise in which component image is reduced compared to the original RGB color image.

[Hint] Consider the conversion equations from RGB to HSI.

6.4.5 To express the color characteristics of an object in the image, one can use ( )

(A) The histogram of the I component;
(B) The contour length of the object;
(C) The result of intensity slicing;
(D) The difference between the R-component histogram and the G-component histogram.

[Hint] The I component and the chrominance components are independent.

References

[1] Plataniotis, K. N. and Venetsanopoulos, A. N. *Color Image Processing and Applications*. Germany, Berlin: Springer, 2000.
[2] Zhang, Y.-J. *Image Engineering (III): Teaching References and Problem Solutions*. China, Beijing: Tsinghua University Press, 2002.
[3] Zhang, Y.-J. *Image Engineering, Vol. 1: Image Processing*. Germany, Berlin: De Gruyter, 2017.

[4] Yu, S. L. *Principles of Television*, 4th Edn. China, Beijing: National Defense Industry Press, 2012.

[5] Koschan, A. and Abidi, M. *Digital Color Image Processing*. USA, New Jersey: Wiley Publishing, Inc., 2009.

[6] Pratt, W. K. *Digital Image Processing: PIKS Scientific Inside*, 4th Edn. USA, Hoboken: Wiley Interscience, 2007.

[7] Gonzalez, R. C. and Woods, R. E. *Digital Image Processing*, 3rd Edn. USA, New Jersey: Pearson, 2008.

Chapter 7

Image Segmentation

Image segmentation refers to the technology and process of dividing an image into regions with common properties and extracting objects of interest. Image segmentation is a key step from image processing to image analysis, and it is also a basic computer vision technology. Image segmentation, object separation, feature extraction, and parameter measurement transform the original image into a more abstract and compact form, making higher-level analysis and understanding possible.

Image segmentation is a large category of image analysis technology, which has been highly valued for many years. The development of image segmentation technology is closely related to many other disciplines and fields. Since there is no universal theory for image segmentation so far, whenever a new mathematical tool or method is proposed, people try to use it for image segmentation, so many special or distinctive segmentation algorithms have been proposed. Some methods extract the object by analyzing and judging each pixel step by step, and some methods directly detect the desired object in the image. The latter method will be introduced in Chapter 8.

The sections of this chapter are arranged as follows:

Section 7.1 first introduces a more formal definition of image segmentation and then discusses the classification framework for various image segmentation techniques.

Section 7.2 discusses the image segmentation methods with differential calculation for object edge detection. Based on the analysis

219

of the principle of differential edge detection, the typical operators that are commonly used for first-order and second-order differential calculations based on masks are introduced.

Section 7.3 introduces a segmentation method that establishes an energy function and optimizes the energy function to adjust the closed curve to determine the precise contour of the object based on the preliminary initiation of a closed boundary of the object.

Section 7.4 introduces a method of separating object pixels and background pixels by selecting a threshold and comparing the pixel value with the threshold. In addition to explaining its principles and steps, some typical methods of determining thresholds are also discussed.

Section 7.5 first introduces a special region in the image—the transition region. Based on its characteristics, the typical method of threshold selection based on the transition region is analyzed.

Section 7.6 introduces a segmentation method that first determines individual pixels in the object and background regions and then gradually determines the attribution of neighboring pixels according to certain combination criteria until all pixels are classified.

7.1   Segmentation Definition and Method Classification

In the research and application of images, people are often only interested in certain parts of the image. These parts are often called **objects** or **foreground** (other parts are called **background**), and they generally correspond to specific regions of the image with unique properties. In order to identify and analyze the object, it is necessary to separate and extract these relevant regions. On this basis, it is possible to further use the object, such as feature extraction and measurement. Image segmentation should be carried out according to the properties of each region, where the properties can be gray scale, color, texture, etc. Image segmentation needs to extract the object; the object can correspond to a single region or multiple regions. Image segmentation has been highly valued for many years. So far, thousands of various types of segmentation algorithms have been proposed, and hundreds of relevant research reports have been published every year in recent years.

Example 7.1 Attention degree of image segmentation

Chapter 1 mentions a survey series of the image engineering literature. This survey series started in 1996 and has made statistics of the
image engineering literature published in 15 journals for 26 consecutive years. Table 1.1 showed the classification of the literature on
image technology categories in the survey, in which image analysis is
divided into five categories. Table 7.1 shows the statistics of the literature on these five types of technologies for the 26 years. Among them,
the total number of papers represents the total number of such papers
mentioned in the survey series. The annual average number of papers
is the average number for the corresponding years. The total ranking
refers to the ranking of the average number of this class of papers in
all image engineering sub-categories (23 sub-categories in total).

It can be seen from Table 7.1 that image segmentation technology is the most noteworthy hot spot and focus of image technology
research and application in the past 26 years, and it occupies the
most important part of the numerous research directions of image
engineering. □

7.1.1 Image segmentation definition

Image segmentation can be defined in a more formal way with the
help of the concept of set theory.

Table 7.1. Statistical result of image analysis literature classification.

Sub-categories	Total number of papers	Annual average number of papers	Total ranking
Image segmentation and primitive detection	1862	71.6	1
Object representation, object description, feature measurement	301	11.6	20
Object feature extraction and analysis	530	20.4	13
Object detection and object recognition	1523	58.6	2
Human body biological feature extraction and verification	1164	55.4	4

Let the set R represent the entire image region. The segmentation of R can be regarded as dividing R into several non-empty subsets (sub-regions) $R_1, R_2, \ldots, R_n$ that meet the following five conditions:

(1) $\bigcup_{i=1}^{n} R_i = R$;
(2) for all i and j, $i \neq j$, there is $R_i \cap R_j = \oslash$;
(3) for $i = 1, 2, \ldots, n$, $P(R_i) = \text{TRUE}$;
(4) for $i \neq j$, $P(R_i \cup R_j) = \text{FALSE}$;
(5) for $i = 1, 2, \ldots, n$, R_i is a connected region.

Here, $P(R_i)$ represents a specified property of all elements in the set R_i and $\oslash$ is the empty set.

The above Condition (1) indicates that the sum (union) of all sub-regions obtained by segmentation should be able to include all pixels in the image or the segmentation should divide each pixel in the image into a certain sub-region. Condition (2) indicates that these sub-regions do not overlap each other or that one pixel cannot belong to two different regions at the same time. Condition (3) points out that the pixels belonging to the same region obtained after segmentation should have certain common properties. Condition (4) indicates that the pixels belonging to different regions obtained after segmentation should have certain different properties. Condition (5) requires that the pixels in the same resultant sub-region should be connected. The image segmentation is always carried out according to some segmentation criteria. Condition (1) and Condition (2) indicate that the segmentation criteria should be applicable to all regions and all pixels, while Condition (3) and Condition (4) indicate that the segmentation criteria should help determine the representative characteristics of pixels in each region.

7.1.2   Image segmentation algorithm classification

Based on the above definitions and discussion, the segmentation algorithms can be classified as follows. First, the segmentation of grayscale images can often be based on two properties between pixel gray values: discontinuity and similarity. Pixels within regions generally have gray-value similarity, while pixels on the boundary between regions generally have gray-value discontinuities. Therefore, the segmentation algorithm can be divided into the boundary-based

Table 7.2. Classification table of segmentation algorithm.

Classification	Boundary (Discontinuity)	Region (Similarity)
Parallel Processing	(i) Parallel boundary category	(iii) Parallel region category
Serial Processing	(ii) Serial boundary category	(iv) Serial region category

algorithm that uses the gray-value discontinuity between regions and the region-based algorithm that uses the gray-value similarity within a region. Second, according to the different processing strategies in the segmentation process, segmentation algorithms can be divided into parallel algorithms and serial algorithms. In parallel algorithms, all judgments and decisions can be made independently and simultaneously, while in serial algorithms, the results of early processing can be used in subsequent processing. Generally, the computation time required for serial algorithms is often longer than that for parallel algorithms, but the robustness against noise is often stronger. The above two criteria do not overlap and complement each other, so the segmentation algorithm can be divided into four categories according to these two criteria (see Table 7.2): (i) parallel boundary category; (ii) serial boundary category; (iii) parallel region category; (iv) serial region category. This classification method can not only meet the five conditions of the above segmentation definition but also include all the various algorithms that have been proposed for image segmentation.

The following sections respectively introduce some basic and typical methods in these four types of technologies. Those belonging to category (i) are in Section 7.2, those belonging to category (ii) are in Section 7.3, those belonging to category (iii) are in Sections 7.4 and 7.5, and those belonging to category (iv) are in Section 7.6.

7.2 Differential Edge Detection

Edge detection is the key step of all boundary-based segmentation methods (including parallel boundary class and serial boundary class). An edge generally exists between two adjacent regions with different gray values, and the gray value has accelerated changes at the edge location.

7.2.1   Principle of differential edge detection

The **edge** is the result of the discontinuity of the gray value. This discontinuity can often be easily detected by differentiation or from the derivative. Generally, the first (-order) derivative and second (-order) derivative are commonly used to detect edges. Let's look at Figure 7.1. Row 1 provides some simplified example of images with edges; Row 2 shows the cross-sectional (profile) view along the horizontal direction of the image; Row 3 and Row 4 are the first and second derivatives of the corresponding cross section, respectively. Due to sampling, the edges in the digital image are always blurred, so the vertical edge profiles here are all represented as having a certain slope.

There are mainly three types of common edge profiles as follows: (i) **step edge**, as shown in Figures 7.1(a) and (b); (ii) **pulse edge**, as shown in Figure 7.1(c); (iii) **roof edge**, as shown in Figure 7.1(d). The step edge is located between two adjacent regions with different gray values in the image; the pulse edge mainly corresponds to the thin strip-shaped mutation region of the gray value, which can be seen as the two step edges in Figures 7.1(a) and (b) that are very close to each other; the rising and falling edges of the roof edge have

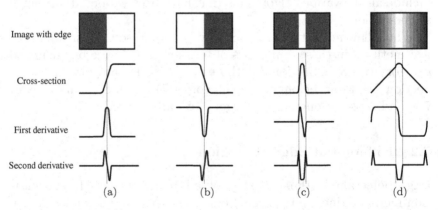

Figure 7.1.   Various edge profiles and corresponding derivatives.

some similarity with the pulse edge of Figure 7.1(c), but the degree of slope change is relatively small.

In Figure 7.1(a), the first derivative of the gray-value profile has an upward step at the position where the image changes from dark to light, and it is zero at other positions. This shows that the amplitude value of the first derivative can be used to detect the presence of an edge, and the peak amplitude generally corresponds to the edge position. For the second derivative of the gray-value profile, there is an upward pulse in the step-up region of the first derivative, and there is a downward pulse in the step-down region of the first derivative. There is a zero-crossing point between these two steps, and its position corresponds to the position of the edge in the original image. Therefore, the zero-crossing point of the second derivative can be used to detect the edge position, and the sign of the second-order derivative near the zero-crossing point can be used to determine the dark region or bright region of the edge pixel at the edge of the image. Similar conclusions can be obtained by analyzing Figure 7.1(b). Here, the image changes from bright to dark, so compared with Figure 7.1(a), the profile is swapped left and right, the first derivative is swapped up and down, and the second derivative is swapped left and right.

In Figure 7.1(c), the shape of cross section of the pulse edge is the same as the first derivative shape of Figure 7.1(a), so the first derivative shape of Figure 7.1(c) is the same as the second derivative of Figure 7.1(a), and its two second derivative zero-crossing points correspond to the rising and falling edges of the pulse, respectively. The range of the pulse can be determined by detecting the zero-crossing points of the two second-order derivatives of the pulse profile.

In Figure 7.1(d), the profile of the roof edge can be regarded as the expansion of the bottom of the pulse edge, so its first derivative can be obtained by pulling apart the rising edge and falling edge of the first derivative of pulse profile in Figure 7.1(c), and its second derivative can be obtained by pulling apart the rising edge and falling edge of the second derivative of pulse profile in Figure 7.1(c). The position of the roof edge can be determined by detecting the zero-crossing point of the first derivative of the roof edge profile.

The detection of the edges in the image can be done through convolution with the help of spatial differential operators. In fact, the differentiation in digital image is approximated by using the difference. In the following, some simple spatial differential operators are presented.

7.2.2   Gradient operator

The spatial differentiation can be achieved by calculating the first and second derivatives.

Gradient operator: The gradient corresponds to the first derivative, and the **gradient operator** is the first derivative operator. For a continuous function $f(x, y)$, its gradient at position (x, y) can be represented as a vector:

$$\nabla f(x, y) = [G_x \ G_y]^{\mathrm{T}} = \left[\frac{\partial f}{\partial x} \ \frac{\partial f}{\partial y} \right]^{\mathrm{T}}. \tag{7.1}$$

The magnitude (often abbreviated directly as gradient) and phase angle of this vector are

$$\mathrm{mag}(\nabla f) = [G_x^2 + G_y^2]^{1/2} \tag{7.2}$$

and

$$\phi(x, y) = \arctan\left(\frac{G_y}{G_x} \right), \tag{7.3}$$

respectively.

In practice, a convolution with a small region mask is often used to approximate the partial derivative in the above gradient calculations. One mask is needed for G_x and another mask is needed for G_y, so two masks are required to be combined to form a gradient operator. According to the size of the masks and the different values of the mask elements (coefficients), many different operators have been proposed. The simplest gradient operator is the **Roberts cross operator**, and its two 2×2 masks are shown in Figure 7.2(a). There are also **Prewitt operator** and **Sobel operator** that are more commonly used. They both use two 3×3 masks, as separately shown in Figures 7.2(b) and (c). Between the two, Sobel operator is the one with the better effect in general.

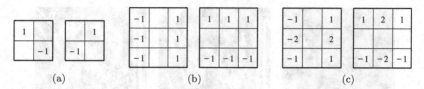

Figure 7.2.   Several commonly used masks of gradient operators.

Example 7.2 Comparison of directional gradient images

Figure 7.3 shows a set of directional gradient images calculated using the masks of the three gradient operators in Figure 7.2 on the image of Figure 1.4(a). In Figure 7.3, the upper ones are the horizontal direction gradient images and the lower ones are the vertical direction gradient images. The two images in Figure 7.3(a) were obtained by using the two Roberts masks of Figure 7.2(a); the two images in Figure 7.3(b) were obtained by using the two Prewitt masks in Figure 7.2(b). The two images in Figure 7.3(c) are obtained by using the two Sobel masks in Figure 7.2(c). It can be seen from these images that the edges obtained with the 2×2 mask are thinner and weaker, and the edges obtained with the 3×3 masks are thicker and stronger. Among the operators using the 3×3 masks, the Sobel operator has a stronger ability to detect weak edges than the Prewitt operator. If one compares the gradient images obtained by using the two masks of the same operator, one can clearly see the directionality of each mask from the spatial position and connectivity of the detected edge points. In other words, each mask would be the most sensitive to gradients in a certain direction. Horizontal masks have the strongest response to vertical edges, while vertical masks have the strongest response to horizontal edges, and the masks in both directions have a certain response to inclined edges.   □

In the computation of the gradient operator, it first uses a mode similar to convolution, that is, it moves each mask on the image and calculates the gradient value of the corresponding center pixel at each position, and then it combines the gradient values of the two masks with different norms to get the integrated gradient (amplitude) value. The norms used here can be seen in Equation (7.2) or Equations (3.19)–(3-21). The result of calculating the gradient (amplitude) value of a gray-scale image is a gradient (amplitude) image. Because the gradient calculation for each pixel is independent of each other,

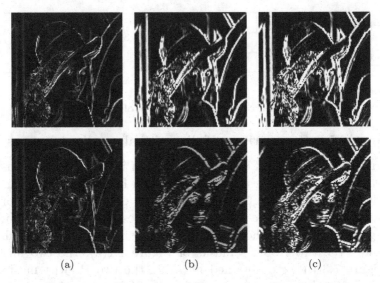

(a)   (b)   (c)

Figure 7.3.   Comparison of directional gradient images.

the calculation of the gradient image can be performed in parallel. When the transition of gray value at edge location is sharp and the noise in the image is relatively small, the gradient operator works quite well.

Example 7.3 Comparison of gradient amplitude images with different norms

Figure 1.4(b) shows an image with edges of various orientations. Figures 7.4(a) to (c) respectively show the gradient amplitude images for which the two masks of the Sobel operator are used to obtain gradient values in two orthogonal directions and the two gradient values are combined in turn using Equations (3.19)–(3.21). The gradient values have undergone a binarization in these three images. White represents a larger gradient value that exceeds the threshold, and black represents a smaller gradient value. Comparing these three images, it can be seen that although they are quite similar in general, the gradient with norm 2 is more sensitive than the gradients with norm 1 or norm ∞. For example, the left silhouette of the tower building in Figure 7.4(b) and the dome next to the tower building in Figure 7.4(c) have not been detected.   □

(a)   (b)   (c)

Figure 7.4.   Examples of gradient amplitude images with different norms.

2. Laplacian operator

The **Laplacian operator** is a kind of second-order derivative operator. For the image $f(x, y)$, its Laplacian value at the position (x, y) is defined as follows:

$$\nabla^2 f = \frac{\partial^2 f}{\partial x^2} + \frac{\partial^2 f}{\partial y^2}. \tag{7.4}$$

In digital images, the calculation of the Laplacian value can also be realized with the help of various masks. The basic requirements for the mask here are that the coefficient corresponding to the central pixel should be positive and the coefficient corresponding to the neighboring pixels of the central pixel should be negative, and the sum of all these coefficients should be zero. The three commonly used typical masks are shown in Figures 7.5(a)–(c), and they all meet the above requirements. The Laplacian operator is a second-order derivative operator, so it is quite sensitive to noise in the image. In addition, it often produces double-pixel-wide edges, and it cannot provide edge direction information. For the above reasons, the Laplacian operator is mainly used to determine whether the edge pixel is on the dark or bright side of the edge in the image after the edge pixel is known, but sometimes it can also be used to detect the location of the edge, according to the nature of the zero-crossing point (see Figure 7.1).

Example 7.4. Edge detection with Laplacian operator

Two images obtained by using the two masks of Figures 7.5(a) and (b) respectively for edge detection on the image of Figure 1.4(a) are

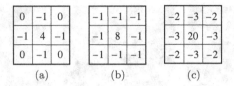

Figure 7.5.   Masks of the Laplacian operator.

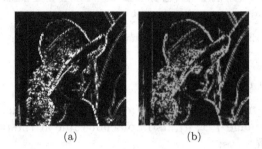

(a)   (b)

Figure 7.6.   Edge points detected by the masks of the Laplacian operator.

shown in Figures 7.6(a) and (b). In Figures 7.6(a) and (b), the zero-crossing points are white and the rest are black. Comparing these two images, the mask in Figure 7.5(b) gives more edge points and a greater intensity. Compared with the gradient images obtained by using various gradient operators in Figure 7.3, the edges detected here are more affected by noise and are not very continuous.   □

In practice, the image can be convolved with the Laplacian of the following 2D Gaussian function to eliminate noise:

$$h(x, y) = \exp\left(-\frac{x^2 + y^2}{2\sigma^2}\right), \tag{7.5}$$

where σ is the mean square error of the Gaussian distribution. If we let $r^2 = x^2 + y^2$ and calculate the Laplace value by finding the second derivative of r, then we have

$$\nabla^2 h = \left(\frac{r^2 - \sigma^2}{\sigma^4}\right) \exp\left(-\frac{r^2}{2\sigma^2}\right). \tag{7.6}$$

This is an axisymmetric function, and its profile is shown in Figure 7.7. It can be seen from the figure that this function curve has a zero-crossing point at $r = \pm\sigma$, which is positive when $|r < \sigma|$ and negative when $|r > \sigma|$.

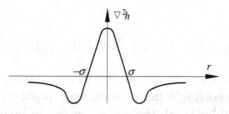

Figure 7.7. Profile of $\nabla^2 h$.

With the help of the function in Equation (7.6), the **Marr operator** can be further constructed for edge detection. It can be proved that the average value of this operator is also zero. If this operator is convolved with the image, it will not change the overall gray-scale range of the image. On the other hand, since the function is quite smooth (see Figure 7.7), if it is convolved with the image, the image will be blurred, and the degree of blur is proportional to σ. Because the smoothing property of $\nabla^2 h$, it can reduce the influence of noise. Therefore, when the edge is blurred or the noise is large, the use of $\nabla^2 h$ for detecting the zero-crossing point can provide a more reliable edge position. This is the advantage of the Marr operator but its computation complexity is relatively large.

7.3 Active Contour Model

The **active contour model** approximates the contour of the object in the image by gradually changing the shape of the closed curve. In this process, each part of the object contour is often represented by straight line segments. The active contour model is also called the **snake model** because in the process of approximating the object contour, the closed curve continuously changes its shape like a snake crawling. In practice, the active contour model is often used to detect an accurate contour when an approximate initial contour of the true object contour in the image is given.

7.3.1 Active contour

An **active contour** is a set of ordered points on the image, which can be represented as

$$V = \{v_1, v_2, \ldots, v_L\}, \tag{7.7}$$

where

$$v_i = (x_i, y_i) \quad i = 1, 2, \ldots, L. \tag{7.8}$$

The points on the contour can iteratively approach the boundary of the object by solving a minimum energy problem. For each point $v_i{}'$ in the v_i neighborhood, the energy term can be calculated as

$$E_i(v_i') = \alpha E_{\text{int}}(v_i') + \beta E_{\text{ext}}(v_i'). \tag{7.9}$$

In this equation, $E_{\text{int}}(\bullet)$ is the **energy function** dependent on the contour shape, $E_{\text{ext}}(\bullet)$ is the energy function dependent on the image properties, and α and β are weighting constants.

Now, Figure 7.8 is used to explain the working principle and steps of the active contour model. The lower-left corner of the figure is a part of the actual object, and its outline is represented by a solid line. The dotted line represents the deformable active contour, which is set in the initial state here (simply set with a part of the elliptical arc).

Segmentation with active contour is the process of approximating the actual contour of the object with points on the contour. This process is a serial process. First, the point v_0 on the active contour is made coincident with the actual contour, and then the points $(v_i, v_{i+1}, \ldots)$ are moved to the actual contour (as shown by the arrows) according to the energy function (see the following). This is an iterative approximation process. If the energy function is properly selected, through continuous adjustment and approximation, the active contour should finally stop on the actual contour of the object (corresponding to the minimum energy).

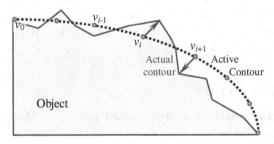

Figure 7.8.   Movement of points on the active contour.

7.3.2 Energy function

Solving the active contour problem is achieved iteratively by solving a minimum energy problem. How to define and determine the energy term could be critical. The energy function takes the active contour as a reference and can be divided into the internal energy function and external energy function.

1. Internal energy

The **internal energy function** is mainly used to promote the change of the active contour shape and to keep the distance between the points on the contour not too far or too close.

Here is an example to describe this process. Define the energy function as

$$\alpha E_{\text{int}}(v_i) = c E_{\text{con}}(v_i) + b E_{\text{bal}}(v_i). \tag{7.10}$$

In this equation, $E_{\text{con}}(\bullet)$ is called **continuous energy**, which is used to promote the change of the shape of the active contour (everywhere); $E_{\text{bal}}(\bullet)$ is called the **expansion force**, which is used to expand or contract the active contour (in the radial direction); c and b are weighting coefficients.

(1) *Continuous energy*

When there are no other factors, the function of continuous energy is to force an unclosed curve into a straight line, while a closed curve into a ring. Define $E_{\text{con}}(v_i{}')$ as follows (note that the energy is proportional to the square of the distance):

$$E_{\text{con}}(v_i') = \frac{1}{I(V)} \|v_i' - \gamma(v_{i-1} + v_{i+1})\|^2. \tag{7.11}$$

In Equation (7.11), γ is the weighting coefficient and the normalization factor $I(V)$ is the average distance between the points in V:

$$I(V) = \frac{1}{L} \sum_{i=1}^{L} \|v_{i+1} - v_i\|^2. \tag{7.12}$$

Using this normalization can make $E_{\text{con}}(v_i)$ independent of the size and position of the points and the orientation between the points in V.

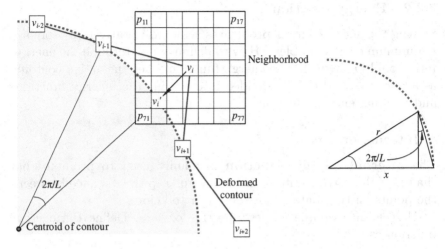

Figure 7.9.   Points on the active contour move due to continuous energy.

For an open curve, take $\gamma = 0.5$. At this time, the minimum energy point is the midpoint between v_{i-1} and v_{i+1}. For a closed curve, the value of V has modulo L. Thus, $v_{L+i} = v_i$. Now, let us define

$$\gamma = \frac{1}{2\cos(2\pi/L)}. \tag{7.13}$$

Here, the point with the smallest energy in $E_{\text{con}}(v_i')$ moves radially outward, causing V to become a ring. This process is shown in Figure 7.9. The point v_i' is at the position of minimum energy because it is on the arc connecting v_{i-1} and v_{i+1}.

(2) *Expansion force*

Expansion force can be used on the closed deformed contour to force the contour to expand or contract without external force. A contour initialized inside a uniform image region will expand under the action of the expansion force until it approaches the edge of the region (the external force at the edge point will affect its movement). Figure 7.10 shows a schematic diagram. Since the object region has a uniform gray value, an expansion force is required to push the active contour to the object boundary.

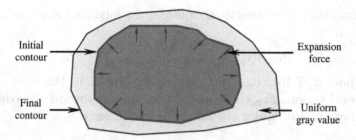

Figure 7.10.   Point movements on the active contour due to the expansion force.

The adaptive expansion force that is inversely proportional to the gradient of the image can be constructed. This adaptive expansion force is stronger in the uniform gray-level region but weaker at the edges and boundaries of the object region. $E_{\mathrm{bal}}(v_i{}')$ can be represented as an inner product (here, the difference between the positions of two points is regarded as the vector of their coordinate difference):

$$E_{\mathrm{bal}}(v_i') = \boldsymbol{n}_i \bullet [\boldsymbol{v}_i - \boldsymbol{v}_i']. \tag{7.14}$$

In this equation, $\boldsymbol{n}_i$ is the unit normal vector outward along V at point v_i. The expansion force is smallest at the point farthest from v_i in the direction of $\boldsymbol{n}_i$. Vector $\boldsymbol{n}_i$ can be obtained by rotating the tangent vector $\boldsymbol{t}_i$ by $90°$, and $\boldsymbol{t}_i$ can be conveniently obtained as follows:

$$\boldsymbol{t}_i = \frac{v_i - v_{i-1}}{\|v_i - v_{i-1}\|} + \frac{v_{i+1} - v_i}{\|v_{i+1} - v_i\|}. \tag{7.15}$$

The adaptive expansion force can be scaled with the help of the image gradient at point v_i (see the discussion on external energy in the following).

2. External energy

The **external energy function** attracts the deformed contour to the features of interest, where the features of interest are often the edges of the object in the image. Any form of energy representation that can achieve this purpose can be used. Image gradient and gray scale are the most commonly used to construct the energy function, and sometimes the size and shape of the object can also be used to construct the energy function. Consider the following external energy function:

$$\beta E_{\text{ext}}(v_i) = m E_{\text{mag}}(v_i) + g E_{\text{grad}}(v_i). \tag{7.16}$$

In Equation (7.16), $E_{\text{mag}}(v_i)$ draws the contour to the high or low gray-level region. $E_{\text{grad}}(v_i)$ pushes the contour toward the edges or boundary, and m and g are weighting coefficients.

(1) Image gray-level energy

The **image gray level energy function** $E_{\text{mag}}(v_i')$ can take the gray level of the corresponding point:

$$E_{\text{mag}}(v_i') = I(v_i'). \tag{7.17}$$

If m is positive, the contour will move to the low gray-level region; if m is negative, the contour will move to the high gray-level region.

(2) Image gradient energy

The **image gradient energy function** draws the deformed contour to the edge of the image. The energy representation proportional to the gradient magnitude is $|\nabla I(v_i')|$. When the active contours are used to detect object contours, the energy functions that can distinguish the boundaries between adjacent objects are often required. The key here is to use the direction of the gradient at the edges of the object. Furthermore, the direction of the gradient at the edges of the object should be close to the unit normal direction of the contour. Refer to Figure 7.9. Assuming that the gradient direction at the boundary of the object of interest is close to the direction of the contour unit normal, then the active contour algorithm will move the contour point $v_i = p_{44}$ to $v_i' = p_{62}$ (the subscript corresponds to the row and column positions). Here, the gradient energy $E_{\text{grad}}(v_i')$ will be assigned by the inner product of the unit normal vector at the corresponding point and the image gradient vector:

$$E_{\text{grad}}(v_i') = -n_i \bullet \nabla I(v_i'). \tag{7.18}$$

3. Normalization

The energy function described above needs to be scaled to make the neighborhood matrix contain comparable coefficient values.

This process is called **normalization** (regularization). Generally, the value of each energy function should be normalized to the interval [0, 1].

In practice, it is often necessary to adjust the expansion energy to adapt to the image gradient. The normalization parameters should be added to the energy terms of gray level and gradient to stabilize the active contour algorithm.

(1) *Continuous energy*

At each point on the deformed contour, the corresponding continuous energy can be scaled to the interval [0, 1] as follows:

$$E'_{\text{con}}(v_i) = \frac{E_{\text{con}}(v_i) - E_{\text{min}}(v_i)}{E_{\text{max}}(v_i) - E_{\text{min}}(v_i)}. \qquad (7.19)$$

In Equation (7.19), $E_{\text{min}}(v_i)$ and $E_{\text{max}}(v_i)$ are the elements with minimum value and maximum value in $E_{\text{con}}(v_i)$, respectively.

(2) *Expansion energy*

The expansion energy is first scaled to the interval [0, 1] and then adjusted according to the image gradient:

$$E'_{\text{bal}}(v_i) = \frac{E_{\text{bal}}(v_i) - E_{\text{min}}(v_i)}{E_{\text{max}}(v_i) - E_{\text{min}}(v_i)} \left[1 - \frac{|\nabla I(v_i)|}{|\nabla I|_{\text{max}}}\right]. \qquad (7.20)$$

In Equation (7.20), $E_{\text{min}}(v_i)$ and $E_{\text{max}}(v_i)$ are the elements with minimum value and maximum value in $E_{\text{bal}}(v_i)$, respectively and $|\nabla I|_{\text{max}}$ is the maximum gradient value in the entire image.

(3) *Gray-level energy*

For normalization, a coefficient k is added to the gray-level energy term, namely:

$$E'_{\text{mag}}(v_i) = \frac{E_{\text{mag}}(v_i) - E_{\text{min}}(v_i)}{\max[E_{\text{max}}(v_i) - E_{\text{min}}(v_i), kI_{\text{max}}]}. \qquad (7.21)$$

In Equation (7.21), $E_{\text{min}}(v_i)$ and $E_{\text{max}}(v_i)$ are the elements with minimum value and maximum value in $E_{\text{mag}}(v_i)$, respectively and I_{max} is the maximum gray level in the whole image. The value range of k is $[0, \infty)$, which determines the sensitivity of the active contour to the local change of the image gray level.

(4) *Gradient energy*

The normalization of gradient energy can use the same method as the normalization of gray-level energy (adding a coefficient l):

$$E'_{\text{grad}}(v_i) = \frac{E_{\text{grad}}(v_i) - E_{\text{min}}(v_i)}{\max[E_{\text{max}}(v_i) - E_{\text{min}}(v_i), l|\nabla I|_{\text{max}}]}. \qquad (7.22)$$

In Equation (7.22), the value range of l is also $[0, \infty)$; a large l will cause the active contour to be more sensitive to weak edges.

7.4   Thresholding Segmentation

Thresholding is the most common parallel method for segmentation, which directly detects the required regions. Other similar methods, such as pixel feature space classification, can be regarded as the extension of thresholding technology.

7.4.1   Principles and steps

Assuming that the image is composed of an object and a background, each with a unimodal gray-scale distribution, the gray values between adjacent pixels inside the object or background are highly correlated (with similarity), but the pixels on both sides of the boundary between the object and the background have a big difference in gray value (with discontinuity). If an image satisfies these conditions, its gray-scale histogram can basically be regarded as a mixture of two unimodal histograms corresponding to the object and background, respectively. Here, if the two distributions are close in size (number of pixels), their means are far enough apart, and the mean square error is small enough, the image histogram should be bimodal. For this kind of images, the threshold method can often be used for better segmentation.

The simplest method to use threshold to segment gray-scale images is as follows. First, determine a gray level threshold $T(0 < T < L - 1)$ for an image with the gray values between 0 and $L - 1$, then compare the gray value of each pixel in the image with the threshold T, and divide the corresponding pixels into two categories according to the comparison result: the pixel whose gray value is greater than the threshold value belongs to one type and the pixel whose gray value is less than the threshold value belongs to the other type (pixels with gray value equal to the threshold value can fall into one of these two categories). These two types of pixels generally correspond to two types of regions in the image. In the above steps, determining the threshold is the key. If an appropriate threshold can be determined, the image can be easily segmented.

No matter what method is used to select the threshold, the image segmented by a single threshold can be defined as

$$g(x, y) = \begin{cases} 1 & \text{if } f(x, y) > T \\ 0 & \text{if } f(x, y) \leq T. \end{cases} \tag{7.23}$$

It should be noted that the information about the spatial distribution of image pixels is not used in the threshold segmentation (only the pixel gray value information is used). A direct result is that if there are multiple disconnected objects in the image, the result of segmentation will be multiple disconnected regions. In other words, threshold segmentation does not necessarily guarantee that the object is one connected region.

Example 7.5 Single threshold segmentation example

Figure 7.11 shows an example of single threshold segmentation. Figure 7.11(a) represents an image with multiple regions of different gray values; Figure 7.11(b) represents its histogram, where z represents the image gray value and T is the threshold for segmentation;

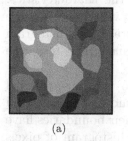
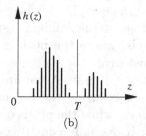
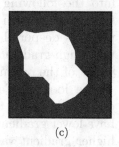

(a) (b) (c)

Figure 7.11. Single threshold segmentation diagram.

Figure 7.11(c) represents the result of segmentation. Pixels larger than the threshold are displayed in white, and pixels smaller than the threshold are displayed in black.   □

7.4.2   Threshold selection

The easiest way to select the **threshold** with the help of histogram is the minimum method. If the envelope of the histogram is regarded as a curve, the valley of the histogram can be selected by finding the minimum value of the curve. Let $h(z)$ represent the histogram, then the minimum point should satisfy

$$\frac{\partial h(z)}{\partial z} = 0 \quad \text{and} \quad \frac{\partial^2 h(z)}{\partial z^2} > 0. \tag{7.24}$$

The gray value corresponding to the minimum point can be used as the segmentation threshold.

In practical applications, the image is often affected by noise, etc., so that the valleys between the originally separated peaks in the histogram are filled, making it difficult to directly detect the valleys. To solve this kind of problem, the local properties of some pixel neighborhoods can be used. Two methods of using pixel gradient values for this purpose are described in the following.

1. Histogram transformation

The basic idea of **histogram transformation** is to use the local properties of some pixel neighborhoods to transform the original histogram to obtain a new histogram. The new histogram can be divided into the following two categories according to the characteristics: (i) histogram with low-gradient pixels, where the valley between the peaks is deeper than that of the original histogram; (ii) histogram with high-gradient pixels, where the peak is transformed from the valley of the original histogram.

We look at Category (i) first. According to the image model described above, the pixels inside the object and the background have lower gradient values, while the pixels on their boundaries have higher gradient values. If one only constructs a histogram of pixels with low gradient values, the peaks corresponding to the internal points in this new histogram should be basically unchanged compared to the original histogram, but because some boundary points are reduced, the valley should be deeper than that of the original histogram.

More generally, a weighted histogram can be calculated, in which pixels with low gradient values are assigned more weight. For example, if the gradient value of a pixel point is g, it can be weighted by $1/(1+g)^2$ when the histogram is counted. In this way, if the gradient value of the pixel is zero, it gets the maximum weight (1); if the pixel has a very large gradient value, the weight it gets becomes negligible. In such a weighted histogram, the peaks are basically unchanged and the valleys become deeper, so the peak–valley gap increases (see Figure 7.12(a), the dashed line is the original histogram); in this case, the valley is easier to be detected and then the segmentation threshold is determined.

The Category (ii) is contrary to the Category (i), a histogram with only high-gradient pixels is to be constructed. This histogram has a peak at the gray level of the boundary (between the object and background) pixels (see Figure 7.12(b), the dashed line is the original histogram). This peak is mainly composed of boundary pixels, then the gray value corresponding to this peak can be selected as a threshold for segmentation.

More generally, a weighted histogram can also be calculated, but pixels with high gradient values are given more weight here. For example, the gradient value g of each pixel can be used as the weight assigned to the pixel. In this way, pixels with a gradient value of zero need not be considered when the histogram is counted, and pixels with a large gradient value will get a larger weight.

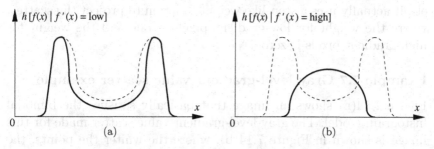

Figure 7.12. Examples of transformed histogram.

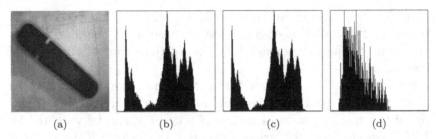

(a)   (b)   (c)   (d)

Figure 7.13.   Examples of transformed histogram.

Example 7.6 Histogram transformation examples

Figure 7.13 shows an example with a set of transformed histograms. Figure 7.13(a) is the original image; Figure 7.13(b) is its histogram; Figures 7.13(c) and (d) are the histograms with low gradient pixels and high gradient pixels, respectively. Comparing Figures 7.13(b) and (c), it can be seen that the valley is deeper in the low-gradient histogram, while comparing Figures 7.13(b) and (d), it can be seen that the highest peak basically corresponds to the original valley.   □

2. Gray level-gradient value scatter

The histogram transformation method introduced above can be obtained by establishing a 2D scatter of gray level versus gradient value and calculating the projection of different weights on the gray-level axis. This **gray level-gradient value scatter** can also be called a 2D histogram, in which one axis is the gray-level axis and the other is the gradient value axis, and its statistical value is the number of pixels with certain gray levels and certain gradient values. For example, when making a histogram with only low-gradient pixels, it actually uses a step-like weight function to project the scatter, where the weight for low-gradient pixels is one and the weight for high-gradient pixels is zero.

Example 7.7 Gray level-gradient value scatter example

Figure 7.14(a) shows an image that basically satisfies the bimodal histogram model. The gray level-gradient value scatter made for this image is shown in Figure 7.14(b), where the whiter the points, the more pixels that meet the conditions.

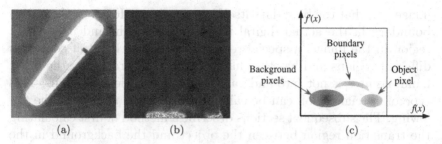

Figure 7.14. A real example of gray level-gradient value scatter.

Figure 7.14(c) shows a real example of a typical gray level-gradient value scatter. The scatter generally has two large clusters close to the gray-level axis (low gradient value) but separated from each other along the gray-level axis. They correspond to the pixels inside the object and the background, respectively. The shape of these two clusters is related to the degree of correlation of these pixels. If the correlation is strong or the gradient operator is not very sensitive to noise, these clusters will be concentrated and close to the gray-level axis. Conversely, if the correlation is weak or the gradient operator is sensitive to noise, these clusters will have some distance from the gray-level axis. There will be fewer points corresponding to the pixels on the boundary between the object and the background in the scatter. The positions of these points are in the middle of the first two clusters along the gray-level axis, but there is a certain distance from the gray-level axis along the gradient value axis due to the larger gradient value. The distribution of these points is related to the shape of the contour and the type of gradient operator. If the boundary edge is sloped and a first-order differential operator is used, then the clustering of boundary pixels will be connected to the clustering of the object and background. This cluster will move away from the gray-level axis in proportion to the edge slope. According to the distribution of pixels in different regions in the scatter, a combination of gray threshold and gradient threshold can be used to separate these clusters. ☐

7.5 Threshold Selection Based on Transition Region

Generally, when discussing region-based and boundary-based algorithms, it is considered that the union of regions covers the entire image and that the boundary itself has no width. However, the object boundary in the actual digital image has a width, and it is also a region in the image, a special region. On the one hand, it separates different regions and has the characteristics of borders; on the other hand, its area is not zero and has the characteristics of regions. This type of special region can be called a **transition region** in the following. The subsequent sections describe a method of first calculating the transition region between the object and the background in the image and then further selecting a threshold for segmentation.

7.5.1   Transition region and effective average gradient

The transition region can be determined by calculating the **effective average gradient** (EAG) of the image and clipping the gray level of the image. Let $f(i, j)$ represent the digital image function in 2D space, where i, j represent the pixel space coordinates and f represents the gray value of the pixel, and they all belong to the integer set Z. Let $g(i, j)$ represent the gradient image of $f(i, j)$, which can be obtained by applying a gradient operator to $f(i, j)$, then EAG can be defined as

$$\text{EAG} = \frac{\text{TG}}{\text{TP}}, \tag{7.25}$$

where

$$\text{TG} = \sum_{i,j \in Z} g(i, j) \tag{7.26}$$

is the total gradient value of the gradient image, and

$$\text{TP} = \sum_{i,j \in Z} p(i, j) \tag{7.27}$$

is the total number of non-zero gradient value pixels because here, $p(i, j)$ is defined as

$$p(i, j) = \begin{cases} 1 & \text{if } g(i, j) > 0 \\ 0 & \text{if } g(i, j) = 0. \end{cases} \tag{7.28}$$

From this definition, it can be seen that only pixels with non-zero gradient value are used when calculating EAG, and the effect of zero-gradient value pixels is neglected, so it is called "effective" gradient.

EAG is the average gradient of non-zero gradient value pixels in the image, and it represents a selective statistic of the image.

Further, in order to reduce the influence of various interferences, the following special clip transformation is defined. The difference between it and the general clip operation is that it sets the clipped part to the clipping value, which avoids the adverse effects of the large contrast caused by the general clip operation on the clipped edge. According to the relationship between the gray value of the clipped part and the gray value of the whole image, this type of clip can be divided into high-end clip and low-end clip. Let L be the clipping value; the clipping results can be represented as

$$f_{\text{high}}(i,j) = \begin{cases} L & \text{if } f(i,j) \geq L \\ f(i,j) & \text{if } f(i,j) < L, \end{cases} \tag{7.29}$$

$$f_{\text{low}}(i,j) = \begin{cases} f(i,j) & \text{if } f(i,j) > L \\ L & \text{if } f(i,j) \leq L. \end{cases} \tag{7.30}$$

If the gradient of the image after such clipping is obtained, the gradient function must be related to the clipping value L, and the resulting EAG becomes the function of the clipping value L, that is, $\text{EAG}(L)$. Note that $\text{EAG}(L)$ is also related to the clipping modes. $\text{EAG}(L)$ corresponding to high-end clipping and low-end clipping can be written as $\text{EAG}_{\text{high}}(L)$ and $\text{EAG}_{\text{low}}(L)$, respectively.

7.5.2 Extreme points of effective average gradient and boundary of transition region

The typical $\text{EAG}_{\text{high}}(L)$ and $\text{EAG}_{\text{low}}(L)$ curves are single-peak curves, that is, they both have an extreme value, which can be obtained by analyzing TG and TP. See Figure 7.15, $\text{EAG}_{\text{low}}(L)$ is the ratio of $\text{TG}_{\text{low}}(L)$ to $\text{TP}_{\text{low}}(L)$.

Both $\text{TG}_{\text{low}}(L)$ and $\text{TP}_{\text{low}}(L)$ decrease with the increase of L. $\text{TP}_{\text{low}}(L)$ is reduced because a large L will clip out more pixels. $\text{TG}_{\text{low}}(L)$ is reduced for two reasons: one is the decrease in the number of pixels and the other is the decrease in the contrast between the remaining pixels. When L increases from 0, the $\text{TG}_{\text{low}}(L)$ and $\text{TP}_{\text{low}}(L)$ curves both decrease from their respective maximums. At the beginning, the $\text{TG}_{\text{low}}(L)$ curve drops relatively slowly because the clipped pixels belong to the background (the gradient is small),

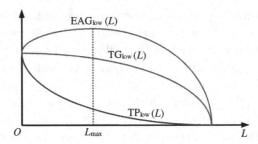

Figure 7.15.   Interpretation of $\text{EAG}_{\text{low}}(L)$ curve: it is a single-peak curve.

while the $\text{TP}_{\text{low}}(L)$ curve drops relatively fast, because the number of pixels clipped out is constantly reduced with the increase of clip level L. The combined effect of these two factors will gradually increase the value of $\text{EAG}_{\text{low}}(L)$ and make it reach a maximum value. Then, the $\text{TG}_{\text{low}}(L)$ curve will drop faster than the $\text{TP}_{\text{low}}(L)$ curve because more pixels with large gradients will be clipped, thus resulting in a decrease in the $\text{EAG}_{\text{low}}(L)$ value.

Suppose the extreme points of the $\text{EAG}_{\text{high}}(L)$ curve and $\text{EAG}_{\text{low}}(L)$ curve are L_{high} and L_{low}, respectively, then

$$L_{\text{high}} = \arg\left\{ \max_L[\text{EAG}_{\text{high}}(L)] \right\}, \tag{7.31}$$

$$L_{\text{low}} = \arg\left\{ \max_L[\text{EAG}_{\text{low}}(L)] \right\}. \tag{7.32}$$

The extreme points of the two $\text{EAG}_{\text{high}}(L)$ and $\text{EAG}_{\text{low}}(L)$ curves calculated above correspond to two special values in the image gray-value set, and they can be used to determine the transition region. In fact, the transition region is a 2D region delimited by two boundaries, in which the gray value of the pixel is defined by the two boundary gray values of the 1D gray-level spaces (see Figure 7.16). The gray values of these two boundaries are L_{high} and L_{low}, respectively, or they define the range of the gray value for transition region.

These two extreme points have three important properties:

(1) For each transition region, L_{high} and L_{low} always exist and only one of each (unique) exists.
(2) The gray values corresponding to L_{high} and L_{low} have obvious ability to distinguish pixel characteristics.

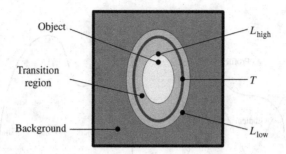

Figure 7.16.   Diagram of transition region.

(3) For the same transition region, L_{high} will not be smaller than L_{low}, and L_{high} is always greater than L_{low} in the actual image.

7.5.3   Threshold selection

Since the transition region is located between the object and the background, and the boundary between the object and the background is inside the transition region, so the transition region can be used for the segmentation. The most direct way is to use the transition region to help select the threshold. First, because the gray values of the pixels contained in the transition region are generally between the gray values of the pixels in the object region and in the background region, a threshold for segmentation can be determined based on these pixels. For example, the average gray value of the pixels in the transition region or the extreme peak values of the histogram of the pixels in the transition region can be taken. Second, since L_{high} and L_{low} define the upper and lower bounds of the gray value of the boundary line, the threshold can also be calculated directly with their help. In addition, the spatial characteristics of the transition region can also be used. Since the transition region is a band-shaped region surrounding the boundary of the object (as shown in Figure 7.16), this region can also be refined or thinned (such as using the **central axis transformation** or seeking the **skeleton**; see Section 9.6) to get the object contour.

The three important properties of the two extreme points indicated above are also valid when there are more than one transition region in the image. Now, look at Figure 7.17, where the

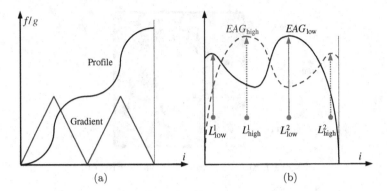

Figure 7.17.   A situation with multiple transition regions.

profile in Figure 7.17(a) has two steps (corresponding to two transition regions), reflecting the two peaks on the gradient curve. Figure 7.17(b) shows the resulting $\text{EAG}_{\text{high}}(L)$ and $\text{EAG}_{\text{low}}(L)$ curves with two sets of extreme points. It can be seen that for the same transition region, the above three important properties of the extreme point still hold. Therefore, the above-described method based on the transition region can not only be used to determine a single threshold to perform binary segmentation of an image but also to determine multiple thresholds to perform multi-threshold segmentation of an image.

7.6   Region Growing

Region growing is a basic serial region segmentation technology, which uses serial processing strategies to achieve image segmentation through direct determination of object regions. The characteristic of the serial segmentation method is to decompose the entire processing procedure into multiple steps in sequence, and the processing of the subsequent steps should be determined according to the processing results of the previously completed steps. The judgment here is based on certain criteria. Generally, if the criterion is based on the gray-scale characteristics of the image, this method can be used for the segmentation of gray-scale images. If the criterion is based on other characteristics of the image (such as texture), the method can also be used for the segmentation of the corresponding image.

7.6.1 Basic method

The basic idea of **region growing** is to combine pixels with similar properties to form regions. Specifically, first find a seed pixel for each region that needs to be segmented as the starting point of growing, then select pixels in the neighborhood around the seed pixel that have the same or similar properties as the seed pixel (determined according to some predetermined growing or similarity criteria) and merge these pixels into the region where the seed pixel is located. Use these new pixels as new seed pixels to continue the above merging process until no more pixels meeting the conditions can be included. In this way, a region can be grown. It can be seen that there are three problems to be solved in the actual application of the region growing method:

(1) Select or determine a group of seed pixels that can correctly represent the required regions.
(2) Determine the similarity criterion that can include adjacent pixels in the growing process.
(3) Establish the conditions or rules for ending the growing process.

The selection of seed pixels can generally be carried out with the help of the characteristics of specific segmentation problems. For example, when detecting a target in a military infrared image, because the target radiation is usually large, the brightest pixel in the image can be selected as the seed pixel. If there is no prior knowledge about a specific problem, it is often possible to calculate each pixel with the help of the criterion used for growing. If the calculation result shows clustering distribution, the pixel close to the center of gravity of the cluster can be taken as the seed pixel.

One of the key points in region growing is to select appropriate growing or similarity criteria. The selection of growing criteria not only depends on the specific problem itself but also on the type of image data used. Growing criteria can be formulated according to different principles, and the use of different growing criteria will affect the process of region growing. The method based on the criterion of gray-value difference mainly has the following steps:

(1) Scan the image line by line to find out the pixels that are not yet belonging to any clusters.

(2) Check its neighborhood pixels with the pixel as the center, that is, compare the pixels in the neighborhood with it one by one, and if the gray-scale difference is less than a predetermined threshold, merge these neighboring pixels.

(3) With the newly merged pixel as the center, return to step (2) and check the neighborhood of the new pixel until the region cannot be expanded further.

(4) Return to step (1) and continue scanning the image until no pixel that is not belonging to any cluster can be found, then end the entire growing process.

Example 7.8 Region growing example

Figure 7.18 shows an example of region growing with known seed pixels. Figure 7.18(a) shows the image to be segmented by region growing. It is assumed that there are two seed pixels (marked as gray squares with different shades), in the respective regions to be grown. Here, the selection of seed pixels can be carried out with the help of the histogram of the image. From the histogram, it can be seen that the numbers of pixels with gray values of 1 and 5 are the most, and these pixels are in the center of the cluster, so one can select one of each with the gray value of the cluster center as seeds. It is assumed that the growing judgment criterion adopted here is: if the absolute value of the difference between the gray values of the considered pixel and the seed pixel is less than a certain threshold T, then the pixel is included in the region where the seed pixel is located. Figure 7.18(b) shows the region growing result when $T = 3$, and the whole image is well divided into two regions; Figure 7.18(c) shows the region growth result when $T = 2$, in which some pixels are unable to be determined (note that the pixel in the upper-right corner cannot

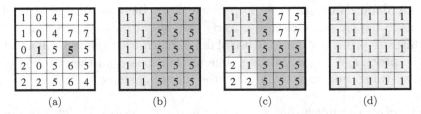

Figure 7.18.   Example of region growing.

be detected); Figure 7.18(d) shows the region growing result when $T = 7$, and the entire image is counted as only one region. This example shows that the choice of threshold is very important. □

7.6.2 Problems and improvements

The results obtained by the above method have a great dependence on the selection of the starting point (seed pixel) of region growing. To overcome this problem, the following improvements can be used:

(1) Set the threshold of gray-level difference to zero, use the above method to expand the region, and merge pixels with the same gray level.
(2) Find the average gray-level difference between all adjacent regions and merge these adjacent regions with the smallest gray-level difference.
(3) Set the termination criterion, repeat the operation in step (2), and merge the regions in sequence until the termination criterion is met.

When there are slowly changing regions in the image, the above method may gradually merge different regions and cause errors. To overcome this problem, instead of comparing the gray value of the new pixel with the gray value of the neighboring pixels, the average gray value of the region where the new pixel is located is used to compare with the gray value of each neighboring pixel.

For an image region R containing N pixels, the mean value is

$$m = \frac{1}{N} \sum_R f(x, y). \tag{7.33}$$

The comparison test for pixels can be represented as

$$\max_R = |f(x, y) - m| < T, \tag{7.34}$$

where T is a given threshold. Now consider the following two cases.

(1) Suppose the region is uniform and the gray value of each pixel is the super-position of the mean value m and a zero mean Gaussian noise. On using Equation (7.34) to test a certain pixel, the probability

that the condition is not established is

$$P(T) = \frac{2}{\sqrt{2\pi}\sigma} \int\limits_{T}^{\infty} \exp\left(-\frac{z^2}{2\sigma^2}\right) dz. \tag{7.35}$$

This is the error function erf(T). If T takes three times the variance, the probability of misjudgment is $1 - (99.7\%)^N$. This shows that when considering the mean gray value, the gray-value variation in the region should be as small as possible.

(2) Let the region be non-uniform and consist of two parts of pixels. The proportions of these two parts of pixels in R are q_1 and q_2, and the gray values are m_1 and m_2, respectively, and the region average value is $q_1 m_1 + q_2 m_2$. For a pixel with a gray value of m_1, the difference between it and the region mean is

$$S_m = m_1 - (q_1 m_1 + q_2 m_2). \tag{7.36}$$

According to Equation (7.35), the probability of correct decision is

$$P(T) = \frac{1}{2}[P(|T - S_m|) + P(|T + S_m|)]. \tag{7.37}$$

Equation (7.37) shows that when considering the average gray value, the gray-value gap between different parts of pixels should be as large as possible.

In addition, the connectivity and proximity between pixels need to be considered when performing the region growing, otherwise meaningless segmentation results will sometimes appear.

7.7   Key Points and References for Each Section

The following indicates the key points of each section and provides some targeted guidance for further references.

1. Segmentation definition and method classification

Image segmentation refers to the technology and process of dividing an image into regions with common properties and extracting the object region of interest. The research on image segmentation has a long history. It has been about 60 years since the Roberts cross operator was proposed. Image segmentation is a key step from image processing to image analysis. It is introduced in all image processing and analysis books; see Refs. [1–5]. A comprehensive discussion on image segmentation can be found in Ref. [6]. Some new developments in image segmentation in recent years can be found in Ref. [7]. A review of image segmentation can be found in Ref. [8], and the data involved in Table 7.1 can be found in Ref. [9].

2. Differential edge detection

Edge detection is the basis of parallel boundary image segmentation algorithms. The edge is the result of the discontinuous gray value, so it can be detected by differentiation or from the derivative. The gradient operator is the earliest edge detection operator proposed. It uses the first derivative to simultaneously detect the strength and direction of the edge. The Laplacian operator uses the second derivative, which can detect the position of the edge and the relative magnitude of the gray values on both sides of the edge. The Marr operator first performs Gaussian filtering on the image and then uses the Laplacian operator, which has strong anti-noise ability. For the detection of sub-pixel-level edges and the detection of edges in 3D images, please refer to Refs. [5,6]. With the help of analytical methods, in addition to the analysis and comparison of 2D edge detection operators, the analysis and comparison of 3D edge detection operators can also be performed; see Ref. [10].

3. Active contour model

Active contour is a segmentation method that belongs to the class of serial boundary techniques; see Ref. [11]. It serially adjusts their positions after determining the initial edge points to obtain an accurate object contour. The adjustment of the contour is controlled by the energy function used (including internal and external energy functions). The design of the energy function is the main task of using active contour segmentation method. The active contour model comprehensively considers the global information of the boundary in the image, so it is relatively insensitive to noise. Similar serial boundary techniques also include graph-based search methods (searching for the least costly path in the graph representation of the image) and dynamic programming-based methods (using heuristic knowledge about specific segmentation applications to reduce the amount of computations); see Ref. [12]. In addition, there are also techniques based on graph cuts, see Ref. [5].

4. Thresholding segmentation

Thresholding segmentation is the most common parallel region segmentation method and the most widely used image segmentation technique. In the threshold segmentation method, selecting the threshold is the key step. The simplest threshold selection method is to use extreme point detection to determine the valley between the two peaks in the histogram and take the gray level corresponding to the valley as the threshold. In order to improve the robustness of threshold selection, the original histogram of the image can be transformed to deepen the valleys between peaks or convert the valleys into peaks so as to make the selection of thresholds more convenient and robust. If one considers the gray-level and gradient values of the pixel at the same time, a 2D histogram (scatter) can be obtained, in which the object, background, and boundary pixels have different distributions. In this way, two thresholds can be selected in the 2D histogram to help segmentation. The 2D histogram method that considers the gray value of the pixel and the average gray value at the same time can be found in Ref. [6]. The various classification methods of thresholding algorithms and the popularization methods of thresholding algorithms can be found in Ref. [6]. After the threshold is used for segmentation, the connected regions need to be extracted and marked, which can be found in Ref. [5].

5. Threshold selection based on transition region

The transition region is a specific region located between adjacent regions in a digital image. The boundary between two adjacent regions is geometrically located in the transition region; see Ref. [13]. The boundary of the transition region itself can be determined by the $\text{EAG}_{\text{high}}(L)$ and $\text{EAG}_{\text{low}}(L)$ curves. It has been proved that these two curves are unimodal curves [6]. The proof of the three important properties of the extreme points of these two curves can be found in

Ref. [13] or Ref. [6]. When there are multiple transition regions in the image, it can be proved that the three properties of extreme points are still valid for the same transition region; see Ref. [14]. The gray value at the extreme point can also be used to directly calculate the segmentation threshold.

6. Region growing

Region growing is a commonly used method for serial region segmentation (another commonly used method of serial region segmentation is split-and-merge method; see Ref. [6]). The basic idea of region growing is to combine pixels with similar properties to form regions. Corresponding to the contour tracking method, there are three specific steps in the region growing method as follows: (i) selecting or determining a set of seed pixels that can correctly represent the desired region as the starting point; (ii) growing the region according to the criterion that adjacent pixels can be included in the growing process; (iii) judging the termination of growing according to the conditions or rules that stop the growing process. The growing criterion has a great influence on the performance of the algorithm, and the discussion on certain criteria can be found in Ref. [6].

Self-Test Questions

The following questions include both single- and multiple-choice questions, so each option should be individually judged.

7.1 Segmentation Definition and Method Classification

7.1.1 Let the set R represent the entire image, then the subsets R_1, $R_2, \ldots, R_n$ are the necessary conditions for the segmentation result of R, excluding the following: ( )

(A) $R_1 \subset R_2 \subset \cdots \subset R_n$;
(B) $P(R_i) = \text{TRUE}, i = 1, 2, \ldots, n$;
(C) $R_i \cap R_j = \oslash \ (i \neq j)$;
(D) Each R_i is connected, $i = 1, 2, \ldots, n$.

[Hint] The image segmentation should divide the image into sub-regions that do not overlap each other.

7.1.2 The following segmentation methods are based on the region-based algorithm: ( )

(A) Edge detection;
(B) Active contour;
(C) Threshold segmentation;
(D) Region growing.

[Hint] The region algorithm uses the similarity of pixels.

7.1.3 Parallel boundary technology and serial region technology in image segmentation respectively uses the following image properties: ( )

(A) Continuity and variability;
(B) Discontinuity and similarity;
(C) Continuity and similarity;
(D) Discontinuity and variability.

[Hint] These properties have nothing to do with parallel or serial.

7.2 Differential Edge Detection

7.2.1 When using the gradient operator, ( )

(A) It always requires two masks;
(B) It can eliminate random noise;
(C) It can detect step edges;
(D) It always produces double-pixel wide edges.

[Hint] Consider the function and composition characteristics of the gradient operator.

7.2.2 Use the Sobel gradient operator to perform edge detection on the image in Figure 7.2.2. The result is (suppose the norm is 1) ( )

1	1	1
2	3	1
2	1	3

Figure 7.2.2.

(A) 3;

(B) 4;

(C) 5;

(D) 6.

[Hint] Put the two masks on the image and calculate them separately.

7.2.3 Laplacian operator ( )

(A) Includes a mask;

(B) Includes two masks;

(C) Is a first-order differential operator;

(D) Is a second-order differential operator.

[Hint] Consider the compositional characteristics of Laplacian operators.

7.2.4 Laplacian operator is mainly used for ( )

(A) Detecting the edge of the image directly;

(B) Detecting the edge of the image after combining with the Roberts operator;

(C) Detecting the direction of the gradient in the image;

(D) Determining the edge pixel in the bright or dark region of the image after knowing the edge pixel.

[Hint] Consider the function of Laplacian operator.

7.2.5 When performing edge detection, the Laplacian operator's response to the following situations is arranged from large to small: ( )

(A) Horizontal and vertical edges > Isolated lines > Oblique edges > Isolated noise points;

(B) Isolated noise points > Oblique edges > Isolated lines > Horizontal and vertical edges;

(C) Slanted edges > Isolated noise points > Horizontal and vertical edges > Isolated lines;

(D) Isolated lines > Oblique edges > Horizontal and vertical edges > Isolated noise points.

[Hint] The response of the Laplacian operator is proportional to the gray-level difference of the image pixels corresponding to its central coefficient and surrounding coefficients.

7.3 Active Contour Model

7.3.1 Active contour ( )

  (A) Is a deformed contour;
  (B) The area enclosed by the deformation is always smaller than that of object;
  (C) Is a collection of a series of points;
  (D) Includes points that can move independently of each other.

[Hint] Consider the definition and working mode of the active contour model.

7.3.2 In order to design the internal energy function, in addition to what has been introduced in Section 7.3, the following factors can also be considered: ( )

  (A) Size of the object region;
  (B) Shape of the object region;
  (C) Smoothness of the object contour;
  (D) Gray-level variance of the object contour points.

[Hint] The general situation that there is no restriction on the object properties before segmentation should be considered.

7.3.3 In order to design the external energy function, the following factors can be considered in addition to those already introduced in Section 7.3: ( )

  (A) Number of pixels in the object of image;
  (B) Gray-level difference between the object and the background in the image;
  (C) Distance between the current contour point and the object boundary point in the image;
  (D) Direction of the line between the current contour point and the adjacent contour point relative to the X axis.

[Hint] The external energy mainly depends on the property value of the image.

7.4 Thresholding segmentation

7.4.1 When using the histogram to take a single threshold method for image segmentation, ( )

  (A) There should be only one object in the image;
  (B) The image histogram should have two peaks;

(C) The sizes of the object and background in the image should be the same;

(D) The gray value of the object in the image should be larger than the gray value of the background.

[Hint] Consider the image model that should be matched at this time.

7.4.2 The influence of noise on the threshold segmentation algorithm using histogram is that ( )

(A) Noise will make the histogram not smooth and there will be many local extreme values;

(B) Noise will reduce the distance between the peaks of the histogram;

(C) Noise will eliminate the peaks of the histogram;

(D) Noise will fill the valleys of the histogram and increase the difficulty of valley detection.

[Hint] Noise will increase or decrease the gray values of some pixels.

7.4.3 Suppose an image has the gray value distribution as shown in Figure 7.4.3, where $p_1(z)$ corresponds to the object and $p_2(z)$ corresponds to the background. If $P_1 = P_2$, the segmentation threshold with the smallest error should be three (corresponding to the intersection). Now, if $P_1 > P_2$, the segmentation threshold with the smallest error will be ( )

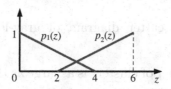

Figure 7.4.3.

(A) Decreased;
(B) Unchanged;
(C) Increased;
(D) Non-existent.

[Hint] Refer to the diagram corresponding to the optimal threshold selection and the equation for calculating the optimal threshold.

7.4.4 When performing histogram transformation, ( )

(A) The gradient value of the pixel must be used;
(B) The input is a histogram and the output is another histogram;
(C) The histogram obtained must have deeper valleys and higher peaks;
(D) The premise is that some pixels in the image have higher gradient values.

[Hint] There are many methods for histogram transformation, and the use of gradient is only one of them.

7.4.5 In order to detect the threshold more conveniently and accurately, one can ( )

(A) Perform median filtering on the histogram to increase the peak-valley difference/gap;
(B) Use histogram equalization to increase the dynamic range of the image;
(C) Use the pixel gradient value to transform the histogram to increase the peak-valley difference/gap;
(D) Perform median filtering on the histogram to remove false peaks caused by noise.

[Hint] In the histogram transformation, one can use the properties of the pixels themselves or the local features of the pixel neighborhood.

7.4.6 Consider the scatter diagram of gray-level versus gradient values. ( )

(A) The number of clusters is as large as the number of objects in the image;
(B) The shape of the cluster has nothing to do with the correlation of the pixels constituting the cluster;
(C) The local property of the pixel neighborhood is used to transform the histogram;
(D) The number of clusters is as large as the number of clusters in the scatter diagram of gray value versus average gray value.

[Hint] In the scatter diagram of gray value versus average gray value, one axis is the gray value and the other axis is the average gray value.

7.5 Threshold Selection Based on Transition Region

7.5.1 In Equation (7.25), ( )

(A) TG is the sum of pixel values in the gradient map of the original image;

(B) TP is the sum of the number of pixels in the gradient map of the original image;

(C) EAG is equal to the sum of all pixel values of the gradient map divided by the sum of the number of non-zero gradient pixels;

(D) EAG is equal to the sum of non-zero gradient pixel values of the gradient map divided by the sum of non-zero gradient pixels.

[Hint] Considering zero gradient pixels when calculating the total gradient value does not affect the result.

7.5.2 In the clip transformed image, which of the following will not happen: ( )

(A) $f_{\text{high}}(i, j) < L$;

(B) $f_{\text{high}}(i, j) > L$;

(C) $f_{\text{low}}(i, j) < L$;

(D) $f_{\text{low}}(i, j) > L$.

[Hint] After clipping at the low end, the minimum gray level is raised to L; after clipping at the high end, the maximum gray level is limited to L.

7.5.3 The reason why the typical $\text{EAG}_{\text{low}}(L)$ curve is a unimodal curve is ( )

(A) $\text{TG}_{\text{low}}(L)$ and $\text{TP}_{\text{low}}(L)$ both increase with the increase of L;

(B) $\text{TG}_{\text{low}}(L)$ decreases faster than $\text{TP}_{\text{low}}(L)$ as L increases;

(C) $\text{TG}_{\text{low}}(L)$ decreases more slowly than $\text{TP}_{\text{low}}(L)$ as L increases;

(D) $TG_{low}(L)$ and $TP_{low}(L)$ both decrease with the increase of L.

[Hint] $TG_{low}(L)$ first drops slowly relative to $TP_{low}(L)$ and drops faster relative to $TP_{low}(L)$ after the extreme value of $EAG_{low}(L)$.

7.6 Region Growing

7.6.1 In order to use the region growing method for image segmentation, it is necessary to determine ( )

(A) The histogram of the image;
(B) The mean value of each region;
(C) The seed pixels of each region;
(D) The criteria for including adjacent pixels in the growing process.

[Hint] Consider the three steps of the region growing method.

7.6.2 Use the region growing method to segment the image in Figure 7.6.2.1.

1	0	2	7	4
5	5	2	7	7
0	1	**5**	5	5
2	0	5	6	5
2	2	5	6	5

Figure 7.6.2.1.

If the central pixel is taken as the seed (marked as a gray square) and the threshold $T = 3$, the 4-connected growing region obtained is ( )

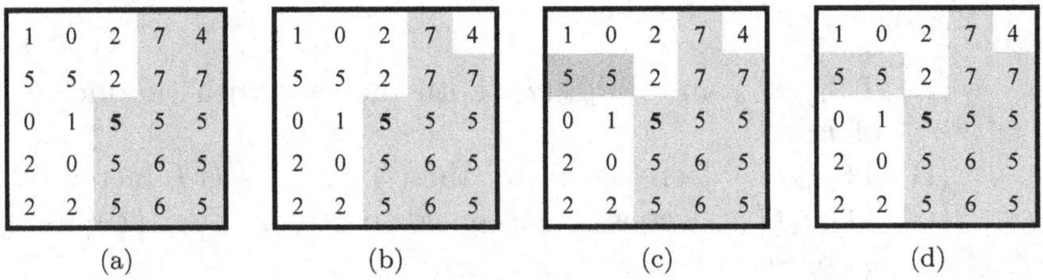

Figure 7.6.2.2.

(A) Figure 7.6.2.2(a);
(B) Figure 7.6.2.2(b);
(C) Figure 7.6.2.2(c);
(D) Figure 7.6.2.2(d).

[Hint] Consider the 4-connected pixels whose gray-level difference from the seed pixel is less than the positive and negative thresholds.

7.6.3 Use the region growing method to segment the image in Figure 7.6.3.1.

Suppose the pixel marked as a gray square is seed, what value the threshold T should take to make the 4-connected growing region obtained as the letter E? ( )

3	1	1	0	0	1	5
0	5	6	6	5	6	1
1	5	6	0	0	3	0
0	5	6	6	5	6	0
1	5	6	0	2	2	0
1	4	5	4	5	6	1
6	1	0	1	1	0	6

Figure 7.6.3.1.

(A) $T = 1$;
(B) $T = 2$;
(C) $T = 3$;
(D) $T = 4$.

[Hint] The position of the letter E in the image is shown in Figure 7.6.3.2.

References

[1] Pratt, W. K. *Digital Image Processing: PIKS Scientific Inside*, 4th Edn. USA, Hoboken: Wiley Interscience, 2007.
[2] Sonka, M., Hlavac, V., and Boyle, R. *Image Processing, Analysis, and Machine Vision*, 4th Edn. Singapore: Cengage Learning, 2014.
[3] Russ, J. C. and Neal, F. B. *The Image Processing Handbook*, 7th Edn. UK, London: CRC Press, 2016.

[4] Gonzalez, R. C. and Woods, R. E. *Digital Image Processing*, 4th Edn. UK, London: Prentice Hall, 2018.

[5] Zhang, Y.-J. *Image Engineering, Vol. 2: Image Analysis*. Germany, Berlin: De Gruyter, 2017.

[6] Zhang, Y.-J. *Image Segmentation*. China, Beijing: Science Press, 2001.

[7] Zhang, Y.-J. (ed.). *Advances in Image and Video Segmentation*. USA, Hershey: Idea Group, Inc. 2006.

[8] Zhang, Y.-J. Half century for image segmentation. *Encyclopedia of Information Science and Technology*, 3rd Edn., 2015, Chapter 584, pp. 5906–5915.

[9] Zhang, Y.-J. Image Engineering in China: 2019. *Journal of Image and Graphics*, 2020, 25(5): 864–878.

[10] Zhang, Y.-J. Quantitative study of 3D gradient operators. *IVC*, 1993, 11: 611–622.

[11] Kass, M., Witkin, A., and Terzopoulos, D. Snakes: Active contour models. *IJCV*, 1988, 1(4): 321–331.

[12] Zhang, Y.-J. *Image Engineering: Processing, Analysis, and Understanding*. Singapore: Cengage Learning, 2009.

[13] Zhang, Y.-J. and Gerbrands, J. J. Transition region determination based thresholding. *PRL*, 1991, 12: 13–23.

[14] Zhang, Y.-J. Transition region and image segmentation. *Acta Electronica Sinica*, 1996, 24(1): 12–17.

Chapter 8

Primitive Detection

The image segmentation method introduced in Chapter 7 mainly considers that an image is composed of many pixels. By judging each pixel one by one to classify it to an object or background, the entire image is segmented. Here, the basic unit of each operation is the pixel. In many cases, if one has more knowledge about the description of the object to be segmented, one can also directly detect the object as a whole (equivalent to the basic unit of each operation is the object region); or, if the structure of the object is known, and its components are well described, it is possible to consider first detecting the components of the object (equivalent to the basic unit of each operation is the component that composes the object) and then combine the detection results according to the object structure to obtain the final segmentation of the object. These are the contents to be introduced in this chapter, which are essentially also image segmentation techniques. The use of larger basic operation units combined with more prior knowledge can often improve the efficiency of segmentation and enhance the robustness of segmentation.

The sections of this chapter are arranged as follows:

Section 8.1 introduces several typical detection methods for points of interest (corner points, edge points, intersection points, etc.) on the object in the image.

Section 8.2 discusses the detection principles and methods for elliptical objects. These methods should be generalized to objects with other shapes.

265

Section 8.3 introduces the Hough transform, which is a general method to detect various object contours and then to segment the image. It uses the global characteristics of the image, is less affected by interference, and may determine the contour to sub-pixel accuracy.

Section 8.4 generalizes the Hough transform, which can not only detect object contours that can be described by analytical representations but also detect more general and arbitrary contours of object.

8.1   Interest Point Detection

Points of interest generally refer to points in an image or on an object that have specific geometric or attribute properties, such as corner points, inflection points, and gradient extreme points. There are many methods for detecting points of interest. The following first introduces the principle of using second-order derivatives to detect corner points and then introduces two more distinctive detection operators that can detect multiple types of points of interest.

8.1.1   Corner detection by second derivative

If a pixel has two distinct edge directions in its small neighborhood, it can often be regarded as a **corner point** (corner, in short). In other words, there are two edge segments in the neighborhood of the corner point, whose orientations are more perpendicular to each other. Some people also regard the edge points with larger local curvature (refer to Section 12.3 for the calculation method of discrete curvature) as corner points. Typical corner detectors are mostly based on the derivative of pixel gray value.

The principle of using the second-order derivative operator to detect corner points is somewhat similar to that of using the first-order derivative operator to detect edges. In a 2D image, the symmetric matrix composed of each second derivative can be written as (the subscript indicates the direction of the partial derivative)

$$I_{(2)} = \begin{bmatrix} I_{xx} & I_{xy} \\ I_{yx} & I_{yy} \end{bmatrix}, \quad I_{xy} = I_{yx}. \tag{8.1}$$

This gives information about the local curvature at the detected point (taken as origin). The above matrix has two eigenvalues, and their three combinations can be considered as follows: (i) Both eigenvalues are very small, indicating that the local neighborhood of the detected point is relatively flat, and the detected point is not an edge point or a corner point; (ii) one eigenvalue is very small and the other eigenvalue is quite large, which means that the local neighborhood of the detected point is ridge-like, that is, it is flat in one direction and rapidly changing in the other direction, and the detected point is an edge point; (iii) Both eigenvalues are very large, indicating that the detected point is a corner point. This detection method is not sensitive to translation and rotational transformations and is stable to changes in illumination and viewing angles.

By rotating the coordinate system, $I_{(2)}$ can be transformed into a diagonal form:

$$\tilde{I}_{(2)} = \begin{bmatrix} I_{\tilde{x}\tilde{x}} & 0 \\ 0 & I_{\tilde{y}\tilde{y}} \end{bmatrix} = \begin{bmatrix} K_1 & 0 \\ 0 & K_2 \end{bmatrix}. \tag{8.2}$$

The second derivative matrix at this time gives the principal curvature at the origin, namely K_1 and K_2.

Back to the matrix of type $\tilde{I}_{(2)}$, its rank and determinant are rotation invariant. Further, the Laplacian and Hessian values can be obtained, respectively:

$$\text{Laplacian} = I_{xx} + I_{yy} = K_1 + K_2, \tag{8.3}$$

$$\text{Hessian} = \det(I_{(2)}) = I_{xx}I_{yy} - I_{xy}^2 = K_1 K_2. \tag{8.4}$$

Based on a square matrix composed of the second-order partial derivative of a function, the **Laplacian operator** and **Hessian operator** calculate the Laplacian and Hessian values, respectively. The former gives a strong response to both edges and straight lines, so it is not suitable for detecting corners. The latter describes the local curvature of the function. Although it does not respond to edges and straight lines, it has a strong response in the neighborhood of the corner point, so it is more suitable for detecting corner points. However, the Hessian operator has zero response at the corner point itself and the signs on both sides of the corner point are not the same, so a more complicated analysis process is required to determine the existence of the corner point and accurately locate the corner point. To avoid this complicated analysis process, it is possible to first calculate the product of curvature and local gray-level gradient as

$$C = Kg = K\sqrt{I_x^2 + I_y^2} = \frac{I_{xx}I_y^2 - 2I_{xy}I_xI_y + I_{yy}I_x^2}{I_x^2 + I_y^2} \tag{8.5}$$

and then to use non-maximum suppression along the edge normal direction to determine the position of the corner point.

8.1.2   Harris interest point operator

Harris interest point operator is also called Harris interest point detector. The representation matrix of the detector can be defined by the gradients I_x and I_y in two directions of the local mask in the image. A commonly used Harris matrix can be written as

$$\boldsymbol{H} = \begin{bmatrix} \sum I_x^2 & \sum I_xI_y \\ \sum I_xI_y & \sum I_y^2 \end{bmatrix}. \tag{8.6}$$

1. Corner detection

The Harris corner detector detects corners by calculating the sum of the squared differences of gray values in the pixel neighborhood. When detecting corner points, the following equation can be used to calculate the **corner strength** (note that the det (determinant) and trace are not affected by the rotation of the coordinate axis):

$$C = \frac{\det(\boldsymbol{H})}{\text{trace}(\boldsymbol{H})}. \tag{8.7}$$

Ideally, consider a local **circular mask**. For the case where there is only a straight line in the mask, $\det(\boldsymbol{H}) = 0$, so $C = 0$. If there is a corner point with an acute angle (the angle between the two sides is less than $90°$) in the mask, as shown in Figure 8.1(a), the Harris matrix can be written as:

$$\boldsymbol{H} = \begin{bmatrix} l_2g^2 \sin^2\theta & l_2g^2 \sin\theta\cos\theta \\ l_2g^2 \sin\theta\cos\theta & l_2g^2 \cos^2\theta + l_1g^2 \end{bmatrix}, \tag{8.8}$$

where l_1 and l_2 are the lengths of the two sides of the corner, respectively, and g is the contrast between two sides of the edge, which is constant in the whole mask.

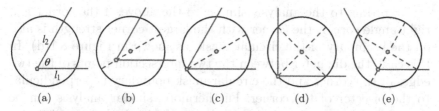

Figure 8.1. Various position relations between corner and mask.

According to Equation (8.8), it can be calculated that

$$\det(\boldsymbol{H}) = l_1 l_2 g^4 \sin^2 \theta, \tag{8.9}$$

$$\text{trace}(\boldsymbol{H}) = (l_1 + l_2)g^2. \tag{8.10}$$

Substituting them into Equation (8.7), the corner strength is obtained:

$$C = \frac{l_1 l_2}{l_1 + l_2} g^2 \sin^2 \theta. \tag{8.11}$$

It includes three items: strength factor $\lambda = l_1 l_2/(l_1 + l_2)$ depending on the length of the edge in the mask; contrast factor g^2; shape factor $\sin^2 \theta$, depending on the degree of acute angle. They are discussed separately in the following.

The strength factor is related to the lengths of the two side parts in the mask. If the sum of l_1 and l_2 is a constant L, then the strength factor $\lambda = (Ll_2 - l_2^2)/L$, and the maximum value is obtained when $l_1 = l_2 = L/2$. This shows that in order to obtain a large corner strength, the two sides of the corner need to be symmetrically placed in the mask region, as shown in Figure 8.1(b), that is, the corner falls on the center line (also the diameter of mask). In order to obtain the maximum strength of the corner point, the two sides of the corner point must be the longest in the mask region. This situation is shown in Figure 8.1(c), that is, the corner point is moved along the median diameter line until the corner points fall on the border of the circular mask.

The contrast factor is constant throughout the mask.

The shape factor depends on the angle θ. The maximum value of shape factor is one when $\theta = \pi/2$, and the minimum value of shape factor is zero when $\theta = 0$ and $\theta = \pi$. According to Equation (8.11), for a straight line, the corner strength is zero.

According to the analysis similar to the above, if the corner is a right-angle corner, the corner with the largest corner strength is also on the boundary of the circular mask, as shown in Figure 8.1(d). In this case, the diameter between the two intersection points of the two edges of the corner and the circular mask boundary is perpendicular to the bisector of the corner. Furthermore, similar analysis can be made for obtuse angle points, and the conclusion is that the diameter between the two intersection points of the two edges of the angle point and the boundary of the circular mask is perpendicular to the bisector of the angle, as shown in Figure 8.1(e).

2. Crossing point detection

In addition to detecting various corner points, the Harris interest point operator can also help to detect other interest points, such as crossing points and T-shaped junctions. The crossing point here can be the intersection of two perpendicular lines (as shown in Figure 8.2(a)) or the intersection of two non-perpendicular (oblique) lines (as shown in Figure 8.2(b)). Similarly, the two straight lines forming the T-junction point can be perpendicular to each other (as shown in Figure 8.2(c)) or not (as shown in Figure 8.2(d)). In Figure 8.2, a same number indicates that the indicated region has the same gray value, and different numbers indicate that the indicated regions have different gray values.

When calculating the strength of the crossing point, Equation (8.11) can still be used, only that the values of l_1 and l_2 are respectively the total length of the straight lines in two directions (the sum of the lines on both sides of the cross point). Also, note that at the crossing point, the contrast signs are reversed in both directions. However, this has no effect on the calculation of cross point

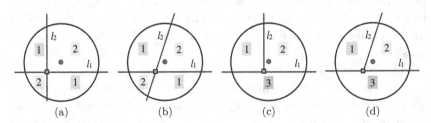

Figure 8.2.   Crossing point and T-junction.

strength because the square of g is used as the contrast factor in Equation (8.11). Therefore, if the crossing point coincides with the central point of the mask, the values of l_1 and l_2 are twice of those of the corner point, respectively, which is also the position with the maximum strength of the crossing point. By the way, this position is the zero-crossing point of the second derivative.

T-junction point can be regarded as a more general point of interest than the corner and crossing points because it involves three regions with different gray levels. In order to consider the situation that there are two kinds of contrast, it is necessary to extend Equation (8.11) to

$$C = \frac{l_1 l_2 g_1^2 g_2^2}{l_1 g_1^2 + l_2 g_2^2} \sin^2 \theta. \tag{8.12}$$

T-junction can have many different configurations. Here, we only consider the case that a weak edge (corresponding to oblique edge) contacts a strong edge (corresponding to horizontal edge) but does not pass through the strong edge, as shown in Figure 8.3.

In Figure 8.3, the T-junction is asymmetric. According to Equation (8.12), the maximum value is obtained when $l_1|g_1| = |l_2 g_2|$. This indicates that the point with the highest detection strength is on the weak edge but not on the strong edge, as shown by the dot in Figure 8.3. In other words, the point with the highest detection strength is not in the geometric position of T-junction because of the influence of gray level.

8.1.3 Integral corner detection

SUSAN operator is a special detection operator. Instead of using differential, it uses integral for detection. It can not only detect the

Figure 8.3.   T-junction and the point with the highest detection strength.

boundary points of the object in the image but also detect the **corner points** of the object robustly.

1. USAN principle

The principle of detection is explained with the help of Figure 8.4. There is a rectangular image, in which the upper part is the bright region and the lower part is the dark region, representing the object and background, respectively. There is a circular mask whose center is called "nuclear", and the size of the mask is limited by the mask boundary. Figure 8.4 shows the schematic situation of the mask in six different positions in the image. Counting from the left, the first mask is totally in the bright region, the second mask is mostly in the bright region, the third mask has one half in the bright region (other half in the dark region), the fourth mask is mostly in the dark region, the fifth mask is totally in the dark region, and the sixth mask has a quarter in the dark region (other three quarters in the dark region). These situations basically summarize the typical positions and responses of the mask.

If the gray level of each pixel in the mask is compared with that of the nuclear pixel in the center of the mask, it is found that the gray level of some mask pixels is the same or similar to that of the nuclear pixel. This part of the region can be called the **univalue segment assimilating nuclear** (USAN), that is, the region with the same or similar value as that of the nuclear. The size of USAN reflects a lot of information related to image structure. As can be seen from Figure 8.4, if the nuclear pixel is in the gray-level consistent region of the image, the area of USAN will reach the maximum, which is the case with the first mask and fifth mask. When the mask crosses two regions but the nuclear is in one of them, the area is more than half. The second mask and fourth mask belong to this case. When the

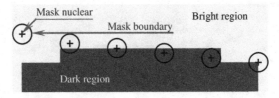

Figure 8.4.   Different positions of the circular mask in the image.

nuclear is at the straight edge, the area is about half of the maximum, which is the case with the third mask. When the nuclear is at the corner, the area is smaller, about one-fourth of the maximum, which is the case with the sixth mask.

Utilizing the above change in the USAN area can detect edges or corners. Specifically, when the area of USAN is larger (more than half), it indicates that the nuclear pixel is in a region with uniform gray values in the image. This area decreases when the mask nucleus is close to the edge, and it decreases more when it approaches the corner. That is, the area at the corner point is the smallest. If the reciprocal of the USAN area is used as the output of the detection, the position of the corner point can be easily determined by calculating the maximum value.

2. Corner detection with SUSAN operator

On the basis of USAN, the SUSAN operator (also known as the smallest univalue segment assimilating nucleus operator) can be discussed.

SUSAN operator uses **circular mask** to get **isotropic response**. In a digital image, the circle can be approximated by a mask with 37 pixels. The 37 pixels are arranged in seven rows, with 3, 5, 7, 7, 7, 5, and 3 pixels, respectively. This is equivalent to a circle with a radius of about 3.4 pixels, as shown in Figure 8.5. If considering the amount of calculation, the common 3×3 mask can also be used to approximate roughly.

Suppose the mask function is $N(x, y)$, place it at the position of each pixel in the image in turn and compare the gray value of

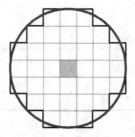

Figure 8.5. Circular mask with 37 pixels.

each pixel under the mask with the gray value of the nuclear at each position:

$$C(x_0, y_0; x, y) = \begin{cases} 1 & |f(x_0, y_0) - f(x, y)| \leq T \\ 0 & |f(x_0, y_0) - f(x, y)| > T, \end{cases} \quad (8.13)$$

where $(x_0,\ y_0)$ is the position coordinates of the nucleus in the image, $(x,\ y)$ is the other position inside the mask $N(x,\ y)$, $f(x_0,\ y_0)$ and $f(x,\ y)$ are the gray values of pixels at $(x_0,\ y_0)$ and $(x,\ y)$, respectively, T is a threshold of gray value difference, and function $C(\cdot;\ \cdot)$ represents the comparison result of the output. An example of this output function is shown in Figure 8.6, where the threshold $T = 27$.

It is required to perform the above comparison for each pixel under the mask, then an output of **running total** can be obtained:

$$S(x_0, y_0) = \sum_{(x,y) \in N(x,y)} C(x_0, y_0; x, y). \quad (8.14)$$

This sum is actually the number of pixels in USAN or it gives the area of USAN. As discussed above, this area will be minimized at the corners. Combining Equations (8.13) and (8.14), it can be seen that the threshold T can be used to help detect the minimum value of the USAN area, and it can also determine the maximum value of noise that can be eliminated.

In actual application of the SUSAN operator, the running total and S need to be compared with a fixed **geometric threshold** G to make a judgment. The threshold is set to $3S_{\max}/4$, where $S_{\max}$ is the maximum value that S can achieve (for a 37-pixel mask, the

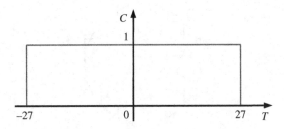

Figure 8.6.   Example of function $C\ (\cdot;\ \cdot)$.

maximum value is 36). The initial edge response $R(x_0, y_0)$ is obtained according to the following equation:

$$R(x_0, y_0) = \begin{cases} G - S(x_0, y_0) & S(x_0, y_0) < G \\ 0 & \text{otherwise.} \end{cases} \tag{8.15}$$

The above equation is obtained according to the USAN principle, that is, the smaller the area of USAN, the greater the response of the edge.

If there is no noise in the image, the geometric threshold may not be required at all. But if there is noise in the image, it is necessary to set $G = 3S_{max}/4$ to give the best noise cancellation performance. Consider a step edge, where the value of S will always be less than $S_{max}/2$ on one of two sides. If the edge is curved, an S value less than $S_{max}/2$ will appear on the concave side. If the edge is a non-ideal step edge (with a slope), the value of S will be smaller, so that the possibility of undetected edges is smaller.

The method described above can usually give quite good results, but there is a more stable equation for calculating $C(\cdot; \cdot)$:

$$C(x_0, y_0; x, y) = \exp\left\{ -\left[\frac{f(x_0, y_0) - f(x, y)}{T} \right]^2 \right\}. \tag{8.16}$$

The curve corresponding to this equation is shown as curve b in Figure 8.7 (curve a corresponds to Equation (8.13), which is a gate function). It can be seen that Equation (8.16) gives a smooth version of Equation (8.13). It allows a certain change in pixel gray level without too much influence on $C(\cdot; \cdot)$.

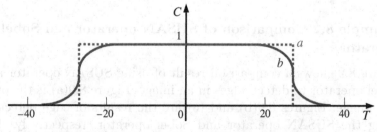

Figure 8.7. Examples of different functions $C\,(\cdot; \cdot)$.

(a)   (b)

Figure 8.8.   Corners detected by SUSAN operator.

Example 8.1 Corner point detection example

Figure 8.8 shows two results obtained by using the SUSAN operator to detect corners in an image.   □

3. Characteristics of SUSAN operator

The SUSAN operator can not only detect corners but also edges. Compared with most edge detection operators, SUSAN operator has some unique properties.

There is no need to calculate the differential when using the SUSAN operator to detect and enhance the edges and corners, which can help explain why the SUSAN operator has better performance when there is noise. This feature, coupled with the nonlinear response characteristics of the SUSAN operator, will help reduce the impact of noise. To understand this, consider an input signal mixed with independently distributed Gaussian noise. As long as the noise is relatively small compared with the area of the USAN, it will not affect the judgment based on the area of the USAN. In other words, the noise is ignored. Here, the operation of summing the value of each pixel in the area calculation further reduces the influence of noise.

Example 8.2 Comparison of SUSAN operator and Sobel operator

Figure 8.9 shows a comparison result of using SUSAN operator and Sobel operator to detect edges in an image. Figure 8.9(a) is the original image; Figures 8.9(b) and (c) are the results of edge detection using the SUSAN operator and Sobel operator, respectively. The boundary extracted by the SUSAN operator is relatively wide, while

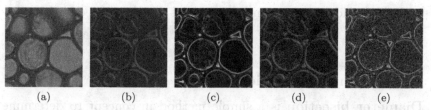

| (a) | (b) | (c) | (d) | (e) |

Figure 8.9. Comparison of edge detection between SUSAN operator and Sobel operator.

the boundary extracted by the Sobel operator is relatively narrow. Figures 8.9(d) and (e) are the results of edge detection using the SUSAN operator and the Sobel operator after adding Gaussian noise to the original image. The effect of noise is greater in Figure 8.9(e) than that in Figure 8.9(d). □

Another feature of the SUSAN operator can be seen from the USAN area in Figure 8.4. When the edge becomes blurred, the USAN area at the center of the edge will decrease. Therefore, the response to the edge will increase as the edge becomes smooth or blurred. This interesting phenomenon is not common in general edge detection operators.

In addition, most of the edge detection operators will change the position of the detected edge with the change of the mask size, but Susan detection operator can provide edge accuracy independent of the mask size. In other words, the calculation of minimum USAN area is a relative concept, which is independent of mask size, so the performance of SUSAN edge detection operator is not affected by mask size. This is a useful expectation feature.

Finally, another advantage of SUSAN operator is that the selection of control parameters is very simple and less arbitrary, so it is easier to realize automatic selection.

8.2 Elliptical Object Detection

The direct detection and extraction of the object often use the properties and prior knowledge of the object. Among them, the geometric properties of the object are widely used. The consideration here is mainly on several detection methods for elliptical objects, but the same idea and strategy can be extended to other objects with various shapes.

8.2.1   Diameter bisection

Diameter bisection is a simple method in concept to determine the center of ellipse of various sizes. First, a list of all edge points in the image is established according to their edge direction. Then, the points are arranged to obtain pairs of parallel points in the opposite direction, which may be on both sides of the diameter of the ellipse. Finally, the midpoint positions of these ellipse diameter lines are voted in the parameter space, and the image space point corresponding to the peak position is the candidate position of the ellipse center. As shown in Figure 8.10, the midpoint (point C) of two edge points (point S and point T) with opposite parallel edge directions should be the candidate point of the center of the ellipse. However, when there are several ellipses with the same orientation in the image, it is possible for the diameter bisection method to find the center point at the midpoint among these ellipses. In order to eliminate these false center points, one needs to only allow the center to vote in the inner position of the edge points.

The above basic method is useful for locating many symmetrical shaped objects (such as circle, square, and rectangle), so it can be used to detect multiple types of objects. On the other hand, when there are multiple objects with these shapes in an image, if only one of them needs to be detected, there will be many false alarms and a lot of computation will be wasted. If only the ellipse is to be detected, another characteristic of the ellipse can be considered, that is, the two orthogonal semi-axes CP and CQ of the ellipse (see Figure 8.10)

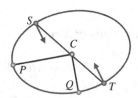

Figure 8.10.   Basic idea of diameter bisection.

satisfy the following equation:

$$\frac{1}{(CP)^2} + \frac{1}{(CQ)^2} = \frac{1}{R^2} = \text{constant}. \tag{8.17}$$

Therefore, one can use the set of edge points that contribute to the same peak in the parameter space to construct a histogram with R histogram bins. If an obvious peak can be found in the histogram, there is likely to be an ellipse at a specific position in the image. If two or more peaks are found, there may be a corresponding number of ellipses overlapping. But if no peak is found, there are only other symmetrical objects in the image.

Finally, it needs a lot of calculation to search the list of edge points with correct orientation by diameter bisection. In order to speed up the processing, the following methods can be used: (i) Add the edge points to a table and then use the orientation to access; (ii) add the appropriate orientation to the table to find the correct edge points. If there are N edge points, the calculation time can be reduced from $O(N^2)$ to $O(N)$.

8.2.2   Chord-tangent method

Chord-tangent method is also a method to determine the center of ellipse of various sizes. As shown in Figure 8.11, a pair of edge points P_1 and P_2 are detected in the image. The tangents passing through these two points intersect at point T. The midpoint of the line between these two points is point B, and the center of the ellipse C and T are on two opposite sides of point B. By calculating the equation of the straight line TB, and similar to the Hough transform (see Section 8.3), the points of BD interval on the straight line

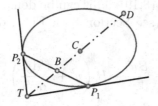

Figure 8.11.   Schematic diagram of the chord-tangent method.

are accumulated in the parameter space, and finally the coordinates (x_c, y_c) of point C can be determined by peak detection.

Because there are many points in the parameter space that need to be accumulated, the amount of calculation may be large. There are three ways to reduce the amount of calculation as follows: (i) to estimate the size and orientation of the ellipse, so as to limit the length of the line BD; (ii) if two edge points are too close or too distant, they will not be paired; (iii) once an edge point has been confirmed to belong to a specific ellipse, it will not be allowed to participate in the subsequent calculation.

8.2.3   Other parameters of the ellipse

Consider the elliptic equation:

$$Ax^2 + 2Hxy + By^2 + 2Gx + 2Fy + C = 0. \qquad (8.18)$$

To distinguish an ellipse from a hyperbola, $AB > H^2$ needs to be satisfied. This shows that A can never be zero, and without loss of generality, $A = 1$ is preferable. This leaves only five parameters, which correspond to the position, orientation, size, and shape (which can be represented by eccentricity) of the ellipse.

The center position (x_c, y_c) of the ellipse has been determined above, and it can be moved to the origin of the coordinate system, so that Equation (8.18) becomes

$$x'^2 + 2Hx'y' + By'^2 + C' = 0, \qquad (8.19)$$

where

$$x' = x - x_c, \quad y' = y - y_c. \qquad (8.20)$$

After determining the center of the ellipse, one can use the edge points to fit Equation (8.19). This can be done with a manner similar to Hough transform (see Section 8.3). First, differentiate Equation (8.19):

$$x' + \frac{By'}{dx'} + H\left(y' + \frac{x'dy'}{dx'}\right) = 0, \qquad (8.21)$$

where dy'/dx' can be determined according to the local edge orientation at (x', y'). At the same time, the accumulation is done in the new parameter space *BH*. If a peak is found, the edge points can be further used to obtain a histogram of the C' value, and the final ellipse parameters can be determined from it.

To determine the orientation θ and the two semi-axes a and b of the ellipse, one needs to use B, H, and C' to calculate as follows:

$$\theta = \frac{1}{2}\arctan\left(\frac{2H}{1-B}\right), \tag{8.22}$$

$$a^2 = \frac{-2C'}{(B+1)-[(B-1)^2+4H^2]^{1/2}}, \tag{8.23}$$

$$b^2 = \frac{-2C'}{(B+1)+[(B-1)^2+4H^2]^{1/2}}, \tag{8.24}$$

where θ is the rotation angle of the quadratic term in the diagonalization of Equation (8.19). After being rotated, the ellipse attains a standard form, and the two semi-axes a and b can be determined.

Summarizing the previous process, the five parameters of the ellipse are determined in three steps: first, the (two) position coordinates, then the orientation, and finally the size and eccentricity.

Example 8.3 Locating an object in image with two types of object

Suppose that there are two types of objects in the image, the small object is a dark rectangle and the large object is a bright ellipse. A design strategy for locating small objects includes the following:

(1) An edge detector is used to make all edge points being value 0, in the image with background being value 1.
(2) The background region is transformed by distance transformation.
(3) The local maximum of distance transformation result is determined.
(4) The numerical value of local maximum position is analyzed.
(5) Further processing is performed to determine the approximately parallel edges of the small object.

In this problem, the key for locating small objects based on the results of distance transformation is to ignore all local maxima that are larger than half the width of the small object (anything significantly smaller than this value can also be ignored). This means that most of the local maxima in the image will be removed, and only some isolated points within the large objects and between the large objects as well as the local maxima along the center line of the small object may remain. Further, using an isolated point elimination algorithm, only the local maxima along the center line of the small object can be retained and then they are expanded to restore the boundary of the small object. The detected edge may be split into multiple fragments, but any discontinuity in the edge generally will not cause the break of the trajectory of local maximum because the distance transform will fill them up more continuously. Although the given values of distance transform will be slightly smaller, it will not affect other parts of the algorithm. Therefore, this method has certain robustness to the factors that affect edge detection.   □

8.3   Hough Transform

The **Hough transform** is a special transformation between the image space and the parameter space and is often used to extract specific objects from an image. This section primarily introduces the basic Hough transform. Section 8.4 will generalize the basic Hough transform to the complete Hough transform.

Considering that there is an object in image space and its contour can be represented by an algebraic equation. Therefore, the algebraic equation contains not only the variables of image space coordinates but also the parameters belonging to parameter space. Hough transform establishes the relationship between spatial variables and parameter variables.

Based on Hough transform, the edge pixels of the object can be connected to form the closed boundary of the object region by using the global characteristics of the image, or the object with known shape can be detected directly in the image, and the boundary to sub-pixel accuracy can be determined. The main advantage of Hough transform is that it is less affected by noise and boundary discontinuity due to the use of the global characteristics of the image.

8.3.1 Point–line duality

The principle of the basic Hough transform can be explained by the following point–line **duality**. In the image space XY, all straight lines passing the point (x, y) satisfy the equation

$$y = px + q, \tag{8.25}$$

where p is the slope and q is the intercept. If a parameter space PQ is established for p and q, then (p, q) denotes a point in the parameter space PQ. This point and the line represented by Equation (8.25) have one-to-one correspondence, that is, a line in XY space corresponds to a point in PQ space. On the other hand, Equation (8.25) can also be written as

$$q = -px + y. \tag{8.26}$$

Equation (8.26) represents a straight line in parameter space PQ, which corresponds to a point (x, y) in XY space.

Now, consider Figure 8.12, where Figure 8.12(a) represents the image space and Figure 8.12(b) represents the parameter space. In the image space XY, the general linear equation passing through the point (x_i, y_i) can be written as $y_i = px_i + q$ according to Equation (8.25) or $q = -px_i + y_i$ according to Equation (8.26); the latter represents a straight line in the parameter space PQ. Similarly, the line passing point (x_j, y_j) has $y_j = px_j + q$, which can also be written as $q = -px_j + y_j$; the latter represents another straight line in the parameter space PQ. Let the two lines intersect at points (p', q') in the parameter space PQ, where the point (p', q') corresponds to

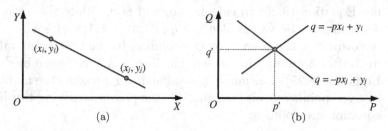

Figure 8.12. Duality of point and line in image space and parameter space.

a straight line passing (x_i, y_i) and (x_j, y_j) in the image space XY because they satisfy $y_i = p'x_i + q'$ and $y_j = p'x_j + q'$. It can be seen that each point on the line passing through points (x_i, y_i) and (x_j, y_j) in image space XY corresponds to a line in parameter space PQ, and these lines intersect at point (p', q').

Therefore, the collinear points in the image space correspond to the intersecting lines in the parameter space. Conversely, all lines intersecting at the same point in the parameter space have collinear points corresponding to them in the image space. This is the point–line duality. According to these dual relations, Hough transform converts the detection problem in the image space into the parameter space and completes the detection task by using simple accumulation statistics in the parameter space.

8.3.2   Calculation steps

The corresponding relationship between the points and lines in image space and parameter space given by Equations (8.25) and (8.26) is the embodiment of point–line duality. According to the point–line duality, the line detection in XY space can be transformed into the point detection in PQ space. For example, if some points in XY space are known, the specific steps of detecting whether they are collinear by using Hough transform are as follows:

(1) Quantify the possible value ranges of the parameters p and q in the parameter space, construct an accumulation array $A(p_{\min} : p_{\max}, q_{\min} : q_{\max})$ according to the quantization result, and initialize it to zero.

(2) For each given point in XY space, let p take all possible values, use Equation (8.26) to calculate q, and accumulate the array A according to the values of p and $q : A(p, q) = A(p, q) + 1$.

(3) According to the p and q corresponding to the maximum value in A after accumulation, a straight line in XY is determined by Equation (8.25). The maximum value in A represents the number of given points on this straight line; the points satisfying this line equation are collinear.

It can be seen from the above that the basic strategy of Hough transform is to calculate the lines in the parameter space from the

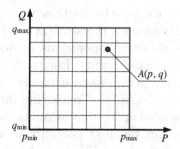

Figure 8.13.   Accumulation array in the parameter space.

points in the image space according to the duality and then calculate the lines in the image space according to the intersection points of the lines in the parameter space.

In the specific calculation, it is necessary to establish a 2D accumulation array in the parameter space PQ. Let the accumulation array be $A(p, q)$, as shown in Figure 8.13, where $[p_{min}, p_{max}]$ and $[q_{min}, q_{max}]$ are the expected value ranges of slope and intercept, respectively. At the beginning, set all the elements in array A to 0; then, for each given point in the image space, let p take all possible values on the P axis and calculate the corresponding q according to Equation (8.26). Then, according to the values of p and q (assuming that they are all rounded), add up A: $A(p, q) = A(p, q) + 1$. After the accumulation, one can know how many points are collinear according to the value of $A(p, q)$, that is, the value of $A(p, q)$ is the number of collinear points at (p, q). At the same time, the value of (p, q) also gives the parameters of the linear equation and further gives the line (function) where the points are.

Note that the accuracy of the collinear statistics of the spatial points here is determined by the size of the accumulated array. The larger the accumulation array, the more accurate the statistics. Assuming that the P axis is divided into K parts, then for each point (x_k, y_k), K values of q can be obtained by using Equation (8.26) (corresponding to p takes K values). If there are n points in the image, then nK operations are required. It can be seen that the calculation amount is a linear function of n. If K is smaller than n (satisfied in practice), the total amount of calculation must be less than n^2. If this problem is calculated by a direct method, it can be seen that several points on a straight line have been detected, and the straight line where they are located needs to be determined. Now, it is necessary to determine all the straight lines defined by any two points (this requires about n^2 operations to determine $n(n-1)/2$ lines) and then find the set of points close to the specific straight line (this requires about n^3 operations to compare each of n points with each of $n(n-1)/2$ straight lines). Comparing the two, the use of the Hough transform has obvious computational advantages.

Hough transform can be used not only to detect the line and connect the points on the same line but also to detect all kinds of curves satisfying the analytic formula $f(\boldsymbol{x}, \boldsymbol{c}) = 0$ and connect the points on the curves. Here, $\boldsymbol{x}$ is a coordinate vector, which is a 2D vector in the 2D image, and $\boldsymbol{c}$ is a coefficient vector. Both $\boldsymbol{x}$ and $\boldsymbol{c}$ can have different dimensions according to different curves, from 2D to 3D, 4D, ... In other words, if one can write the curve equation, one can use the Hough transform to detect this curve. The following is a brief introduction on how to detect circles. The general equation of a circle is

$$(x - a)^2 + (y - b)^2 = r^2. \tag{8.27}$$

Because Equation (8.27) has three parameters a, b, and r, it is necessary to create a 3D accumulation array A in the parameter space, and its elements can be written as $A(a, b, r)$. In this way, a and b can be changed in turn to calculate r according to Equation (8.27) and accumulate A: $A(a, b, r) = A(a, b, r) + 1$. It can be seen that the principle here is the same as that of detecting points on a straight line, but the complexity has increased. The coefficient vector $\boldsymbol{c}$ is now a 3D vector. In theory, the amount of calculation and the size of the accumulator increase exponentially with the increase in the number of parameters, so in practice, the Hough transform is most suitable for detection of points on a simple curve (that is, the number of parameters in its analytical representation is less).

Example 8.4 Example of circle detection using Hough transform

Figure 8.14 shows a set of example images for circle detection with Hough transform. Figure 8.14(a) is a composite image of 256×256, 256-level gray-scale image. There is a circular object with a gray value of 160 and a radius of 80. The object is in the center of the

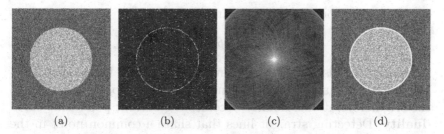

(a)　　　　　　(b)　　　　　　(c)　　　　　　(d)

Figure 8.14.　Use of the Hough transform to detect a circle.

background that has a gray value of 96. Random noises uniformly distributed between $[-48, 48]$ are added to the entire image. Now, consider using the Hough transform to detect the center of this circle (assuming the radius is known). The first step here is to calculate the gradient image of the original image (e.g., the Sobel operator can be used) and then threshold the gradient image to get some edge points of the object. Due to noise interference, if the threshold here is lower, the contour line composed of edge points will be wider. However, if the threshold is higher, the contour line composed of edge points will be discontinuous, and there will still be many noise points, as shown in Figure 8.14(b). This also shows that the detection of complete boundaries is a difficult problem if there is noise. Now, the Hough transform can be calculated on the thresholded gradient image, and the resulting accumulator image is shown in Figure 8.14(c), where each edge point draws a circle with the given radius. The coordinates of the center of the circle can be determined according to the maximum value (that is, the brightest point) in the accumulator image. Because the radius is known, the contour (boundary) of the circular object can be immediately obtained, as shown by the white circle in Figure 8.14(d). The circle in Figure 8.14(d) is superimposed on the original image to show the effect. □

8.3.3　Polar coordinate equation

Now, go back to the problem of line detection with Hough transform. When using the linear equation of Equation (8.25), if the straight line is close to the vertical direction, the amount of calculation will be greatly increased as the values of p and q may be close to infinity (the size of the accumulator will be very large). In this case, the polar coordinate equation of the line can be used:

$$\lambda = x \cos \theta + y \sin \theta. \tag{8.28}$$

According to this equation, a point in the original image space corresponds to a sine curve in the new parameter space $\Lambda\Theta$, that is, the original point–line duality becomes the current point–sine curve **duality**. Detecting straight lines that share a common point in the image space requires detecting the intersection of sinusoids in the parameter space. Specifically, let θ take all possible values on the Θ axis and calculate the corresponding λ according to Equation (8.28). Then, accumulate the accumulation array $A(\theta, \lambda)$ according to the values of θ and λ (all have been rounded) and get the number of collinear points from the value of $A(\theta, \lambda)$. The method of creating an accumulation array in the parameter space is still similar to that described in Section 8.3.2, except that no matter how the straight line changes, the value ranges of θ and λ are both in finite intervals.

Now, take a look at Figure 8.15, where Figure 8.15(a) shows five points in the image space XY (they can be regarded as the center point and four vertices of an image), Figure 8.15(b) gives five curves corresponding to them in the parameter space $\Lambda\Theta$. Here, the value range of θ is $[-90°, +90°]$ and the value range of λ is $[-2^{1/2}N, +2^{1/2}N]$, where N is the image side length.

It can be seen from Figure 8.15 that each end point in the image can be obtained and their corresponding curves in the parameter space can be made. The Hough transform of any other point in the

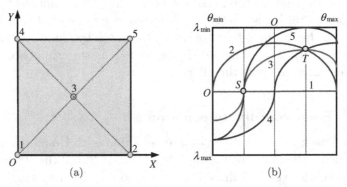

Figure 8.15.   Five points in the image space and their corresponding sinusoid curves in the parameter space.

image should be between these curves. It has been pointed out above that the points in the image space corresponding to the intersecting sinusoids in the parameter space are connected on the same straight line. In Figure 8.15(b), curves 1, 3, and 5 all cross point S, which indicates that the points 1, 3, and 5 in the image space in Figure 8.15(a) are on the same straight line. In the same way, points 2, 3, and 4 in the image space in Figure 8.15(a) are on the same straight line because in Figure 8.15(b), the curves 2, 3, and 4 all cross point T. Moreover, because λ changes sign when θ is at $\pm 90°$, which can be calculated according to Equation (8.28), the Hough transform has a reflection-connected relationship between the left and right limits of the parameter space, e.g., curves 4 and 5 have two intersections at $\theta = \theta_{min}$ and $\theta = \theta_{max}$, respectively, and these intersections are symmetrical about the line with $\lambda = 0$.

Example 8.5 Hough transform based on foot-of-normal

There are many ways to improve the basic Hough transform. Among them, there is a method that uses **foot-of-normal** to speed up the calculation. Refer to Figure 8.16, when detecting a straight line based on the Hough transform of polar coordinates, (ρ, θ) can be used to represent the parameter space. Let the coordinate of the intersection of the line represented by (ρ, θ) and the line to be detected as (x_f, y_f), the intersection can be called the foot-of-normal. (ρ, θ) and (x_f, y_f) have a one-to-one correspondence, so (x_f, y_f) can also be used to represent the parameter space. In this way, the Hough transform based on foot-of-normal can be obtained.

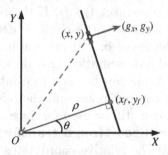

Figure 8.16. Hough transform based on foot-of-normal.

Consider here that a point (x, y) on the line needs to be detected, and the gray-level gradient at that point is (g_x, g_y). According to Figure 8.16, we can get

$$g_y/g_x = y_f/x_f,$$

$$(x - x_f)x_f + (y - y_f)y_f = 0.$$

By solving these two equations, we can obtain

$$x_f = g_x \times (xg_x + yg_y)/(g_x^2 + g_y^2),$$

$$y_f = g_y \times (xg_x + yg_y)/(g_x^2 + g_y^2).$$

Every point on the same line will vote for (x_f, y_f) in the parameter space. This Hough transform based on foot-of-normal has the same robustness as the basic Hough transform. However, its computation is faster in practice because we do not need to compute the arctangent function to get θ, and we do not need to compute the square root to get ρ. □

8.4   Generalized Hough Transform

By generalizing Hough transform to generalized Hough transform, more objects with various shapes can be detected.

8.4.1   Principle of generation

From the detection of a circle, it can be seen that relative to the point (x, y) on the circle, the center coordinate (p, q) of the circle is a reference point, and all the points (x, y) take the radius r as the parameter to connect (p, q). If the reference point (p, q) can be determined (detected), the circle is determined. According to this idea, when the curve or object contour to be detected does not have an analytical representation or is difficult to be represented in a closed form, the table can be used to establish the relationship between the curve or contour point and the reference point, so that the Hough transform can still be used for detection. This is the basic principle of the **generalized Hough transform**.

Here, the case that the relative coordinates of each point on the curve or object contour are known and only the absolute coordinates need to be determined is first considered. That is, the shape, orientation, and scale of the curve or object contour are known and only the position information needs to be detected. In practice, the gradient information of curve or contour points can be used to help establish the table. The following describes the specific method.

First of all, it is necessary to "encode" the known object contour (curve), that is, establish the connection/relation between the reference point and the contour point, so that the object contour is discretely represented by a table without analytical formula. Refer to Figure 8.17; first take a reference point (p, q) inside the given contour. For any contour point (x, y), let the vector from (x, y) to (p, q) be r and the angle between r and the positive X axis is ϕ. Draw the tangent and normal of the contour point (x, y) and set the angle (gradient angle) between the normal and the positive X axis to be θ. Here, r and ϕ are both functions of θ. Note that each contour point corresponds to a gradient angle θ, but in turn, one θ may correspond to multiple contour points. The number of corresponding contour points is related to the contour shape and the quantization interval $\Delta\theta$ of θ.

Following the above definition, the coordinates of the reference point can be calculated from the coordinates of the contour point:

$$p = x + r(\theta)\cos[\phi(\theta)],\tag{8.29}$$

$$q = y + r(\theta)\sin[\phi(\theta)].\tag{8.30}$$

It can be seen from the above that taking θ as the independent variable, a reference table — called **R-table** — can be made according to the functional relationship of r, ϕ, and θ, in which r varies

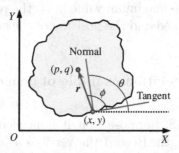

Figure 8.17. Corresponding relationship between reference points and contour points.

Table 8.1.   R-table example.

Gradient angle θ	Vector radius $r(\theta)$	Vector angle $\phi(\theta)$
θ_1	$r_1^1, r_1^2, \ldots, r_1^{N_1}$	$\phi_1^1, \phi_1^2, \ldots, \phi_1^{N_1}$
θ_2	$r_2^1, r_2^2, \ldots, r_2^{N_2}$	$\phi_2^1, \phi_2^2, \ldots, \phi_2^{N_2}$
$\ldots$	$\ldots$	$\ldots$
θ_M	$r_M^1, r_M^2, \ldots, r_M^{N_M}$	$\phi_M^1, \phi_M^2, \ldots, \phi_M^{N_M}$

in size and direction with different contour points. The R-table itself has nothing to do with the absolute coordinates of the contour. It only uses relative coordinates to help describe the contour. However, the reference points calculated by Equations (8.29) and (8.30) have absolute coordinates (because of x and y having absolute coordinates). If there are a total of N points on the contour and a total of M gradient angles, there should be $N \geq M$. The format of the built R-table is shown in Table 8.1, where $N = N_1 + N_2 + \cdots + N_M$.

It can be seen from Table 8.1 that given a θ, a possible reference point position can be determined (equivalent to establishing an equation). After the contour is encoded in this way, it can be detected by the generalized Hough transform. The next steps correspond to those in the basic Hough transform:

(1) Establish an accumulation array in the parameter space: $A(p_{min} : p_{max}, q_{min} : q_{max})$.
(2) For each point (x, y) on the contour, first calculate its gradient angle θ, then calculate p and q from Equations (8.29) and (8.30), and accumulate A accordingly: $A(p, q) = A(p, q) + 1$.
(3) According to the maximum value in A, the reference point of the contour is obtained and the position of the entire contour can be determined.

Example 8.6 Calculation example of generalized Hough transform

Consider Figure 8.18. Suppose that it is needed to detect a square with a unit side length. Record the vertices as a, b, c, d, which can be considered to belong to the four sides of the square, respectively, and a', b', c', d' are the midpoints of each side. The above eight

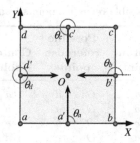

Figure 8.18. Square detection schematic.

Table 8.2. Vector from contour point to reference point.

Contour point	a	a'	b	b'	c	c'	d	d'
Vector radius $r(\theta)$	$\sqrt{2}/2$	1/2	$\sqrt{2}/2$	1/2	$\sqrt{2}/2$	1/2	$\sqrt{2}/2$	1/2
Vector angle $\phi(\theta)$	$1\pi/4$	$2\pi/4$	$3\pi/4$	$4\pi/4$	$5\pi/4$	$6\pi/4$	$7\pi/4$	$8\pi/4$

Table 8.3. R-table corresponding to the square in Figure 8.18.

Gradient angle θ	Vector radius $r(\theta)$		Vector angle $\phi(\theta)$	
$\theta_a = \pi/2$	$\sqrt{2}/2$	1/2	$\pi/4$	$2\pi/4$
$\theta_b = 2\pi/2$	$\sqrt{2}/2$	1/2	$3\pi/4$	$4\pi/4$
$\theta_c = 3\pi/2$	$\sqrt{2}/2$	1/2	$5\pi/4$	$6\pi/4$
$\theta_d = 4\pi/2$	$\sqrt{2}/2$	1/2	$7\pi/4$	$8\pi/4$

points are all square contour points. The points on each side have the same gradient angle, which are θ_a, θ_b, θ_c, θ_d, respectively. If the center point of the square is set as the reference point, the vector radius and vector angle of each contour point to the reference point are shown in Table 8.2.

According to Table 8.2, the R-table of the square can be established. As shown in Table 8.3, each gradient angle corresponds to two contour points.

The possible reference points corresponding to the eight contour points on the square in Figure 8.18 are determined, respectively. The results are shown in Table 8.4.

Table 8.4.   Possible reference points from Figure 8.18.

Gradient angle	Contour point	Possible reference points	Contour point	Possible reference points	
θ_a	a	O	d'	a'	b'	O
θ_b	b	O	a'	b'	c'	O
θ_c	c	O	b'	c'	d'	O
θ_d	d	O	c'	d'	a'	O

Because the θ of two points on each edge are the same, for each θ there are two r and two ϕ corresponding to it. It can be seen from Table 8.4 that from the frequency of reference points, point O appears most (it is the possible reference point of each contour point), so if it is accumulated, the maximum value will be obtained, that is, the detected reference point is point O.   □

8.4.2 Complete generalized Hough transform

In the actual coordinate transformation, not only the translation of the contour but also the scaling and rotation of the contour must be considered. Here, the parameter space increases from 2D to 4D. That is, the orientation parameter β (the angle between the principal direction of contour and the X axis) of the contour needs to be added, and the scale transformation coefficient S also needs to be added, but the basic method of the generalized Hough transformation remains unchanged. Now, we only need to expand the accumulation array to $A(p_{\min} : p_{\max}, q_{\min} : q_{\max}, \beta_{\min} : \beta_{\max}, S_{\min} : S_{\max})$, and change Equations (8.29) and (8.30) to the following (note that the orientation angle β and the scale transformation coefficient S are not functions of θ):

$$p = x + S \times r(\theta) \cos[\phi(\theta) + \beta], \tag{8.31}$$

$$q = y + S \times r(\theta) \sin[\phi(\theta) + \beta]. \tag{8.32}$$

Finally, the accumulation rule for the accumulation array becomes $A(p, q, \beta, S) = A(p, q, \beta, S) + 1$.

For the case of the parameter dimension increasing, other methods can also be used to consider the scaling and rotation of the contour.

For example, it can be done by transforming the **R-table**. First, consider the R-table as a multi-vector valued function $R(\theta)$. Here, if S is used to represent the scale transformation coefficient, and the scale transformation is recorded as Ts, then $Ts[R(\theta)] = SR(\theta)$. If β is used to represent the angle of rotation, and the rotation transformation is recorded as $T\beta$, then $T\beta[R(\theta)] = R[(\theta - \beta)\mathrm{mod}(2\pi)]$. In other words, for each θ in R, give an increment $-\beta$ and take the modulus of 2π, which is equivalent to rotating the corresponding vector radius r by β angle on the contour.

To achieve this goal, θ in the R-table can be changed to $\theta + \beta$, while $r(\theta)$ and ϕ are unchanged. Now, Equations (8.31) and (8.32) can still be used to calculate p and q, but the interpretation is different. The meaning here is as follows: (i) First, calculate the gradient angle after rotation; (ii) then, calculate the new vector angle to obtain a new R-table; (iii) finally, use the new R-table to calculate the reference point according to the original method.

Example 8.7 Calculation example of complete generalized Hough transform

The square in Figure 8.18 is now rotated counterclockwise around point a (taken as origin), and the result obtained is shown in Figure 8.19. It is required to calculate the position of reference point at this time.

The R-table corresponding to the rotated square obtained according to the previous method is shown in Table 8.5.

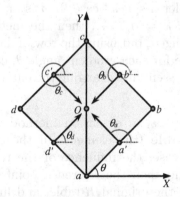

Figure 8.19. Detection after square rotation.

Table 8.5.　*R*-table corresponding to the square in Figure 8.19.

Original gradient angle θ	New gradient angle θ'	Vector radius $r(\theta)$		New vector angle $\phi(\theta)$	
$\theta_a = \pi/2$	$\theta'_a = 3\pi/4$	$\sqrt{2}/2$	1/2	$2\pi/4$	θ'_a
$\theta_b = 2\pi/2$	$\theta'_b = 5\pi/4$	$\sqrt{2}/2$	1/2	$4\pi/4$	θ'_b
$\theta_c = 3\pi/2$	$\theta'_c = 7\pi/4$	$\sqrt{2}/2$	1/2	$6\pi/4$	θ'_c
$\theta_d = 4\pi/2$	$\theta'_d = \pi/4$	$\sqrt{2}/2$	1/2	$8\pi/4$	θ'_d

Table 8.6.　Table of possible reference points obtained from Figure 8.19.

Gradient angle	Contour point	Possible reference points		Contour point	Possible reference points	
θ'_a	a	O	d'	a'	b'	O
θ'_b	b	O	a'	b'	c'	O
θ'_c	c	O	b'	c'	d'	O
θ'_d	d	O	c'	d'	a'	O

For the eight contour points on the square (see Figure 8.19), their possible reference points are calculated, and the results are shown in Table 8.6 (compare it with Table 8.4). According to the frequency of the reference points, it can be known that the point O should be the most possible reference point.

Now, let's consider a special case. If β is an integral multiple of $\Delta\theta$, i.e., $\beta = k\Delta\theta$, $k = 0, 1, \ldots$, then the method of keeping the R-table itself unchanged, but using the row of data corresponding to $\theta + \beta$ in the R-table for each gradient angle θ, can also be adopted. This can be seen as essentially changing the entry of the R-table with the changing of β.　$\square$

In addition, there is an extension method that does not need to modify the **R-table** (the elements in the original R-table are still used). In this case, the influence of the rotation angle β can be omitted first, and then the reference point coordinates can be calculated by using the original R-table, and finally the calculated reference point coordinates can be rotated by β angle. That is, we find out first

$$r_x = r(\theta - \beta)\cos[\phi(\theta) - \beta] \qquad (8.33)$$

$$r_y = r(\theta - \beta)\sin[\phi(\theta) - \beta], \qquad (8.34)$$

then rotate the angle β again, and finally get

$$p = r_x \cos\beta - r_y \sin\beta = r(\theta - \beta)\cos[\phi(\theta - \beta) + \beta], \qquad (8.35)$$

$$q = r_x \cos\beta + r_y \sin\beta = r(\theta - \beta)\sin[\phi(\theta - \beta) + \beta]. \qquad (8.36)$$

When using the Hough transform to detect the object, it has certain robustness to the problem of partial occlusion of the object. This is because the Hough transform only looks for evidence and can ignore the missing data due to partial occlusion. Therefore, it can infer the existence of an object from limited information (whether caused by noise, object distortion, occlusion, etc.).

8.5 Key Points and References for Each Section

The following indicates the key points of each section and provides some targeted guidance for further references.

1. Interest point detection

The point of interest is a general term, which can include various distinctive object points. There are many corner detection methods; in addition to Harris corner detectors, there are Moravec detectors, Zuniga–Haralick detectors, Kitchen–Rosenfeld detectors, etc.; see Ref. [1]. The SUSAN operator is an integral-based detection operator, which is relatively anti-noise; see Ref. [2]. It can not only detect corners but also edges; it can not only detect edge strength but also edge direction; see Ref. [3]. The SUSAN operator is relatively robust, its accuracy is not affected by the size of the mask, and the parameter selection can be realized automatically regardless of the image.

2. Elliptical object detection

The direct detection of elliptical objects is introduced as an example of object detection using object geometric characteristics and prior knowledge. For more detection methods of similar objects, please refer to Ref. [4].

3. Hough transform

Hough transform can use the global characteristics of the image to connect the contour pixels or directly detect the known shape objects, so as to achieve the goal of object segmentation. The introduction of Hough transform can be found in many books, such as Refs. [3,5–7]. For the method of foot-of-normal, please refer to Ref. [8]. The effect of Hough transform is better when detecting large-scale circular objects. If the object is small, lateral histogram technology can be considered; see Ref. [9]. When there are many parameters in Hough transform, the amount of calculation will be greatly increased. In order to speed up the calculation, gradient can be used for dimension reduction, which can be found in Ref. [10]. In addition, some parameters can be fixed first, only adjusting the remaining parameters, and then the adjusted parameters can be fixed, only adjusting the previously fixed parameters. In this way, the high-dimensional Hough transform can be decomposed into several low-dimensional Hough transforms, and a specific method can be found in Ref. [11].

4. Generalized hough transform

The Hough transform is suitable for the object contour that can be represented analytically, and the generalized Hough transform can be extended to the contour of the object without analytical representation. More introduction can be found in Ref. [3].

Self-Test Questions

The following questions include both single- and multiple-choice questions, so each option should be individually judged.

8.1 Interest Point Detection

8.1.1 The calculations of Laplace value and Hessian value are based on the second-order partial derivative. ( )

(A) The Laplacian value and Hessian value both have strong response at the edge;

(B) The Laplace value and Hessian value both have a strong response at the corner points;

(C) The Laplacian value has a strong response at the edge and the Hessian value has a strong response at the corner;

(D) The Laplacian value has a strong response at the corners and the Hessian value has a strong response at the edges.

[Hint] The Laplacian value also has a strong response to a straight line.

8.1.2 Harris interest point operator can detect ( )

(A) Isolated points;

(B) Corner points;

(C) Cross points;

(D) T-junction points.

[Hint] The cross point and T-junction point can be regarded as corner points in common.

8.1.3 If the mask used contains 37 pixels, when the SUSAN operator detects edges and corners, the areas of USAN will respectively be ( )

(A) 18 pixels and 9 pixels;

(B) 27 pixels and 9 pixels;

(C) 18 pixels and 27 pixels;

(D) 27 pixels and 18 pixels.

[Hint] The angle between the two sides of the corner point is about 90°.

8.1.4 SUSAN operator ( )

(A) Is a linear operator;

(B) Increases the performance as the object size increases;

(C) Is better in the detection effect of the image affected by noise, compared with the differential operator;

(D) Has stronger response to the edge in the smoother image, compared with the differential operator.

[Hint] The SUSAN operator includes two steps: first take the threshold and then make the summation.

8.1.5 When using SUSAN operator to detect edges or corners, ( )

(A) There is no parameter that needs to be determined in advance;

(B) There is a parameter that needs to be determined in advance;

(C) There are two parameters that need to be determined in advance;

(D) The parameters can be determined adaptively.

[Hint] SUSAN operator judges the detection result according to the area of USAN.

8.2 Elliptical Object Detection

8.2.1 Using diameter bisection method to detect the ellipse can get ( )

(A) The major axis of the ellipse;

(B) The minor axis of the ellipse;

(C) The center of the ellipse;

(D) The orientation of the ellipse.

[Hint] The diameter of ellipse always bisects the ellipse.

8.2.2 When using the chord-tangent method to detect the ellipse, in order to reduce the amount of calculation, we need to ( )

(A) Reduce the number of edge points involved in the calculation;

(B) Avoid calculating the tangent of the edge point;

(C) Reduce the number of candidates for the center point of the ellipse;

(D) Let the line between the two edge points pass through the center of the ellipse as much as possible.

[Hint] Analyze the three aspects to reduce the amount of calculation.

8.2.3 In order to completely determine the ellipse, after obtaining the center of the ellipse, it is also necessary to determine the direction, size, and shape of the ellipse. ( )

(A) These parameters can be determined together;

(B) The orientation parameters must be determined before the size parameters;

(C) The orientation parameters must be determined before the shape parameters;

(D) The size parameters must be determined before the shape parameters.

[Hint] Pay attention to the relationship between size parameters and shape parameters.

8.3 Hough Transform

8.3.1 According to the point–line duality, ( )

(A) A point in the image space corresponds to a line in the parameter space;

(B) A point in the parameter space corresponds to a line in the image space;

(C) The three collinear points in the image space correspond to the intersection of the two lines in the parameter space;

(D) The three collinear points in the image space correspond to the intersection of the three lines in the parameter space.

[Hint] Each of the three collinear points in the image space corresponds to a line in the parameter space.

8.3.2 The maximum value in accumulation array $A(p, q)$ corresponds to ( )

(A) The number of points in the image;

(B) The number of collinear points in the image;

(C) The maximum slope of the line in the image;

(D) The maximum value of line intercept in the image.

[Hint] If the points in the image are not collinear, they will appear in different positions of the accumulation array.

8.3.3 Assume that there are n points in the image, if one wants to calculate the lines with common points directly, ( )

(A) It needs n^2 operations;

(B) It needs n^3 operations;

(C) It needs $n^2 + n^3$ operations;

(D) It needs $n^2 \times n^3$ operations.

[Hint] The two operations are consecutive.

8.3.4 Assuming that there are nine points in the image evenly distributed on a cross, the maximum value in the accumulated array is ( )

(A) Four;

(B) Five;

(C) Eight;

(D) Nine.

[Hint] The points in the image are on two straight lines.

8.4 Generalized Hough Transform

8.4.1 Using generalized Hough transform, one ( )

(A) Needs to know the absolute coordinates of the contour points;

(B) Can detect the contour of the object with unknown shape;

(C) Needs to "code" every point of the object;

(D) Can detect the object contour without analytical representation.

[Hint] Analyze the composition and function of R-list.

8.4.2 In the generalized Hough transform, the R-table establishes ( )

(A) The relationship between the gradient angle and the vector radius;

(B) The relationship between the gradient angle and the vector angle;

(C) The relationship between the gradient angle and the contour point;

(D) The relationship between the gradient angle and possible reference points.

[Hint] The R-table is created before the start of detection.

8.4.3 Using generalized Hough transform to detect objects, it requires to know ( )

(A) The shape, orientation, and scale of the object contour;
(B) The shape and orientation of the object contour;
(C) The shape of the object contour;
(D) The position of the object contour.

[Hint] The accumulation array of the complete generalized Hough transform has four parameters.

References

[1] Sonka, M., Hlavac, V., and Boyle, R. *Image Processing, Analysis, and Machine Vision*, 3rd Edn. Canada, Toronto: Thomson, 2008.

[2] Smith, S. M. and Brady, J. M. SUSAN — A new approach to low level image processing. *IJCV*, 1997, 23(1): 45–78.

[3] Zhang, Y.-J. *Image Engineering (II): Image Analysis*, 4th Edn. Tsinghua University Press, 2018.

[4] Davies, E. R. *Computer and Machine Vision: Theory, Algorithms, Practicalities*, 4th Edn. The Netherlands, Amsterdam: Elsevier, 2012.

[5] Sonka, M., Hlavac, V., and Boyle, R. *Image Processing, Analysis, and Machine Vision*, 4th Edn. Singapore: Cengage Learning, 2014.

[6] Russ, J. C. and Neal, F. B. *The Image Processing Handbook*, 7th Edn. USA, New York: CRC Press, 2016.

[7] Gonzalez, R. C. and Woods, R. E. *Digital Image Processing*, 4th Edn. UK, London: Prentice Hall, 2018.

[8] Davies, E. R. *Machine Vision: Theory, Algorithms, Practicalities*, 3rd Edn. Singapore: Elsevier, 2005.

[9] Zhang, Y.-J. *A Course of Computer Vision*, 2nd Edn. China, Beijing: Post and Telecom Press, 2011.

[10] Zhang, Y.-J. *Image Engineering, Vol. 2: Image Analysis*. Germany, Berlin: De Gruyter, 2017.

[11] Li, R. and Zhang, Y.-J. Automated image registration using multi-resolution based Hough transform. *SPIE*, 2005, 5960: 1363–1370.

Chapter 9

Object Representation

After image segmentation, the region of interest in the image analysis application is obtained, which is usually called the **object**. Generally, the object is often represented in a suitable form different from the original image. Similar to segmentation, a region in an image can be represented by its interior (such as the set of pixels that make up the region) or its exterior (such as the set of pixels that make up the contour of the region). Generally, if one is more concerned about the reflective properties of the region, such as gray scale, color, and texture, one often chooses the internal representation; if one is more concerned about the shape of the region, one often chooses the external representation.

The sections of this chapter are arranged as follows:

Section 9.1 introduces the chain code representation method of object contour. In order to ensure the consistency of the representation of the object contour chain code, the methods of normalizing the starting point of the chain code and normalizing the rotation of the chain code are also introduced.

Section 9.2 discusses the 1D functional representation method that uses contour signatures to represent contours. Contour signature is produced by means of projection. Four typical contour signature methods are introduced.

Section 9.3 introduces the method of performing polygonal approximation to the contour first (listing three techniques) and then representing the object contour with the help of corresponding polygons.

Section 9.4 discusses the hierarchical representation method of the object region using the pyramidal data structure and specifically introduces the quad-tree representation and binary tree representation methods.

Section 9.5 introduces the method of establishing the bounding region of the object region (including Feret box, minimum enclosing rectangle, and convex hull) to approximate the representation of the object region.

Section 9.6 introduces the skeleton technology that can represent the object region abstractly and concisely and describes specifically a practical algorithm for obtaining the skeleton of the binary object region.

9.1   Chain Code Representation of Contour

Chain code is a kind of coding representation method for the region contour points, which is simple and practical.

9.1.1   Chain code representation

The chain code uses a series of connected straight line segments with specific length and direction to represent the contour of the object. Because the length of each line segment is fixed and the number of directions is limited, only the starting point of the contour needs to be represented in (absolute) coordinates, and the remaining points can simply use the connection direction to represent the offset. Since the number of bits required to represent one direction value is less than that of one coordinate value, and only one direction number for each point can replace two coordinate values, the chain code representation can greatly reduce the amount of data needed for contour representation. Digital images are generally collected on a grid with a fixed interval, so the simplest chain code is obtained by tracking the contour and assigning a direction value to the connecting line between every two adjacent pixels. The commonly used 4-direction and 8-direction chain codes are shown in Figures 9.1(a) and (b), respectively. Their common feature is that the length of the straight line segment is fixed, the direction value is limited, and the numbers of direction bits are 2 and 3, respectively. Figure 9.1(c) and (d)

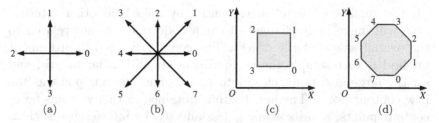

Figure 9.1. 4-direction and 8-direction chain codes.

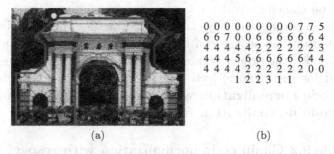

Figure 9.2. 8-direction chain code representation example.

separately show the examples of using 4-direction and 8-direction chain codes to represent the region contour.

Example 9.1 Contour representation example with 8-direction chain code

Figure 9.2 shows an example of contour representation with 8-direction chain code. The arch in Figure 9.2(a) is the object of interest, and its approximate contour is represented by a series of line segments. Encoding can start clockwise from the starting point (white point) marked in the upper-left corner and return to the starting point around the contour. The resulting chain code sequence (gray line) is shown in Figure 9.2(b). □

9.1.2 Chain code normalization

In practice, directly encoding the object contour obtained by segmentation may cause the following two problems: (i) For non-smooth contours, the code string generated in this way is often very long;

(ii) the small contour changes caused by noise and other interference will make large changes of chain code that are not related to the overall shape of the object. The commonly used improvement method is to resample the original contour with a larger grid and set the large grid point closest to the original contour point as the new contour point. The new contour obtained in this way has fewer contour points, and its shape is less affected by interference such as noise. This new contour can be represented by a shorter chain code. This method can also be used to eliminate the impact of object scale changes on the chain code.

When encoding the object contour, starting the encoding from different positions on the contour will result in different chain code strings; and if the object rotates, different chain code strings will be obtained for the same object. To this end, it is necessary to make **chain code normalization with respect to starting point** and **chain code normalization for rotation**.

Example 9.2 Chain code normalization with respect to starting point

When using chain codes, the choice of starting point is often critical. For the same contour, if different contour points are used as the starting point of the chain code, the obtained chain codes are different. In order to solve this problem, the chain code can be normalized. A specific method is to treat a chain code generated from an arbitrary point as a natural number composed of numbers representing various directions. Circulate these directional numbers in one direction to minimize the value of the natural number they constitute. Take the starting point of the chain code corresponding to this conversion as the starting point of the normalized chain code of this contour; see Figure 9.3. □

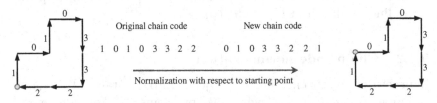

Figure 9.3.   Chain code normalization with respect to starting point.

Example 9.3 Chain code normalization for rotation

When a chain code is used to represent the contour of a given object, if the object is translated, the chain code will not change, but if the object rotates, the chain code will change. To solve this problem, the first-order difference of the chain code can be used to reconstruct a sequence (a new sequence representing the direction change between the segments of the original chain code). This is equivalent to rotating and normalizing the chain code. This difference can be obtained by subtracting the numbers in two adjacent directions (in opposite directions). Refer to Figure 9.4, in which the upper row is the original chain code (the rightmost directional number is cycled to the leftmost and is in parentheses) and the lower row is the differential code obtained by subtracting pairwise. The object on the left becomes the shape on the right after rotating 90° counterclockwise. The original chain code has changed, but the differential code has not changed.

According to the contour chain code, a kind of contour shape descriptor, **shape number**, can also be obtained. The shape number of a contour is a sequence with the smallest value in the contour difference code. In other words, the shape number is the differential code (of chain code) with the smallest value. For example, the 4-direction-based chain code of the object before normalization in Figure 9.4 is 10103322, the difference code is 33133030, and the shape number is 03033133. □

9.2 Contour Signature

In the representation methods for contours, the method of using **signature** is a 1D functional representation method of contours. There are many ways to generate **contour signatures**, but no matter what method is used to generate signatures, the basic idea is

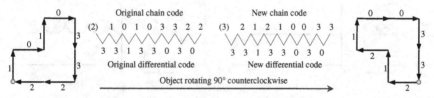

Figure 9.4. Chain code normalization for rotation (using first-order difference).

to represent 2D contours in the form of easy-to-describe functions of 1D. If one is originally interested in the shape of the 2D contour, this method can transform the problem of 2D shape description into the problem of analyzing the 1D waveform.

In a broader sense, signatures can be produced by generalized projections. Here, the projection can be horizontal, vertical, diagonal, or even radial, rotating, etc. One thing to note is that projection is not a transformation that always retains information. Transforming the contour of a region on a 2D plane into a 1D curve may lose information.

Four different contour signatures are introduced in the following.

9.2.1   Distance-angle signature

This kind of signature first finds the center of gravity for a given object and then makes the distance between the contour point and the center of gravity as a function of angle (**distance-angle signature**). Figures 9.5(a) and (b) show the signatures thus obtained for round and square objects, respectively. In Figure 9.5(a), r is a constant, and in Figure 9.5(b), $r = A \sec \theta$. This kind of signature is not affected by the object's translation but will change with the object's rotation or scaling. The impact of scaling is that the amplitude value of the signature changes. This problem can be solved by normalizing the maximum amplitude value to a unit value. There are many ways to solve the rotation effect. If one can specify a starting point that does not change with the orientation of the object and produce a signature, it can eliminate the influence of rotation changes. For example, the point farthest from the center of gravity can be selected as the starting point for generating the signature. If there is only one such point, the signature obtained has nothing to do with the orientation of the object. A more robust method is to

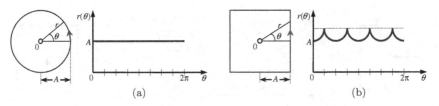

Figure 9.5.   Two distance-angle signatures.

first obtain the equivalent ellipse of the object region and then take the farthest point on its long axis as the starting point for generating the signature. Since the equivalent ellipse is determined by all points in the object region, the calculation amount is relatively large but the method is also relatively reliable.

9.2.2 Tangent angle-arc length signature

If it is circled along the contour of object and a tangent line is made at each position, then the angle value between the tangent line and a reference direction (such as the horizontal axis) gives a signature. The **tangent angle-arc length signature** (also called the ψ-s curve signature) is obtained based on this idea, where s is the length of the contour to be passed and ψ is the angle between the reference direction and the tangent line. The tangent angle-arc length signature is somewhat like a continuous form of chain code representation. Figures 9.6(a) and (b) show the signatures thus obtained for round and square objects, respectively.

It can be seen from Figure 9.6 that the horizontal straight line segment in the tangent angle-arc length signature corresponds to the straight line segment on the contour (ψ unchanged), while the inclined straight line segment in the tangent angle-arc length signature corresponds to the circular arc segment on the contour (ψ changes with a constant value). In Figure 9.6(b), the four horizontal straight segments of ψ correspond to the four sides of the square object.

9.2.3 Slope density signature

The **slope density signature** can be regarded as the result of projecting the ψ-s curve along the ψ axis. This signature is the histogram

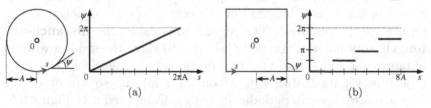

(a)   (b)

Figure 9.6. Two tangent angles-arc length signatures.

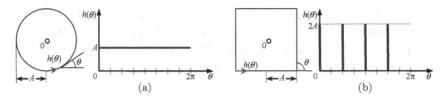

Figure 9.7.   Two slope density signatures.

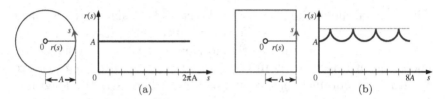

Figure 9.8.   Two distance-arc length signatures.

$h(\theta)$ of the tangent angle. Since the histogram is a measure of the concentration of values, the slope density signature will have a stronger response to the straight line segment on the contour with a constant tangent angle, and the straight line segment with a faster change in the tangent angle corresponds to a deeper valley. Figures 9.7(a) and (b) show the signatures obtained in this way for round and square objects, respectively. The slope density signature for the round object has the same form as the distance-angle signature, but the slope density signature for the square object is very different compared with the form of the distance-angle signature.

9.2.4   Distance-arc length signature

Contour-based signatures can be made by gradually produced in surrounding the object along the contour from a starting point. If the distance between each contour point and the center of gravity of object is taken as a function of the contour point sequence, a signature can be obtained. This signature is called the **distance-arc length signature**. Figures 9.8(a) and (b) show the signatures thus obtained for round and square objects, respectively. For the round object in Figure 9.8(a), r is a constant; for the square object in Figure 9.8(b), r varies periodically with s. Compared with Figure 9.5, for round objects, the two signatures are the same (set $A = 1$); for square objects, the two signatures are dissimilar (the horizontal axes are different).

9.3 Polygonal Approximation of Contour

Digital contours in practical applications often have many smaller irregularities due to the influence of noise and sampling. These irregularities often have obvious interference effects on the contour representation by chain code. A method of better anti-interference performance and saving the amount of data required for representation is to approximate the object contour with polygons. A polygon is a closed collection of a series of line segments, which can be used to approximate most practical curves to arbitrary precision. In digital images, if the number of line segments of the polygon is equal to the number of points on the contour, the polygon can represent the contour completely and accurately (the chain code is a special case). In practice, the purpose of polygon representation is often to use as few line segments as possible to represent the contour and maintain the basic shape of the contour, so that the contour can be represented and described with less data and a more concise form. The following describes the polygons obtained by three different methods.

9.3.1 Minimum perimeter polygon

The **minimum perimeter polygon** is a polygon with an approximate contour obtained based on contraction. It regards the original object contour as a group of flexible/elastic lines, and the inner and outer sides of the pixel sequence constituting the contour as a wall. The object contour is located between the inner and outer walls. In the meantime, if the line is tightened, the minimum perimeter polygon of the object can be obtained.

Example 9.4 Minimum perimeter polygon example

Figure 9.9(a) shows an object region (inside shaded) and its contour pixels (pixels through which the thick line passes). The contour is surrounded by the boundary of the pixel. If the contour line is tightened and the shortest distance of each contour segment is taken, then

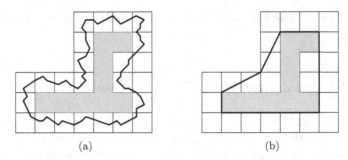

Figure 9.9.　Minimum perimeter polygon method.

the minimum perimeter polygon, as shown in Figure 9.9(b), can be obtained.　　　　　　　　　　　　　　　　　　　　　　□

9.3.2　Merging polygon

The **merging polygon** is a polygon obtained by approximating the contour with the aid of the minimum mean square error line segment. It connects each pixel on the contour in turn along the contour. It first selects a contour point as the starting point and uses a straight line to connect this point with adjacent contour points in turn. It then calculates the (approximation) fitting error between each straight line and the contour, respectively, to determine the line segment before the error exceeds a certain limit as a side of the polygon and sets the error to zero. It continues to connect the contour points with the other end point of the line segment as the starting point until it completely circles the contour round. In this way, an approximate polygon of the contour is obtained.

Example 9.5 Merging and approximating polygon example

Figure 9.10 shows an example of polygon approximation based on merging. The original contour is a polygon represented by points a, b, c, d, e, f, g, h, etc. Now, start from point a and make straight lines ab, ac, ad, ae, etc. in turn. For each line segment starting from ac, the distance between the previous contour point and the line segment is calculated as the fitting error. In Figure 9.10, suppose that the lengths of bi and cj do not exceed the predetermined error limit and the length of dk exceeds the limit, so point d is chosen as

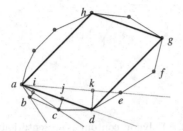

Figure 9.10. Merging and approximating polygon.

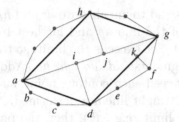

Figure 9.11. Splitting and approximating polygon.

the polygon vertex next to point a. From point d, proceed as above, and the vertices of the approximate polygon finally obtained are a, d, g, h. □

9.3.3 Splitting polygon

The **splitting polygon** is a polygon obtained by approximating the contour with the aid of the minimum mean square error line segment. It first connects the two most distant pixels on the contour (that is, it divides the contour into two parts) and then further decomposes the contour (parts) according to a certain fitting error criterion by gradually forming a polygon to approximate the contour until the fitting error meets a certain limit.

Example 9.6 Splitting and approximating polygon example

Figure 9.11 shows an example of splitting the contour based on the maximum distance between the contour point and the existing polygon. As in Figure 9.10, the original contour is a polygon represented by points a, b, c, d, e, f, g, h, etc. The first step is to draw line ag

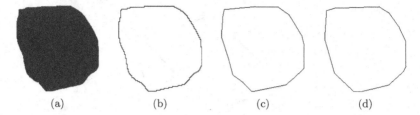

Figure 9.12.   Polygon contour representation examples.

(connecting a and g) and then calculate di and hj (point d and point h are on two sides of the line ag and farthest from the line ag). In Figure 9.11, each distance exceeds the limit, so the contour is further divided into four segments: ad, dg, gh, ha. Additional calculations for the distances between each contour point, such as b, c, e, f, and each corresponding straight line are performed. Assuming that none of them exceeds the limit (e.g., fk), then the polygon with vertices a, d, g, and h is the required polygon.   □

Example 9.7 Polygonal contour representation example

Figure 9.12 shows several examples of using different ways for representing polygon contours. Figure 9.12(a) is an irregularly shaped object in a segmented image; Figure 9.12(b) is the result of subsampling the contour and represented by chain code, which uses 112 bits; Figure 9.12(c) is the result obtained by the merging and approximating polygon method, which uses 22 bits; Figure 9.12(d) is the result obtained by the splitting and approximating polygon method, which uses 24 bits.   □

9.4   Hierarchical Representation of Objects

The object can be regarded as the collection of all the pixels that make up the object region. From the point of view of the set, the set can be decomposed into subsets, and each subset can continue to be decomposed to individual elements. The hierarchical representation of the object is based on this idea, which uses a pyramidal data structure to represent the object. The most commonly used methods of representing the object hierarchy use the structures of quad tree and binary tree. They are introduced separately in the following.

9.4.1 Quad-tree representation

The **quad-tree** representation method divides the image into four parts each time during decomposition. When the image is square and the number of pixels is an integer power of two, the quad-tree method is most suitable (so that it can be decomposed all the time). In this tree representation (refer to Figure 9.13), all nodes can be divided into the following three categories: (i) object node (indicated by white); (ii) background node (indicated by black); (iii) mixed node (indicated by gray). The root of the quad tree corresponds to the entire image, and the leaves correspond to individual pixels or a square of pixels with the same properties. Generally, the tree root nodes are often mixed nodes, while leaf nodes are definitely not mixed nodes. The quad tree is composed of multiple levels; the root is at level zero and one fork adds one more level (each node is divided into four sub-nodes). For a quad tree with $n+1$ levels, the total number of nodes N is at most (for the actual image, because there is always object without complete decomposition, it is generally less than this number)

$$N = \sum_{k=0}^{n} 4^k = \frac{4^{n+1} - 1}{3} \approx \frac{4}{3} 4^n. \tag{9.1}$$

Example 9.8 A method to build a quad tree

A specific method of building a quad tree is as follows. Suppose the image size is $2^n \times 2^n$ represented in octal. The image is first scanned, reading two lines at a time. The image is divided into four

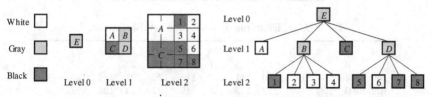

Figure 9.13. Diagram of quad-tree representation.

blocks. The subscripts of each block are: $2k$, $2k + 1$, $2^n + 2k$, $2^n + 2k + 1$ $(k = 0, 1, 2, \ldots, 2^{n-1} - 1)$. The corresponding gray values are f_0, f_1, f_2, f_3. Based on this result, the following four new gray levels can be obtained:

$$g_0 = \frac{1}{4} \sum_{i=0}^{3} f_i, \tag{9.2}$$

$$g_j = f_j - g_0 \quad j = 1, 2, 3. \tag{9.3}$$

In order to build the upper level of the tree, the first pixel of each block (calculated by Equation (9.2)) is formed into the first row, and the three differences calculated by Equation (9.3) are put into another array to get Table 9.1.

In this way, when the next two rows are read, the subscript of the first pixel will be increased by 2^{n+1}, and the result of Table 9.2 will be obtained.

Continue like this way to get a $2^{n-1} \times 2^{n-1}$ image and a $3 \times 2^{2n-2}$ array. Repeating the above process, the number of pixels in the image is reduced and the area of each pixel is increased. When the entire image becomes only one pixel, the information is collected into the array. An example is given in Table 9.3.   □

Table 9.1.   First step in building a quad tree.

g_0	g_4	g_{10}	g_{14}	g_{20}	g_{24}	$\cdots$
(g_1, g_2, g_3)	(g_5, g_6, g_7)	(g_{11}, g_{12}, g_{13})	(g_{15}, g_{16}, g_{17})	(g_{21}, g_{22}, g_{23})	(g_{25}, g_{26}, g_{27})	$\cdots$

Table 9.2.   Second step in building a quad tree.

g_0	g_4	g_{10}	g_{14}	g_{20}	g_{24}	$\cdots$
g_{100}	g_{104}	g_{110}	g_{114}	g_{120}	g_{124}	$\cdots$

Table 9.3.   Example of quad-tree establishment.

0	1	4	5	10	11	14	15	20	21	24	25	$\cdots$
2	3	6	7	12	13	16	17	22	23	26	27	$\cdots$
100	101	104	105	110	111	114	115	120	121	124	125	$\cdots$
102	103	106	107	112	113	116	117	122	123	126	127	$\cdots$

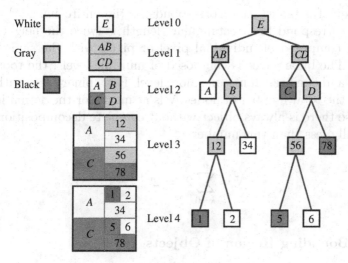

Figure 9.14. Binary tree representation.

The advantage of the quad-tree representation is that it is easy to generate, and it can also easily calculate the various features of the region. In addition, its structural characteristics make it commonly usable in the display of "rough information first". Its disadvantage is that if the level of the node in the tree is determined, the resolution cannot be further improved. In addition, operations between quad trees can only be performed between nodes of the same level. The correspondence of quad-tree representation in 3D space is octree representation.

9.4.2 Binary tree representation

The binary tree representation method divides the image into two parts each time during decomposition. The **binary tree** can be regarded as a variant of the quad tree. Compared with the quad tree, the change in resolution between levels is smaller. A representation of a binary tree is shown in Figure 9.14.

Similar to the quad-tree representation, in the binary tree representation, all nodes are still divided into the following three categories: (i) object node (indicated by white); (ii) background node (indicated by black); (iii) mixed node (indicated by gray). Similarly, the root of a binary tree corresponds to the entire image, but the leaves correspond to a rectangular (length is twice the height) or a square composed of individual pixel or pixels with the same properties. The binary tree is composed of multiple levels; the root is at level 0 and one branch has one more level. For a binary tree with $n+1$ levels, the total number of nodes N is at most (for the actual image, because there is always object without complete decomposition, it is generally less than this number)

$$N = \sum_{k=0}^{n} 2^k = 2^{n+1} - 1. \tag{9.4}$$

9.5   Bounding Region of Objects

There are many object representation methods based on the **bounding region** (**surrounding region**), and their common point is to approximate the object with a region that contains the object. Here are three commonly used methods.

9.5.1   Feret box

The **Feret box** is the smallest rectangle that contains the object region (its orientation can be determined with the help of a specific reference direction), hence the name.

Example 9.9 Size and shape of the Feret box change with the rotation of the object

The Feret box of the object region is a rectangle, and its two pairs of sides are always parallel to two coordinate axes in practice. In this way, when the object is rotated, a series of Feret boxes with different sizes and shapes will be produced. Figure 9.15(a) shows a group of Feret boxes obtained when the same object is in different orientations (the angle with the horizontal axis is from 0° to 90° and the interval is 10°); Figures 9.15(b) and (c) give the size parameter (normalized size ratio) and shape parameter (normalized length ratio of short-long sides) of each corresponding Feret box with the change in rotation, respectively.   □

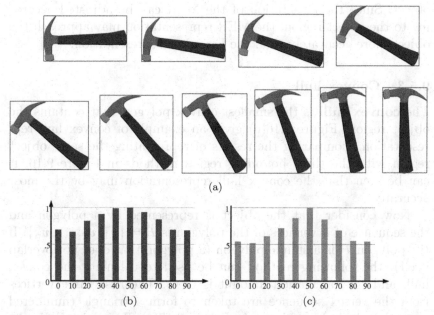

(a)

(b)   (c)

Figure 9.15. Change in the size and shape of the Feret box with the rotation of object.

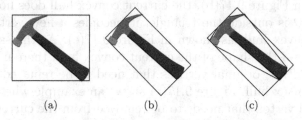

(a)   (b)   (c)

Figure 9.16. Representation results of three bounding regions of the same object.

9.5.2 Minimum enclosing rectangle

The **minimum enclosing rectangle** (MER) is also called the enclosure. It is defined as the smallest rectangle that contains the object region (which can be any orientation, that is, its four sides are not always parallel to the coordinate axis). Both the Feret box and MER are rectangles, but their orientations are often different. Figures 9.16(a) and (b) respectively give examples of the representations of the Feret box and the minimum rectangle for the same object. Since the orientation of the MER can be adjusted according to the object region, the MER representation may approach the object more accurately than the Feret box representation.

9.5.3 Convex hull

The **convex hull** is the smallest convex polygon that contains the object region. Figure 9.16(c) gives an example of convex hull representation. Comparing the results of representing the same object region with the three bounding region methods in Figure 9.16, it can be seen that the convex hull representation may be the most accurate.

Now consider that the object is represented by a polygon and the sequence of n vertices of the polygon is $P = \{v_1, v_2, \ldots, v_n\}$. If the polygon P is a simple polygon (a polygon that does not overlap itself), the following method can be used to calculate the convex hull, and the calculation amount is $O(n)$. The first three vertices from the vertex sequence are taken to form a triangle (numbered counterclockwise), as shown in Figure 9.17(a). This triangle is the current convex hull. Then, we need to determine whether the next vertex D is inside or outside the triangle. If D is inside the triangle, as shown in Figure 9.17(b), the current convex hull does not change. If vertex D is outside the triangle, it becomes a new vertex of the current convex hull, as shown in Figure 9.17(c). At the same time, depending on the shape of the current convex hull, there may be no, one, or multiple original vertices that need to be removed from the current convex hull. Figure 9.17(c) shows an example where there is no original vertex that needs to be removed from the current convex hull, while Figure 9.17(d) shows that there is one original vertex (vertex B) that needs to be removed from the current convex hull.

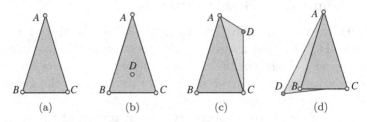

Figure 9.17.   Schematic of convex hull calculation.

The above process must be performed on all subsequent vertices, and the final polygon obtained is the required convex hull.

9.6 Skeleton Representation of the Object

The skeleton representation of the object is a simplified method of representing the object region, which can reflect the structural shape characteristics of the object in many cases.

9.6.1 Skeleton and skeleton point

The skeleton of the region can be obtained with thinning techniques. **Medial axis transform** (MAT) is a thinning technique commonly used to determine the skeleton of an object. The transformation of the central axis can also be more vividly called the **grassland fire technology**. Suppose there is a grass land with the shape of the required skeleton region and a fire is set around it at the same time. As the fire gradually burns inward, the trajectory of fire will intersect the medial axis of the region. In other words, the medial axis (or skeleton) burns last. The MAT of the region R with the contour B is determined as follows. For each point p in R, the closest point in B is searched. If more than one such point can be found for p (that is, there are two or more points in B that are closest to p at the same time), then p can be considered to belong to the medial axis or skeleton of R, that is, p is a skeleton point. The set of all skeleton points constitutes the skeleton of the region.

Theoretically, each skeleton point maintains its minimum distance from the contour point, so if a set of circles centered on each skeleton points (using a suitable distance measurement) are used as the basis, the original region can be restored. Specifically, each skeleton point is taken as the center of the circle, and the aforementioned minimum distance is taken as the radius of the circle. Their envelope constitutes the contour of the region, and the entire region can be obtained by filling all the circles. In other words, take each skeleton point as the center and all the lengths less than or equal to the minimum distance as the radius to make a circle, then the union of these circles covers the entire region.

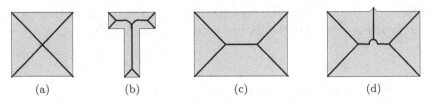

Figure 9.18.   Examples of some skeletons calculated using Euclidean distance.

From the above discussion, the skeleton d_s is defined by the minimum distance between a point p and a point set B, which can be written as

$$d_s(p, B) = \inf\{d(p, z)|z \subset B\}. \tag{9.5}$$

The distance metric can be Euclidean, city block, or chessboard. Because the closest distance depends on the distance metrics used, the result of MAT is also related to the distance metrics used.

Example 9.10 Skeleton example

Figure 9.18 shows some regions and their skeletons calculated using Euclidean distance. From Figures 9.18(a) and (b), it can be seen that the skeleton of a slender object can often provide more shape information, while for a thicker object, the information provided by the skeleton would be less. Note that sometimes a region represented by the skeleton is greatly affected by noise. For example, compare Figures 9.18(c) and (d), where the region in Figure 9.18(d) is similar to that in Figure 9.18(c), with only a slight difference (it can be considered to be caused by noise), but the two skeletons are quite different. □

9.6.2   Skeleton algorithm

The following introduces a practical algorithm for obtaining the skeleton of a binary object region. Set the known object point as one and the background point as zero. The contour point is defined as the point that is marked as one and at least one point in its 8-connected neighborhood is marked as zero. The algorithm performs the following two steps on the contour points:

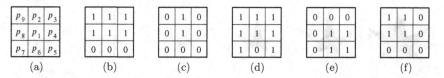

Figure 9.19. Calculation of the skeleton of the binary object region.

(1) Consider the 8-neighborhood centered on the contour point, denote the center point as p_1, and the eight points in the neighborhood clockwise around the center point as p_2, p_3, ..., p_9, where p_2 is on the top of p_1; see Figure 9.19(a). Now, consider a specific example shown in Figure 9.19(b). First, mark the contour points that meet the following conditions at the same time:

  (1.1) $2 \leq N(p_1) \leq 6$;
  (1.2) $S(p_1) = 1$;
  (1.3) $p_2 \bullet p_4 \bullet p_6 = 0$ (that is, if any point is zero, the result is zero);
  (1.4) $p_4 \bullet p_6 \bullet p_8 = 0$,

  where $N(p_1)$ is the number of non-zero neighbors of p_1, which is five in Figure 9.19(b) and $S(p_1)$ is the number of times these points changes from $0 \to 1$ when it goes around p_1 in the order of p_2, p_3, ..., p_9, p_2, which is one in Figure 9.19(b). After all the contour points are checked, all the marked points are removed.

(2) Same as step (1), only change the previous condition (1.3) to condition (2.3) $p_2 \bullet p_4 \bullet p_8 = 0$ and condition (1.4) to condition (2.4) $p_2 \bullet p_6 \bullet p_8 = 0$. Similarly, after checking all contour points, remove all marked points.

The above two steps constitute one iteration. The algorithm iterates repeatedly until no more points meet the marking condition, and then the remaining points form the skeleton of the region. Among the above marking conditions, condition (1.1) removes the case that p_1 has only one adjacent point marked as one, that is, as shown in Figure 9.19(c), when p_1 is the end point of the line segment, and removes the case that p_1 has seven marked neighboring points of one, that is, the situation where p_1 is too deep into the region, as shown in Figure 9.19(d). Condition (1.2) removes the case of operating on the line segment with a width of a single pixel to avoid cutting the skeleton. Conditions (1.3) and (1.4) remove the case where p_1 is the

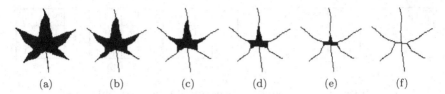

Figure 9.20.   Skeleton calculation example.

right end or lower end point of the contour ($p_4 = 0$ or $p_6 = 0$), or as shown in Figure 9.19(e), where p_1 is the upper-left corner point of the contour ($p_2 = 0$ and $p_8 = 0$), that is, it is not a skeleton point. Similarly, conditions (2.3) and (2.4) remove the case where p_1 is the left or upper end point of the contour ($p_2 = 0$ or $p_8 = 0$), or as shown in Figure 9.19(f), where p_1 is the lower-right corner points of the contour ($p_4 = 0$ and $p_6 = 0$), that is, it is not a skeleton point. Finally, notice that if p_1 is the upper-right end point of the contour, we have $p_2 = 0$ and $p_4 = 0$, and if p_1 is the lower-left end point of the contour, we have $p_6 = 0$ and $p_8 = 0$. They both satisfy the conditions (1.3) and (1.4) as well as conditions (2.3) and (2.4).

Example 9.11 Skeleton calculation example

Figure 9.20 shows a set of skeleton calculation examples. Figure 9.20(a) is a binary image after segmentation and Figures 9.20(b) to (e) are the intermediate results calculated according to the aforementioned method for four consecutive iterations. Figure 9.20(f) shows the final skeleton.   □

9.7   Key Points and References for Each Section

The following indicates the key points of each section and provides some targeted guidance for further references.

1. Chain code representation of contour

The chain code representation of the contour is an accurate representation of the object region in the image, which relies on the coding of the contour points; see Ref. [1]. The chain code representation of the contour uses a series of connected straight line segments with specific length and direction to represent the contour of the object, which can greatly reduce the amount of data required for contour representation. The normalization of the starting point of the chain code can eliminate the influence of the starting point position on the generated chain code, and the normalization of the rotation of the chain code can eliminate the influence of the object contour rotation on the chain code. The introduction of the smoothing of chain codes and a modification of chain codes, crack codes, can be found in Ref. [2]. For further discussion on the shape number based on chain code and its application in image matching, please refer to Refs. [2,3].

2. Contour signature

The signature representation of contour is a method of transforming the contour of a 2D object region into a 1D function form. It is closely related to other external representation methods; see Ref. [4]. For example, the tangent angle-arc length signature is similar to the continuous form of chain code representation; see Ref. [5]. Signatures can be produced by various generalized projections; see Ref. [6]. Although projection does not always retain information, in many cases, it is possible for signatures to accurately represent contours; see Ref. [7].

3. Polygonal approximation of contour

Using polygons to approximate the contour is an approximation representation of the object contour; see Ref. [2]. A polygon is a closed collection of a series of line segments. It can represent and describe the contour with less data and in a more concise form, as well as maintain the basic shape of the contour. After the object contour is converted into an approximating polygon, the complexity of the contour representation and the amount of data required for the representation can be greatly reduced.

4. Hierarchical representation of objects

Regarding the object region as a set of pixels, then gradually decomposing the set into subsets, and subsequently decomposing the subsets into pixels is the basic idea of hierarchical representation of the object region; see Ref. [7]. Both quad tree and binary tree are common hierarchical representations. These two representation methods must establish a representation tree. In the tree, the root of the tree corresponds to the entire image, and the nodes are divided into the following three categories: (i) object node; (ii) background node; (iii) mixed node. The quad-tree representation method divides one node into four (sub-nodes) each time during decomposition, and the binary tree representation method divides one node into two (sub-nodes) each time during decomposition. Considering the correlation of the object pixels in the image, the total number of nodes in the tree will be less than the number of pixels in the original image. The generalization of quad-tree representation in 3D is octree representation; see Ref. [8].

5. Bounding region of objects

The bounding region is the region that contains the object, which can approximately represent the object's location, size, and even certain shape information. The three methods introduced in this section have a trend of increasing accuracy from the Feret box, to the minimum enclosing box, and then to the convex hull. With the help of the contour decomposition of the convex hull, another object contour representation method, boundary segment, can be obtained, which can be found in Ref. [2]. The convex hull can also be obtained by means of mathematical morphology; see Appendix A.

6. Skeleton representation of the object

The regional skeleton representation is a simplified method of object representation, which can be found in Ref. [7]. The skeleton reflects the shape of the object region to a certain extent, but it may be greatly affected by noise. There are many ways to obtain the skeleton. This section introduced a commonly used iterative method. The contour points of the region are scanned in both positive and negative directions, and the contour points that do not meet the conditions of the skeleton point are removed one by one, leaving only the skeleton points. Another method of using mathematical morphology to obtain the skeleton can be found in Appendix A. The skeleton can also be obtained through iterative thinning, from which the original region can be restored or the region can be reconstructed; see Ref. [9].

Self-Test Questions

The following questions include both single- and multiple-choice questions, so each option should be individually judged.

9.1 Chain Code Representation of Contour

9.1.1 Using 4-direction chain code, which graph in Figure 9.1.1 is represented by the chain code 010303322211? ( )

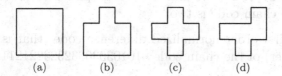

(a)   (b)   (c)   (d)

Figure 9.1.1.

(A) Figure 9.1.1(a);
(B) Figure 9.1.1(b);
(C) Figure 9.1.1(c);
(D) Figure 9.1.1(d).

[Hint] Draw the graph according to the definition of the chain code.

9.1.2 Which of the following chain code(s) correctly represent(s) the closed contour? ( )

(A) 030322122100;
(B) 123323300103;
(C) 212232300001;
(D) 323230010101.

[Hint] For a closed contour, the value of its head and tail chain codes (with respect to adjacent chain codes) will not be exactly two.

9.1.3 If an 8-direction chain code is used to encode the graph in Figure 9.1.3, the resulting chain code should be ( )

Figure 9.1.3.

(A) 12345670;
(B) 31276450;
(C) 64531207;
(D) 76543210.

[Hint] There are two places in the graph where the change value of the chain code is two.

9.1.4 The first-order normalized difference code (that is, the shape number) of the chain code 0101030303323232212111 is ( )

(A) 3 1 3 1 3 3 1 3 1 3 0 3 1 3 1 3 0 3 1 3 0 0;
(B) 3 1 3 0 3 1 3 1 3 0 3 1 3 0 0 3 1 3 1 3 3 1;
(C) 3 1 3 0 3 1 3 0 0 3 1 3 1 3 3 1 3 1 3 0 3 1;
(D) 0 0 3 1 3 1 3 3 1 3 1 3 0 3 1 3 1 3 0 3 1 3.

[Hint] Calculate according to the definition of difference code.

9.1.5 Among the first-order difference codes of 4-directional chain codes, which code(s) do(es) not appear? ( )

(A) 0;
(B) 1;
(C) 2;
(D) 3.

[Hint] Note that the direction chain codes 0 and 2 as well as the direction chain codes 1 and 3 will not be connected.

9.1.6 If a 4-direction chain code is used to encode the (segmented) contour of the graph in Figure 9.1.6, then the shape number of the graph is ( )

(A) 0 0 0 3 0 3 3 1 0 1 3 3 0 3;
(B) 3 0 0 3 0 3 3 1 1 1 1 3 3 0;

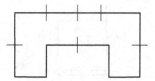

Figure 9.1.6.

(C) 0 0 0 3 3 2,1 2 2 2 3 2 1 1;
(D) 0 2 1 2 3 2 1 1 1 0 0 0 3 3.

[Hint] Computer the difference of the chain code, as the shape number is the difference code with the smallest value.

9.2 Contour Signature

9.2.1 In Figure 9.5(b), if the maximum value of r is linearly normalized to 1, the minimum value of r is ( )

(A) 0;
(B) 1/2;
(C) 1;
(D) $1/(2)^{1/2}$.

[Hint] For $r = A \sec \theta$, it is the smallest when $\theta = 0$ and the largest when $\theta = \pi/4$.

9.2.2 A regular octagon can be regarded as a geometric shape between a circle and a square. Among the four types of signatures introduced in Section 9.2, which of its signature(s) is/are the least like between a circle signature and a square signature? ( )

(A) Distance-angle signature;
(B) Tangent angle-arc length signature;
(C) Slope density signature;
(D) Distance-arc length signature.

[Hint] The circle signature and the square signature can be superimposed together as a reference.

9.2.3 In Figure 9.2.3.1, if the X axis is taken as the reference line and the contour is traced in the counterclockwise direction, the signature obtained is ( )

Figure 9.2.3.1.

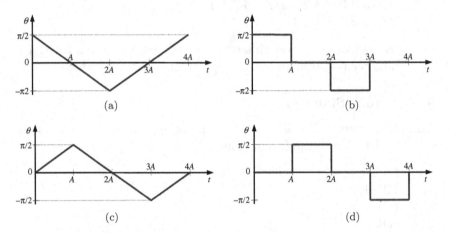

Figure 9.2.3.2.

(A) Figure 9.2.3.2(a);
(B) Figure 9.2.3.2(b);
(C) Figure 9.2.3.2(c);
(D) Figure 9.2.3.2(d).

[Hint] Note to start from the origin.

9.3 Polygonal Approximation of Contour

9.3.1 Suppose the distance between adjacent pixels is one, if the minimum perimeter polygon is calculated, the maximum error generated inside each pixel would be ( )

(A) $\sqrt{2}/3$;
(B) $\sqrt{2}/2$;
(C) $\sqrt{2}$;
(D) $1/\sqrt{2}$.

[Hint] The distance between adjacent pixels is one, that is, the side length of the pixel is one.

9.3.2 Among the three methods of approximating contours with polygons, ( )

(A) The polygons obtained by merging line segments clockwise and counterclockwise are different;

(B) The perimeter of the polygon obtained by the line segment approximation method based on merging is always greater than the original contour length;

(C) The perimeter of the polygon obtained by the line segment approximation method based on splitting is always smaller than the original contour length;

(D) The polygon obtained by the contraction method is the same as the polygon obtained by the line segment approximation method based on splitting.

[Hint] Consider the specific steps and characteristics of the three methods.

9.3.3 For the contour of a round object, ( )

(A) The polygons obtained by merging-based methods are always symmetrical;

(B) The polygons obtained by the splitting-based method are always symmetrical;

(C) The number of sides of the polygon obtained by the merging-based method doubles as the fitting error limit decreases;

(D) The number of sides of the polygon obtained by the splitting-based method increases exponentially with the decrease of the fitting error limit.

[Hint] The round object is symmetrical, but when using the merging method to form a polygon, one can start from certain points along a certain direction, so the result is not always symmetrical.

9.4 Hierarchical Representation of Objects

9.4.1 For a quad tree with four levels in total, how many nodes does it have at most? ( )

(A) 75;
(B) 85;
(C) 95;
(D) 105.

[Hint] Calculate according to the quad-tree node calculation formula.

9.4.2 A quad tree of a 4×4 image is shown in Figure 9.4.2.1. The object node is represented by white, the background node is represented by black, and the mixed node is represented by gray.

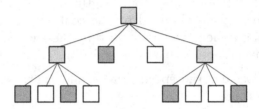

Figure 9.4.2.1.

Based on the quad tree, try to determine which of the original image(s) is/are in Figure 9.4.2.2? ( )

(A) Figure 9.4.2.2(a);
(B) Figure 9.4.2.2(b);
(C) Figure 9.4.2.2(c);
(D) Figure 9.4.2.2(d).

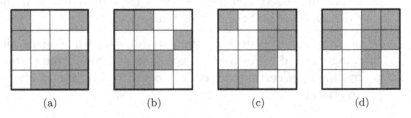

(a)   (b)   (c)   (d)

Figure 9.4.2.2.

[Hint] Draw the image level by level from top to bottom according to the quad tree.

9.4.3 Binary tree ( )

(A) Is a special case of quad-tree;

(B) Has nodes in its representation in two types;

(C) Every node always corresponds to a rectangle composed of pixels with the same characteristics;

(D) Requires always less number of nodes to represent the image than the number of nodes required by the quad tree.

[Hint] Consider the definition of a binary tree.

9.5 Bounding Region of Objects

9.5.1 For an object, if the obtained Feret box is exactly the same as the minimum enclosing rectangle, then ( )

(A) This object is a round object;

(B) This object is an elliptical object;

(C) This object is a square object;

(D) This object is a square object with one side parallel to the X axis.

[Hint] Note that if there is no restriction on the object, the object can have any orientation.

9.5.2 For which of the following object(s), the minimum enclosing rectangle and the convex hull have the most difference in area? ( )

(A) Square object;

(B) Equilateral triangle object;

(C) Regular hexagonal object;

(D) Regular octagonal object.

[Hint] The area of the convex hull here is the area of the object.

9.5.3 Suppose there is a rod-like object with a length 10 times its diameter, initially lying flat on the ground, and then lifting one end and becoming gradually vertical. In this process, considering its profile image (the optical axis of the camera is perpendicular to its rotation plane), how will the size of the Feret box of the image change? ( )

(A) The size gradually increases;

(B) The size gradually decreases;

(C) The size increases first and then it decreases gradually;

(D) The size decreases first and then it increases gradually.

[Hint] Pay attention to the changes of the long and short sides of the Feret box during this process.

9.6 Skeleton Representation of the Object

9.6.1 For the triangular region in Figure 9.6.1, indicate which skeleton(s) is/are correct? ( )

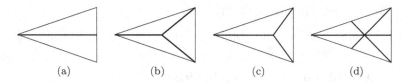

Figure 9.6.1.

(A) Figure 9.6.1(a);

(B) Figure 9.6.1(b);

(C) Figure 9.6.1(c);

(D) Figure 9.6.1(d).

[Hint] According to the skeleton definition and characteristic analysis, the three line segments in Figure 9.6.1(b) have the same length.

9.6.2 For the quadrilateral region in Figure 9.6.2, indicate which skeleton(s) is/are correct? ( )

(A) Figure 9.6.2(a);

(B) Figure 9.6.2(b);

(C) Figure 9.6.2(c);

(D) Figure 9.6.2(d).

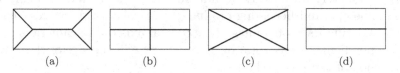

Figure 9.6.2.

[Hint] Analyze according to the skeleton definition and characteristics.

9.6.3 For a square image affected by noise, which of the skeleton(s) in Figure 9.6.3 is/are correct? ( )

(A) Figure 9.6.3(a);
(B) Figure 9.6.3(b);
(C) Figure 9.6.3(c);
(D) Figure 9.6.3(d).

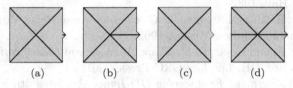

(a)　　　(b)　　　(c)　　　(d)

Figure 9.6.3.

[Hint] Pay attention to the influence of noise on the skeleton.

9.6.4 Consider the operation of the introduced skeleton algorithm at point p in Figure 9.6.4 and determine which of the following statements is correct. ( )

1	1	1
1	p	1
0	0	1

Figure 9.6.4.

(A) $N(p) = 2$;
(B) $S(p) = 0$;
(C) $p_2 \bullet p_4 \bullet p_6 = 0$;
(D) p is the point that should be removed according to the skeleton algorithm.

[Hint] Make analysis according to the skeleton algorithm of the binary object region.

References

[1] Gonzalez, R. C. and Woods, R. E. *Digital Image Processing*, 4th Edn. UK, London: Prentice Hall. 2018.

[2] Zhang, Y.-J. *Image Engineering, Vol. 2: Image Analysis*. Germany, Berlin: De Gruyter, 2017.

[3] Zhang, Y.-J. *Image Engineering, Vol. 3: Image Understanding*. Germany, Berlin: De Gruyter, 2017.

[4] Russ, J. C. and Neal, F. B. *The Image Processing Handbook*, 7th Edn. UK, London: CRC Press, 2016.

[5] Ballard, D. H. and Brown, C. M. *Computer Vision*. UK, London: Prentice-Hall, 1982.

[6] Haralick, R. M. and Shapiro. L. G. *Computer and Robot Vision, Vol. 1*. UK, London: Addison-Wesley, 1992.

[7] Costa, L. F. and Cesar, R. M. *Shape Analysis and Classification: Theory and Practice*. UK, London: CRC Press, 2001.

[8] Zhang, Y.-J. *Image Engineering (II) Image Analysis*, 4th Edn. China, Beijing: Tsinghua University Press, 2018.

[9] Sonka, M., Hlavac, V. and Boyle, R. *Image Processing, Analysis, and Machine Vision*, 4th Edn. Singapore: Cengage Learning, 2014.

Chapter 10

Object Description

In addition to the proper representation of the segmented object, it is also necessary to describe the object so that the computer can make full use of the segmentation results obtained. The goal of **Object representation** is to represent the object directly and concretely, and that of **object description** is to represent the properties of object more abstractly. A good description should be insensitive to the scale, translation, and rotation of the object on the basis of distinguishing different objects as much as possible. Such a description is more general.

Similar to the representation of the object based on the region or contour of the object, the description of the object can also be divided into the description of the contour and the description of the region, which can also be called the external description and internal description of the object, respectively. In addition, the relationship between contours and contours or between regions and regions of different objects often needs to be described.

The description parameters corresponding to the representation of the image region are also called **features**. To describe the object, one can use some more general basic parameters, but if one wants to describe some special characteristics of object, there are also many corresponding methods. This chapter introduces some general and typical descriptors, and the description of more specific feature categories can also be found in Chapters 11 and 12.

The sections of this chapter are arranged as follows:

Section 10.1 introduces several basic object contour description parameters, including contour length, contour diameter, as well as the parameters for describing slope, curvature, and corner points. Section 10.2 introduces several basic object region description parameters, including region area, region center of gravity, and some region gray characteristics.

Section 10.3 introduces the description of the contour with the help of Fourier transform. When the contour is translated, rotated, and scaled, the transformed description can be directly derived from the already obtained description according to Fourier transform theorem.

Section 10.4 introduces the contour description method based on wavelet transform, which has some unique advantages over the contour description method based on Fourier transform.

Section 10.5 introduces the central moments of regions, including seven region invariant moments based on normalized central moments and four region affine invariant moments based on central moments.

Section 10.6 discusses two methods of describing the relationship between objects, one based on string description and the other based on tree structure description.

10.1   Basic Contour Description Parameters

The description parameters corresponding to the external representation of the object in the image can be obtained from the object contour. The following introduces several basic parameters for describing contours and the measurement methods.

10.1.1   Contour length

The **contour length** is a simple global feature, which is the circumference/perimeter of the enclosed object region. The region in the image can be seen as composed of the internal points of the region plus the contour points (i.e., boundary points). The contour B of the region R is composed of all the contour points of R connected in the 4-direction or 8-direction, and other points in the region are called the internal points of the region. For region R, each of its contour point p should meet the following two conditions: (i) p itself belongs to region R; (ii) there are pixels in the neighborhood of p that do not belong to region R. It should be noted here that if the internal points of the region R are determined by 8-direction connectivity, the contour obtained is 4-direction connected; if the internal points of the region R are judged by 4-direction connectivity, the contour obtained is 8-direction connected.

The 4-direction connected contour B_4 and the 8-direction connected contour B_8 can be respectively defined as follows:

$$B_4 = \{(x, y) \in R | N_8(x, y) - R \neq 0\}, \tag{10.1}$$

$$B_8 = \{(x, y) \in R | N_4(x, y) - R \neq 0\}. \tag{10.2}$$

The first condition on the right side of Equations (10.1) and (10.2) indicates that the contour point itself belongs to the region, and the second condition indicates that there are points in the neighborhood of the contour point, which do not belong to the region. If the contour has been represented by a chain code of unit length, the number of horizontal and vertical codes plus the number of diagonal codes multiplied by $\sqrt{2}$ can be used as the contour length. Arrange all the points of the contour from 0 to $K - 1$ (suppose there are K points in total), and the lengths of the two types of contours B_4 and B_8 can be calculated by the following equation:

$$\|B\| = \#\{k | (x_{k+1}, y_{k+1}) \in N_4(x_k, y_k)\}$$

$$+\sqrt{2}\#\{k | (x_{k+1}, y_{k+1}) \in N_D(x_k, y_k)\}, \tag{10.3}$$

where $\#$ means quantity, and $k + 1$ is calculated by modulo K. The first term on the right side of the above equation corresponds to a straight line segment between two pixels, and the second term on the right side of the above equation corresponds to a diagonal line segment between two pixels.

Example 10.1 Calculation of contour length

The shaded part in Figure 10.1(a) is a polygonal region, its 4-direction connected contour is shown in Figure 10.1(b) and its 8-direction connected contour is shown in Figure 10.1(c). Because

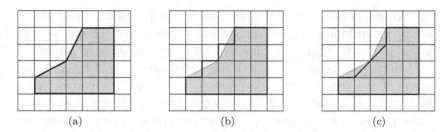

(a)   (b)   (c)

Figure 10.1.   Calculation of contour length.

there are 18 straight line segments on the 4-direction connected contour, the contour length is 18. There are 14 straight line segments and two diagonal line segments on the 8-direction connected contour, so the contour length is about 16.8.   □

10.1.2   Contour diameter

The **contour diameter** is the distance between the two furthest points on the contour, that is, the length of the straight line between these two points. Sometimes, this line is also called the major axis or long axis of the contour (the longest line segment perpendicular to this major axis and between the two intersection points of the contour is also called the minor axis of the contour). Both the length and orientation of the major axis can be used to describe the contour. The diameter $\text{Dia}_d(B)$ of contour B can be calculated by the following equation:

$$\text{Dia}_d(B) = \max_{i,j}[D_d(b_i, b_j)] \quad b_i \in B, \quad b_j \in B, \tag{10.4}$$

where $D_d(\cdot)$ can be any distance metric. If $D_d(\cdot)$ are measured with different distance metrics, the obtained $\text{Dia}_d(B)$ will be different. There are three commonly used distance metrics, namely $D_E(\cdot)$, $D_4(\cdot)$, and $D_8(\cdot)$ distance (see Section 3.5).

Example 10.2 Calculation of contour diameter

Figure 10.2 shows the three diameter values obtained by using three different distance metrics to calculate the same object contour (here, $D_8(\cdot)$ distance calculation refers to Equation (10.3) using $2^{1/2}$ to

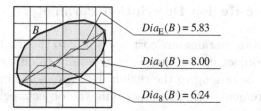

Figure 10.2. Calculation of contour diameter.

represent the diagonal length). It can be seen that when different distance measurements are selected, the contour diameters of the same line segment length may be quite different. □

10.1.3 Slope, curvature, and corner point

The contour consists of a series of points. The **slope** can indicate the local orientation of each point on the contour. **Curvature** is the change rate of slope, which describes the changes of points on the contour along the contour direction. At a given contour point, the sign of curvature describes the concavity and convexity of the contour at that point. If the curvature is greater than zero, the curve is concave toward the positive direction of the normal to that point. If the curvature is less than zero, the concave direction of the curve is toward the negative direction of the normal to that point. When tracking the contour in the clockwise direction, if the curvature of a point is greater than zero, the point is part of the convex segment, otherwise it is part of the concave segment. The local extreme points of curvature are called **corner points**, which are more prominent points on the contour, reflecting the complexity of the contour to a certain extent (see also Section 8.1). The above concepts are also applicable to non-closed contours.

Calculating the curvature of a certain point on the contour of a discrete image often becomes unreliable due to the roughness and unevenness of the discrete boundary. However, if the contour has been approximated by a polygon (see Section 9.3), it will be more convenient and reliable to calculate the curvature at the intersection of adjacent line segments of the contour (that is, the vertex of the polygon).

10.2   Basic Region Description Parameters

The description parameters corresponding to the internal representation of the object in the image are generally calculated using the set of all pixels belonging to the region. Here are some basic parameters and measurement formulas describing the object region.

10.2.1   Region area

The **region area** is a basic property of the region; it describes the size of the region. For a region R, assuming that the side length of a square pixel is the unit length, the calculation equation for its area A is as follows:

$$A = \sum_{(x,y)\in R} 1. \tag{10.5}$$

It can be seen from the above equation that calculating the region area is to count the number of pixels belonging to the region.

It should be pointed out that in addition to using Equation (10.6) to calculate the area of the region, some people also suggest other methods. But it can be proved that using the method of counting pixels to find the area of the region is not only the simplest but also the best estimate of the unbiased and consistent area of the original simulation region.

Example 10.3 Region area calculation

Figure 10.3 shows the results of using different area calculation methods for the same region (set the pixel side length to one). The method in Figure 10.3(a) corresponds to Equation (10.5), and the result is 10 (pixels). The two methods shown in Figures 10.3(b) and (c) both use the triangle area calculation formula. Figure 10.3(b) takes the distance between two pixels, d (here one) as the unit, Figure 10.3(c) takes the pixel side length n (here one) as the unit, and the results obtained are 4.5 and 8, respectively. Although these two methods are more reasonable for continuous regions on the plane, they have larger errors for digital images.   □

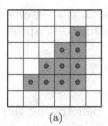 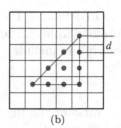 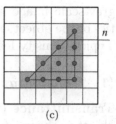

(a) (b) (c)

Figure 10.3. Examples of several area calculation methods.

10.2.2 Centroid of region

The **centroid of region** is also called regional center of gravity and is also a type of regional global descriptor. The coordinates of the centroid of region are calculated based on all points belonging to the region:

$$\bar{x} = \frac{1}{A} \sum_{(x,y)\in R} x, \tag{10.6}$$

$$\bar{y} = \frac{1}{A} \sum_{(x,y)\in R} y. \tag{10.7}$$

Although the coordinates of each point in the region are always integers, the coordinates of the centroid of region calculated as above are often not integers. When the size of the region itself is relatively small compared to the distance between different regions, the region can be approximated by the mass point located at its center of gravity (count as the point object), so that the spatial position of the region can be represented.

10.2.3 Regional gray-scale characteristics

The purpose of describing the region is often to describe the characteristics of the object in the original scene, including the properties reflecting the object's gray-scale and color information. Different from the calculation of the area and the centroid of the region in which only the segmented image is needed, the measurement of the object gray-scale characteristics should combine the original gray-scale image and segmented image. The gray-scale characteristics of the object can be obtained from the density feature descriptor. Typical density feature descriptors include:

(1) *Transmittance*

Transmittance (T) is the ratio of the light (flux) penetrating the object to the incident light, reflecting the transmittance of the object:

$$T = \text{light (flux) penetrating the object/incident light.} \quad (10.8)$$

(2) *Optical density*

Optical density (OD) is defined as the ratio of the incident light to the light penetrating the object (reciprocal, the inverse of the transmittance) and then taking the logarithm to the base 10:

$$\text{OD} = \lg(1/T) = -\lg T. \quad (10.9)$$

The value of the optical density ranges from 0 (100% transmission) to infinity (completely no transmission), reflecting the opacity of the object.

(3) *Integrated optical density*

The **integrated optical density** (IOD) is a commonly used region gray-scale parameter. It is an internal feature of an image, and it can also be classified as a gray-scale feature. It can be seen as a measure of the "mass" of the object. For an image $f(x, y)$ of $M \times N$, the integrated optical density IOD is defined as:

$$\text{IOD} = \sum_{x=0}^{M-1} \sum_{y=0}^{N-1} f(x, y). \quad (10.10)$$

If the histogram of the image is $H(\cdot)$ and the gray level of the image is G, then according to the definition of the histogram, we have

$$\text{IOD} = \sum_{k=0}^{G-1} kH(k). \quad (10.11)$$

That is, the integrated optical density is the weighted sum of the gray levels in the histogram.

Based on the above density feature descriptors, statistics such as their maximum, minimum, median, average, variance, and high-order moments can also be calculated to describe regional gray-scale characteristics.

10.3 Fourier Description of Contour

In addition to direct representation and description of the object in space domain, the object is often transferred to other domains for representation and description. Taking the description of the object contour as an example, it can be performed in the frequency domain with the help of Fourier coefficients or in the wavelet domain with the help of wavelet coefficients (see Section 10.4).

10.3.1 Fourier description of contour

Discrete Fourier transform representation of contour can be used as the basis for quantitative description of contour shape. One advantage of using Fourier's description is that the 2D problem can be simplified to a 1D problem. The specific method is to coincide the XY plane, where the contour is located, with a complex plane UV, where the real part U axis coincides with the X axis and the imaginary part V axis coincides with the Y axis. In this way, a complex number $u + jv$ can be used to represent each point (x, y) on a given contour, and the curve segment in the XY plane can be transformed into a sequence on the complex plane. It should be pointed out that the two representations on the space plane XY and the complex plane UV are essentially identical, and the points correspond to each other, as shown in Figure 10.4.

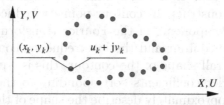

Figure 10.4. Two ways of representing contour points.

Now, consider a closed contour composed of N points, starting from any one point and going around the contour one round, a complex number sequence is obtained:

$$s(k) = u(k) + jv(k) \quad k = 0, 1, \ldots, N - 1. \tag{10.12}$$

The discrete Fourier transform of $s(k)$ is

$$S(w) = \frac{1}{N} \sum_{k-0}^{N-1} s(k) \exp[-j2\pi k/N] \quad w = 0, 1, \ldots, N - 1. \tag{10.13}$$

$S(w)$ can be called the **Fourier contour descriptor**, and its inverse Fourier transform is

$$s(k) = \sum_{w=0}^{N-1} S(w) \exp[-j2\pi wk/N] \quad k = 0, 1, \ldots, N - 1. \tag{10.14}$$

It can be seen from Equations (10.13) and (10.14) that because the discrete Fourier transform is a reversible linear transform, the information neither increases nor decreases in this process. However, the above representation methods provide the convenience for selectively describing contours. Suppose that only the first $M(M < N)$ coefficients of $S(w)$ are used, so that one approximation of $s(k)$ can be obtained:

$$s_e(k) = \sum_{w=0}^{M-1} S(w) \exp[j2\pi wk/N] \quad k = 0, 1, \ldots, N - 1. \tag{10.15}$$

Comparing Equation (10.14) with Equation (10.15), the range of the number of coefficients k remains unchanged, that is, the number of points on the approximate contour is still the same, but the range of w is reduced, that is, the number of high-frequency components used to reconstruct the contour points is reduced. Because the high-frequency components of the Fourier transform correspond to the details of the contour and the low-frequency components correspond to the overall shape of the contour, this is equivalent to only using some Fourier coefficients corresponding to the low-frequency components to approximately describe the shape of the contour, so as to reduce the amount of data required for the representation of the contour.

Example 10.4 Approximately represent the contour with the help of Fourier description

According to Equation (10.15), using the first M coefficients of Fourier descriptor to represent the contour is equivalent to using relatively fewer data volume to represent the basic shape of the contour. Figure 10.5 shows a square contour composed of $N = 64$ points and some results obtained by reconstructing this contour with different M values in Equation (10.15).

It can be seen from Figure 10.5 that for small M values ($M = 2$ and $M = 4$), the reconstructed contour is circular, which is very different from the original square. The reason is that the corners of the square contour correspond to high-frequency components, and only a few low-frequency coefficients cannot provide corner information. When M is increased to 8, the reconstructed contour begins to look like a rounded square. Afterward, with the increase of M (from $M = 16$ to $M = 48$), the reconstructed contour basically does not change much. Only when $M = 56$, the four corner points become more obvious. When the value of M continues increasing to 61, the four sides become straight. Finally, on adding another coefficient, $M = 62$, the reconstructed contour is almost the same as the original contour. It can be seen that, although the general shape can be

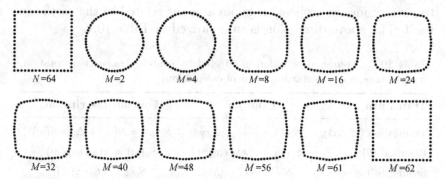

Figure 10.5. Approximate representation of a contour with the help of Fourier description.

reflected when fewer coefficients are used, it is necessary to continue
to add a lot of coefficients to accurately describe some shape features
such as corner points.   □

10.3.2   Fourier description changes with contour

The **Fourier contour descriptor** will be affected by contour translation, rotation, scale transformation, etc. as well as the starting
point of calculation (Fourier description is related to the starting
point of establishing complex sequence pairs from contour points).
However, this effect can be described by some theorems of Fourier
transform. For example, according to the translation theorem of
the Fourier transform, the translation of the contour in the spatial
domain is equivalent to adding a constant amount of translation to
all coordinates, which does not bring about changes in the Fourier
transform domain except at the origin $k = 0$. At $k = 0$, the Fourier
transform of the constant is the impulse function at the origin, it can
be seen that there is one $\delta(k)$. For another example, according to the
rotation theorem of the Fourier transform, rotating the contour by
an angle in the spatial domain is equivalent to rotating the contour
by the same angle in the frequency domain. In the same way, according to the scaling theorem of Fourier transform, scaling the contour
in the spatial domain is equivalent to applying the same scaling to
its Fourier transform in the frequency domain. The change of the
starting point is equivalent to shifting the sequence origin in the spatial domain, while in the Fourier transform domain, it is equivalent
to performing multiplication by an amount related to the coefficient
itself. The above discussion is summarized in Table 10.1.

Table 10.1.   Fourier description is affected by contour translation, rotation,
scale change, and the starting point of calculation.

Transform	Contour	Fourier description
Translation $(\Delta x, \Delta y)$	$s_t(k) = s(k) + \Delta xy$	$S_t(w) = S(w) + \Delta xy \cdot \delta(w)$
Rotation (θ)	$S_r(k) = s(k)\exp(\mathrm{j}\theta)$	$S_r(w) = S(w)\exp(\mathrm{j}\theta)$
Scaling (C)	$S_c(k) = C \cdot s(k)$	$S_c(w) = C \cdot S(w)$
Starting point (k_0)	$s_p(k) = s(k - k_0)$	$S_p(w) = S(w)\exp(-\mathrm{j}2\pi k_0 w/N)$

Note: $\Delta xy = \Delta x + j\Delta y$.

10.4 Wavelet Description of Contour

After transforming the object contour to the wavelet domain by means of **wavelet transform** (WT), the object contour can be described by means of wavelet contour descriptor.

10.4.1 Wavelet transform basics

Consider the 1D function $f(x)$, which can be represented by a linear combination of a series of expansion functions:

$$f(x) = \sum_k a_k u_k(x), \qquad (10.16)$$

where k is an integer, the sum can be finite or infinite; a_k is a real number, called the expansion coefficient; $u_k(x)$ is a real number function, called the expansion function.

Now, consider using the above expansion function as the scaling function, and perform translation and binary scaling to get the set $\{u_{j,k}(x)\}$:

$$u_{j,k}(x) = 2^{j/2} u(2^j x - k). \qquad (10.17)$$

It can be seen that k determines the position of $u_{j,k}(x)$ along the X axis and j determines the width of $u_{j,k}(x)$ along the X axis (so, $u(x)$ is also called a scaling function), and the coefficient $2^{j/2}$ determines the magnitude of $u_{j,k}(x)$. Given j, a scaling space U_j can be determined, and the size of U_j increases or decreases as j increases or decreases, respectively. In addition, each scaling space U_j, $j = -\infty, \ldots, 0, 1, \ldots, \infty$ is nested, that is, $U_j \subset U_{j+1}$. If $f(x) \in U_j$, then $f(x)$ can be expanded with $\{u_{j,k}(x)\}$ as in Equation (10.16):

$$f(x) = \sum_k a_k u_{j,k}(x). \qquad (10.18)$$

Similarly, let $v(x)$ denote the wavelet function, and perform translation and binary scaling on the wavelet function to obtain the set $\{v_{j,k}(x)\}$:

$$v_{j,k}(x) = 2^{j/2} v(2^j x - k). \qquad (10.19)$$

The wavelet space corresponding to the wavelet function $v_{j,k}(x)$ is represented by V_j. If $f(x) \in V_j$, then $f(x)$ can also be expanded

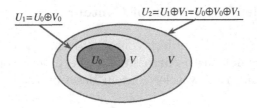

Figure 10.6.   Relationship between scaling space and wavelet space.

by $\{v_{j,k}(x)\}$:

$$f(x) = \sum_k a_k v_{j,k}(x). \tag{10.20}$$

The scaling spaces U_j, U_{j+1} and the wavelet space V_j have the following relationship (see the example of $j = 0, 1$ given in Figure 10.6):

$$U_{j+1} = U_j \oplus V_j, \tag{10.21}$$

where $\oplus$ represents the union of spaces (similar to the union of sets). It can be seen that in U_{j+1}, the complement of U_j is V_j and the V_j space is also nested.

The wavelet transform of $f(x)$ is to expand $f(x)$ with the sets $\{u_{j,k}(x)\}$ and $\{v_{j,k}(x)\}$. The commonly used expansion form is

$$f(x) = \frac{1}{\sqrt{M}} \sum_k h_u(0, k) u_{0,k}(x)$$

$$+ \frac{1}{\sqrt{M}} \sum_{j=0}^{\infty} \sum_k h_v(j, k) v_{j,k}(x), \tag{10.22}$$

where $h_u(0, k)$ and $h_v(j, k)$ are respectively called scaling (approximation) coefficients and wavelet (detail) coefficients. Generally, M is an integer power of two, so the above summation is performed for $x = 0, 1, 2, \ldots, M-1$, $j = 0, 1, 2, \ldots, J-1$, and $k = 0, 1, 2, \ldots, 2^j - 1$.

10.4.2   Wavelet contour descriptor

Wavelet contour descriptor is a kind of contour descriptor based on wavelet transform, which can describe contour features, and the description result is not affected by contour translation or scaling. Define the following wavelet function family $\{W_{j,k}(x)\}$:

$$W_{j,k}(x) = \frac{1}{\sqrt{2^j}} W\left(\frac{x - 2^j k}{2^j}\right) = 2^{-j/2} W(2^{-j} x - k). \quad (10.23)$$

For a given (contour) function $f(x)$, all wavelet transform coefficients construct the wavelet descriptors corresponding to $f(x)$, which can be used to describe the contour. The wavelet contour descriptor defined in this way has uniqueness (one-to-one correspondence between the descriptor and the contour) and comparability (for the description vector of two contours, the distance between them can be defined by the inner product to judge the similarity of these contours).

The wavelet contour descriptor has some characteristics comparable with the **Fourier contour descriptor**. One of its characteristics is that the local change of the contour only affects the corresponding local coefficients of the wavelet descriptor and has no obvious influence on other coefficients, which is different from the Fourier descriptor. The result of the Fourier transform is a global description in the frequency domain, so local changes in the contour will bring about intuitively unpredictable changes in the values of the Fourier descriptor. In addition, according to the duality of the transformation, it can be known that the local fluctuation of the wavelet descriptor corresponds to the local change of the original contour and the local fluctuation of the Fourier descriptor corresponds to the global irregular distortion of the original contour.

Example 10.5 Comparison of wavelet contour descriptor and Fourier descriptor when the contour changes locally

Figure 10.7 shows two contour images (denoted as A and B) with only minor differences locally. The two contours are basically the same, with only slight differences in the central parts.

Assuming that the descriptors of image A are $\{x_a\}$ and $\{y_a\}$ and the descriptors of image B are $\{x_b\}$ and $\{y_b\}$, define $\delta = (x_a - x_b)^2 + (y_a - y_b)^2$ as the difference between the two images. Figures 10.8 and 10.9 show the difference when using wavelet contour descriptor and Fourier contour descriptor, respectively. In the figures, the abscissa corresponds to the coefficient points of the 64 descriptors

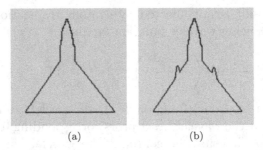

(a)   (b)

Figure 10.7.   Two contour images with local differences.

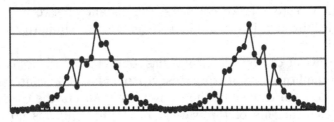

Figure 10.8.   Difference change of the wavelet descriptor after the local contour distortion.

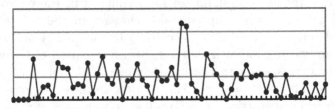

Figure 10.9.   Difference change of the Fourier descriptor after the local contour distortion.

and the ordinate corresponds to δ. It can be seen from Figure 10.8 that the local changes of the contour bring about regular changes in the wavelet descriptor (note that the starting point of the encoding is the head of the object, so the peak value of the wavelet coefficient change is also spatially symmetric). It can be seen from Figure 10.9 that the local changes of the contour bring about irregular changes in the Fourier descriptor.

Another characteristics of the wavelet contour descriptor is that it has a higher contour description accuracy than the Fourier descriptor, so that fewer coefficients can be used to achieve higher contour description accuracy, or in other words, under the same

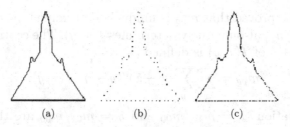

(a) (b) (c)

Figure 10.10. Comparison of description accuracy of two descriptors.

length, the wavelet contour descriptor has higher description accuracy than the Fourier contour descriptor. □

Example 10.6 Comparison of the description accuracy of two contour descriptors

Figure 10.10 shows a comparison example of the description accuracy of the two descriptors. For the contour shown in Figure 10.10(a), both descriptors use 64 coefficients, but it can be seen from Figure 10.10(b) that only 64 discrete points are obtained from the Fourier descriptor, and it is not able to give the information between discrete points. It can be seen from Figure 10.10(c) that the whole original contour is obtained from the wavelet descriptor and the amount of information included actually exceeds 64 spatial points. □

10.5   Region Description with Invariant Moments

The **region moment** is a physical quantity calculated with the help of all points belonging to the region, so its ability to describe the region is not affected by noise. For the image function $f(x, y)$, if it is piecewise continuous and only a finite number of points on the XY plane is not zero, it can be proved that all its moments exist. In practice, there are different calculation methods for region moments.

10.5.1   Central moment

The $p + q$ order moment of an image $f(x, y)$ is defined as

$$m_{pq} = \sum_x \sum_y x^p y^q f(x, y). \qquad (10.24)$$

It can be proved that m_{pq} is uniquely determined by $f(x, y)$, and vice versa, m_{pq} also uniquely determines $f(x, y)$. The central moment of order $p + q$ of $f(x, y)$ is defined as

$$m_{pq} = \sum_x \sum_y (x - \bar{x})^p (y - \bar{y})^q f(x, y). \tag{10.25}$$

In the equation, $\bar{x} = m_{10}/m_{00}$ and $\bar{y} = m_{01}/m_{00}$ are the centroid coordinates of $f(x, y)$. Equations (10.6) and (10.7) can calculate the centroid coordinates of the binary image, and the definitions of $\bar{x}$ and $\bar{y}$ can also be used for gray-scale images. Finally, the normalized central moment of $f(x, y)$ can be represented as

$$N_{pq} = \frac{M_{pq}}{M_{00}^\gamma} \quad \text{where } \gamma = \frac{p + q}{2} + 1. \quad p + q = 2, 3, \ldots. \tag{10.26}$$

Example 10.7 Calculation of central moment

Figure 10.11 shows some simple example images for calculating moments. Among them, the image size is 8×8, pixel size is 1×1, dark pixels are object pixels (value of one), and white pixels are background pixels (value of zero).

Table 10.2 shows the values of three second-order central moments and two third-order central moments calculated from each image in Figure 10.11 according to Equation (10.25). Here, each pixel is regarded as a mass point whose quality is located at the center of the pixel, the moments are relative to the center of gravity of the object, and the values have been rounded up. Since the center of the image is taken as the origin of the coordinate system, the central moment that contains an odd number of orders in a certain direction may have a negative value.

Observing and comparing Figure 10.11 and Table 10.2, it can be seen that if the object is symmetrical along the X direction or Y direction, the region moment along the symmetry direction can be obtained according to the symmetry of the region.   □

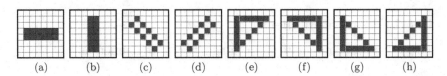

(a)   (b)   (c)   (d)   (e)   (f)   (g)   (h)

Figure 10.11.   Some example images used to calculate moments.

Table 10.2. Central moment values calculated from the example images in Figure 10.11.

Serial number	Central moment	(a)	(b)	(c)	(d)	(e)	(f)	(g)	(h)
1	M_{02}	3	35	22	22	43	43	43	43
2	M_{11}	0	0	−18	18	21	−21	−21	21
3	M_{20}	35	3	22	22	43	43	43	43
4	M_{12}	0	0	0	0	−19	19	−19	19
5	M_{21}	0	0	0	0	19	19	−19	−19

10.5.2 Region invariant moments

The following seven **region invariant moments** that do not change with translation, rotation, and scale transformation are composed of a combination of normalized second-order central moments and third-order central moments:

$$T_1 = N_{20} + N_{02}, \tag{10.27}$$

$$T_2 = (N_{20} - N_{02})^2 + 4N_{11}^2, \tag{10.28}$$

$$T_3 = (N_{30} - 3N_{12})^2 + (3N_{21} - N_{03})^2, \tag{10.29}$$

$$T_4 = (N_{30} + N_{12})^2 + (N_{21} + N_{03})^2, \tag{10.30}$$

$$T_5 = (N_{30} - 3N_{12})(N_{30} + N_{12})\left[(N_{30} + N_{12})^2 - 3(N_{21} + N_{03})^2\right]$$
$$+ 3(N_{21} - N_{03})(N_{21} + N_{03})\left[3(N_{30} + N_{12})^2 - (N_{21} + N_{03})^2\right], \tag{10.31}$$

$$T_6 = (N_{20} - N_{02}) + \left[(N_{30} + N_{12})^2 - (N_{21} + N_{03})^2\right]$$
$$+ 4N_{11}(N_{30} + N_{12})(N_{21} + N_{03}), \tag{10.32}$$

$$T_7 = (3N_{21} - 3N_{03})(N_{30} + N_{12})\left[(N_{30} + N_{12})^2 - 3(N_{21} + N_{03})^2\right]$$
$$+ 3(N_{12} - N_{30})(N_{21} + N_{03})\left[3(N_{30} + N_{12})^2 - (N_{21} + N_{03})^2\right]. \tag{10.33}$$

Example 10.8 Object invariant moment calculation example

Figure 10.12 shows a set of different variants obtained from the same image to verify the invariance of the seven moments defined by Equations(10.27)–(10.33). Figure 10.12(a) is the original image used for calculation; Figure 10.12(b) is the result obtained by rotating Figure 10.12(a) by 45°; Figure 10.12(c) is the result of reducing the scale of Figure 10.12(a) by half; Figure 10.12(d) is the mirror symmetry image of Figure 10.12(a).

For each image in Figure 10.12, the values of the seven moments calculated according to Equations (10.27)–(10.33) are listed in Table 10.3. It can be seen from the Table 10.3 that the values of these seven region invariant moments basically remain unchanged (some minor differences can be attributed to the numerical calculation error of the discrete image) when the image undergoes the above several changes. According to the characteristics of these invariant moments, they can be used to detect specific objects, regardless of object rotation or scaling.   □

(a)   (b)   (c)   (d)

Figure 10.12.   Different variants of the same image.

Table 10.3.   Region invariant moment calculation results.

Invariant moment	Original image	Rotating 45°	Scaling by half	Mirror symmetry
T_1	1.510494 E−03	1.508716 E−03	1.509853 E−03	1.510494 E−03
T_2	9.760256 E−09	9.678238 E−09	9.728370 E−09	9.760237 E−09
T_3	4.418879 E−11	4.355925 E−11	4.398158 E−11	4.418888 E−11
T_4	7.146467 E−11	7.087601 E−11	7.134290 E−11	7.146379 E−11
T_5	−3.991224 E−21	−3.916882 E−21	−3.973600 E−21	−3.991150 E−21
T_6	−6.832063 E−15	−6.738512 E−15	−6.813098 E−15	−6.831952 E−15
T_7	4.453588 E−22	4.084548 E−22	4.256447 E−22	−4.453826 E−22

10.5.3　Region affine invariant moments

The seven region invariant moments introduced in Section 10.5.2 are only invariant to translation, rotation, and scaling. A set of four **region affine invariant moments** that do not change for more general affine transformations (they are all based on the second and third moments) are as follows:

$$I_1 = \{M_{20}M_{02} - M_{11}^2\}/M_{00}^4, \tag{10.34}$$

$$I_2 = \{M_{30}^2 M_{03}^2 - 6M_{30}M_{21}M_{12}M_{03} + 4M_{30}M_{12}^2$$
$$+ 4M_{21}^2 M_{03} - 3M_{21}^2 M_{12}^2\}/M_{00}^{10}, \tag{10.35}$$

$$I_3 = \{M_{20}(M_{21}M_{03} - M_{12}^2) - M_{11}(M_{30}M_{03} - M_{21}M_{12})$$
$$+ M_{02}(M_{30}M_{12} - M_{21}^2)\}/M_{00}^7, \tag{10.36}$$

$$I_{04} = \{M_{20}^3 M_{03}^2 - 6M_{20}^2 M_{11}M_{12}M_{03} - 6M_{20}^2 M_{02}M_{21}M_{03}$$
$$+ 9M_{20}^2 M_{02}M_{12}^2 + 12M_{20}M_{11}^2 M_{21}M_{00}$$
$$+ 6M_{20}M_{11}M_{02}M_{30}M_{03} - 18M_{20}M_{11}M_{02}M_{21}M_{12}$$
$$- 8M_{11}^3 M_{30}M_{03} - 6M_{20}M_{02}^2 M_{30}M_{12} + 9M_{20}M_{02}^2 M_{21}^2$$
$$+ 12M_{11}^2 M_{02}M_{30}M_{12} - 6M_{11}M_{02}^2 M_{30}M_{21} + M_{02}^3 M_{30}^2\}/M_{00}^{11}. \tag{10.37}$$

10.6　Object Relationship Description

When there are multiple objects in the image, the description of the relationship between these objects is also very important. Two basic methods are introduced in the following.

10.6.1　String description

With the help of Figure 10.13, the concept and method of using character **string descriptions** to describe relationships can be introduced. Assuming that Figure 10.13(a) is a stepped structure (which can be understood as a geometric distribution of the object) obtained from the segmented image, a formal method (using formal grammar) can be used to describe it. First, two basic elements (characters) a and b, as shown in Figure 10.13(b) are defined. Then, the stepped

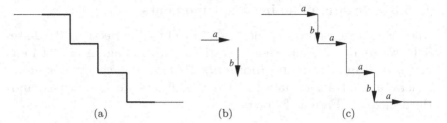

Figure 10.13.   Using character strings to describe the relationship structure.

structure can be represented as a combination of these two basic elements, as shown in Figure 10.13(c).

As can be seen from Figure 10.13, an outstanding feature of this representation is the repetition of basic elements.

Now, establish a way to use the basic elements to describe the above structure. Suppose S and A are variables, S is also the start symbol and a and b are constants corresponding to the basic elements defined above, then a description grammar (**formal grammar**) can be established or the following rewriting (replacement) rules can be determined:

(1) $S \rightarrow aA$ (the starting symbol can be replaced by element a and variable A);
(2) $A \rightarrow bS$ (variable A can be replaced with element b and start symbol S);
(3) $A \rightarrow b$ (variable A can be replaced with a single element b).

According to Rule (2), if A is replaced with b and S, it returns to Rule (1) and the whole process can be repeated. According to Rule (3), if A is replaced with b, the whole process ends because there are no more variables in the expression. Note that these rules force each a to be followed by one b, so the relationship between a and b remains unchanged.

Example 10.9 Using rewriting rules to generate structure

Figure 10.14 shows several examples of using these rewriting rules to generate various structures. The numbers in parentheses under each structure represent the numbers of the rules used in turn. The first structure is obtained by applying Rule (1) and Rule (3) in sequence;

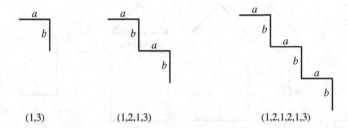

(1,3)   (1,2,1,3)   (1,2,1,2,1,3)

Figure 10.14.　Several examples of using rewriting rules.

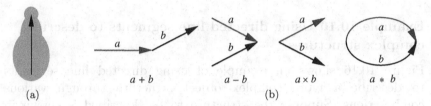

(a)   (b)

Figure 10.15.　Directed line segments and typical operations.

the second structure is obtained by applying Rule (1), Rule (2), and then Rule (1) and Rule (3) in sequence; finally, the third structure is obtained by applying Rule (1), Rule (2), Rule (1), Rule (2), then Rule (1) and Rule (3) in sequence. It can be seen that various similar structures can be generated by repeatedly using the above three rewriting rules.

The character string is a 1D structure. When used to describe a 2D image, the 2D spatial position information needs to be converted into a 1D form. When describing the contour of an object, a commonly used method is to trace the contour from a point, represent the contour with a line segment of a specific length and direction (the chain code is essentially based on this idea), and then use the character to represent the line segment to obtain the character string description. Another more general method is to first use directed line segments to (abstractly) describe the image region, these line segments can be combined with other operations in addition to connecting head and tail. Figure 10.15(a) shows a schematic diagram of extracting directed line segments from a region. Figure 10.15(b) gives some examples of typical combinations of directed line segments. Using combination operations can build up complex composite structures.　□

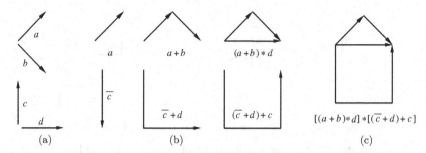

Figure 10.16.   Using directed line segments to describe complex structures.

Example 10.10 Using directed line segments to describe complex structures

Figure 10.16 shows an example of using directed line segments to describe a more complex object structure through various combinations. Suppose the structure to be described is shown in Figure 10.16(c). According to the analysis, it is composed of four types of directed line segments with different orientations. First, the basic directed line segments for four orientations are defined, as shown in Figure 10.16(a). By performing various typical combined operations as shown in Figure 10.16(b) step by step on these basic directed line segments, the structure shown in Figure 10.16(c) can be finally formed.   □

10.6.2   Tree structure description

String description can only describe a simple sequence structure and tree structure can describe multiple structures with common parts. A **tree** is a finite set of one or more nodes, which is a special case of a **graph**. In a sense, the tree structure is a 2D structure. For each tree structure, there is a unique root node and the remaining nodes are divided into several subsets that are not directly connected to each other. Each subset is a subtree. The bottom node of each tree is called the leaf node. The quad tree and binary tree introduced in Section 9.4 of Chapter 9 are both special tree structure data types. They are more regular, so it is more compact and effective to represent the pixel region.

The discussion of tree structure here is mainly to describe the relationship between the objects in the image, which is more general.

There can be many types of connections between objects, and there should not be *a priori* requirements for the size, position, and shape of each object. Broadly speaking, there are two types of important information in the tree. One is the information about nodes, which can be recorded by a set of characters or symbols; the other is the information about the relationship between a node and its connected nodes, which can be recorded by a set of pointers directed to these nodes.

Among the two types of information in the tree structure, the first type determines the basic pattern elements in the image description, and the second type determines the physical connection relationship between the basic pattern elements. Figure 10.17 shows an example of using a tree structure to describe the inclusion relationship between objects. Figure 10.17(a) is a combined region (combined from multiple regions, each region corresponds to a node in the tree, which are represented with lowercase letters), which can be described by the tree shown in Figure 10.17(b) with the help of the relationship "inside...." The root node R in Figure 10.17 represents the whole image, the nodes a and c are the root nodes of the two subtrees corresponding to the two sub-regions in R, and the remaining nodes are their sub-nodes. Comparing Figures 10.17(a) and (b), it shows that e is in d, d and f are in c, b is in a, and a and c are in R.

The structure of **tree description** in Figure 10.17(b) shows a special case of a **region neighborhood graph**. The region neighborhood graph represents each region in the image as a node, and the nodes of each region in the neighborhood are connected by edges.

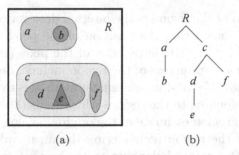

(a)   (b)

Figure 10.17. Using the "inside ..." to describe the relationship between regions in the combined region with the help of tree structure description.

The nodes contain the attributes of the regions, and the edges indicate the relationships between the regions. The relationship between different regions in the image can be "on ... ", "above ... ", etc., in addition to "inside ...." If the regions are in contact with each other, the region neighborhood graph becomes the **region adjacency graph**.

10.7   Key Points and References for Each Section

The following indicates the key points of each section and provides some targeted guidance for further references.

1. Basic contour description parameters

The description of the contour is the external description of the object. The contour point of a region is a point that belongs to the region but has pixels in its neighborhood that do not belong to the region. This is related to the definition of the neighborhood. The basic parameters of the contour include: length of the contour (circumference of the enclosed region); diameter of the contour (distance between the two farthest-apart points of object region); slope and curvature of the contour points and corner points on the contour (the slope corresponds to the tangent direction of the point, the curvature is the rate of change of the slope, and the corner points are the points with local extreme of the curvature). There are also some other parameters that can be found in Refs. [1,2].

2. Basic region description parameters

The description of the region is the internal description of the object. In addition to considering the position of the pixel, it is often necessary to consider the attribute value of the pixel (such as the gray value). The basic parameters of the region include: area of the region (size of the region, the best measurement method is to count the number of pixels belonging to the region, which is also the best (unbiased and consistent) region estimate of the original analog region; see Ref. [3]; centroid of the region (considering the mean value of the coordinates of all the points belonging to the region); gray level of the region (including various statistics based on the pixel gray level), for which the original image should be used in addition to the segmented image. For other parameters, please refer to Refs. [1,2,4].

3. Fourier description of contour

The Fourier descriptor of the contour is composed of discrete coefficients obtained by Fourier transform of the object contour. Specifically, the contour points are first represented as a complex sequence and then the Fourier transform is calculated. The Fourier description provides a basis for the approximate description of the contour. By discarding a certain number of transform coefficients, the amount of data representing the contour can be reduced and the basic shape of the contour can be maintained. According to the nature of the Fourier transform, the influence caused by the translation, rotation, scaling, and other coordinate transformations on contour to the Fourier description can be inferenced. Related discussions can also be found in Ref. [1] and its cited references.

4. Wavelet description of contour

The contour wavelet descriptor is composed of discrete coefficients obtained by performing wavelet transformation on the object contour. A complete introduction to wavelet transform can be found in specialized books (such as [5,6]). The wavelet contour descriptors defined in this section are unique and comparable, and the description results are not affected by contour translation or scaling. Compared with the Fourier descriptor, the wavelet descriptor is less affected by the local changes of the contour and the description accuracy is higher. Please refer to Ref. [7].

5. Region description with region invariant moments

Moment can be regarded as a statistical physical quantity, which is easy to realize and has physical meaning to describe the object contour and region. Describing the contour with moments is to regard the contour as the connecting body of line segments and to represent the 2D plane curve as a 1D function along the curve, with the help of various order statistics of the function. Using moments to describe the region directly uses all the points in the region. By calculating the central moment and normalizing it, the second- and third-order moments can be combined to obtain seven moments that are invariant to translation, rotation, and scale transformation. In addition, the second- and third-order moments can be combined to produce four moments that are invariant to general affine transformations; see Ref. [2].

6. Object relationship description

Both string description and tree structure description can describe the abstract connections between the various parts of an overall object, and they often correspond to the spatial relationship between different regions in the image. For more complex relationships, the graph structure in graph theory (for example, see Ref. [8]) is often used for representation and description. The description method of the relationship between objects abstracted as point objects can also be found in Ref. [2].

Self-Test Questions

The following questions include both single- and multiple-choice questions, so each option should be individually judged.

10.1 Basic Contour Description Parameters

10.1.1 Suppose p is a contour point of the 8-direction connected region R, then ( )

 (A) Point p belongs to the complement of region R;
 (B) There are pixels in the 4-neighborhood of point p that belong to the complement of region R;
 (C) There are pixels in the 8-neighborhood of point p that belong to the complement of region R;
 (D) Both the 4-neighborhood and 8-neighborhood of point p have pixels belonging to the complement of region R.

 [Hint] There are two key elements to judge a contour point.

10.1.2 For the (gray) region in Figure 10.1.2.1, if its internal points are determined by 4-connectivity, then the boundary point sequence is as follows: ( )

Figure 10.1.2.1.

(A) Figure 10.1.2.2(a);
(B) Figure 10.1.2.2(b);
(C) Figure 10.1.2.2(c);
(D) Figure 10.1.2.2(d).

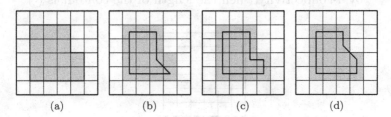

| (a) | (b) | (c) | (d) |

Figure 10.1.2.2.

[Hint] Here, the boundary should be 8-connected.

10.1.3 For the (gray) region in Figure 10.1.3.1, if its internal points are determined by 8-connectivity, then the boundary point sequence is as follows: ( )

Figure 10.1.3.1.

(A) Figure 10.1.3.2(a);
(B) Figure 10.1.3.2(b);
(C) Figure 10.1.3.2(c);
(D) Figure 10.1.3.2(d).

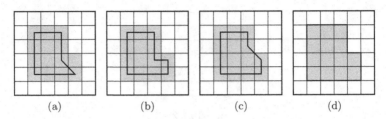

(a)   (b)   (c)   (d)

Figure 10.1.3.2.

[Hint] The boundary should be 4-connected here.

10.1.4 Suppose the side length of each small square in Figure 10.1.4 is one. If the internal points in the (gray) region are determined by 4-connectivity, then the length of the contour is ( )

Figure 10.1.4.

(A) $12 + 2\sqrt{2}$;
(B) $12 + 4\sqrt{2}$;
(C) $10 + 4\sqrt{2}$;
(D) $10 + 2\sqrt{2}$.

[Hint] Draw an 8-connected contour; the length of each diagonal segment is $\sqrt{2}$.

10.1.5 Suppose the side length of each small square in Figure 10.1.5 is one. If the internal points of the (gray) region are judged by 8-connectivity, then the length of the contour is ( )

Figure 10.1.5.

(A) 12;
(B) 14;
(C) 16;
(D) 18.

[Hint] Draw a 4-connected contour, and the length of each line segment is 1.

10.2 Basic Region Description Parameters

10.2.1 Suppose the side length of each small square in Figure 10.2.1 is one, then the area of the shaded part in the figure is approximately ( )

Figure 10.2.1.

(A) 7;
(B) 8;
(C) 9;
(D) 10.

[Hint] First, determining the pixel should be considered according to whether the shaded part in each pixel occupies more than 50% of the area and then count the pixels to be considered.

10.2.2 The centroid coordinates of the shaded region in Figure 10.2.2 are approximately ( )

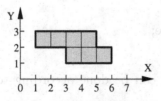

Figure 10.2.2.

(A) (3.6, 2.0);
(B) (3.6, 2.1);
(C) (3.7, 2.0);
(D) (3.7, 2.1).

[Hint] Take the center of each pixel as the centroid of the pixel, and then calculate their common centroid.

10.2.3 In the region gray-scale characteristics, ( )

(A) The transmittance is the reciprocal of the optical density, so the value of the transmittance ranges from infinity (100% transmission) to zero (no transmission at all);
(B) Integral optical density is the integral of optical density;
(C) Integral optical density can be regarded as a measure of the "quality" of the object, where the quality corresponds to the pixel gray level;
(D) According to Equation (10.11), the integrated optical density is the weighted sum of the gray levels in the histogram, where the weight is k;

[Hint] Analyze according to the definition formula of gray-scale characteristics.

10.3 Fourier Description of Contour

10.3.1 It is known that the complex number sequence obtained by representing each point (x, y) on an object contour in the form of a complex number $u + jv$ is as follows: $s(0) = 0$, $s(1) = 1$, $s(2) = 2$, $s(3) = 2 + j$, $s(4) = 2 + 2j$, $s(5) = 1 + 2j$, $s(6) = 2j$, $s(7) = j$. The object is ( )

(A) A triangle;
(B) A hexagon;
(C) A rectangle;
(D) A square.

[Hint] Drawing can be done according to the coordinates of each point.

10.3.2 On performing discrete Fourier transform for complex number sequence, $s(0) = 0$, $s(1) = 1$, $s(2) = 2$, $s(3) = 2+j$, $s(4) = 2+2j$, $s(5) = 1+2j$, $s(6) = 2j$, $s(7) = j$, if only the first six coefficients are taken, the approximation error is ( )

(A) Zero;
(B) One;
(C) Two;
(D) Three.

[Hint] Calculate the Fourier transform coefficients and rank them.

10.3.3 Which of the following description parameter(s) will be affected by the translation and rotation of the object contour? ( )

(A) Length of the contour;
(B) Orientation of the contour;
(C) Number of points on the contour;
(D) Fourier descriptor of the contour.

[Hint] The translation is related to the coordinates, and the rotation is related to the starting point.

10.3.4 If there are only real numbers in the Fourier descriptor of a contour, then the data sequence representing this contour ( )

(A) Is an odd sequence;
(B) Is an even sequence;
(C) Is symmetric about the origin;
(D) Consists only positive numbers.

[Hint] Expand the representation of the Fourier descriptor and take the imaginary number term as zero for analysis.

10.4 Wavelet Description of Contour

10.4.1 In $u_{j,k}(x) = 2^{j/2}u(2^j x - k)$, ( )

(A) The j determines its amplitude, k determines its position along the X axis, and $2^{j/2}$ determines its width along the X axis;

(B) The j determines its amplitude, k determines its width along the X-axis, and $2^{j/2}$ determines its position along the X-axis;

(C) The j determines its width along the X-axis, k determines its position along the X-axis, and $2^{j/2}$ determines its amplitude;

(D) The j determines its position along the X-axis, k determines its width along the X-axis, and $2^{j/2}$ determines its amplitude.

[Hint] Pay attention to the position of the translation and binary scaling factor in the function.

10.4.2 The scaling function corresponds to the scaling space and the wavelet function corresponds to the wavelet space. Considering the nesting of two spaces, then ( )

(A) The scaling space and wavelet space are both nested with each other;

(B) The scaling space and wavelet space are both coincident and nested;

(C) The scaling space and wavelet space of the same level are nested in the wavelet space of the upper level;

(D) The scaling space and wavelet space of the same level are nested in the scaling space of the upper level;

[Hint] Consider the connection between the scaling space and the wavelet space (see Figure 10.6).

10.4.3 Wavelet contour descriptor is ( )

(A) Unaffected by contour translation;

(B) Unaffected by contour rotation;

(C) Unaffected by contour scaling;

(D) Unaffected by contour deformation.

[Hint] Analyze according to the wavelet transform formula.

10.4.4 Compared with Fourier contour descriptor, the wavelet contour descriptor ( )

(A) Focuses more on the description of the local part of the contour;

(B) Has less affected coefficients when the contour changes locally;

(C) Has a higher contour description accuracy when having the same coefficient length;

(D) Has relatively irregular influence for local fluctuations on the original contour.

[Hint] Consider the characteristics of the two transformations separately.

10.4.5 When discussing the contour description precision of the wavelet contour descriptor, ( )

(A) The precision is defined by the amount of information included in the descriptor;

(B) The precision is defined by the number of coefficients used in the descriptor;

(C) The accuracy is defined by the number of contour points recovered by the descriptor;

(D) The accuracy is defined by the discreteness of the contour recovered by the descriptor.

[Hint] Refer to the discussion in the text under Section 10.4.

10.5 Region Description with Region Invariant Moments

10.5.1 The central moment of the object has the following characteristics: ( )

(A) There is a direct connection with the shape;

(B) There is no change in mirror symmetry transformation;

(C) It is the region moment of the object;

(D) It has nothing to do with the position of the object in space.

[Hint] Analyze according to the calculation formula of central moment.

10.5.2 In region-invariant moments, T_3, T_5, and T_7 are respectively ( )

(A) The 6th order moment, 8th order moment, and 10th order moment;

(B) The 6th order moment, 8th order moment, and 12th order moment;

(C) The 6th order moment, 10th order moment, and 12th order moment;

(D) The 6th order moment, 12th order moment, and 12th order moment.

[Hint] On squaring, the moments are added.

10.5.3 In region affine invariant moments, the highest orders of I_2, I_3, I_4 are respectively ( )

(A) The 12th order moment, 10th order moment, 12th order moment;

(B) The 12th order moment, 8th order moment, 12th order moment;

(C) The 12th order moment, 10th order moment, 12th order moment;

(D) The 12th order moment, 8th order moment, 10th order moment.

[Hint] The order of each item in the same moment may be different.

10.6 Object Relationship Description

10.6.1 According to the structural representation $\{[(a^- + b) * c^-] + d\} * (d + c^-)$, the structure obtained by using the four basic directed line segments given in Figure 10.16(a) is ( )

(A) Figure 10.6.1(a);
(B) Figure 10.6.1(b);
(C) Figure 10.6.1(c);
(D) Figure 10.6.1(d).

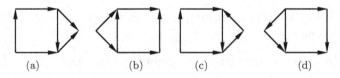

(a)   (b)   (c)   (d)

Figure 10.6.1.

[Hint] Refer to the combined operation rules in Figure 10.15.

10.6.2 The structural representation corresponding to Figure 10.6.2 is (using the four basic directed line segments given in Figure 10.16(a)) ( )

Figure 10.6.2.

(A) $\{[(\bar{a}+b)*c]+d\}*\{[(a+b)*d]+[\bar{c}*(\bar{b}+\bar{a})]\}$;

(B) $\{[(\bar{a}+b)*c]+d\}*\{[(a+\bar{b})*d]+[\bar{c}*(a+\bar{b})]\}$;

(C) $\{[(\bar{a}+b)*c]+d\}*\{[(a+\bar{b})*d]+[\bar{c}*(\bar{b}+a)]\}$;

(D) $\{[(\bar{a}+b)*c]+d\}*\{[(a+\bar{b})*d]+[\bar{c}*(\bar{b}+\bar{a})]\}$.

[Hint] First, consider the three triangles on the upper side as well as the left and right sides.

10.6.3 In a scene, there is a table T. On the table a computer n, a cup c, and a book b are placed. There are also a pen p and a ruler r on the book. If described by the relationship "above ...", the resulting tree is ( )

(A) Figure 10.6.3(a);
(B) Figure 10.6.3(b);
(C) Figure 10.6.3(c);
(D) Picture 10.6.3(d).

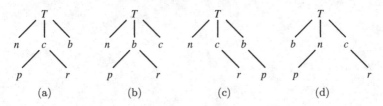

Figure 10.6.3.

[Hint] The judgment can be made only by considering the physical connection.

References

[1] Sonka, M., Hlavac, V., and Boyle, R. *Image Processing, Analysis, and Machine Vision*, 4th Edn. Singapore: Cengage Learning, 2014.

[2] Zhang, Y.-J. *Image Engineering, Vol. 2: Image Analysis*. Germany, Berlin: De Gruyter, 2017.

[3] Young, I. T. Three-dimensional image analysis. *Proc. VIP' 93*, 1993, 35–38.

[4] Ballard, D. H. and Brown, C. M. *Computer Vision*. UK, London: Prentice-Hall, 1982.

[5] Chui, C. K. *An Introduction to WAVELETS*. USA, Salt Lake City: Academic Press, 1992.

[6] Goswami, J. C. and Chan, A. K. *Fundamentals of Wavelets — Theory, Algorithms, and Applications*. USA, New Jersey: John Wiley & Sons, Inc. 1999.

[7] Yang, X. Y. and Zhang, Y.-J. Wavelet boundary descriptors and its application in image querying. *Chinese Journal of Computers*, 1999, 22(7): 752–757.

[8] Sun, H. Q. *Graph Theory and Its Applications*. China, Beijing: Science Press, 2004.

Chapter 11

Texture Description

Texture is a commonly used concept in image analysis and has a wide range of applications. **Texture description** can provide many characteristics of the region, mainly reflecting the nature of the surface of the object, but there is currently no formal (or no consistent) definition for it. Generally, texture can be considered to be composed of many elements that are close to each other and weave each other, and they are often full of periodicity. Intuitively, the texture description can provide features such as smoothness, sparseness, and regularity of the region. Quantifying the texture content of a region is an important region description method. Three commonly used texture description methods are as follows: (i) statistical method; (ii) structure method; (iii) spectrum method.

The sections of this chapter are arranged as follows:

Section 11.1 introduces the statistical description method of texture, mainly including co-occurrence matrix and texture descriptor based on co-occurrence matrix, and texture descriptor based on energy.

Section 11.2 discusses the structure description method of texture. On the basis of the principle of structural description, the techniques of realizing texture description by means of texture tessellation and local binary pattern are respectively introduced.

Section 11.3 introduces the spectral description method of texture and specifically discusses texture description technology based on Fourier spectrum and Fourier–Bessel spectrum.

11.1   Statistical Description of Texture

In the **statistical method** of describing texture, some information about the image (including pixel position and pixel value) needs to be counted. The statistical method is more suitable for describing natural textures.

11.1.1   Co-occurrence matrix

The description of the texture is often done with the aid of the **co-occurrence matrix** of the regional gray scale. Suppose S is the set of pixel pairs with specific spatial relationships in the object region R, then the (element of) co-occurrence matrix P can be defined as

$$P(g_1, g_2) = \frac{\#\left\{[(x_1, y_1), (x_2, y_2)] \in S | f(x_1, y_1) = g_1 \& f(x_2, y_2) = g_2\right\}}{\#S}.$$

(11.1)

The numerator on the right side of the equal sign in the above equation is the number of pixel pairs with a certain spatial relationship and gray values of g_1 and g_2, respectively, and the denominator is the sum of pixel pairs (# represents the amount). The P thus obtained is normalized.

Example 11.1 Position operator and co-occurrence matrix

In the statistical description of texture, the co-occurrence matrix can be calculated with the help of the position operator in order to use the spatial information. Suppose W is a position operator and P is a $k \times k$ matrix, where each element a_{ij} is the number of occurrences of a point with a gray value g_i relative to a point with a gray value g_j determined by W, we have $1 \leq i, j \leq k$. For example, for an image with only three gray levels in Figure 11.1(a), $g_1 = 0$, $g_2 = 1$, $g_3 = 2$, if W is defined as the position relationship of "one pixel to the right and one pixel down", the resulting matrix P will be as shown in Figure 11.1(b).

If the total number of pixel pairs satisfying W is N, then each element of P is divided by N to get the estimation of the occurrence probability of pixel pairs satisfying the relation defined by W, and the corresponding (normalized) co-occurrence matrix will be obtained.   □

$$
\begin{array}{ccccc}
0 & 0 & 0 & 1 & 2 \\
1 & 1 & 0 & 1 & 1 \\
2 & 2 & 1 & 0 & 0 \\
1 & 1 & 0 & 2 & 0 \\
0 & 0 & 1 & 0 & 1
\end{array}
\qquad
P = \begin{bmatrix} P_{11} & P_{12} & P_{13} \\ P_{21} & P_{22} & P_{23} \\ P_{31} & P_{32} & P_{33} \end{bmatrix} = \begin{bmatrix} 4 & 2 & 0 \\ 2 & 3 & 2 \\ 1 & 2 & 0 \end{bmatrix}
$$

(a)   (b)

Figure 11.1. Calculation of the co-occurrence matrix with the help of position operator.

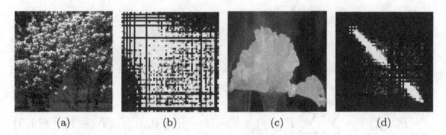

(a)   (b)   (c)   (d)

Figure 11.2. Image and its co-occurrence matrix diagram.

Example 11.2 Image and its co-occurrence matrix

Different images will have different gray-level co-occurrence matrices due to the variation of texture scales. This is said to be the basis for further calculation of texture descriptors with the help of gray-level co-occurrence matrix. Figure 11.2 shows two groups of examples. Figures 11.2(a) and (b) respectively show an image with many details and its co-occurrence matrix diagram. Because the gray scale in Figure 11.2(a) has higher frequency changes both along the horizontal and vertical directions, that is, the distribution of gray-scale changes is relatively uniform, so most of the items in the co-occurrence matrix in Figure 11.2(b) are not zero. Figures 11.2(c) and (d) respectively show an image with a larger similar region and its co-occurrence matrix. Because the gray scale in Figure 11.2(c) changes slowly over a large range (many low-frequency components), so only the elements on the main diagonal in the co-occurrence matrix take larger values in Figure 11.2(d). Comparing the two groups of images, it can be seen that the co-occurrence matrix can indeed reflect the spatial information of the relative positions of different pixels to help describe and distinguish textures. □

11.1.2 Texture descriptors based on co-occurrence matrix

The **texture descriptors** can be defined on the basis of the co-occurrence matrix, if set:

$$P_x(i) = \sum_{j=1}^{N} P(i,j) \quad i = 1, 2, \ldots, N, \tag{11.2}$$

$$P_y(j) = \sum_{i=1}^{N} P(i,j) \quad j = 1, 2, \ldots, N, \tag{11.3}$$

$$P_{x+y}(k) = \sum_{i=1}^{N}\sum_{j=1}^{N} P(i,j) \quad k = i+j = 2, 3, \ldots, 2N, \tag{11.4}$$

$$P_{x-y}(k) = \sum_{i=1}^{N}\sum_{j=1}^{N} P(i,j) \quad k = |i-j| = 0, 1, \ldots, N-1. \tag{11.5}$$

Then, the following 14 texture descriptors can be further obtained (their values reflect the characteristics of the texture):

(1) Angular second moment:

$$W_1 = \sum_{i=1}^{N}\sum_{j=1}^{N} P^2(i,j). \tag{11.6}$$

(2) Contrast:

$$W_2 = \sum_{t=0}^{N-1} t^2 \left\{ \sum_{i=1}^{N}\sum_{j=1}^{N} P(i,j) \right\} \quad |i-j| = t. \tag{11.7}$$

(3) Correlation:

$$W_3 = \frac{1}{\sigma_x \sigma_y} \left\{ \sum_{i=1}^{N}\sum_{j=1}^{N} ij P(i,j) - \mu_x \mu_y \right\}, \tag{11.8}$$

where μ_x and σ_x are the mean and mean square deviation of $P_x(i)$, respectively, and μ_y and σ_y are the mean and mean square deviation of $P_y(j)$, respectively.

(4) Difference moment:

$$W_4 = \sum_{i=1}^{N} \sum_{j=1}^{N} (i - \mu)^2 P(i,j) = \sum_{i=1}^{N} (i - \mu)^2 P_x(i), \qquad (11.9)$$

where μ is the mean value of $P(i,j)$.

(5) Inverse difference moment (uniformity):

$$W_5 = \sum_{i=1}^{N} \sum_{j=1}^{N} \frac{1}{1 + (i - j)^2} P(i,j). \qquad (11.10)$$

(6) Sum average:

$$W_6 = \sum_{i=2}^{2N} i P_{x+y}(i). \qquad (11.11)$$

(7) Sum variance:

$$W_7 = \sum_{i=2}^{2N} (i - W_6) P_{x+y}(i). \qquad (11.12)$$

(8) Sum entropy:

$$W_8 = - \sum_{i=2}^{2N} P_{x+y}(i) \log \left[P_{x+y}(i) \right]. \qquad (11.13)$$

(9) Entropy:

$$W_9 = - \sum_{i=1}^{N} \sum_{j=1}^{N} P(i,j) \log \left[P(i,j) \right]. \qquad (11.14)$$

(10) Variance of difference:

$$W_{10} = \sum_{i=2}^{2N} (i - d)^2 P_{x-y}(i), \qquad (11.15)$$

where $d = \Sigma_{i=2}^{2N} i P_{x-y}(i)$.

(11) Difference entropy:

$$W_{11} = - \sum_{i=2}^{2N} P_{x-y}(i) \log \left[P_{x-y}(i) \right]. \qquad (11.16)$$

(12) Related information metric 1:

$$W_{12} = \frac{W_9 - E_1}{\max(E_x, E_y)}, \qquad (11.17)$$

where $E_1 = -\Sigma_{i=1}^{N}\Sigma_{j=1}^{N}P(i,j)\log\left[P_x(i)P_y(j)\right]$, $E_x = -\Sigma_{i=1}^{N}$ $P_x(i)\log\left[P_x(i)\right]$, and $E_y = -\Sigma_{j=1}^{N}P_y(j)\log\left[P_y(j)\right]$.

(13) Related information metric 2:

$$W_{13} = \sqrt{1 - \exp\left[-2(E_2 - W_9)\right]}, \qquad (11.18)$$

where $E_2 = -\Sigma_{i=1}^{N}\Sigma_{j=1}^{N}P_x(i)P_y(j)\log\left[P_x(i)P_y(j)\right]$.

(14) Maximum correlation coefficient:

W_{14} = The second largest eigenvalue of matrix $\mathbf{R}$

$$R(i,j) = \sum_{k=1}^{N} \frac{P(i,k)P(j,k)}{P_x(i)P_y(j)}. \qquad (11.19)$$

11.1.3   Energy-based texture descriptor

By using a mask (also called a kernel) to calculate the energy of the local texture, the information of the gray-level change can be obtained. Suppose the image is $f(x, y)$ and a set of masks are respectively $M_1, M_2, \ldots, M_N$, then the convolution $g_n = f \otimes M_n$ $(n = 1, 2, \ldots, N)$ gives the representation of the texture energy component of the texture feature in the neighborhood of each pixel. If the mask size is $k \times k$, the element of texture image corresponding to the nth mask is

$$T_n(x,y) = \frac{1}{k \times k} \sum_{i=-(k-1)/2}^{(k-1)/2} \sum_{j=-(k-1)/2}^{(k-1)/2} |g_n(x+i, y+j)|. \qquad (11.20)$$

So, corresponding to each pixel position (x, y), there is a texture feature vector $[T_1(x, y)T_2(x, y)\ldots T_N(x, y)]^{\mathrm{T}}$.

The commonly used mask sizes are 3×3, 5×5, and 7×7. Let L stand for level, E stand for edge, S stand for shape, W stand for wave, R stand for ripple, and O stand for oscillation, then various 1D masks can be obtained. For example, the 1D vectors (written as a row vectors) corresponding to a 5×5 mask are in the form

$$
\begin{aligned}
\boldsymbol{L}_5 &= [1\ 4\ 6\ 4\ 1], \\
\boldsymbol{E}_5 &= [-1\ -2\ 0\ 2\ 1], \\
\boldsymbol{S}_5 &= [-1\ 0\ 2\ 0\ -1], \\
\boldsymbol{W}_5 &= [-1\ 2\ 0\ -2\ 1], \\
\boldsymbol{R}_5 &= [1\ -4\ 6\ -4\ 1],
\end{aligned}
\tag{11.21}
$$

where, $\boldsymbol{L}_5$ gives the center-weighted local average, $\boldsymbol{E}_5$ detects edges, $\boldsymbol{S}_5$ detects points, $\boldsymbol{W}_5$ detects waves, and $\boldsymbol{R}_5$ detects ripples.

The effect of the 2D mask used in the image can be obtained by convolving two 1D masks (row mask and column mask). For each pixel in the original image, the above convolution result obtained in its neighborhood is used to replace its value, and a map corresponding to the texture energy of its neighborhood is obtained. With the help of the energy map, each pixel can be replaced with an N^2D feature quantity that represents the texture energy in the neighborhood.

In many practical applications, nine 5×5 masks are often used to calculate **texture energy**. These nine masks can be obtained by using four 1D vectors of $\boldsymbol{L}_5$, $\boldsymbol{E}_5$, $\boldsymbol{S}_5$, and $\boldsymbol{R}_5$. The 2D mask can be obtained by calculating the outer product of the 1D mask, for example,

$$
\boldsymbol{E}_5^{\mathrm{T}} \boldsymbol{L}_5 =
\begin{bmatrix}
-1 \\
-2 \\
0 \\
2 \\
1
\end{bmatrix}
\times [1\ 4\ 6\ 4\ 1] =
\begin{bmatrix}
-1 & -4 & -6 & -4 & -1 \\
-2 & -8 & -12 & -8 & -2 \\
0 & 0 & 0 & 0 & 0 \\
2 & 8 & 12 & 8 & 2 \\
1 & 4 & 6 & 4 & 1
\end{bmatrix}
\tag{11.22}
$$

When using four 1D vectors, 16 5×5 2D masks can be obtained. Using these 16 masks for the original image can get 16 filtered images. Let $F_n(x,y)$ be the result of filtering with the nth mask at the position (x, y), then the texture energy map E_n corresponding to the nth mask is (c and r represent rows and columns, respectively)

$$E_n(r, c) = \sum_{x=c-2}^{c+2} \sum_{y=r-2}^{r+2} |F_n(x, y)|. \tag{11.23}$$

Each texture energy map is a full-size image, representing the result obtained with the nth mask.

Once the 16 texture energy maps are obtained, the symmetrical map pairs can be further combined (the pair of maps are replaced by their mean maps) to obtain nine final maps. For example, $E_5^T L_5$ measures horizontal edges and $L_5^T E_5$ measures vertical edges, and their average value can measure all edges. The nine texture energy maps obtained in this way are $L_5^T E_5 / E_5^T L_5$, $L_5^T S_5 / S_5^T L_5$, $L_5^T R_5 / R_5^T L_5$, $E_5^T E_5$, $E_5^T S_5 / S_5^T E_5$, $E_5^T R_5 / R_5^T E_5$, $S_5^T S_5$, $S_5^T R_5 / R_5^T S_5$, $R_5^T R_5$. The nine texture energy maps obtained above can also be regarded as one map, and each pixel position has a vector containing nine texture attributes.

11.2   Structural Description of Texture

In the **structural method** of describing texture, texture is regarded as the result of a set of texture primitives combined with a certain regular or repeated relationship. This method attempts to describe texture primitives based on some placement/arrangement rules describing geometric relationships. The structural method can often obtain some texture features related to visual perception, such as coarseness, contrast, directionality, linearity, regularity, roughness or unevenness.

11.2.1   Basis of structure description method

There are two keys to the structural method. One is to determine texture primitives; the other is to establish arrangement rules. In order to describe the texture, it is necessary to describe the nature of the gray-scale texture primitives and the spatial arrangement rules between them.

1. Texture primitives

The nature of the texture region in the image is related to the nature and quantity of the basic units/primitives that make up the texture. If a region contains primitives with almost constant gray levels, the main attribute of the region is gray scale; if a region contains many primitives with varying gray levels, the main attribute of the region is texture. The key factors here are the size of the image region, the type of primitives, as well as the number and arrangement of different primitives. When the number of different primitives is reduced, the gray-scale characteristics will be enhanced. In fact, if the image region is just a single pixel, this region has only gray-scale properties; when the number of different primitives in the image region increases, the texture characteristics gradually increase. If the spatial patterns of gray scale are random and the gray-scale changes of different primitives are relatively large, a coarser texture is obtained; when the spatial pattern becomes finer and the image region contains more and more pixels, it gets a finer texture.

Currently, there is no standard (or commonly recognized) texture primitive collection. It is generally considered that a **texture primitive** is a set of connected pixels described by a set of attributes. The simplest primitive is a pixel, and its attribute is its gray scale. A more complicated primitive is a set of connected pixels with uniform properties. Such a primitive can be described by size, orientation, shape, and average value.

Assuming that the texture primitive is represented by $h(x, y)$ and the arrangement rule is represented by $r(x, y)$, the texture $t(x, y)$ can be represented as

$$t(x,y) = h(x,y) \otimes r(x,y). \tag{11.24}$$

The arrangement rule determines the position of the primitive, so it is equivalent to the pulse sampling function:

$$r(x,y) = \sum \delta(x - x_m, y - y_m). \tag{11.25}$$

Here, x_m and y_m are the position coordinates of the pulse function. According to the convolution theorem, in the frequency domain,

$$T(u,v) = H(u,v)R(u,v). \tag{11.26}$$

So,

$$R(u, v) = \frac{T(u, v)}{H(u, v)}. \tag{11.27}$$

In this way, given the description of the texture primitive $h(x, y)$, the deconvolution filter $H^{-1}(u, v)$ can be derived. Applying this filter to the texture image, the pulse array in the texture region is obtained, in which each pulse is in the center of the texture primitive. Texture primitives describe local texture features, and the statistics on the distribution of different texture primitives in the entire image can provide comprehensive texture information of the image. Here, the histogram (texture spectrum) of the texture image can be obtained by labeling the texture primitive as the horizontal axis and their appearance frequency as the vertical axis.

2. Arrangement rules

In order to describe the texture with the structural method, on the basis of obtaining the texture primitives, it is necessary to establish the rules for arranging them. If some rules for arranging primitives can be defined, it is possible to organize the given texture primitives into the required texture pattern in a prescribed way. The rules and methods here can be defined by **formal grammar**, similar to the description of the object relationship in Section 10.6.

Consider the following four rewriting rules (where t represents texture primitives, a represents rightward movement, and b represents downward movement):

(1) $S \rightarrow aS$ (variable S can be replaced by aS).
(2) $S \rightarrow bS$ (variable S can be replaced by bS).
(3) $S \rightarrow tS$ (variable S can be replaced by tS).
(4) $S \rightarrow t$ (variable S can be replaced by t).

Different 2D texture regions can be generated by combining different rewriting rules.

For example, let t be a texture primitive as shown in Figure 11.3(a), which can also be regarded as obtained by directly using Rule (4). If Rule (3), Rule (1), Rule (3), Rule (1), Rule (3), Rule (1), and Rule (4) are used in sequence, it produces "*tatatat*", that is, the pattern in Figure 11.3(b) is generated. If Rule (3), Rule (1), Rule (3),

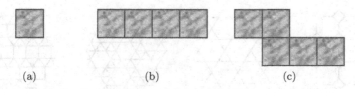

Figure 11.3. Generation of various 2D texture patterns.

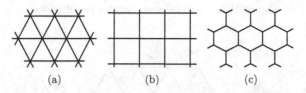

Figure 11.4. Three kinds of regular polygon tessellation.

Rule (2), Rule (3), Rule (1), Rule (3), Rule (1), and Rule (4) are used in sequence, it produces "*tatbtatat*", which can generate the pattern as shown in Figure 11.4(c).

11.2.2 Texture tessellation

More regular textures can be constructed by **texture tessellation** (also called texture mosaic) in an orderly form in space. The most typical tessellation pattern in **regular tessellation** is regular polygon tessellation. In Figure 11.4, Figure 11.4(a) shows a pattern composed of regular triangles; Figure 11.4(b) shows a pattern composed of regular squares; Figure 11.4(c) shows a pattern composed of regular hexagons.

If two regular polygons with various sides are used for tessellation at the same time, it constitutes a **semi-regular tessellation**. Several typical semi-regular tessellation patterns are shown in Figure 11.5.

To describe these tessellation patterns, the number of sides of the polygon around the vertex can be listed in sequence. For example, for the pattern in Figure 11.4(c), it can be represented as (6, 6, 6), that is, there are three hexagons surrounding each vertex. For the pattern in Figure 11.5(c), there are four triangles and one hexagon surrounding each vertex, so it is represented as (3, 3, 3, 3, 6). Depending on the starting polygon, the representation of pattern

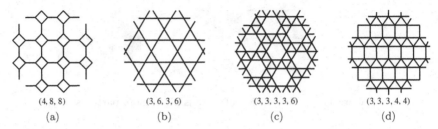

(4, 8, 8)   (3, 6, 3, 6)   (3, 3, 3, 3, 6)   (3, 3, 3, 4, 4)

(a)   (b)   (c)   (d)

Figure 11.5.   Several semi-regular tessellations.

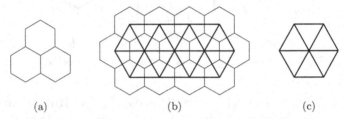

(a)   (b)   (c)

Figure 11.6.   Duality of tessellation of primitives and tessellation of arrangements.

can be looped. The important thing here is the arrangement of the primitives, not the primitives themselves. It should be pointed out that **primitive tessellation pattern** and **arrangement tessellation pattern** have **duality**. In Figure 11.6, Figures 11.6(a) and (c) correspond to the tessellation of primitives and tessellation of arrangements, respectively and Figure 11.6(b) is the result of their combination.

11.2.3   Local binary pattern

Local binary pattern (LBP) is a texture analysis operator, which is a texture metric defined by the local neighborhood. It belongs to the point sample estimation method, which has the advantages of scale invariance, rotation invariance, and low computational complexity. Only the basic principles are described in the following.

The original LBP operator makes the **thresholding** of the pixels in the 3×3 neighborhood of a pixel in sequence, then treats the result as a binary number and serves as the label of the center pixel. Figure 11.7 shows an example. The left side is a texture image, from

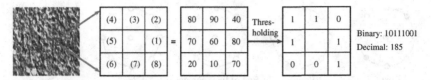

Figure 11.7.   Basic LBP operator.

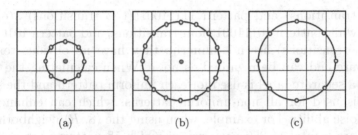

(a)   (b)   (c)

Figure 11.8.   Neighborhood sets corresponding to different (P, R).

which a 3×3 neighborhood is taken out. The order of the pixels in the neighborhood is indicated by the numbers in parentheses. The gray values of these pixels are determined by the next window representation. If the threshold value of 50 is used to threshold the pixels in the neighborhood, a binary image is obtained, and the binary label of each pixel is 10111001 in turn, and it is 185 in decimal. The histogram obtained from 256 different labels can be further used as the texture descriptor of the region.

The basic LBP operator can be extended by using neighborhoods of different sizes and shape. First, the neighborhood can be circular, and bilinear interpolation can be used to calculate pixel values for non-integer coordinate positions to eliminate the restrictions on the radius of the neighborhood and the number of pixels in the neighborhood. In the following, (P, R) is used to represent a pixel neighborhood, where there are P pixels in the neighborhood and the circle radius is R. Figure 11.8 gives several examples of circular neighborhoods.

Another extension to the basic LBP operator is the **uniform pattern**. Consider the pixels in a neighborhood in a sequential cycle. If it contains at most two transitions from zero to one or from one to zero, the binary pattern is uniform. For example, pattern 00000000

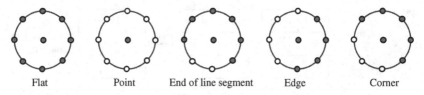

| Flat | Point | End of line segment | Edge | Corner |

Figure 11.9.   Local primitives obtained with LBP labeling.

(zero transitions) and pattern 11111001 (two transitions) are uniform, while pattern 10111001 (four transitions) and pattern 10101010 (seven transitions) are not uniform; they have no obvious texture structure and can be regarded as noise. When calculating the LBP label, a separate label is used for each uniform pattern and the same label is used for all non-uniform patterns, which can enhance its anti-noise ability. For example, when using the $(8, R)$ neighborhood, there are a total of 256 patterns, of which 58 patterns are uniform patterns, so there are a total of 59 labels. In summary, it can use $\mathrm{LBP}_{P,R}^{(\mathrm{u})}$ to represent such a uniform pattern LBP operator.

According to the label of LBP, different local primitives can be obtained, corresponding to different local texture structures. Figure 11.9 gives some (meaningful) examples, where the hollow dot represents one and the solid point represents zero.

If the image $f_L(x, y)$ marked with the LBP label is calculated, the LBP histogram can be defined as

$$H(i) = \sum_{x,y} I\{f_{\mathrm{L}}(x,y) = i\}, \quad i = 0, \ldots, n-1, \tag{11.28}$$

where n is the number of different labels given by the LBP operator, and the function $I(z)$ is

$$I(z) = \begin{cases} 1 & z \text{ is TRUE} \\ 0 & z \text{ is FALSE}. \end{cases} \tag{11.29}$$

11.3   Spectral Description of Texture

The spectral method of describing texture generally uses the distribution of the Fourier spectrum (obtained by Fourier transform), especially the high-energy narrow pulse in the spectrum, to describe the global periodic nature of the texture pattern.

11.3.1   Fourier spectrum

The frequency characteristics of the **Fourier spectrum** can be used to describe the directionality of periodic or nearly periodic 2D image modes. Specifically, the main direction of the texture pattern is determined by the protruding peaks in the Fourier spectrum, and the position of these peaks in the frequency domain plane is used to determine the basic period of the pattern.

In the actual spectrum feature detection, the spectrum can be converted into a polar coordinate system for simplicity. Here, the frequency spectrum can be represented by the function $S(r, \theta)$. For each given direction θ, $S(r, \theta)$ is a 1D function $S_\theta(r)$; for each given frequency r, $S(r, \theta)$ is a 1D function $S_r(\theta)$. For a given θ, analyzing $S_\theta(r)$ can get the behavioral characteristics of the spectrum along the direction departing from the origin; for a given r, analyzing $S_r(\theta)$ can get the behavioral characteristics of the spectrum on a circle centered at the origin. Further summing these functions for the subscripts can provide a more global description, namely

$$S(r) = \sum_{\theta=0}^{\pi} S_\theta(r), \tag{11.30}$$

$$S(\theta) = \sum_{r=1}^{R} S_r(\theta). \tag{11.31}$$

In Equations (11.30) and (11.31), R is the radius of a circle centered at the origin. $S(r)$ and $S(\theta)$ constitute the description of the texture spectrum energy of the entire image or image region, where $S(r)$ is also called the ring feature (the route of summation for θ is circular), and $S(\theta)$ is also called the wedge feature (the summation route for r is wedge-shaped). Figures 11.10(a) and (b) show schematic diagrams of two texture regions and their frequency spectra. Comparing the two spectral curves, we can see the difference in orientation of the two textures. In addition, the position of their maximum value can be calculated from the spectrum curve.

If the texture has spatial periodicity, or has a certain directionality, the energy spectrum will have a peak at the corresponding frequency. Based on these peaks, the features required for pattern recognition can be obtained. One way to determine these features is to divide the Fourier space into blocks and then calculate the energy

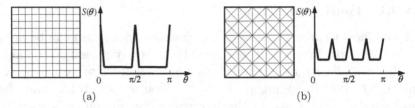

Figure 11.10. Corresponding schematic diagram of texture and frequency spectrum.

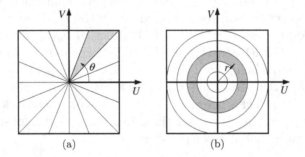

Figure 11.11. Two forms of partitioning of Fourier space.

in each block. There are two types of block commonly used, namely the angle type and radial type. The former corresponds to a wedge filter or sector filter, and the latter corresponds to an annular filter or a loop filter, as shown in Figures 11.11(a) and (b), respectively.

The features of the angle orientation can be defined as follows ($|F|^2$ is the Fourier power spectrum):

$$A(\theta_1, \theta_2) = \sum \sum |F|^2(u, v). \tag{11.32}$$

Among them, the sum limits are

$$\begin{aligned} \theta_1 \leq \arctan(v/u) &< \theta_2 \\ 0 < u, v &\leq N - 1. \end{aligned} \tag{11.33}$$

The feature of angle orientation represents the sensitivity of energy spectrum to texture direction. If the texture contains many straight lines or edges in a given direction θ, the value of $|F|^2$ will be clustered near the direction of $\theta + \pi/2$ in the frequency space.

The radial feature can be defined as

$$R(r_1, r_2) = \sum \sum |F|^2(u, v). \tag{11.34}$$

Among them, the sum limits are

$$
\begin{aligned}
r_1^2 \leq u^2 + v^2 < r_2^2 \\
0 < u, v \leq N - 1.
\end{aligned}
\tag{11.35}
$$

The radial feature is related to the roughness of the texture. A smooth texture will have a larger $R(r_1, r_2)$ value at a small radius, while a rough-grained texture will have a larger $R(r_1, r_2)$ value at a large radius.

11.3.2 Bessel–Fourier spectrum

Bessel–Fourier spectrum combines Bessel function and Fourier spectrum and has the following form:

$$G(R, \theta) = \sum_{m=0}^{\infty} \sum_{n=0}^{\infty} (A_{m,n} \cos m\theta + B_{m,n} \sin m\theta) J_m \left(Z_{m,n} \frac{R}{R_v} \right). \tag{11.36}$$

In Equation (11.36), $G(R, \theta)$ is the gray-scale function (θ is the angle), $A_{m,n}$ and $B_{m,n}$ are Bessel–Fourier coefficients, J_m is the first-type mth order Bessel function, $Z_{m,n}$ is the zero root of Bessel function, and R_v is the radius of the field of view.

Using this spectrum, the following important texture features can be obtained:

(1) *Bessel–Fourier coefficient*: That is, the coefficients $A_{m,n}$ and $B_{m,n}$ of the Bessel–Fourier transform; see Equation (11.36).
(2) *Moment of gray-scale distribution function (gray-scale histogram)*: That is, the various moments of the histogram of the Bessel–Fourier spectrum $G(R, \theta)$.
(3) *Partial rotational symmetry coefficient*: The texture is composed of discrete gray levels. An R-fold symmetric operation can be done by comparing the gray level in $G(R, \theta)$ with the gray level

in $G(R, \theta + \Delta\theta)$. The partial rotational symmetry coefficients of the texture can be obtained as follows:

$$C_R = \frac{\sum_{m=0}^{\infty} \sum_{n=0}^{\infty} [H_{m,n} R^2 \cos m(2\pi/R)] J_m^2(Z_{m,n})}{\sum_{m=0}^{\infty} \sum_{n=0}^{\infty} (H_{m,n} R^2) J_m^2(Z_{m,n})}. \qquad (11.37)$$

In Equation (11.37), $R = 1, 2, \ldots, H_{m,n} R^2 = A_{m,n} R^2 + B_{m,n} R^2$.

(4) *Partial translational symmetry coefficient*: When the gray scale is compared along the radius (e.g., $G(R, \theta)$ is compared with $G(R + \Delta R, \theta)$), the property of partial translational symmetry can be found. The partial translational symmetry coefficient of the texture can be defined as

$$C_T = \frac{\sum_{m=0}^{\infty} \sum_{n=0}^{\infty} H_{m,n}^2 J_m^2(Z_{m,n}) - (A_{m,n} A_{m-1,n} + B_{m,n} B_{m-1,n}) J_m^2(Z_{m,n}) \frac{\Delta R}{2R_v}}{2 \sum_{m=0}^{\infty} \sum_{n=0}^{\infty} H_{m,n}^2 J_m^2(Z_{m,n})}.$$

$$(11.38)$$

It satisfies $0 < C_T < 1$.

(5) *Roughness*: **Roughness** can be defined as the gray-level difference between four neighboring pixels surrounding a pixel (x, y). The analysis shows that the roughness has the following relationship with partial rotational symmetry coefficient and partial translation symmetry coefficient:

$$F_{\text{crs}} = 4 - 2(C_R + C_T). \qquad (11.39)$$

(6) *Contrast*: If the values of some variables are distributed near the mean of these values, the distribution is said to have a large kurtosis. **Contrast** can be defined by means of kurtosis σ^4 as

$$F_{\text{con}} = \frac{\mu_4}{\sigma^4}, \qquad (11.40)$$

where μ_4 is the fourth-order moment of the gray-scale distribution pattern with respect to the mean and σ^2 is the variance.

(7) *Unevenness*: The **unevenness** is related to roughness and contrast as follows:

$$F_{\text{rou}} = F_{\text{crs}} + F_{\text{con}}. \qquad (11.41)$$

(8) *Regularity*: **Regularity** is a function of the (translation and rotation) changes of texture elements in the image, which can be defined as

$$F_{\text{reg}} = \sum_{r=1}^{m} C_R + \sum_{t=1}^{n} C_T. \qquad (11.42)$$

An image with high rotational symmetry and high translational symmetry has great regularity.

11.4 Key Points and References for Each Section

The following indicates the key points of each section and provides some targeted guidance for further references.

1. Statistical description of texture

Statistical method is an important method to describe texture. Different images have very different gray-level co-occurrence matrices due to different texture sizes, periods, and shapes. Therefore, statistical methods often use regional gray-level co-occurrence matrices to describe texture. Many texture descriptors can be defined on the basis of the co-occurrence matrix. The 14 texture descriptors defined by the regional gray-level co-occurrence matrix and introduced in this section can be found in Ref. [1]. The texture descriptor defined by the regional gray-gradient co-occurrence matrix can be found in Ref. [2]. In addition, texture images can similarly be generated according to the parameters obtained by statistical methods for random processes; see Ref. [3].

2. Structural description of texture

In the description of texture structure, texture is regarded as the result of a set of texture primitives combined in a certain regular or repetitive relationship; see Ref. [4]. In other words, the structural method attempts to describe texture primitives according to some placement/arrangement rules describing geometric relationships; see Ref. [3]. Therefore, the structural texture description method is most suitable for more regular textures. The regularity here refers to the more consistent texture primitives and more orderly arrangement. The basic form of the local binary pattern is extended to the spatial-temporal representation to become a 3D local binary pattern operator, and dynamic texture analysis can also be performed; see Ref. [5]. In order to overcome the problem that the local binary pattern is more sensitive to noise interference, the local three-value pattern (LTP) has been proposed to improve the robustness; see Ref. [6]. In addition, the fractal corresponds to the regularity on different scales and the fractal model can also be used to describe the texture better; see Refs. [5,7].

3. Spectral description of texture

In addition to the use of Fourier spectrum and Bessel–Fourier spectrum, the spectrum description can also use the Gaber spectrum; see Ref. [5]. For the sample graph of the Gaber spectrum, refer to Ref. [8]. Three types of texture descriptors are recommended in the international standard MPEG-7. In addition to edge histograms, homogeneous texture descriptors and texture browsing descriptors are also based on the nature of the frequency domain; see the Ref. [9]. A comparison of these three texture descriptors can be found in Ref. [10]. An example of using transform domain coefficients to describe texture properties for image retrieval can be found in Ref. [11].

Self-Test Questions

The following questions include both single- and multiple-choice questions, so each option should be individually judged.

11.1 Statistical Description of Texture

11.1.1 Suppose that the upper-left pixel value of a 5×5 chessboard image is zero, its adjacent pixels value are one, and the position operator W is defined as one pixel to the right. In this case, the co-occurrence matrix of the image is ( )

(A) $\begin{bmatrix} 10 & 0 \\ 0 & 0 \end{bmatrix}$;

(B) $\begin{bmatrix} 10 & 0 \\ 0 & 10 \end{bmatrix}$;

(C) $\begin{bmatrix} 0 & 10 \\ 10 & 0 \end{bmatrix}$;

(D) $\begin{bmatrix} 10 & 10 \\ 10 & 10 \end{bmatrix}$.

[Hint] Draw the 5 × 5 chessboard image described first, and then analyze the regularity.

11.1.2 Suppose that a given 6 × 6 image is shown in Figure 11.1.2. Define the position operator W to be one pixel to the right. At this time, the co-occurrence matrix of the image is ( )

0	1	2	0	1	2
1	2	0	1	2	0
2	0	1	2	0	1
0	1	2	0	1	2
0	1	2	0	1	2
1	2	0	1	2	0

Figure 11.1.2.

(A) $\begin{bmatrix} 0 & 10 & 0 \\ 0 & 0 & 11 \\ 9 & 0 & 0 \end{bmatrix}$;

(B) $\begin{bmatrix} 10 & 0 & 0 \\ 0 & 0 & 10 \\ 0 & 10 & 0 \end{bmatrix}$;

(C) $\begin{bmatrix} 0 & 0 & 0 \\ 0 & 0 & 10 \\ 0 & 10 & 10 \end{bmatrix}$;

(D) $\begin{bmatrix} 10 & 0 & 0 \\ 0 & 10 & 0 \\ 0 & 0 & 10 \end{bmatrix}$.

[Hint] Pay attention to the analysis of the order of the three numbers.

11.1.3 There are 14 texture descriptors that can be obtained from the gray-level co-occurrence matrix. ( )

(A) Their values are proportional to the values of the co-occurrence matrix;
(B) They are all related to the gray scale and gradient of the image;
(C) They all have dimensions;
(D) They are all related.

[Hint] Look carefully at the calculation equations of each texture descriptor.

11.1.4 The texture energy maps $S_5^T S_5$ and $R_5^T R_5$ can detect, respectively, ( )

(A) Edges and ripples;
(B) Points and ripples;
(C) Ripples and points;
(D) Ripples and edges.

[Hint] The effect of one 2D mask can be obtained by convolution of two 1D masks (row mask and column mask).

11.1.5 Texture energy map $R_5^T E_5$ can detect ( )

(A) Edges and ripples;
(B) Ripples and edges;
(C) Vertical ripples;
(D) Inclined ripples.

[Hint] The effect of one 2D mask combines the effects of two 1D masks (row mask and column mask).

11.2 Structural Description of Texture

11.2.1 Refer to Figure 11.3. If it is required to generate the pattern in Figure 11.2.1, one needs to use the following rules in sequence: ( )

(A) (3), (1), (3), (1), (1), (3), (2), (1), (3), (2), (3), (1), (4);
(B) (3), (1), (3), (1), (3), (2), (3), (1), (1), (3), (3), (1), (4);

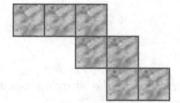

Figure 11.2.1.

(C) (3), (1), (3), (1), (3), (2), (3), (1), (3), (2), (3), (1), (4);
(D) (3), (1), (3), (1), (3), (2), (3), (1), (3), (2), (1), (3), (4).

[Hint] It can be specifically generated once according to the given pattern.

11.2.2 Consider the pattern shown in Figure 11.2.2, which is a ( )

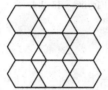

Figure 11.2.2.

(A) Semi-regular tessellation: (3, 3, 6, 6);
(B) Non-semi-regular tessellation;
(C) Semi-regular tessellation: (3, 6, 3, 6);
(D) Regular polygon tessellation.

[Hint] Consider the definition of semi-regular tessellation.

11.2.3 Given the neighborhood as shown in Figure 11.2.3, if 50 is used to threshold it, the decimal label of its LBP is ( )

10	40	70
20	50	80
30	60	90

Figure 11.2.3.

(A) 15;
(B) 43;
(C) 135;
(D) 195.

[Hint] Pay attention to the starting point and order when numbering pixels.

11.2.4 Consider the neighborhood (P, R) given in Figure 11.2.4, where ( )

Figure 11.2.4.

(A) $P = 10, R = 1$;
(B) $P = 12, R = 1$;
(C) $P = 12, R = 1.5$;
(D) $P = 14, R = 1.5$.

[Hint] The radius here is from the center of a pixel to the edge of the adjacent pixel.

11.3 Spectral Description of Texture

11.3.1 If the angle type of feature takes the maximum value in a given direction θ, this indicates that ( )

(A) There are many high-frequency components along the θ direction in the image;
(B) There are many straight lines or edges along the θ direction in the image;
(C) There are many high-frequency components perpendicular to the θ direction in the image;
(D) There are many lines or edges perpendicular to the θ direction in the image.

[Hint] The energy is proportional to the change in gray level.

11.3.2 If the radial type of feature of image I increases with the increasing of radius and the radial type of feature of image J decreases with the increasing of radius, which shows ( )

(A) The texture in image I is relatively smooth and the texture in image J is relatively rough;

(B) The texture in image I is relatively rough and the texture in image J is relatively smooth;

(C) There are more high-frequency components in image I and more low-frequency components in image J;

(D) There are more low-frequency components in image I and more high-frequency components in image J.

[Hint] Smooth texture has more low-frequency components, while rough texture has more high-frequency components.

11.3.3 Regularity, roughness, and unevenness are respectively related to partial rotational symmetry coefficients and partial translational symmetry coefficients: ( )

(A) Positive relationship, positive relationship, positive relationship;

(B) Positive relationship, positive relationship, and negative relationship;

(C) Positive relationship, negative relationship, and positive relationship;

(D) Positive relationship, negative relationship, and negative relationship.

[Hint] Judge according to the definition formulas.

References

[1] Haralick, R. M. and Shapiro, L. G. *Computer and Robot Vision, Vol. 1.* UK, London: Addison-Wesley, 1992.

[2] Zhang, Y.-J. *Image Engineering (III): Teaching References and Problem Solutions.* China, Beijing: Tsinghua University Press, 2002.

[3] Russ, J. C. and Neal, F. B. *The Image Processing Handbook*, 7th Edn. UK, London: CRC Press, 2016.

[4] Shapiro, L. and Stockman, G. *Computer Vision.* UK, London: Prentice Hall, 2001.

402   *2D Computer Vision: Principles, Algorithms and Applications*

[5] Zhang, Y.-J. *Image Engineering (II) Image Analysis*, 4th Edn. China, Beijing: Tsinghua University Press, 2018.

[6] Tan, X. Y. and Bill, T. Enhanced local texture feature sets for face recognition under difficult lighting conditions. *Proc. AMFG*, 2007, 168–182.

[7] Wu, G. H., Zhang, Y.-J., and Lin, X, G. Fractal–based autocorrelation description and classification of natural texture images. *Journal of Tsinghua University (Science and Technology)*, 2000, 40(3): 90–93.

[8] Forsyth, D. and Ponce, J. *Computer Vision: A Modern Approach.* UK, London: Prentice Hall, 2003.

[9] Zhang, Y.-J. *Content-Based Visual Information Retrieval.* China, Beijing: Science Press, 2003.

[10] Xu, F. and Zhang, Y.-J. Comparison and evaluation of texture descriptors proposed in MPEG-7. *International Journal of Visual Communication and Image Representation*, 2006, 17: 701–716.

[11] Huang, X. Y., Zhang, Y.-J., and Hu, D. Image retrieval based on weighted texture features using DCT coefficients of JPEG images. *Proc. 4th IEEE PCM*, 2003, 3: 1571–1575.

Chapter 12

Shape Description

Shape is a commonly used concept in image analysis. When people observe an object of interest in the scene, they can often quickly find the boundary between it and the surrounding environment, compose the outline of the object, and describe its appearance based on experience. Experience is used here because the description of the shape often uses a method of comparing with the known shape, that is, the shape description mainly uses the relative method.

A dictionary interpretation of shape terms is "the appearance of an object or figure combined by external surfaces or contours". The shape of an object can be defined as a pattern composed of points on the boundary of the object. The main difficulty in quantitative description of shape is the lack of precise and uniform definition of shape. Therefore, the properties of a shape are often described by different theoretical techniques or descriptors. This chapter will mainly discuss two important shape properties: compactness and complexity (also called extensibility/elongation and irregularity, respectively). To describe these two properties, a variety of descriptors have been designed. In addition, this chapter also introduces the shape descriptors based on discrete curvature and the shape description methods based on topology.

The sections of this chapter are arranged as follows:

Section 12.1 introduces the description methods for shape compactness and mainly introduces the five shape descriptors: aspect ratio, shape factor, eccentricity, sphericity, and circularity, and also compares their characteristics.

Section 12.2 introduces how to describe the complexity of shapes. In addition to giving some simple descriptors of shape complexity, the technique of blurring images to help describe shape complexity and the saturation-based descriptors are also discussed.

Section 12.3 reviews the calculation of discrete curvatures and presents the curvature-based shape descriptors.

Section 12.4 briefly introduces the topology description method and discusses an important description parameter, namely Euler's number, as well as two other derived description parameters, crossing number and connection number.

12.1   Shape Compactness Descriptor

Compactness is an important shape property, which is closely related to the **elongation** of the shape. Many different descriptors have been used to describe the compactness of the object region (several descriptors can also describe some other properties of the region). These descriptors basically correspond to the geometric parameters of the object, so they are all related to scale (different from topological parameters).

The compactness of an object region can be calculated directly or can be indirectly described by comparing the region with typical/ideal shaped regions (such as circles and rectangles). The following presents a few commonly used parameters that describe the compactness of the object.

12.1.1   Aspect ratio

The **aspect ratio** R is often used to describe the shape (the degree of slenderness) of the object after plastic deformation. It can be defined as

$$R = \frac{L}{W},\qquad(12.1)$$

where L and W are the length and width of the minimum enclosing rectangle of object, respectively, and some people use the length and width of the Feret box of object (see Section 9.5). For square or round objects, the value of R is the smallest (one); for slender objects, the value of R is greater than one and increases with the degree of slenderness.

12.1.2 Form factor

The **form factor** F is calculated based on the perimeter of the region and the area of the region:

$$F = \frac{\|B\|^2}{4\pi A}. \tag{12.2}$$

It can be seen from Equation (12.2) that F is one when a continuous region is a circle and F is greater than 1 when the region is another shape. That is, the value of F reaches the minimum when the region is a circle. It has been proved that for digital images, if the contour length is calculated according to 4-connectivity, the minimum F value is reached for the regular octagonal region; if the contour length is calculated according to 8-connectivity, the minimum F value is reached for the regular diamond region.

Example 12.1 Form factor calculation example

When calculating the form factor of a discrete object, the distance definition used needs to be considered. Figure 12.1 shows a circular object. Its 8-connected contour is approximately an octagon, as shown in Figure 12.1(a); its 4-connected contour is also approximately an octagon, but all four bevel edges are polyline segments, as shown in Figure 12.1(b). For Figure 12.1(a), the form factor $F = (8 + 12\sqrt{2})^2/4\pi(46) \approx 1.0787$, calculated with 8-connectivity. For Figure 12.1(b), the shape factor $F = 32^2/4\pi(52) \approx 1.5671$, calculated with 4-connectivity. Although from the approximation of the

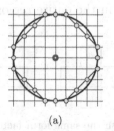 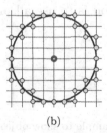

(a) (b)

Figure 12.1. Calculation of form factor.

contour of the circle object, the contour of Figure 12.1(a) is worse than that of Figure 12.1(b), from the value of the form factor, the contour of Figure 12.1(a) is closer to a circle than the contour of Figure 12.1(b).   □

The form factor describes the compactness of the region to a certain extent. It has no dimension, so it is not sensitive to changes in the region scale. The error caused by the rotation of discrete regions is eliminated because the form factor is not very sensitive to region rotation.

Example 12.2 Form factor and region shape

The shape of the region and the form factor of the region are related to a certain degree, but they do not have one-to-one correspondence. In some cases, using the form factor F alone cannot distinguish regions of different shapes. Figure 12.2 shows a group of examples. Each of the four regions in the figure includes five pixels, so their areas are the same. Their 4-connected contour lengths are also the same, all are 12, so they have the same form factor $(7.2/\pi)$, but it can be seen from the figure that their shapes are obviously different from each other.   □

12.1.3   Eccentricity

Eccentricity E is also called **elongation**, and it describes the **compactness** of the region to a certain extent. There are multiple calculation formulas for eccentricity E. A commonly used simple method is to calculate the ratio of the length of the major axis (diameter) of the region to the length of the minor axis, but the value calculated in this way is greatly affected by the shape of the object and the noise. A better method is to use all pixels in the entire region, so that the

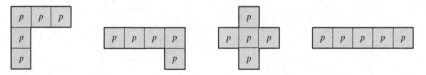

Figure 12.2.   Example to show objects with the same form factors but very different shapes.

ability to resist noise and other interference is stronger. The following introduces a calculation method of eccentricity derived from the moment of inertia.

Rigid body dynamics tells us that the inertia of a rigid body when it rotates can be measured by its moment of inertia. Suppose a rigid body object has N mass points, their masses are $m_1, m_2, \ldots, m_N$ and their coordinates are $(x_1, y_1, z_1), (x_2, y_2, z_2), \ldots, (x_N, y_N, z_N)$, then the moment of inertia I of this rigid body around a certain axis L can be expressed as

$$I = \sum_{i=1}^{N} m_i d_i^2, \tag{12.3}$$

where d_i represents the vertical distance between the mass point m_i and the axis of rotation L. If L passes through the origin of the coordinate system and its direction cosines are α, β, γ, then Equation (12.3) can be written as

$$I = A\alpha^2 + B\beta^2 + C\gamma^2 - 2F\beta\gamma - 2G\gamma\alpha - 2H\alpha\beta, \tag{12.4}$$

where $A = \Sigma m_i(y_i^2 + z_i^2)$, $B = \Sigma m_i(z_i^2 + x_i^2)$, and $C = \Sigma m_i(x_i^2 + y_i^2)$ are the moments of inertia of the rigid body around the X, Y, and Z coordinate axes and $F = \Sigma m_i y_i z_i$, $G = \Sigma m_i z_i x_i$, and $H = \Sigma m_i x_i y_i$ are called the products of inertia.

Equation (12.4) can be explained in a simple geometric way. First, the equation

$$I = Ax^2 + By^2 + Cz^2 - 2Fyz - 2Gzx - 2Hxy \tag{12.5}$$

represents a second-order surface (cone) whose center is at the origin of the coordinate system. If r is used to represent the vector from the origin to the surface, and the direction cosines of the vector are α, β, γ, then substituting Equation (12.4) into Equation (12.5) can give

$$r^2 \left(A\alpha^2 + B\beta^2 + C\gamma^2 - 2F\beta\gamma - 2G\gamma\alpha - 2H\alpha\beta\right) = r^2 I = 1. \tag{12.6}$$

From the above equation, $r^2 I = 1$. We know that because I is always greater than zero, r must be a finite value, that is, the surface is closed. Considering that this is a second-order surface, it must be an ellipsoid, called an ellipsoid of inertia. It has three main axes perpendicular to each other. For a homogeneous ellipsoid of inertia, the cross-section with any two principal axes coplanar is an ellipse, which is called an **ellipse of inertia**. The object in a 2D image can be regarded as a planar uniform rigid body, and a corresponding ellipse of inertia can be calculated as above, which reflects the distribution of points on the object.

An ellipse of inertia can be completely determined by the direction and length of its two principal axes. The directions of the two principal axes of the ellipse of inertia can be obtained by the method of finding eigenvalues in linear algebra. Suppose the slopes of the two main axes are k and l, respectively, then

$$k = \frac{1}{H}\left[(A - B) - \sqrt{(A - B)^2 + 4H^2}\right], \qquad (12.7)$$

$$l = \frac{1}{H}\left[(A - B) + \sqrt{(A - B)^2 + 4H^2}\right]. \qquad (12.8)$$

It can be further solved so that the lengths of the two semi-major axes (p and q) of the ellipse of inertia are respectively

$$p = \sqrt{\frac{2}{(A + B) - \sqrt{(A - B)^2 + 4H^2}}}, \qquad (12.9)$$

$$q = \sqrt{\frac{2}{(A + B) + \sqrt{(A - B)^2 + 4H^2}}}. \qquad (12.10)$$

The eccentricity of the object region can be obtained by the ratio of p and q, namely

$$E = \frac{p}{q}. \qquad (12.11)$$

It is easy to see that the eccentricity defined in this way is not affected by translation, rotation, and scale transformation. It is derived from the 3D space, so it can also describe the object in the 3D image. Equations (12.7) and (12.8) can also give a description of the orientation of the object region.

Example 12.3 Ellipse matching method for geometric correction

With the help of the calculation of the ellipse of inertia, the equivalent ellipse can be further constructed. The geometric transformation needed to correct the geometric distortion between the two image regions can be obtained by matching between the corresponding equivalent ellipses. The basic process of this method is shown in Figure 12.3.

First, the moment of inertia of the image region is calculated and the two semi-axis lengths of the ellipse of inertia are obtained. Then, the eccentricity of the ellipse of inertia is found from the two semi-axis lengths. According to this eccentricity value (take $p/q = a/b$) and the region area to normalize the axis length, the equivalent ellipse can be obtained. In the area normalization, if the area of the image region is M, then the semi-major axis of the equivalent ellipse (set $A < B$ in Equation (12.4)) a is

$$a = \sqrt{\frac{2\left[(A+B) - \sqrt{(A-B)^2 + 4H^2}\right]}{M}}. \tag{12.12}$$

The center coordinates of the equivalent ellipse can be determined by the center of gravity of the image region, and the orientation of the equivalent ellipse is the same as the orientation of the ellipse of inertia. Here, the orientation of the ellipse can be calculated by means of the orientation angle, which is defined as the angle between its major axis and the positive X axis. The orientation angle of the equivalent ellipse ϕ can be determined by the slope of the two principal axes of the ellipse of inertia:

$$\phi = \begin{cases} \arctan(k) & \text{if } A < B \\ \arctan(l) & \text{if } A > B. \end{cases} \tag{12.13}$$

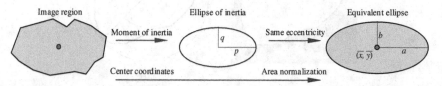

Figure 12.3.   Using the ellipse of inertia to construct an equivalent ellipse.

When performing geometric correction, first obtain the equivalent ellipses of the distortion image and the correction image and then obtain the required three basic parameters for translation, rotation, and scaling transformation according to the center coordinates, orientation angle, and length of the major semi-axis of the two equivalent ellipses, respectively.   □

12.1.4   Sphericity

Sphericity S is a parameter describing the shape of a 2D object, which is defined as

$$S = \frac{r_i}{r_c}. \tag{12.14}$$

In Equation (12.14), r_i represents the radius of the inscribed circle of the region and r_c represents the radius of the circumscribed circle of the region. The centers of these two circles can be at the center of gravity of the region, as shown in Figure 12.4.

The value of sphericity reaches the maximum when the region is a circle ($S = 1$), and when the region is of other shapes, it is $S < 1$. It is not affected by regional translation, rotation, and scale changes.

12.1.5   Circularity

Different from the several parameters already introduced above, the descriptor **circularity** C is a feature defined by all the contour points

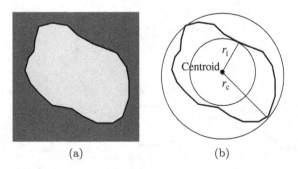

(a)   (b)

Figure 12.4.   Schematic diagram of the definition of sphericity.

of the region R:

$$C = \frac{\mu_R}{\sigma_R}, \tag{12.15}$$

where μ_R is the average distance from the center of gravity of the region to the contour point and σ_R is the mean square error of the distance from the center of gravity of the region to the contour point:

$$\mu_R = \frac{1}{k} \sum_{k=0}^{K-1} \|(x_k, y_k) - (\bar{x}, \bar{y})\|, \tag{12.16}$$

$$\sigma_R^2 = \frac{1}{k} \sum_{k=0}^{K-1} [\|(x_k, y_k) - (\bar{x}, \bar{y})\| - \mu_R]^2. \tag{12.17}$$

Circularity C approaches infinity when the region R tends to a circle, and it is not affected by regional translation, rotation, and scale changes.

12.1.6 Descriptor comparison

The following two examples are used to give some connections between the aforementioned shape compactness descriptors.

Example 12.4 Values of the shape compactness descriptors for some special-shaped objects

Table 12.1 gives the numerical values of the five shape compactness descriptors introduced above for several simple geometrical regions.

It can be seen from Table 12.1 that the numerical values of the aforementioned shape compactness descriptors have their own characteristics in distinguishing different objects. □

Example 12.5 Digital calculation of descriptors

So far, discussions on various compactness descriptors have been basically considered in continuous space. Figure 12.5 shows an example of calculating each descriptor for a discrete square, where Figures 12.5(a) and (b) correspond to B and A in the calculation of the form factor, respectively; Figures 12.5(c) and (d) correspond to r_i and r_c in the calculation of sphericity; Figure 12.5(e) corresponds to

Table 12.1.   Shape compactness descriptors of some special-shaped objects.

Object	R	F	E	S	C
Square (side length $= 1$)	1	$4/\pi(\approx 1.273)$	1	$\sqrt{2}/2(\approx 0.707)$	9.102
Hexagon (side length $= 1$)	1.1542	1.103	1.010	0.866	22.613
Regular octagon (side length $= 1$)	1	1.055	1	0.924	41.616
Rectangle (length $= 2$, width $= 1$)	2	1.432	2	0.447	3.965
Ellipse (major axis $= 2$, minor axis $= 1$)	2	1.190	2	0.500	4.412

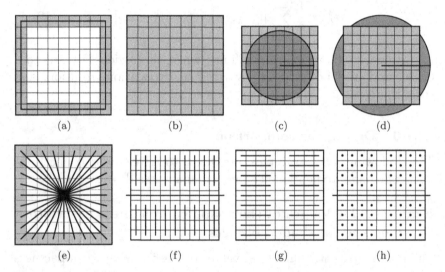

Figure 12.5.   Schematic diagram of discrete calculation of compactness descriptors.

μ_R in the calculation of circularity; Figures 12.5(f) to (h) correspond to A, B, and H in the calculation of eccentricity, respectively.   □

12.2   Shape Complexity Descriptor

Complexity is also an important shape property. In many practical applications, objects need to be classified according to their complexity. For example, in the morphological classification of neurons, the complexity of the branched tree often plays an important role.

The complexity of a shape is sometimes difficult to define directly, so it is necessary to relate it to other properties of the shape (especially geometric properties). For example, a commonly used concept is **spatial coverage**, which is closely related to the ability to fill space. The **space-filling capability** represents the ability of the organism to fill the surrounding space, and it defines the intersection of the object and the surrounding background. If the shape of a bacterium is more complex, that is, the spatial coverage is higher, then it is easier to find food. In another example, the amount of water that a tree root can absorb is proportional to its spatial coverage of the surrounding land.

12.2.1 Simple descriptors of shape complexity

It should be pointed out that although the concept of shape complexity has been widely used, there is no precise definition for it. People often use various measures of object shape to describe the concept of complexity. Here are some examples (where B and A represent the perimeter and area of the object region, respectively):

(1) **Thinness ratio:** It is the reciprocal of the form factor given by Equation (12.2), namely $4\pi(A/B^2)$.
(2) **Area perimeter ratio:** A/B.
(3) **Rectangularity:** Defined as A/A_{MER}, where A_{MER} represents the area of the **minimum enclosing rectangle** (see Section 9.5) of object. The rectangularity reflects the concavity–convexity of the object contour.
(4) **Mean distance to the boundary:** It is defined as A/μ_R^2; see Equation (12.16).
(5) **Boundary temperature:** According to the principle of thermodynamics, it is defined as $T = \log_2[(2B)/(B-H)]$, where H is the perimeter of the **convex hull** (see Section 9.5) of the object region.

12.2.2 Using the histogram analysis of the blurred image to describe the shape complexity

Since the histogram does not use the spatial distribution information of the pixels in image, the general histogram measure cannot be used as a shape feature. For example, the two images in Figures 12.6(a)

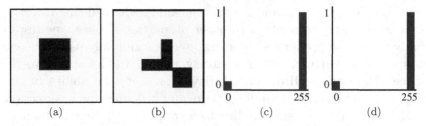

Figure 12.6.   Two images containing objects of different shapes and their histograms.

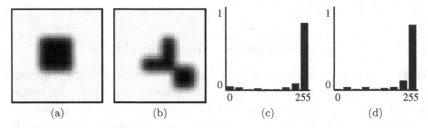

Figure 12.7.   Two smoothed images containing different shapes of objects and their histograms.

and (b) each contain an object with a different shape. The two objects have the same size (area), so the two images have the same histogram, as shown in Figures 12.6(c) and (d), respectively.

Now, the average filter is used to smooth the two images in Figures 12.6(a) and (b), and the results obtained are shown in Figures 12.7(a) and (b), respectively. Since the object shapes in the original two images are different, the histograms of the smoothed images are no longer the same in this case, as shown in Figures 12.7(c) and (d), respectively. Further, information can be extracted from the histogram of the smoothed image to define the shape feature.

12.2.3   Saturation

There is often a certain relationship between the compactness and complexity of the object, and the more compactly distributed objects often have a relatively simple shape.

For example, the saturation reflects the compactness of the object in a certain sense, and it considers how full the object is in its

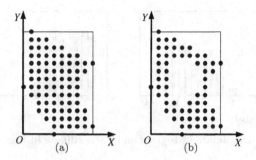

Figure 12.8. Example of object saturation.

minimum enclosing rectangle. Specifically, it can be calculated by the ratio of the number of pixels belonging to the object to the number of pixels contained in the entire minimum enclosing rectangle. Figure 12.8 shows the two objects (each pixel is marked) used to discuss this problem and their minimum enclosing rectangles. The two objects have the same minimum enclosing rectangles, but there is a hole in the center of the object in Figure 12.8(b). The saturations of the two images are $81/140 = 57.8\%$ and $63/140 = 45\%$, respectively. Comparing the saturation shows that the pixel distribution of the object in Figure 12.8(a) is more concentrated or the distribution density is greater than that of the object in Figure 12.8(b). When comparing these two objects, the object in Figure 12.8(b) also gives people a more complicated filling.

The above statistics on saturation are similar to the statistics on histograms which do not reflect spatial distribution information, so they do not provide general shape information. For this reason, consider calculating the projection histogram of the object. Here, the X-coordinate histogram is obtained by counting the number of object pixels by column and the Y-coordinate histogram is obtained by counting the number of object pixels by row. The X-coordinate histogram and Y-coordinate histogram obtained by statistics of Figure 12.8(a) are shown in Figure 12.9(a). The X-coordinate histogram and Y-coordinate histogram obtained by statistics of Figure 12.8(b) are shown in Figure 12.9(b). Among them, the X-coordinate histogram and Y-coordinate histogram in Figure 12.9(b) are not monotonic or single-peak histograms, and there are obvious valleys in the middle, which are caused by the hole in the object in Figure 12.8(b).

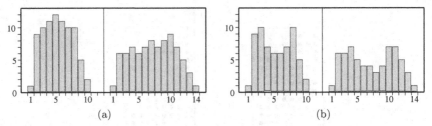

Figure 12.9. X-coordinate histogram and Y-coordinate histogram of an object.

12.3   Descriptor Based on Discrete Curvature

Curvature describes the changes in the points on the contour of an object along the boundary tangent direction (see Section 10.1), which is regarded as a basic and important feature that can be extracted from the contour. The study of curvature has a strong biological background and motivation. The human visual system often uses curvature as an important clue to observe the scene.

12.3.1   Curvature and geometric features

Many geometric features can be described with the help of **curvature**. Table 12.2 gives some examples.

12.3.2   Discrete curvature

In discrete space, curvature often refers to the direction change of a sequence of discrete points composing the object along the contour. Therefore, it is necessary to define the order of the discrete point sequence before determining the discrete curvature.

A formal definition of **discrete curvature** is given as follows. For a set of discrete points $P = \{p_i\}_{i=0,\ldots,n}$, a **digital curve** (that is, an ordered sequence of discrete points, in which, except for the two **end** pixels of the curve, each pixel has exactly two neighboring pixels and each end pixel of the curve has only one neighboring pixel) is defined. The kth order curvature at point $p_i \in P$ is $\rho_k(p_i) = |1 - \cos\theta_k^i|$, where $\rho_k(p_i) = |1 - \cos\theta_k^i|$ is the angle between the two line segments $[p_{i-k}, p_i]$ and $[p_i, p_{i+k}]$ and the order $k \in \{i, \ldots, n-i\}$. Figure 12.10 shows the calculation of the third-order discrete curvature $\overset{\rho}{3}(p_{10})$ at the point p_{10} for the digital curve $P_{pq} = \{p_i\}_{i=0,\ldots,17}$.

Table 12.2. Some geometric features that can be described by curvature.

Curvature	Geometric feature
Continuous zero curvature	Straight line segment
Continuous non-zero curvature	Arc segment
Absolute local maximum curvature	Corner point
Positive local maximum curvature	Convex corner point
Negative local maximum curvature	Concave corner point
Curvature zero crossing point	Inflection point
Mean absolute or square value of large curvature	Shape complexity

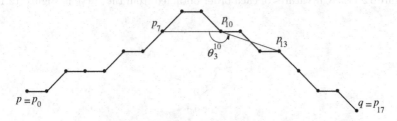

Figure 12.10. Calculation of discrete curvature.

The order number k is introduced to reduce the influence of the curvature on local changes in the boundary direction. The higher-order discrete curvature can more accurately approximate the overall curvature determined by the discrete point sequence. Figure 12.11 shows the results of calculating curvatures of different orders $(k = 1, \ldots, 6)$ for the curve in Figure 12.10. Obviously, the first-order curvature only considers very local changes, so it is not an accurate representation of discrete curvature. As the order increases, the calculated curvature gradually reflects the overall behavior of a curve. The peak (at point p_8 or p_9) in each figure corresponds to the place where the global direction changes greatly on the boundary.

12.3.3 Calculation of discrete curvature

For a parametric curve $c(t) = [x(t), y(t)]$, its curvature function $k(t)$ is defined as

$$k(t) = \frac{x'(t)y''(t) - x''(t)y'(t)}{[x'(t)^2 + y'(t)^2]^{3/2}}. \qquad (12.18)$$

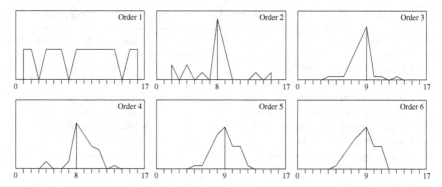

Figure 12.11.   Curvatures of each order obtained from the curve in Figure 12.10.

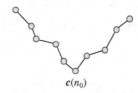

$$c(n_0)$$

Figure 12.12.   Curvature calculation based on interpolation.

Different methods can be used to calculate higher-order derivatives in discrete space:

(1) First, sample $x(t)$ and $y(t)$, and then calculate the derivative. Suppose it is needed to calculate the curvature at point $c(n_0)$, first obtain a certain number of sampling points on both sides of $c(n_0)$, as shown in Figure 12.12.

  Then, different methods can be used to calculate the curvature analytically using these sampling points. The simplest method is to use the finite difference method. First, calculate the first and second derivatives as follows:

$$
\begin{aligned}
x'(n) &= x(n) - x(n-1), \\
y'(n) &= y(n) - y(n-1),
\end{aligned}
\tag{12.19}
$$

$$
\begin{aligned}
x''(n) &= x'(n) - x'(n-1), \\
y''(n) &= y'(n) - y'(n-1).
\end{aligned}
\tag{12.20}
$$

Substituting the results of Equations (12.19) and (12.20) into Equation (12.18), the curvature can be calculated. This method is simple to implement but very sensitive to noise.

In order to reduce the influence of noise, B-spline can be used to approximate the above sampling points. Assuming that a third-order polynomial is needed to approximate the sampling points between $t \in [0, 1]$, the $x(t)$ and $y(t)$ between the start point ($t = 0$) and the end point ($t = 1$) can be approximated by the following polynomials :

$$
\begin{aligned}
x(t) &= a_1 t^3 + b_1 t^2 + c_1 t + d_1, \\
y(t) &= a_2 t^3 + b_2 t^2 + c_2 t + d_2,
\end{aligned}
\tag{12.21}
$$

In Equation (12.21), all a, b, c, and d are coefficients of a polynomial. Calculate the derivative of the above parameter curve and substitute it into Equation (12.18) to get

$$
k = 2 \frac{c_1 b_2 - c_2 b_1}{\left[c_1^2 + c_2^2 \right]^{3/2}}.
\tag{12.22}
$$

In Equation (12.22), the coefficients b_1, b_2, c_1, and c_2 can be calculated as follows:

$$
\begin{aligned}
b_1 &= \frac{1}{12} \left[(x_{n-2} + x_{n+2}) + 2(x_{n-1} + x_{n+1}) - 6x_n \right], \\
b_2 &= \frac{1}{12} \left[(y_{n-2} + y_{n+2}) + 2(y_{n-1} + y_{n+1}) - 6y_n \right],
\end{aligned}
\tag{12.23}
$$

$$
\begin{aligned}
c_1 &= \frac{1}{12} \left[(x_{n-2} + x_{n+2}) + 4(x_{n-1} + x_{n+1}) \right], \\
c_2 &= \frac{1}{12} \left[(y_{n-2} + y_{n+2}) + 4(y_{n-1} + y_{n+1}) \right].
\end{aligned}
\tag{12.24}
$$

(2) Define the equivalent curvature measure according to the angle between the vectors.

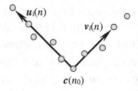

Figure 12.13.   Angle-based curvature calculation.

Assuming that the curvature at point $c(n_0)$ needs to be calculated, let $c(n) = [x(n), y(n)]$ be a digital curve, then the following two vectors can be defined:

$$\boldsymbol{u}_i(n) = [x(n) - x(n - i)\ y(n) - y(n - i)],$$
$$\boldsymbol{v}_i(n) = [x(n) - x(n + i)\ y(n) - y(n + i)]. \tag{12.25}$$

These two vectors are respectively determined by the point $c(n_0)$ and the ith neighbor in front of it, and the point $c(n_0)$ and the ith neighbor behind it; see Figure 12.13.

It is more appropriate to use the above two vectors to calculate the curvature of a point of large curvature. Here, the cosine of the angle between $\boldsymbol{u}_i(n)$ and $\boldsymbol{v}_i(n)$ satisfies

$$r_i(n) = \frac{\boldsymbol{u}_i(n)\boldsymbol{v}_i(n)}{\|\boldsymbol{u}_i(n)\|\|\boldsymbol{v}_i(n)\|}. \tag{12.26}$$

Thus, $-1 \le r_i(n) \le 1$, where $r_i(n) = -1$ corresponds to a straight line and $r_i(n) = 1$ corresponds to the coincidence of two vectors.

12.3.4   Descriptor based on curvature

The curvature of each point on the object contour itself can be used as a descriptor (see Section 10.1), but the amount of data is often large and redundant. After the curvature of each point of the contour is calculated, the following curvature descriptors can be further calculated for the entire object contour:

(1) *Statistical histogram of curvature*

The histogram of curvature can provide some useful global measures, such as mean curvature, median, variance, entropy, and moment.

(2) *Maximum point, minimum point, and inflection point of the curvature values*

Not all points on a contour are equally important. The points where the curvature reaches the maximum positive and the minimum negative or the inflection point carries more information. The number of these points, their positions in the contour, and the curvature values of the positive maximum and negative minimum points can all be used to describe the shape.

(3) *Bending energy*

The **bending energy** (BE) of a curve is the energy required to bend a straight line into a specific curve shape. It can be obtained by adding up the squares of the curvature along the curve (it can also be calculated with the Fourier transform coefficient of the curve with the aid of Parseval's theorem). Suppose the curve length is L and the curvature of a point t on it is $k(t)$, then the bending energy is

$$BE = \sum_{t=1}^{L} k^2(t). \tag{12.27}$$

The average value of the bending energy of the entire contour curve is also called the contour energy, which can also describe the shape characteristics.

Example 12.6 Bending energy calculation example

If the object contour is represented by a chain code, a calculation example of its bending energy is shown in Figure 12.14. Suppose the chain code of the boundary segment is 0, 0, 2, 0, 1, 0, 7, 6, 0, 0, as shown in Figure 12.14(a); calculate the curvature of each point to get 0, 2, −2, 1, −1, −1, −1, 2, 0, as shown in Figure 12.14(b); find the sum of the squares of curvature to get the bending energy, as shown in Figure 12.14(c); the final smooth version is shown in Figure 12.14(d). □

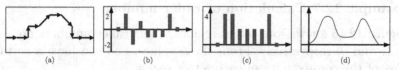

Figure 12.14.   Bending energy calculation example.

(4) Symmetry measure

For curve segments, the **symmetry measure** is defined as

$$S = \int_0^L \left(\int_0^t k(l)dl - \frac{A}{2} \right) dt. \qquad (12.28)$$

The internal integral is the angle change amount up to the current position. A is the angle change amount of the entire curve, L is the length of the entire curve, and $k(l)$ is the curvature along the contour.

12.4   Topological Descriptor

Topology studies the nature of graphics that are not affected by distortion (not including tearing or sticking). The topological properties of the region are useful for the global description of the region. These properties do not depend on the distance or other characteristics based on distance measurement. Topological parameters describe the structure of the entire region by representing the interaction between various parts of the region.

12.4.1   Euler number

Euler number is a typical regional topology descriptor, describing the connectivity of the region. For a given plane region, the number C of connected components in the region (any two points can be connected by a curve completely inside the region) and the number H of the holes in the region (point set surrounded by connected components) are common topological properties, and they can be further used to define Euler's number (E):

$$E = C - H. \qquad (12.29)$$

Example 12.7 Calculation of Euler number

Figure 12.15 shows four letter regions, their Euler numbers are -1, 2, 1, and 0, respectively. From these values, one can have a certain idea of the connectivity of each letter region.   □

Bird

Figure 12.15. Euler number of the letter region.

Table 12.3. Euler numbers of some object regions with simple structures.

No.	A	$C_4(A)$	$C_8(A)$	$H_4(A)$	$H_8(A)$	$E_4(A)$	$E_8(A)$
1	✛	1	1	0	0	1	1
2	⠇	5	1	0	0	5	1
3	◫	1	1	1	1	0	0
4	⬡	4	1	1	0	4	0
5	▦	2	1	4	1	1	−3
6	▨	1	1	5	1	0	−4
7	▣	2	2	1	1	1	1

For a binary image A, two Euler numbers can be defined, denoted as $E_4(A)$ and $E_8(A)$. The difference between them is the connectivity used by the object and the hole. The 4-connected Euler number $E_4(A)$ is defined as the 4-connected object number $C_4(A)$ minus the 8-connected hole number $H_8(A)$:

$$E_4(A) = C_4(A) - H_8(A). \tag{12.30}$$

The 8-connected Euler number $E_8(A)$ is defined as the 8-connected target number $C_8(A)$ minus the 4-connected hole number $H_4(A)$:

$$E_8(A) = C_8(A) - H_4(A). \tag{12.31}$$

Table 12.3 shows the Euler numbers calculated for some simple structure object regions.

12.4.2 Crossing number and connectivity number

The **crossings number** and **connectivity number** are also two topological parameters, both of which reflect the structural information of the region.

Consider the eight neighborhood pixels q_i ($i = 0, \ldots, 7$) of a pixel p, start from any 4-neighborhood position, and arrange them in a clockwise direction around p. According to whether the pixel q_i is white or black of, assign it $q_i = 0$ or $q_i = 1$, respectively, then the following definitions can be made:

(1) The crossing number $S_4(p)$ represents the number of 4-connected components in the 8-neighborhood of p, which can be written as

$$S_4(p) = \prod_{i=0}^{7} q_i + \frac{1}{2} \sum_{i=0}^{7} |q_{i+1} - q_i|. \tag{12.32}$$

(2) The connectivity number $C_8(p)$ represents the number of 8-connected components in the 8-neighborhood of p, which can be written as

$$C_8(p) = q_0 q_2 q_4 q_6 + \sum_{i=0}^{3} (\bar{q}_{2i} - \bar{q}_{2i}\bar{q}_{2i+1}\bar{q}_{2i+2}). \tag{12.33}$$

In Equation (12.33), $\bar{q}_i = 1 - q_i$.

With the help of the above definitions, each pixel p in a 4-connected component C can be distinguished according to the value of $S_4(p)$:

(1) If $S_4(p) = 0$, then p is an isolated point (i.e., $C = \{p\}$).
(2) If $S_4(p) = 1$, then p is an end point (boundary point) or an intermediate point (internal point).
(3) If $S_4(p) = 2$, then p is an essential point for maintaining the 4-connectivity of C.
(4) If $S_4(p) = 3$, then p is a bifurcation point.
(5) If $S_4(p) = 4$, then p is an intersection point.

The above situations are summarized in Figure 12.16, where Figure 12.16(a) shows two connected regions (each small box represents a pixel) and the number in each small box represents the value of $S_4(p)$. Simplify Figure 12.16(a) to obtain the topological structure diagram shown in Figure 12.16(b), which is a **graph** representation of all connected components in Figure 12.16(a) and represents the topological properties of Figure 12.16(a). Because this is a 2D plan, Euler's formula holds. That is, if V represents the set of nodes in the graph structure and A represents the set of arcs connected by

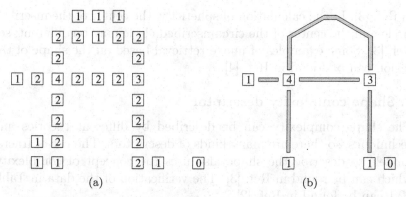

Figure 12.16. Examples of introduction to the crossing number and connectivity number.

the nodes in the graph structure, then the number of holes in the graph $H = 1 + |A| - |V|$, where $|A|$ and $|V|$ represent the number of elements in the A set and V set (in this example, both are five).

The graph structure is used to highlight the holes and endpoints in the connected components, and the connections between the different parts of the object are given. It should be noted that objects of different shapes may be mapped to the same topology graph structure.

12.5 Key Points and References for Each Section

The following indicates the key points of each section and provides some targeted guidance for further references.

1. Shape compactness descriptor

The description of the shape of a region is often indirectly described by comparing the region with typical/ideal shapes (such as circles and rectangles); see Ref. [1]. Most commonly used regional shape descriptors are not affected by regional translation, rotation, and scale changes. The form factor calculated from the perimeter of the region and area of the region describes the compactness of the region. When using different connectivity to calculate the contour length, the shape of the region where the form factor takes the smallest value is also different; see Ref. [2]. The calculation of eccentricity based on the moment of inertia of the region and its application can be found in Ref. [3]. In the calculation of sphericity, the center of the inscribed circle and the center of the circumscribed circle may be different; see Ref. [3]. Some examples of image retrieval based on the shape of the region can be found in Ref. [4].

2. Shape complexity descriptor

The shape complexity can be described by different theories and techniques, so there are many kinds of descriptors. The use of fractal models to describe the shape also uses the concept of complexity, which can be found in Ref. [3]. The verification of the data in Table 12.1 can be found in Ref. [2].

3. Descriptor based on discrete curvature

The description based on discrete curvature is an example of describing different shape characteristics based on the same technology. The key to this type of description method is to have a more general representation technique or a more suitable mathematical tool. In fact, many mathematical tools introduced in the image field in recent years, such as wavelet transform, have contributed to shape description. The formal definition of discrete curvature can be found in Ref. [1]. Different methods can be used for the calculation of higher-order derivatives in discrete space; see Ref. [5].

4. Topological descriptor

Euler number is based on topological properties and is not affected by regional deformation. The Euler numbers with two different connectivity can also be found in Ref. [6]. The crossing number and connectivity number are two parameters that reflect regional topology information. The topological structure information of the region is, to a large extent, closely related to the shape information of the object itself and the spatial relationship between the objects. Further discussions can be found in Ref. [4].

Self-Test Questions

The following questions include both single- and multiple-choice questions, so each option should be individually judged.

12.1 Shape Compactness Descriptor

12.1.1 Suppose the side length of each small square in Figure 12.1.1 is one, then the form factor of the shaded part in the figure is approximately (the perimeter is calculated along the outer contour) ( )

Figure 12.1.1.

(A) 2.6;
(B) 2.7;
(C) 2.8;
(D) 2.9.

[Hint] Calculate the perimeter and area of the shaded part first.

12.1.2 Point out the incorrect ones in the following statements: ( )

(A) The form factor is a dimensional quantity;
(B) The form factor reflects the compactness of the described region to a certain extent;
(C) If the form factors of the two objects are the same, then their shapes are the same;
(D) If the form factor of an object is one, then the object is round.

[Hint] Analyze the calculation formula of the form factor.

12.1.3 In Figure 12.1.3, which of the graph(s) has/have the largest eccentricity? ( )

(A) Figure 12.1.3(a);
(B) Figure 12.1.3(b);
(C) Figure 12.1.3(c);
(D) Figure 12.1.3(d).

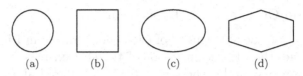

(a)   (b)   (c)   (d)

Figure 12.1.3.

[Hint] Draw the long axis and short axis of each graph first.

12.1.4 The sphericity parameter S of a square with side length 2 is equal to ( )

(A) $\sqrt{2}/2$;
(B) $\sqrt{2}$;
(C) 2;
(D) $2\sqrt{2}$.

[Hint] The inscribed circle and circumscribed circle of the square have four intersections with the square.

12.1.5 The circularity parameter C of a square with side length 3 is approximately equal to ( )

(A) 3;
(B) 6;
(C) 9;
(D) 12.

[Hint] The circularity is related to the shape of the object, not to the scale.

12.2 Shape Complexity Descriptor

12.2.1 For an object in a digital image, the maximum value of its thinness ratio ( )

(A) Is obtained from the diamond-shaped region (the contour length is calculated with 4-connectivity);
(B) Is obtained from the diamond-shaped region (the contour length is calculated with 8-connectivity);
(C) Is obtained from the regular octagonal region (the contour length is calculated by 4-connectivity);
(D) Is obtained from the regular octagonal region (the contour length is calculated by 8-connectivity).

[Hint] The thinness ratio is the inverse of the form factor.

12.2.2 When using the histogram analysis of the blurred image to describe the complexity of the object shape, ( )

    (A) The more the black pixels and white pixels in the histogram of the blurred image, the more complex the object shape;

    (B) The fewer the black pixels and white pixels in the histogram of the blurred image, the more complex the object shape;

    (C) The more the black pixels and white pixels in the histogram of the blurred image, the less complex the object shape;

    (D) The fewer the black pixels and white pixels in the histogram of the blurred image, the less complex the object shape;

[Hint] There are only black pixels and white pixels in the image before blurring.

12.2.3 Use saturation to judge the shape complexity of the five objects in Figure 12.2.3 (all sub-regions R are the same). ( )

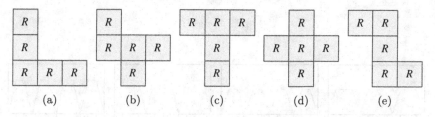

Figure 12.2.3.

    (A) Figure 12.2.3(a) has the highest complexity;

    (B) Figure 12.2.3(b) is more complicated than Figure 12.2.3(c);

    (C) Figure 12.2.3(d) has the lowest complexity;

    (D) Figure 12.2.3(e) has the same complexity as the other four objects.

[Hint] Judge according to the definition of saturation.

12.3 Descriptor Based on Discrete Curvature

12.3.1 Calculate the discrete curvatures of different orders for the same curve. ( )

(A) The higher-order discrete curvature can reflect the local change of the curve better;
(B) The lower-order discrete curvature can reflect the local change of the curve better;
(C) The higher-order discrete curvature can reflect the overall curvature of the curve better;
(D) The lower-order discrete curvature can reflect the overall curvature of the curve better.

[Hint] Analyze the definition of order.

12.3.2 A straight line is digitized as shown in Figure 12.3.2.1 (part of the fragment), and the discrete curvatures of different orders are calculated. Which of the discrete curvature curve(s) in 12.3.2.2 is/are correct? ( )

Figure 12.3.2.1.

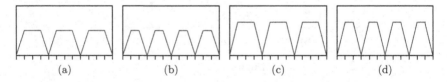

Figure 12.3.2.2.

(A) Figure 12.3.2.2(a);
(B) Figure 12.3.2.2(b);
(C) Figure 12.3.2.2(c);
(D) Figure 12.3.2.2(d).

[Hint] The period of the discrete straight line is three.

12.3.3 Two of the discrete curvature curves in Figure 12.3.2.2 are of order two and the other two curves are of order three, then ( )

(A) Figure 12.3.2.2(a) and Figure 12.3.2.2(b) are of order two;
(B) Figure 12.3.2.2(b) and Figure 12.3.2.2(c) are of order two;
(C) Figure 12.3.2.2(c) and Figure 12.3.2.2(d) are of order two;
(D) Figure 12.3.2.2(d) and Figure 12.3.2.2(a) are of order two.

[Hint] With the increase in the order, the curvature value gradually decreases toward zero.

12.4 Topological Descriptor

12.4.1 The Euler numbers of the 8-letter regions that make up the word "Birthday" are: ( )

(A) $-1, 2, 1, 1, 1, 0, 1, 1$;
(B) $-1, 2, 1, 1, 0, 1, 0, 1$;
(C) $-1, 2, 1, 1, 0, 1, 1, 1$;
(D) $-1, 2, 1, 1, 1, 0, 0, 1$;

[Hint] Calculate according to Euler number calculation formula.

12.4.2 For the same object region, ( )

(A) The 4-connected Euler number is always smaller than or equal to the 8-connected Euler number;
(B) The 4-connected Euler number is always greater than or equal to the 8-connected Euler number;
(C) The 4-connected Euler number is always equal to the 8-connected Euler number;
(D) The 4-connected Euler number is always not equal to the 8-connected Euler number;

[Hint] Analyze according to the two connected definitions.

12.4.3 The maximum crossing number of a pixel is four, then ( )

(A) The maximum connectivity number of a pixel is eight;
(B) The maximum connectivity number of a pixel is six;
(C) The maximum connectivity number of a pixel is four;
(D) The maximum connectivity number of a pixel is two.

[Hint] The 8-neighborhood of a pixel is composed of four 4-neighbor pixels plus four diagonal neighbor pixels.

References

[1] Marchand-Maillet, S. and Sharaiha, Y. M. *Binary Digital Image Processing — A Discrete Approach.* USA, Salt Lake City: Academic Press, 2000.

[2] Zhang, Y.-J. *Image Engineering (III): Teaching References and Problem Solutions.* China, Beijing: Tsinghua University Press, 2002.

[3] Zhang, Y.-J. *Image Engineering (II) Image Analysis*, 4th Edn. China, Beijing: Tsinghua University Press, 2018.

[4] Zhang, Y.-J. *Content-Based Visual Information Retrieval.* China, Beijing: Science Press, 2003.

[5] Costa, L. F. and Cesar, R. M. *Shape Analysis and Classification: Theory and Practice.* UK, London: CRC Press, 2001.

[6] Ritter, G. X. and Wilson. J. N. *Handbook of Computer Vision Algorithms in Image Algebra.* UK, London: CRC Press, 2001.

Chapter 13

Object Classification

Based on the representation and description of the object as well as the description and measurement of various features, the object can be classified further. The so-called **object classification** is to divide the object into a group with similar characteristics or attributes.

The object classification should be based on the description of the object features or the measurement of the object features. In order to classify objects accurately and robustly, there are certain requirements (such as invariance) for feature selection and extraction. A key issue of classification is to design an effective classifier, which will be the focus of this chapter.

The sections of this chapter are arranged as follows:

Section 13.1 introduces the cross-ratio which is a commonly used invariant in object classification. On the basis of the essential definition of cross-ratio, some extended forms and application examples are also discussed.

Section 13.2 introduces the method of classification using statistical models. According to the basic classification principles, the commonly used minimum distance classifiers and optimal statistical classifiers, as well as the adaptive boosting strategy combining weak classifiers, are discussed.

Section 13.3 discusses support vector machines (SVMs) based on statistical learning theory, which is an optimal design methodology for linear classifiers and also refers to the classifiers designed in this way.

13.1 Invariant Cross-Ratio

In object classification, the invariant feature of the object plays a very important role. **Invariant** refers to a metric that does not change with certain transformations (such as translation and rotation). They can help to uniquely describe the object without considering the position and orientation, which is particularly important in complex 3D situations. The following introduces a commonly used invariant cross-ratio. The idea here is to overcome the scale problem during imaging by discovering the distance ratio. The use of the ratio of ratios is to overcome the geometric problems caused by the projection angle by discovering the ratio value of the ratio.

13.1.1 Cross-ratio

Cross-ratio is a ratio of ratios or rate of rates. It is used when projecting the object to give an invariant independent of the position and orientation of the observation point. Let's first look at the situation where there are four collinear points on the object. As shown in Figure 13.1, the four collinear points P_1, P_2, P_3, and P_4 give points Q_1, Q_2, Q_3, and Q_4 after the imaging transformation (the perspective transformation with the optical center at C), respectively. Choose the coordinate system appropriately so that the coordinates of P_1, P_2, P_3, and P_4 can be $(x_1, 0)$, $(x_2, 0)$, $(x_3, 0)$, and $(x_4, 0)$ and the coordinates of Q_1, Q_2, Q_3, and Q_4 are $(0, y_1)$, $(0, y_2)$, $(0, y_3)$, and $(0, y_4)$, respectively.

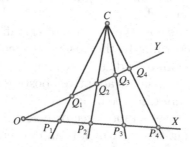

Figure 13.1.   Perspective transformation of four collinear points.

Suppose the coordinate of point C is (x_o, y_o), then there is a relational expression according to the distance ratio:

$$\frac{x_o}{x_i} + \frac{y_o}{y_i} = 1 \quad i = 1, 2, 3, 4. \tag{13.1}$$

Consider the difference between the relational expressions of two points (indicated by i and j respectively), which can be written as

$$\frac{x_o(x_j - x_i)}{x_i x_j} = -\frac{y_o(y_j - y_i)}{y_i y_j}. \tag{13.2}$$

The ratio of two such relations can eliminate the unknown x_o and y_o, for example,

$$\frac{x_3(x_2 - x_1)}{x_2(x_3 - x_1)} = -\frac{y_3(y_2 - y_1)}{y_2(y_3 - y_1)}. \tag{13.3}$$

However, there are also terms that depend on absolute coordinates, such as x_3/x_2. To eliminate the influence of absolute coordinates, the following ratio can be used:

$$\frac{(x_2 - x_4)/(x_3 - x_4)}{(x_2 - x_1)/(x_3 - x_1)} = -\frac{(y_2 - y_4)/(y_3 - y_4)}{(y_2 - y_1)/(y_3 - y_1)}. \tag{13.4}$$

It can be seen that from any projection point of view, the cross-ratios obtained from the four collinear points have the same value. This can be written as

$$C(P_1, P_2, P_3, P_4) = \frac{(x_3 - x_1)/(x_2 - x_4)}{(x_2 - x_1)/(x_3 - x_4)} = R. \tag{13.5}$$

Denote this special cross-ratio by R, then for four collinear points on a straight line, there are $4! = 24$ possible arrangements. However, only six of them are established, that is, only six kinds of values. In addition to the one given by Equation (13.5), there are three more common ones:

$$C(P_2, P_1, P_3, P_4) = \frac{(x_3 - x_2)/(x_1 - x_4)}{(x_1 - x_2)/(x_3 - x_4)} = C(P_1, P_2, P_4, P_3)$$

$$= \frac{(x_4 - x_1)/(x_2 - x_3)}{(x_2 - x_1)/(x_4 - x_3)} = 1 - R, \tag{13.6}$$

$$C(P_1, P_3, P_2, P_4) = \frac{(x_2 - x_1)/(x_3 - x_4)}{(x_3 - x_1)/(x_2 - x_4)} = C(P_4, P_2, P_3, P_1)$$

$$= \frac{(x_3 - x_4)/(x_2 - x_1)}{(x_2 - x_4)/(x_3 - x_1)} = \frac{1}{R}, \tag{13.7}$$

$$C(P_3, P_2, P_1, P_4) = \frac{(x_1 - x_3)/(x_2 - x_4)}{(x_2 - x_3)/(x_1 - x_4)} = C(P_1, P_4, P_3, P_2)$$

$$= \frac{(x_3 - x_1)/(x_4 - x_2)}{(x_4 - x_1)/(x_3 - x_2)} = \frac{R}{R - 1} \tag{13.8}$$

and two rarer ones:

$$C(P_3, P_1, P_2, P_4) = 1 - C(P_1, P_3, P_2, P_4)$$

$$= 1 - \frac{1}{R} = \frac{R - 1}{R}, \tag{13.9}$$

$$C(P_2, P_3, P_1, P_4) = \frac{1}{C(P_2, P_1, P_3, P_4)} = \frac{1}{1 - R}. \tag{13.10}$$

It can be seen from the above that reversing the sequence of the points (equivalent to observing these lines from the other side) will not change the value of the cross-ratio.

If the intersection of the four collinear points (equivalent to the optical center) of the coplanar straight lines are also considered, they define a special structure, "a pencil of lines" (this is a more vivid name). A cross-ratio can be defined for the "a pencil of lines" to be equal to the cross-ratio of any four collinear points. For this, consider the angle between these lines, as shown in Figure 13.2.

For the cross-ratio $C(P_1, P_2, P_3, P_4)$, the sine rule is used four times to obtain:

$$\frac{x_3 - x_1}{\sin \alpha_{13}} = \frac{OP_1}{\sin \beta_3} \quad \frac{x_2 - x_4}{\sin \alpha_{24}} = \frac{OP_4}{\sin \beta_2}$$

$$\frac{x_2 - x_1}{\sin \alpha_{21}} = \frac{OP_1}{\sin \beta_2} \quad \frac{x_3 - x_4}{\sin \alpha_{34}} = \frac{OP_4}{\sin \beta_3}. \tag{13.11}$$

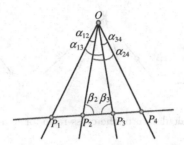

Figure 13.2. Calculation of the cross-ratio for the group forming the "a pencil of line".

Combining these equations to eliminate OP_1, OP_4, $\sin\beta_2$, and $\sin\beta_3$, we get

$$C(P_1, P_2, P_3, P_4) = \frac{\sin\alpha_{13}\sin\alpha_{24}}{\sin\alpha_{12}\sin\alpha_{34}}. \tag{13.12}$$

It can be seen that the cross-ratio depends only on the angle between the lines.

13.1.2 Invariant of non-collinear points

The above results can be generalized to the case of four parallel planes, that is, considering the **invariants for non-collinear points** to solve more general problems.

If the four points are not collinear, it is not enough to just calculate the cross-ratio information. Consider the case where one point is not in a straight line with the other three points. At this time, if there is another single coplanar point (the fifth point, indicated by $\Diamond$), as shown in Figure 13.3(a), one can connect a line from this point to that single point and intersect this line with the straight lines from the other three points. Using such five points, the cross-ratio of non-collinear points can be calculated.

It can be proved that for a more general situation, five points can always be used to obtain an invariant cross-ratio, as shown in Figure 13.3(b). Figure 13.3(b) also has a point denoted by $\Diamond$. It is used to illustrate that only calculating a cross-ratio cannot distinguish it from other points on the same straight line. Furthermore, Figure 13.3(c) shows that taking two reference points to calculate two cross-ratios can uniquely determine the orientation relationship

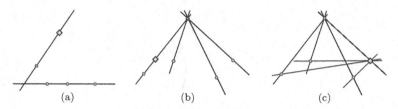

Figure 13.3.   Calculation of the cross-ratio for non-collinear points.

between all remaining points. Here, the fifth point (indicated by $\Diamond$) is the origin of the second "a pencil of lines". So, the conclusion is that five coplanar points can be used to calculate two different cross-ratios, so that the point distribution/structure pattern can be described.

In addition to that the cross-ratio can be described by the sine of the angle between the lines, it can also be described by the area of the relevant triangle. Here, the area of the triangle can be expressed as (take the triangle OP_1P_3 in Figure 13.2 as an example and consider point O as the fifth point)

$$\Delta_{513} = \frac{1}{2}d_{51}d_{53}\sin\alpha_{13}. \qquad (13.13)$$

Among them, d_{51} and d_{53} are respectively the length of the line segment between point O and point P_1 as well as point O and point P_3.

The area can also be expressed as a function of point coordinates:

$$\Delta_{513} = \frac{1}{2}\begin{vmatrix} p_{5x} & p_{1x} & p_{3x} \\ p_{5y} & p_{1y} & p_{3y} \\ p_{5z} & p_{1z} & p_{3z} \end{vmatrix} = \frac{1}{2}|p_5\ p_1\ p_3|. \qquad (13.14)$$

Using Equation (13.14), a pair of equations for calculating the cross-ratio invariant can be written as

$$C_a = \frac{\Delta_{513}\Delta_{524}}{\Delta_{512}\Delta_{534}}, \qquad (13.15)$$

$$C_b = \frac{\Delta_{124}\Delta_{135}}{\Delta_{123}\Delta_{145}}. \qquad (13.16)$$

Although three other equations can be written, they are not independent of Equations (13.15) and (13.16) and they do not provide further information.

If the determinant in Equation (13.14) is zero or infinite, it means that the three points are collinear, that is, the area of the triangle is zero. This is the situation in Figure 13.3(a). A cross-ratio with such a determinant cannot provide useful information.

13.1.3 Symmetrical cross-ratio function

When using a cross-ratio for a set of points on a line, often the order of the points is known, and the question that causes ambiguity is in which direction to scan the line. However, the cross-ratio has nothing to do with the linear scanning direction because $C(P_1, P_2, P_3, P_4) = C(P_4, P_3, P_2, P_1)$. But sometimes the order of the points is uncertain. For example, in Figure 13.3, some points are not belonging to just a single straight line and sometimes only a conic section is known but the specific equation is unknown. In these cases, it is better to have invariance in all possible ordering situations. In other words, a **symmetrical cross-ratio function** is required at this time.

If the ambiguity comes from the indistinguishability of whether the value of the cross-ratio is R or $(1 - R)$, the function $f(R) = R(1-R)$ can be used, which satisfies $f(R) = f(1-R)$ and is symmetrical. If the ambiguity comes from the indistinguishability of whether the value of the cross-ratio is R or $1/R$, the function $g(R) = R + 1/R$ can be used, which satisfies $g(R) = g(1/R)$. However, if the value of the cross-ratio is not distinguished between R, $(1 - R)$, or $1/R$, the situation is much more complicated. For this reason, a function $h(R) = h(1 - R) = h(1/R)$ that can satisfy the double condition is needed. The simplest should be

$$S(R) = \frac{(1 - R + R^2)^3}{R^2(1 - R^2)^2} \tag{13.17}$$

because it can be written in two forms to satisfy the symmetrical idea:

$$S(R) = \frac{[1 - R(1 - R)]^3}{R^2(1 - R^2)^2} = \frac{(R + 1/R - 1)^3}{R + 1/R - 2}. \tag{13.18}$$

Along this line of thought, one can discuss the values of six cross-ratios, namely R, $(1 - R)$, $1/R$, $1/(1 - R)$, $(R - 1)/R$, and $R/(1 - R)$. Although it would be very complicated, fortunately they can be deduced from each other with the help of negation and reciprocal.

13.1.4   Cross-ratio application examples

The following examples illustrate some situations where the cross-ratio is used to determine the ground plane in practical applications. These situations often occur in self-movements such as vehicle navigation. Here, a set of four collinear points can be observed in successive frames of images. If they are all on a single plane, the cross-ratio remains constant; if they are not on a single plane, the cross-ratio changes with time. Refer to Figure 13.4. Figure 13.4(a) shows the situation where the four collinear points are all on the ground level. Figure 13.4(b) shows the situation where the ground is uneven and the cross-ratio cannot be kept constant. Figure 13.4(c) is the case where the cross-ratio remains constant but the four collinear points are not all on the ground level. Figure 13.4(d) is the case where the four points are not coplanar, so the cross-ratio is not a constant.

Now consider the case of conic curve further. Suppose there are four fixed coplanar points (F_1, F_2, F_3, and F_4) and another moving point P on a conic curve, as shown in Figure 13.5. The straight line connecting the four fixed points to the point P forms the "a pencil of lines", and the value of its cross-ratio generally varies with the position of point P. The Chasles theorem in algebraic geometry states that if point P moves and keeps the value of the cross-ratio constant, the trajectory of point P is a conic curve. Similar to the case

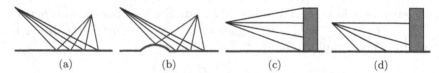

(a)   (b)   (c)   (d)

Figure 13.4.   Determination of the ground plane with the help of cross-ratio.

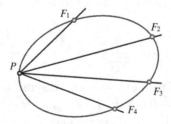

Figure 13.5.   Using the cross-ratio to determine the conic curve.

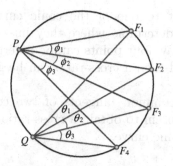

Figure 13.6.   Use of a circle to prove Chasles theorem.

of determining the ground plane above, this gives a way to determine whether a set of points is on a plane conic (such as an ellipse, hyperbola, or parabola).

Under the condition of perspective projection, one conic curve can always be transformed into another conic curve. In other words, the characteristics obtained from one conic curve can be extended to other conic curves. Let's use a circle to prove Chasles theorem. As shown in Figure 13.6, the angles φ_1, φ_2, and φ_3 are equal to θ_1, θ_2, and θ_3, respectively. So, "a pencil of lines" formed by PF_1, PF_2, PF_3, and PF_4 as well as "a pencil of lines" formed by QF_1, QF_2, QF_3, and QF_4 have the same included angle, and their relative directions overlap. It can be seen that when P moves along a circle, "a pencil of lines" will maintain a constant cross-ratio. This proves that the Chasles theorem holds true for the circle. Under the condition of perspective projection, it can also be extended to other types of conic curves.

Example 13.1 Two conic curves define a cross-ratio

For two conic curves, there are three relationships between them:

(1) They intersect at four points.
(2) They intersect at two points.
(3) They do not intersect at all but have the same tangent.

In these three cases, there are ways to define a constant cross-ratio:

(1) Use Chasles theorem for one of the conic curves and use four intersection points to give a cross-ratio.

(2) Make a tangent to one of the conic curves at the intersection point and determine where they intersect the other conic curve. In this way, four points can be determined on the second conic curve, and then a cross-ratio can be given by the Chasles theorem.

(3) Take the four common tangents of two conic curves and use the Chasles theorem to obtain a cross-ratio for the four contact points of any conic curve.   □

13.2   Statistical Pattern Classification

Object classification is essentially a **pattern classification** problem, also often called pattern recognition. **Statistical pattern classification** refers to the use of a series of automatic techniques to determine the decision function and assign and classify the given pattern according to the statistical characteristics of the pattern. The main work is to select the characteristic representation pattern and design a classifier for classification. In statistical pattern recognition, classification is based on statistical parameters. Generally, the pattern used to estimate the statistical parameter (of which the class is known) is called the training pattern, and a group of such patterns is called a training set. The process of using a training set to obtain the decision function is called learning or training. Two simple classifiers are introduced in the following. The training patterns in each class are directly used to calculate the corresponding decision function parameters. Once these parameters are obtained, the structure of the classifier is determined, and the performance of the classifier depends on the extent to which the actual pattern samples meet the statistical assumptions in the classification method.

13.2.1   Principle of pattern classification

Pattern is a broad concept. The **image pattern** is mainly considered here (the gray-scale distribution of the image constitutes a brightness pattern).

Image pattern can be defined as a quantitative or structured description of the object or other interesting parts in the image. Usually a pattern is composed (or arranged into) one or more pattern symbols, which can also be called features. A pattern class is composed of a group of patterns with some common characteristics. Generally, the pattern classes are often represented by $s_1, s_2, \ldots, s_M$, where M is the number of classes. **Pattern recognition** refers to the function and technology of analyzing, describing, and classifying patterns.

The pattern vector is generally represented in lowercase bold font. An n-dimensional pattern vector can be written as

$$x = [x_1 \ x_2 \ \cdots \ x_n]^{\mathrm{T}}. \tag{13.19}$$

Among them, x_i represents the ith descriptor and n is the number of descriptors. In the pattern vector x, the content of each component depends on the measurement technique used to describe the physical actual pattern. In the pattern space, a pattern vector corresponds to one of the points.

The classification of patterns is mainly based on decision theory, and decision theory methods use **decision functions**. Let x in Equation (13.19) represent an nD pattern vector. For the given M pattern classes $s_1, s_2, \ldots, s_M$, we must now determine M discriminant functions $d_1(x), d_2(x), \ldots, d_M(x)$. If a pattern x belongs to the class s_i, then we have

$$d_i(x) > d_j(x) \quad j = 1, 2, \ldots, M \ j \neq i. \tag{13.20}$$

In other words, for an unknown pattern x, if it is substituted into all decision functions and the $d_i(x)$ value is the largest, then x belongs to the ith class. If for the value of x, there is $d_i(x) = d_j(x)$, then the decision boundary separating class i from class j can be obtained. The above conditions can also be written as

$$d_{ij}(x) = d_i(x) - d_j(x) = 0. \tag{13.21}$$

In this way, if $d_{ij}(x) > 0$, the pattern belongs to s_i; if $d_{ij}(x) < 0$, the pattern belongs to s_j.

Based on the decision function, various classifiers can be designed for pattern classification, while different methods are needed to determine the decision function.

13.2.2 Minimum distance classifier

The **minimum distance classifier** is a simple pattern classifier, which estimates the statistical parameters of various patterns based on sampling the patterns and is completely determined by the mean and variance of each class. When the distance between the means of the two classes of patterns is larger than the distribution of the corresponding means inside the same class, the minimum distance classifier can work well.

Suppose that each pattern class is represented by a mean vector as follows:

$$m_j = \frac{1}{N_j} \sum_{x \in s_j} x \quad j = 1, 2, \ldots, M, \tag{13.22}$$

where N_j represents the number of patterns in the class s_j. The way to classify an unknown pattern vector is to assign this pattern to the class closest to it. If the Euclidean distance is used to determine the degree of proximity, the problem is transformed into a measurement of distance, that is

$$D_j(x) = \|x - m_j\| \quad j = 1, 2, \ldots, M, \tag{13.23}$$

where $\|a\| = (a^{\mathrm{T}} a)^{1/2}$ is the Euclidean modulus. Because the smallest distance represents the best match, if $D_j(x)$ is the smallest distance, x is assigned to the class s_j. It can be shown that this is equivalent to calculating

$$d_j(x) = x^{\mathrm{T}} m_j - \frac{1}{2} m_j^{\mathrm{T}} m_j \quad j = 1, 2, \ldots, M \tag{13.24}$$

and assigning x to class s_j when $d_j(x)$ gives the maximum value.

According to Equations (13.21) and (13.24), for a minimum distance classifier, the decision boundary between classes s_i and s_j is as follows:

$$d_{ij}(x) = d_i(x) - d_j(x) = x^{\mathrm{T}} (m_i - m_j)$$
$$- \frac{1}{2} (m_i - m_j)^{\mathrm{T}} (m_i - m_j) = 0. \tag{13.25}$$

The above equation actually gives a vertical dichotomy connecting the line segment between m_i and m_j. For $M = 2$, the vertical dichotomy is a line; for $M = 3$, the vertical dichotomy is a plane; for $M > 3$, the vertical dichotomy is a hyperplane.

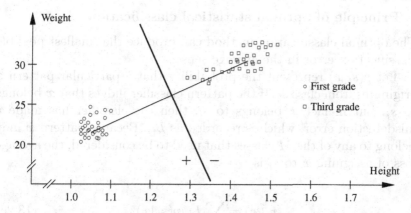

Figure 13.7. Decision boundary of the minimum distance classifier.

Example 13.2 Minimum distance classification example

Suppose we need to measure the height and weight of pupils in two different grades (set as the first and third grades) to represent and reflect their growth and development. Let $x = [x_1 x_2]^T$, where x_1 corresponds to height and x_2 corresponds to weight. Pupils in each grade form a pattern class, which can be denoted as s_1 and s_2, respectively. Figure 13.7 shows these two pattern classes. Each pupil corresponds to a point in the figure (in the vector space).

Suppose the mean vector of the two pattern classes are $m_1 = [1.05 \ 22]^T$ and $m_2 = [1.45 \ 30]^T$, respectively. According to Equation (13.24), the two decision functions are $d_1(x) = x^T m_1 - 0.5 m_1^T m_1 = 1.05x_1 + 22x_2 - 242.55$ and $d_2(x) = x^T m_2 - m_2^T m_2 = 1.45x_1 + 30x_2 - 456.05$.

According to Equation (13.25), the boundary equation is $d_{12}(x) = d_1(x) - d_2(x) = -0.4x_1 - 8.0x_2 + 213.5 = 0$, as shown by the solid line in Figure 13.7. If any pattern belonging to the class s_1 is substituted, $d_{12}(x) < 0$, and if any pattern belonging to the class s_2 is substituted, $d_{12}(x) > 0$. It can be seen that only the sign of $d_{12}(x)$ can determine the class to which the pattern belongs. $\square$

13.2.3 Optimum statistical classifier

The **optimum statistical classifier** is a probability-based pattern classifier and is suitable for classifying randomly generated patterns.

1. Principle of optimal statistical classification

The optimal classification method can produce the smallest possible classification error in the average sense.

Let $p(s_i|x)$ represent the probability that a particular pattern x originates from class s_i. If the pattern classifier judges that x belongs to s_j, but in fact x belongs to s_i, then the classifier has made a misdetection error, which is recorded as L_{ij}. Because pattern x may belong to any of the M classes that need to be considered, the average loss of assigning x to s_j is

$$r_j(x) = \sum_{k=1}^{M} L_{kj} p(s_k|x). \tag{13.26}$$

In discriminant theory, Equation (13.26) is often called conditional average risk loss. According to the basic probability theory, $p(a|b) = [p(a)p(b|a)]/p(b)$, then Equation (13.26) can be rewritten as

$$r_j(x) = \frac{1}{p(x)} \sum_{k=1}^{M} L_{kj} p(x|s_k) P(s_k), \tag{13.27}$$

where $p(x|s_k)$ is the probability density function of pattern x belonging to s_k and $P(s_k)$ is the probability of class s_k. Because $1/p(x)$ is positive and is the same for all $r_j(x)$, $j = 1, 2, \ldots, M$, so $1/p(x)$ can be omitted from the above equation without affecting the ordering of these functions from largest to smallest. Thus, the representation of average risk can be written as

$$r_j(x) = \sum_{k=1}^{M} L_{kj} p(x|s_k) P(s_k). \tag{13.28}$$

The classifier has M possible choices for any given unknown pattern. If $r_1(x), r_2(x), \ldots, r_M(x)$ are calculated for each x and x is assigned to the class that can produce the smallest loss, the total average loss relative to all decisions will be the smallest. A classifier that can minimize the total average loss is called a **Bayesian classifier**. For Bayesian classifiers, if $r_i(x) < r_j(x)$, $j = 1, 2, \ldots, M$ and

$j \neq i$, then $\boldsymbol{x}$ is assigned to s_i. In other words, if

$$\sum_{k=1}^{M} L_{ki} p(\boldsymbol{x}|s_k) P(s_k) < \sum_{l=1}^{M} L_{lj} p(\boldsymbol{x}|s_l) P(s_l), \qquad (13.29)$$

then assign $\boldsymbol{x}$ to s_i.

In many recognition problems, if a correct judgment is made, the loss is zero, and for any wrong judgment, the loss is the same non-zero number (such as one). In this case, the loss function becomes

$$L_{ij} = 1 - \delta_{ij}. \qquad (13.30)$$

Substituting Equation (13.30) into Equation (13.28) can get

$$r_j(\boldsymbol{x}) = \sum_{k=1}^{M} (1 - \delta_{ij}) p(s_k|\boldsymbol{x}) P(s_k) = p(\boldsymbol{x}) - p(s_j|\boldsymbol{x}) P(s_j). \quad (13.31)$$

The Bayesian classifier assigns $\boldsymbol{x}$ to the class s_i if the following conditions are met:

$$p(s_i|\boldsymbol{x}) P(s_i) > p(s_j|\boldsymbol{x}) P(s_j) \quad j = 1, 2, \ldots, M; \ j \neq i. \qquad (13.32)$$

Looking back at the previous derivation of Equation (13.20), it can be seen that for the 0-1 loss function, the Bayesian classifier is equivalent to implementing the following decision function:

$$d_j(\boldsymbol{x}) = p(\boldsymbol{x}|s_j) P(s_j) \quad j = 1, 2, \ldots, M, \qquad (13.33)$$

where the vector $\boldsymbol{x}$ will be assigned to the class s_i (for all $j \neq i$) if $d_i(\boldsymbol{x}) < d_j(\boldsymbol{x})$.

The decision function of Equation (13.33) is optimal in the sense of minimizing the average loss of misclassification, but to obtain this optimal function, we need to know the probability density function of the pattern in each class and the probability of each class itself. The latter requirement mentioned earlier can often be met. For example, when all classes of themselves have the same possibility of appearance, $p(s_j) = 1/M$. But estimating the probability density function $p(\boldsymbol{x}|s_i)$ is another matter. If the pattern vector is nD, then $p(\boldsymbol{x}|s_i)$ is a function with n variables. If its form is unknown, it needs to be estimated using methods in multi-variate probability theory. Generally, Bayesian classifiers are used only when it is assumed that there are analytical representations for the probability density function, and these representation parameters can be estimated from pattern sampling. The most commonly used assumption so far is that $p(x|s_i)$ conforms to the Gaussian probability density.

2. Bayesian classifier for Gaussian pattern class

Consider the 1D problem first. Suppose that there are two $(M = 2)$ pattern classes that obey the Gaussian probability density. The mean values are m_1 and m_2, and the standard deviations are σ_1 and σ_2. According to Equation (13.33), the Bayesian decision function is as follows (the pattern is scalar):

$$d_j(x) = p(x|s_j)P(s_j) = \frac{1}{\sqrt{2\pi}\sigma_j} \exp\left[-\frac{(x - m_j)^2}{2\sigma_j^2}\right] \quad j = 1, 2.$$

$$(13.34)$$

Image segmentation with threshold (see Section 7.4) is a special case of pattern classification. Assuming that the image is composed of an object and background that have gray values with Gaussian distribution, the threshold can be determined by the Bayesian decision function of Equation (13.34).

Example 13.3 Determining the threshold with Bayesian decision function

Refer to Figure 13.8, which shows the probability density functions that represent the object and background patterns. The boundary between the two classes of patterns is now a point, denoted by x_0. If the probability of these two classes is the same, that is, $P(s_1) = P(s_2) = 1/2$, then we have $p(x_0|s_1) = p(x_0|s_2)$ at the decision boundary. This corresponds to the point of intersection of two probability density functions in Figure 13.8. Selecting the gray value of this point as the segmentation threshold, all points on the right of x_0 are assigned to class s_1 and all points on the left of x_0 are assigned to class s_2. If the probabilities of these two classes are different, if $P(s_1) > P(s_2)$, x_0 moves to the left; if $P(s_1) < P(s_2)$, x_0 moves to

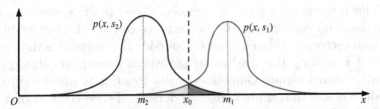

Figure 13.8. Probability density functions of two Gaussian distributions of object and background.

the right. In the extreme case, if $P(s_2) = 0$, then assigning all patterns to class s_1 (that is, moving x_0 to negative infinity) will never cause an error. □

In the case of nD, the Gaussian density vector of the jth pattern class has the following form:

$$p(\boldsymbol{x}|s_j) = \frac{1}{(2\pi)^{n/2} |C_j|^{1/2}} \exp\left[-\frac{1}{2}(\boldsymbol{x} - \boldsymbol{m}_j)^{\mathrm{T}} C_j^{-1}(\boldsymbol{x} - \boldsymbol{m}_j)\right].$$

$$(13.35)$$

The density of each pattern is completely determined by its mean vector and variance matrix. They are

$$\boldsymbol{m}_j = E_j\{\boldsymbol{x}\}, \tag{13.36}$$

$$C_j = E_j\{(\boldsymbol{x} - \boldsymbol{m}_j)(\boldsymbol{x} - \boldsymbol{m}_j)^{\mathrm{T}}\}, \tag{13.37}$$

where $E_j\{\cdot\}$ represents the expected value of the pattern argument in the class s_j. In Equation (13.35), n is the dimension of the pattern vector and $|C_j\|$ is the determinant of matrix C_j. The mean vector and covariance matrix given by using the mean to approximate the expected value are as follows:

$$\boldsymbol{m}_j = \frac{1}{N} \sum_{x \in s_j} \boldsymbol{x}, \tag{13.38}$$

$$C_j = \frac{1}{N_j} \sum_{x \in s_j} \boldsymbol{x}\boldsymbol{x}^{\mathrm{T}} - m_j m_j^{\mathrm{T}}, \tag{13.39}$$

where N_j is the number of pattern vectors in the class s_j; the summation is performed on all pattern vectors.

The covariance matrix is symmetric and positive semi-definite. The diagonal element C_{kk} is the variance of the kth element in the pattern vector, and the element C_{jk} outside the diagonal is the covariance of x_j and x_k. If x_j and x_k are statistically independent, $C_{jk} = 0$, then the multi-variate Gaussian density function is simplified to the product of the univariate Gaussian density of each element of x.

According to Equation (13.34), the Bayesian decision function for class s_j is $d_j(x) = p(x|s_j)P(s_j)$, but considering the exponential form of the Gaussian density function, the natural logarithmic form expression is usually more convenient. In other words, the decision function can be represented in the following form:

$$d_j(x) = \ln[p(x|s_j)P(s_j)] = \ln p(x|s_j) + \ln P(s_j). \qquad (13.40)$$

From the classification effect, Equations (13.40) and (13.34) are equivalent because the logarithm is a single increasing function. In other words, the rank of the decision function in Equations (13.34) and (13.40) are the same. Substituting Equation (13.35) into Equation (13.40), we can get

$$d_j(x) = \ln P(s_j) - \frac{n}{2}\ln 2\pi - \frac{1}{2}\ln |C_j| - \frac{1}{2}\Big[(x - m_j)^{\mathrm{T}}C_j^{-1}(x - m_j)\Big].$$
$$(13.41)$$

Because the term $(n/2)\ln 2\pi$ is the same for all classes, it can be omitted from Equation (13.41). Equation (13.41) becomes the following form:

$$d_j(x) = \ln P(s_j) - \frac{1}{2}\ln |C_j| - \frac{1}{2}\Big[(x - m_j)^{\mathrm{T}}C_j^{-1}(x - m_j)\Big]. \quad (13.42)$$

Equation (13.42) represents the **Bayesian decision function** of **Gaussian pattern class** under the condition of 0-1 loss function.

The decision function given by Equation (13.42) is a super-quadratic function (a quadratic function in nD space), in which no component of x is higher than the second order. It can be seen that for the Gaussian pattern, the best effect that the Bayesian classifier can obtain is to put a generalized second-order decision surface between every two pattern classes. If the pattern sample is indeed Gaussian, then this decision surface can give the least loss classification.

If all the covariance matrices are equal, that is, $C_j = C$, $j = 1, 2, \ldots, M$, with all items independent of j omitted, then Equation (13.42) becomes the following form:

$$d_j(\boldsymbol{x}) = \ln P(s_j) + \boldsymbol{x}^{\mathrm{T}} \boldsymbol{C}^{-1} \boldsymbol{m}_j - \frac{1}{2} \boldsymbol{m}_j^{\mathrm{T}} \boldsymbol{C}^{-1} \boldsymbol{m}_j. \tag{13.43}$$

For $j = 1, 2, \ldots, M$, they are **linear decision functions**.

Further, if $C = I$, I is the identity matrix and $P(s_j) = 1/M$ for $j = 1, 2, \ldots, M$, then

$$d_j(\boldsymbol{x}) = \boldsymbol{x}^{\mathrm{T}} \boldsymbol{m}_j - \frac{1}{2} \boldsymbol{m}_j^{\mathrm{T}} \boldsymbol{m}_j \quad j = 1, 2, \ldots, M. \tag{13.44}$$

Equation (13.44) gives the same decision function as Equation (13.24) for the minimum distance classifier. Under the following three conditions, the minimum distance classifier is optimal in the Bayesian sense: (i) The pattern class is Gaussian; (ii) all covariance matrices are equal to the identity matrix; (iii) all classes have the same probability of appearance. The Gaussian pattern class that meets these conditions is in the form of a sphere in nD, called hypersphere. The minimum distance classifier establishes a hyperplane between each pair of classes, and this hyperplane equally divides the straight line connecting the centers of each pair of spheres. In the 2D case, the clusters form circular regions, and the boundary becomes a straight line that bisects the center line segments of each pair of circular regions.

Example 13.4 Distribution of patterns in 3D space

Figure 13.9 shows the distribution of two classes of patterns (represented by solid circles and hollow circles, respectively) in 3D space. Assuming that the patterns in each class are all samples of the Gaussian distribution, they can be used to explain the mechanism of establishing Bayesian classifiers.

Applying Equation (13.38) to the patterns shown in Figure 13.9, we can obtain

$$\boldsymbol{m}_1 = \frac{1}{4}[3 \ 1 \ 1]^{\mathrm{T}} \quad \boldsymbol{m}_2 = \frac{1}{4}[1 \ 3 \ 3]^{\mathrm{T}}.$$

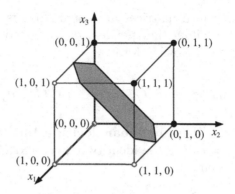

Figure 13.9.   Decision surface in 3D space.

Similarly, applying Equation (13.39) to these two patterns can get two equal covariance matrices as follows:

$$C_1 = C_2 = \frac{1}{16} \begin{bmatrix} 3 & 1 & 1 \\ 1 & 3 & -1 \\ 1 & -1 & 3 \end{bmatrix}.$$

Because the two covariance matrices are equal, the Bayesian decision function can be given by Equation (13.42). If it is assumed that $P(s_1) = P(s_2) = 1/2$ and the logarithmic term is omitted, then

$$d_j(x) = x^{\mathrm{T}} C^{-1} m_j - \frac{1}{2} m_j^{\mathrm{T}} C^{-1} m_j,$$

where

$$C^{-1} = \begin{bmatrix} 8 & -4 & -4 \\ -4 & 8 & 4 \\ -4 & 4 & 8 \end{bmatrix}.$$

Expanding the representation of $d_j(x)$ to get $d_1(x) = 4x_1 - 1.5$, $d_2(x) = -4x_1 + 8x_2 + 8x_3 - 5.5$, then the decision surface that separates the two classes of pattern will be $d_1(x) - d_2(x) = -8x_1 - 8x_2 - 8x_3 + 4 = 0$. The shading in Figure 13.9 shows a part of this plane (inside the cube), which effectively separates the space where the two classes of pattern are located.   □

13.2.4　AdaBoost

In practice, the classification effect of many classifiers is only slightly higher than 50% for two classes of samples, which is called **weak classifier**. It is necessary to combine multiple such independent classifiers to achieve better results. Specifically, these classifiers are applied to different training sample subsets in sequence, which is called **boosting**. The boosting algorithm combines multiple weak classifiers into a new **strong classifier** that is better than each weak classifier. There are two key issues here, one is how to select a subset of training sample inputs to each weak classifier; the other is how to combine them to form a strong classifier. The solution to the former problem is to give more weight to samples that are difficult to classify; the solution to the latter problem is to vote for the results of each weak classifier.

The most commonly used boosting algorithm is adaptive boosting (Adaboost). Suppose the pattern space is X, the training set contains m patterns x_i, and their corresponding class identifiers are c_i. In the two types of classification problems, $c_i \in \{-1, 1\}$. The main steps of the adaptive boosting algorithm are as follows:

(1) Initialize K, where K is the number of weak classifiers to be used.
(2) Let $k = 1$ and initialize the weight $W_1(i) = 1/m$.
(3) For each k, use the training set and a set of weights $W_k(i)$ to train the weak classifier C_k and assign a real number to each pattern x_i, namely $C_k : X \to R$.
(4) Select coefficient $a_k > 0 \in R$.
(5) Update the weight (where G_k is the normalization coefficient to make $\sum_{i=1}^{m} W_{k+1}(i) = 1$), where

$$W_{k+1}(i) = \frac{W_k(i) \exp[-a_k c_i C_k(x_i)]}{G_k}. \tag{13.45}$$

(6) Set $k = k + 1$.
(7) If $k \leq K$, go back to step (3).
(8) The final strong classifier is

$$S(x_i) = \text{sign}\left[\sum_{k=1}^{K} a_k C_k(x_i)\right]. \tag{13.46}$$

In the above algorithm, the weak classifier C_k is used for the training set; the importance of correct classification of a single sample in each step is different, and each step k is determined by a set of weights $W_k(i)$, where the sum of the weights is one. At the beginning, the weights are all equal. But after every iteration, the weight of the sample that is misclassified increases relatively because the exponential item in step (5) is classified as positive, which makes the weight of $W_k(i)$ larger, that is, the weak classifier C_{k+1} will pay more attention to the samples that are misclassified in kth iterations.

At each step, the weak classifier C_k must be determined to adapt its performance to the weight distribution $W_k(i)$. In the case of binary classification, the objective function to be minimized for weak classifier training is

$$e_k = \sum_{i=1}^{m} P_{i \sim W_k(i)}[C_k(x_i) \neq c_i], \qquad (13.47)$$

where $P[\cdot]$ represents the experience probability obtained from the training sample. The error e_k depends on the weight distribution $W_k(i)$, and the weight distribution $W_k(i)$ is related to whether the classification is correct. Each classifier is trained to be better than random classification for each part of the training set.

There are different methods for determining a_k, and the following is advisable for the binary classification problem:

$$a_k = \frac{1}{2} \ln \left(\frac{1 - e_k}{e_k} \right). \qquad (13.48)$$

13.3   Support Vector Machines

Support vector machine (SVM) is an optimal design methodology for linear classifiers (also refers to the classifiers designed in this way).

13.3.1   Linearly separable classes

Consider a problem of classifying two classes of patterns. Assuming that the feature vector of the training set X is x_i, $i = 1, 2, \ldots, N$, they either belong to the first class s_1 or the second class s_2. Now,

let them be **linearly separable**. The design purpose of the linear
classifier is to design a hyperplane such that

$$g(x) = \boldsymbol{w}^{\mathrm{T}} x + w_0 = 0, \tag{13.49}$$

where $\boldsymbol{w} = [w_1, w_2, \ldots, w_l]^{\mathrm{T}}$ is the weight vector and w_0 is the threshold. The previously mentioned classifier should be able to correctly
classify all training set samples. The hyperplanes that meet the conditions are generally not unique. For example, the two straight lines
(a thick solid line and a thin dashed line) shown in Figure 13.10
are examples of two possible hyperplanes (the straight lines here can
be regarded as special cases of the hyperplane). When the actual
situation is considered, which hyperplane is better? It must be the
hyperplane represented by the thick line because it is far from both of
the two classes. When the samples of the two classes are distributed
more scattered or considering the actual test samples, the result of
using this hyperplane to make classification will be better and the
possible error rate will be smaller.

The previous discussion shows that in the design of the classifier,
its ability and performance of generalization need to be considered.
In other words, the classifier designed with the training set should
consider whether it can get satisfactory results when it is applied
to samples other than the training set. In a linear classifier of two
classes, the one whose classification hyperplane has the largest distance from both of the two classes should be the best.

Each hyperplane can be characterized by its orientation and the
distance from the origin, the former is determined by $\boldsymbol{w}$ and the
latter by w_0. If there is no bias to the two classes of patterns, then
for each orientation, the hyperplane with the same distance from

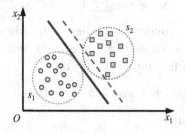

Figure 13.10. Linearly separable classes and two hyperplanes.

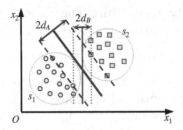

Figure 13.11.   Two hyperplanes with different distances.

the two classes of patterns should have the largest distance from the two classes of patterns, so the problem becomes to determine a hyperplane of certain orientation with the largest distance between two classes of patterns. Figure 13.11 shows an example given on the basis of Figure 13.10, where orientation A is required and orientation B gives an example of other orientations.

The distance from a point to a hyperplane can be expressed as

$$d = \frac{|g(x)|}{\|\boldsymbol{w}\|}. \tag{13.50}$$

By normalizing $\boldsymbol{w}$ and w_0, the value of $g(x)$ at the closest point in s_1 can be made 1 and the value of $g(x)$ at the closest point in s_2 is -1. This is also equivalent to the distance

$$\frac{1}{\|\boldsymbol{w}\|} + \frac{1}{\|\boldsymbol{w}\|} = \frac{1}{\|\boldsymbol{w}\|} \tag{13.51}$$

and meets

$$\boldsymbol{w}^{\mathrm{T}} x + w_0 \geq 1 \quad \forall x \in s_1,$$
$$\boldsymbol{w}^{\mathrm{T}} x + w_0 \leq 1 \quad \forall x \in s_2. \tag{13.52}$$

For each class s_i, denote its label as t_i, where $t_1 = 1$, $t_2 = -1$. Now, the problem becomes to calculate the $\boldsymbol{w}$ and w_0 of the hyperplane. If the following conditions are met:

$$t_i(\boldsymbol{w}^{\mathrm{T}} \boldsymbol{x} + w_0) \geq 1 \quad i = 1, 2, \ldots, N \tag{13.53}$$

it requires to minimize

$$C(w) = \frac{1}{2}\|\boldsymbol{w}\|^2. \tag{13.54}$$

The above problem is a problem of optimizing a quadratic (nonlinear) cost function under the condition of satisfying a set of linear inequalities. This problem can be solved by the Lagrangian multiplier method, specifically by solving the following equation:

$$L(\boldsymbol{w}, \boldsymbol{w}_0, \lambda) \equiv \frac{1}{2}\boldsymbol{w}^{\mathrm{T}}\boldsymbol{w} - \sum_{i=1}^{N} \lambda_i[t_i(\boldsymbol{w}^{\mathrm{T}}\boldsymbol{x}_i + w_0) - 1]. \qquad (13.55)$$

We get the following results:

$$\boldsymbol{w} = \sum_{i=1}^{N} \lambda_i t_i x_i. \qquad (13.56)$$

$$\sum_{i=1}^{N} \lambda_i t_i = 0. \qquad (13.57)$$

Because the Lagrangian multiplier can take a positive value or zero, the vector parameter $\boldsymbol{w}$ of the optimal solution is a linear combination of N_s $(N_s \leq N)$ eigenvectors related to $\lambda_i \neq 0$:

$$\boldsymbol{w} = \sum_{i=1}^{N_s} \lambda_i t_i x_i. \qquad (13.58)$$

These vectors are called support vectors, and the optimal hyperplane classifier is called a **support vector machine**. For $\lambda_i \neq 0$, the support vector always coincides with one of the two hyperplanes:

$$\boldsymbol{w}^{\mathrm{T}}\boldsymbol{x} + w_0 \pm 1. \qquad (13.59)$$

In other words, the support vector gives the training vector closest to the linear classifier. The feature vector corresponding to $\lambda_i = 0$ is either on the outside of the "classification band" defined by the two hyperplanes of Equation (13.59) or on one of the two hyperplanes (this is a degenerate situation). The hyperplane classifier thus obtained is insensitive to the number and position of feature vectors that do not cross the classification band.

Because the cost function in Equation (13.54) is strictly convex and the inequality in Equation (13.53) (used as a constraint) is a linear function, it can be seen that any local minimum is also the only global minimum. In other words, the optimal hyperplane classifier obtained from the support vector is unique.

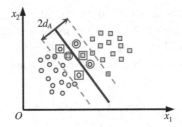

Figure 13.12.   Sample falling into classification band when the classes are non-separable.

13.3.2   Linearly non-separable classes

In the case that the pattern classes are **linearly non-separable**, the previous discussion needs to be considered separately. Take Figure 13.12 as an example. Here, the samples of the two classes cannot be separated (with a straight line) anyway, or no matter how we choose the hyperplane, there will always be samples falling into the classification band (between the two dotted lines).

In this case, the training feature vector can be divided into the following three categories:

(1) The vectors fall outside the classification band and are correctly classified. These vectors satisfy Equation (13.53).

(2) The vectors fall within the classification band and are correctly classified. These vectors correspond to the samples enclosed by the big boxes in Figure 13.12. They satisfy the following inequality:

$$0 \leq t_i\left(\boldsymbol{w}^\mathrm{T} \boldsymbol{x} + w_0 \right) < 1. \tag{13.60}$$

(3) The vectors are classified incorrectly. These vectors correspond to the samples surrounded by large circles in Figure 13.12. They satisfy the following inequality:

$$t_i\left(\boldsymbol{w}^\mathrm{T} \boldsymbol{x} + w_0 \right) < 0. \tag{13.61}$$

The above three cases can be unified by introducing a set of relaxation variables:

$$t_i\left(\boldsymbol{w}^\mathrm{T} \boldsymbol{x} + w_0 \right) \geq 1 - r_i. \tag{13.62}$$

The first case corresponds to $r_i = 0$, the second case corresponds to $0 \leq r_i \leq 1$, and the third case corresponds to $r_i > 1$. The optimization goal here is to make the distance from the nearest point to the hyperplane as small as possible while keeping the number of points with $r_i = 0$ as few as possible. The cost function to be minimized at this time is

$$C(\boldsymbol{w}, w_0, \boldsymbol{r}) \equiv \frac{1}{2}\|\boldsymbol{w}\|^2 + k\sum_{i=1}^{N} I(r_i), \qquad (13.63)$$

where $\boldsymbol{r}$ is a vector composed of parameters r_i, k is a parameter that controls the relative influence of the first and second items (in the previous classifiable situation, $k \to \infty$), and

$$I(r_i) = \begin{cases} 1 & r_i > 0 \\ 0 & r_i = 0, \end{cases} \qquad (13.64)$$

Since $I(r_i)$ is a discrete function, it is not easy to optimize Equation (13.63). For this reason, the problem is approximated as satisfying the following conditions:

$$t_i(w^{\mathrm{T}}x + w_0) > 1 - r_i \quad i = 1, 2, \ldots, N,$$
$$r_i > 0 \quad i = 1, 2, \ldots, N, \qquad (13.65)$$

to minimize

$$C(w, w_0 r) \equiv \frac{1}{2}\|w\|^2 + k\sum_{i=1}^{N} r_i. \qquad (13.66)$$

The Lagrangian function at this time is

$$L(\boldsymbol{w}, w_0, \boldsymbol{r}, \lambda, \mu) = \frac{1}{2}\|w\|^2 + k\sum_{i=1}^{N} r_i - \sum_{i=1}^{N} \mu_i r_i$$

$$- \sum_{i=1}^{N} \lambda_i \left[t_i(\boldsymbol{w}^{\mathrm{T}}\boldsymbol{x}_i + w_0) - 1 + r_i \right]. \qquad (13.67)$$

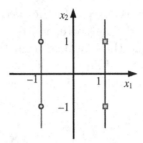

Figure 13.13.   Classification of two classes of samples.

Example 13.5 Classification of two classes of samples

Consider the following problem for classification of two classes of samples. Refer to Figure 13.13. The four sample points are known: $[1, 1]^{\mathrm{T}}$ and $[1, -1]^{\mathrm{T}}$ belonging to s_1, $[-1, 1]^{\mathrm{T}}$ and $[-1, -1]^{\mathrm{T}}$ belonging to s_2. These four points are at the four vertices of the square centered on the origin. The optimal hyperplane is a line here, and the equation is $g(\boldsymbol{x}) = w_1 x_1 + w_2 x_2 + w_0 = 0$.

Since the geometric relationship is relatively simple, one can directly obtain $w_2 = w_0 = 0$ and $w_1 = 1$ through observation, that is, the optimal hyperplane $g(\boldsymbol{x}) = x_1 = 0$. In this example, all four points are support vectors. $\qquad\square$

Finally, it needs to be pointed out that the problem of multiple classes can also be solved by **support vector machines**. There are many specific methods. A simple idea is to directly extend the aforementioned two-class method and consider the problem of M classes as the M problems of two classes. Design an optimal discriminate function $g_i(\boldsymbol{x})$, $i = 1, 2, \ldots, M$ for each class pattern, such that $g_i(\boldsymbol{x}) > g_j(\boldsymbol{x})$, $\forall i \neq j$, $\boldsymbol{x} \in s_i$. According to the method of SVM, a discriminating function $g_i(\boldsymbol{x})$ is designed for each class s_i in order to distinguish the class s_i from other classes. The linear function thus obtained gives $g_i(\boldsymbol{x}) > 0$ for $\boldsymbol{x} \in s_i$ and $g_i(\boldsymbol{x}) < 0$ for other cases.

13.4   Key Points and References for Each Section

The following indicates the key points of each section and provides some targeted guidance for further references.

1. Invariant cross-ratio

Cross-ratio is a commonly used invariant parameter in pattern classification and recognition. For more details, please refer to Ref. [1]. In order to make the cross-ratio invariant, four points are required to define the cross-ratio by means of collinear points and five points are required to define the cross-ratio by means of non-collinear points. The method of constructing symmetric cross-ratio function inspires us to construct other symmetric functions. A work that uses cross-ratio design to quickly and effectively match icon descriptors can be found in Ref. [2].

2. Statistical pattern classification

Statistical pattern classification is the main content of statistical pattern recognition, and there are many related reference books, such as Ref. [3]. For the design of the classifier, please refer to Refs. [4,5]. A work using de-noising auto-encoder model for object classification can be found in Ref. [6]. A work that uses the manifold structure to perform dictionary learning to achieve object classification can be found in Ref. [7]. A work that uses sparse representation technology to classify objects can be found in Refs. [8,9]. A method that combines sparse coding and dictionary learning can be found in Ref. [10]. Some extended introductions on adaptive boosting can also be found in Ref. [11]. An example and fast algorithm using adaptive boosting can be found in Ref. [12]. A review of deep learning methods in object recognition can be found in Ref. [13].

3. Support vector machines

Support vector machine is the first practical result of statistical learning theory. Its initial application was in pattern recognition and became an important means of statistical pattern classification. For more information on support vector machines, please refer to Ref. [14]. For a comprehensive description of statistical learning theory and support vector machines, please refer to Ref. [15]. In the optimal linear classifier of the two classes, the conclusion that the classification hyperplane has the maximum distance from the two classes can be proved mathematically; see Ref. [5].

Self-Test Questions

The following questions include both single- and multiple-choice questions, so each option should be individually judged.

13.1 Invariant Cross-Ratio

13.1.1 Given: $R = \frac{(x_3-x_1)/(x_2-x_4)}{(x_2-x_1)/(x_3-x_4)}$, then ( )

    (A) $R = (x_3 - x_1)/(x_2 - x_4)/(x_1 - x_2)/(x_3 - x_4)$;
    (B) $R = (x_3 - x_1)/(x_4 - x_2)/(x_2 - x_1)/(x_3 - x_4)$;
    (C) $R = (x_3 - x_1)/(x_2 - x_4)/(x_2 - x_1)/(x_3 - x_4)$;
    (D) $R = (x_3 - x_1)/(x_2 - x_4)/(x_2 - x_1)/(x_4 - x_3)$.

[Hint] Compare the definitions of R.

13.1.2 Which of the following cross-ratio(s) is/are established? ( )

    (A) $\dfrac{(x_2 - x_1)/(x_4 - x_3)}{(x_4 - x_1)/(x_2 - x_3)}$;

    (B) $\dfrac{(x_2 - x_3)/(x_1 - x_4)}{(x_1 - x_3)/(x_2 - x_4)}$;

    (C) $\dfrac{(x_4 - x_1)/(x_3 - x_2)}{(x_3 - x_1)/(x_4 - x_2)}$;

    (D) $\dfrac{(x_2 - x_1)/(x_3 - x_4)}{(x_3 - x_1)/(x_4 - x_2)}$.

[Hint] There are six forms of cross-ratio.

13.1.3 Consider the order of points in the calculation of the cross-ratio, it has ( )

    (A) $C(P_1, P_3, P_2, P_4) = C(P_3, P_1, P_2, P_4)$;
    (B) $C(P_1, P_3, P_2, P_4) = C(P_4, P_2, P_3, P_1)$;
    (C) $C(P_1, P_4, P_3, P_2) = C(P_3, P_2, P_1, P_4)$;
    (D) $C(P_2, P_1, P_3, P_4) = C(P_1, P_2, P_4, P_3)$.

[Hint] The same cross-ratio may have different forms.

13.1.4 To calculate the invariant cross-ratio of non-collinear points, ( )

    (A) It is necessary to calculate two cross-ratios;

(B) It is necessary to use five coplanar points;

(C) It is not enough to calculate only one cross-ratio;

(D) Two of the five points must be collinear.

[Hint] The same cross-ratio may have different forms.

13.1.5 Symmetrical cross-ratio functions include ( )

(A) $R + 1/R$;

(B) $R(1 - R)$;

(C) $[R + 1/R] [R(1 - R)]$;

(D) $[R + 1/R] + [R(1 - R)]$.

[Hint] The individual conditions are incompatible.

13.2 Statistical Pattern Classification

13.2.1 There are three sets of points, $\{(0,5), (0,6), (1,5), (1,6), (1,7)\}$, $\{(5,1), (5,2), (6,1), (6,2), (7,1)\}$, $\{(8,6), (9,5), (9,7), (10,6), (10,7)\}$; in order to divide them, a straight line can be used: ( )

(A) $x = 3$ and $y = x$;

(B) $y = 3$ and $y = x$;

(C) $y = x$ and $x = 10 - y$;

(D) $y = x$ and $y = 10 - x$.

[Hint] Draw the given points in the coordinate system, and then consider the equation of each straight line.

13.2.2 It is known that the two pattern classes are S_1 and S_2, and their mean vector is $m_1 = [4 \ 2]^T$ and $m_2 = [2 \ 5]^T$, respectively. Then, for the patterns $x_1 = [3 \ 2]^T$ and $x_2 = [-3 \ 1]^T$, according to the minimum distance classifier, they belong separately to ( )

(A) S_1 and S_1;

(B) S_1 and S_2;

(C) S_2 and S_1;

(D) S_2 and S_2.

[Hint] Try to make a decision boundary.

13.2.3 For Bayesian classifier, ( )

(A) The loss function is always a 0-1 function;

(B) The decision function is only related to $P(s_k)$ and $p(\boldsymbol{x}|s_k)$;

(C) It can minimize the total average loss caused by classification;

(D) The possibility of each pattern appearing is always the same.

[Hint] Some conclusions are only valid when the assumption is satisfied.

13.3 Support Vector Machines

13.3.1 Support vector machine ( )

(A) Is a nearest neighbor classifier;

(B) Is an optimal classifier design method;

(C) Cannot have the same classification effect as other classifiers;

(D) Is the only classifier that can give the classification hyperplane having the same distance to the two classes.

[Hint] Compare the characteristics of support vector machines with other classifiers.

13.3.2 When using feature vectors to train linearly separable support vector machines, ( )

(A) The support vector is the feature vector;

(B) The number of support vectors is greater than or equal to the number of feature vectors;

(C) The support vector is a combination of feature vectors;

(D) The number of support vectors is less than or equal to the number of feature vectors.

[Hint] The support vector is obtained with the help of the feature vector of the training set.

13.3.3 When using feature vectors to train nonlinear separable support vector machines, ( )

(A) All training feature vector samples can always be correctly classified;

(B) The samples falling in the classification band can always be correctly classified;

(C) There will be situations where all samples cannot be correctly classified;

(D) There will be cases where some samples are correctly classified and some are incorrectly classified.

[Hint] Consider the situations where there are three types of training feature vectors.

References

[1] Davies, E. R. *Computer and Machine Vision: Theory, Algorithms, Practicalities*, 4th Edn. The Netherlands, Amsterdam: Elsevier, 2012.

[2] Aoki, T. and Kaminishi, K. A local descriptor for high-speed and high-performance pictogram matching. *Proc. ICIP*, 2017, 1062–1066.

[3] Bishop, C. M. *Pattern Recognition and Machine Learning*. Germany, Berlin: Springer, 2006.

[4] Duda, R. O., Hart, P. E., and Stork, D. G. *Pattern Classification*, 2nd Edn. USA, New Jersey: John Wiley & Sons, Inc., 2001.

[5] Theodoridis, S. and Koutroumbas, K. *Pattern Recognition*, 3rd Edn. The Netherlands, Amsterdam: Elsevier Science, 2009.

[6] You, Q. H. Z. and Zhang, Y.-J. A new training principle for stacked denoising autoencoders. *Proc. 7th ICIG*, 2013, 384–389.

[7] Liu, B. D., Wang, Y. X., Zhang, Y.-J., *et al.* Learning dictionary on manifolds for image classification. *Pattern Recognition*, 2013, 46(7): 1879–1890.

[8] Liu, B. D., Wang, Y. X., Shen, B., *et al.* Self-explanatory convex sparse representation for image classification. *Proc. ICSMC*, 2013, 2120–2125.

[9] Liu, B. D., Wang, Y. X., Shen, B., *et al.* Self-explanatory sparse representation for image classification. *Proc. ECCV*, Part II, LNCS 8690: 600–616, 2014.

[10] Liu, B. D., Wang, Y. X., Shen, B., *et al.* Blockwise coordinate descent schemes for efficient and effective dictionary learning. *Neurocomputing*, 2016, 178: 25–35.

[11] Zhang, Y.-J., *et al. Sub-Space-Based Face Recognition*. China, Beijing: Tsinghua University Press, 2009.

[12] Jia, H. X. and Zhang, Y.-J. Fast Adaboost training algorithm by dynamic weight trimming. *Chinese Journal of Computers*, 2009, 32(2): 336–341.

[13] Zheng, Y., Chen, Q. Q., and Zhang, Y.-J. Deep learning and its new progress in object and behavior recognition. *Journal of Image and Graphics*, 2014, 19(2): 175–184.

[14] Snyder, W. E. and Qi, H. *Machine Vision*. UK, Cambridge: Cambridge University Press, 2004.

[15] Schölkopf, B. and Smola, A. J. *Learning with Kernels: Support Vector Machines, Regularization, Optimization, and Beyond*. USA, Cambridge: MIT Press, 2002.

Appendix A

Mathematical Morphology

Mathematical morphology is a commonly used mathematical tool in image processing and analysis. Its basic idea is to use structuring elements with a certain shape to measure and extract the corresponding shapes in the image to achieve the purpose of image analysis and recognition. The application of mathematical morphology in the field of computer vision can simplify image data, maintain their basic shape characteristics, and remove irrelevant structures. The algorithm of mathematical morphology has a natural parallel implementation structure.

The operating object (operand) of mathematical morphology can be a binary image or a gray-scale image. This appendix only introduces the mathematical morphology for binary images.

Section A.1 outlines some basic concepts and definitions about sets and lays a foundation for the following sections.

Section A.2 introduces the basic operations of binary morphology: dilation, erosion, opening, closing, and their properties.

Section A.3 first introduces the hit-or-miss transform and then combines it with the basic operations to form the binary morphological combination operations that can realize some basic image processing and analysis functions.

Section A.4 discusses some practical algorithms of binary mathematical morphology composed of basic operations and combination operations, and gives several examples to solve practical image processing and analysis problems.

A.1   Basic Set Definition

The mathematical foundation and language of **mathematical morphology** is set theory. Therefore, the definitions of some basic nouns/concepts of **set** are first given as follows:

(1) *Set*: The totality of definite and differentiated things with a certain nature (set is also a thing in itself). Commonly represented by capital letters, A, B, ..., etc. If something does not exist, it is said that the whole of such things is an empty set. It is stipulated that any empty set is just the same set, denoted as $\varnothing$. In the following introduction, assume that A, B, C, etc. are all sets in the Euclidean space, E^N.

(2) *Elements*: Things that make up a set. Commonly represented by lowercase letters, a, b, ..., etc. Nothing is an element in $\varnothing$.

(3) *Subset*: If and only if all the elements of set A belong to set B, then call A one subset of B.

(4) *Union*: The set composed of all the elements of A and B is called the union of A and B.

(5) *Intersection*: The set consisting of the common elements of A and B is called the intersection of A and B.

(6) *Complement*: The complement of A, denoted as A^c, is defined as

$$A^c = \{x | x \notin A\}. \tag{A.1}$$

(7) *Displacement*: Set A with displacement of x, denoted as $(A)_x$, is defined as

$$(A)_x = \{y | y = a + x, a \in A\}. \tag{A.2}$$

(8) *Reflection*: Set A's reflection (also called mapping), denoted as $\hat{A}$, is defined as

$$\hat{A} = \{x | x = -a, a \in A\}. \tag{A.3}$$

(9) *Difference set*: The difference between two sets A and B, denoted as A–B, is defined as

$$A - B = \{x | x \in A, x \notin B\} = A \cap B^c. \tag{A.4}$$

Example A.1 Basic set definition examples

If a is an element of set A, denote it as: $a \in A$ (pronounced a belongs to A). If a is not an element of A, denote it as: $a \notin A$ (pronounced a does not belong to A). Because $\in$ and $\notin$ negate each other logically, the above two cases cannot be both established and cannot be both non-established.

When a set consists of only a finite number of elements, it can be written specifically, such as $A = \{a, b, c\}$. To indicate the characteristics of the set, the characteristics of the elements are often marked. It is generally represented by $\{x : x$ has property $P\}$ or $\{x|x$ has property $P\}$.

If there is only one certain thing, this thing is assumed to be recorded as a, then the whole of this kind of things is set $\{a\}$ and a is the only element in $\{a\}$. It should be noted that a and $\{a\}$ are generally different concepts. For example, $\{\varnothing\}$ has a unique element $\varnothing$, but there is no element in $\varnothing$.

If A is a subset of B, record it as: $A \subseteq B$ (pronounced A is contained in B) or $B \supseteq A$ (pronounced B contains A). If A is not a subset of B, denoted as $A \not\subseteq B$ (pronounced A is not included in B). Because $\subseteq$ and $\not\subseteq$ negate each other logically, these two cases cannot be both established and cannot be both non-established.

The union of sets A and B is denoted as $A \cup B$ (that is, $x \in A \cup B$ $\Leftrightarrow x \in A$ or $x \in B$). The intersection of sets A and B is denoted as $A \cap B$ (that is, $x \in A \cap B \Leftrightarrow x \in A$ and $x \in B$). Here, "$\Leftrightarrow$" is pronounced as "equivalent to".

Figure A.1 shows some diagrams for basic set definitions. Figure A.1(a) shows set A (shaded region, black dots indicate reference origin) and its complement (other regions); Figure A.1(b) gives the displacement $(A)_{\mathbf{x}}$ of A, which is the translation result

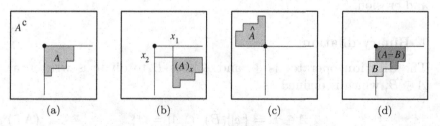

Figure A.1. Some basic set definition examples.

of A, where $x = (x_1, x_2)$; Figure A.1(c) gives the reflection $\hat{A}$ of A (rotated by 180° on the plane). The reflection set and the original set are symmetrical, which can also be said to be transposed to each other. Figure A.1(d) shows the difference set $A - B$ (dark-shaded region) between the set A and the other set B (light-shaded region), which belongs to the set A but not to the set B. □

The basic operations between sets discussed above are closely related to the basic logical operations for binary images introduced in Section 3.1. In fact, the concept of complement corresponds to the logical complement operation: the union operation corresponds to the logical OR operation and the intersection operation corresponds to the logical AND operation.

A.2   Basic Operations of Binary Morphology

The operation objects in binary morphology involve two sets. Generally, A is called an image set, B is a **structuring element** (it is still an image set), and mathematical morphology operations are considered as using B to operate on A. Each structuring element has an origin, which is the reference point for the structuring element to participate in morphological operations, but the origin does not necessarily belong to the structuring element. The following uses shading to represent the region with a value of one and white to represent the region with a value of zero. The calculation is performed on the region of the image with a value of one.

A.2.1   Binary dilation and erosion

The most basic pair of operations in binary morphology is dilation and erosion.

1. Binary dilation

The **dilation** operator is $\oplus$, and A uses B to dilate is written as $A \oplus B$, which is defined as

$$A \oplus B = \{x | [(\hat{B})_x \cap A] = \varnothing\}. \qquad (A.5)$$

The above equation shows that the process of dilating A with B is to map B about the origin first and then translate its reflection by x, where the intersection of A with the reflection of B is not an empty set. In other words, the set obtained by dilating A with B is the set of the origin of B when the displacement of $\hat{B}$ intersects with at least one non-zero element in A. According to this explanation, Equation (A.5) can also be written as

$$A \oplus B = \{x | [(\hat{B})_x \cap A] \subseteq A\}. \tag{A.6}$$

The above equation can help people understand the dilation operation with the concept of convolution. If B is regard as a convolutional **mask**, the dilation is achieved by first mapping B respect to the origin and then moving the reflection on A continuously.

Example A.2 Dilation operation diagram

Figure A.2 shows an example of the dilation operation. The shaded part in Figure A.2(a) is set A, and the shaded part in Figure A.2(b) is structuring element B (the origin is marked with "+"), the reflection is shown in Figure A.2(c), and the two shaded parts (the darker part is the enlarged part) in Figure A.2(d) are combined into a set $A \oplus B$. It can be seen from the figure that dilation has expanded (increased) the original region. □

2. Binary erosion

The **erosion** operator is $\ominus$, and A uses B to erode is written as $A \ominus B$, which is defined as

$$A \ominus B = \{x | (B)_x \subseteq A\}. \tag{A.7}$$

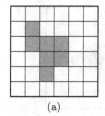
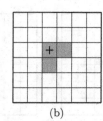
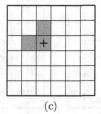
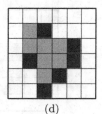

(a)   (b)   (c)   (d)

Figure A.2.   Example of dilation operation.

The above equation shows that the erosion result of A with B is the set of all $\boldsymbol{x}$, where B is still in A after being translated by $\boldsymbol{x}$. In other words, the set obtained by eroding A with B is the set of B's origin position when B is completely included in A. The above equation can also help people understand erosion operations with the help of correlation concepts.

Example A.3 Erosion calculation diagram

Figure A.3 shows a simple example of the erosion calculation. The set A in Figure A.3(a) and the structuring element B in Figure A.3(b) are the same as those in Figure A.2, while the dark-shaded part in Figure A.3(c) gives $A \ominus B$ (the light color indicates the part that was originally belonging to A but now is eroded). It can be seen from the figure that erosion has contracted (reduced) the original region.   □

3. Using vector operations to achieve dilation and erosion

In addition to the more intuitive definitions mentioned earlier, there are some equivalent definitions of dilation and erosion. Each of these definitions has its own characteristics. For example, dilation and erosion operations can be realized by vector operations or displacement operations, and it is more convenient to actually use computers to complete dilation and erosion operations.

Let's look at vector operations first. Considering both A and B as vectors, dilation and erosion can be represented as

$$A \oplus B = \{x | x = a + b \quad \text{for some } a \in A \text{ and } b \in B\}, \quad (A.8)$$

$$A \ominus B = \{x | (x + b) \in A \quad \text{for every } b \in B\}. \quad (A.9)$$

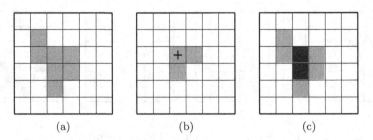

Figure A.3.   Erosion calculation example.

Example A.4 Using vector operations to achieve dilation and erosion operations

Refer to Figure A.2. Taking the upper-left corner of the image as the origin $(0, 0)$, A and B can be represented as $A = \{(1,1), (1,2), (2,2), (3,2), (2,3), (3,3), (2,4)\}$ and $B = \{(0,0), (1,0), (0,1)\}$. Dilation with vector operations can be represented as $A \oplus B = \{(1,1), (1,2), (2,2), (3,2), (2,3), (3,3), (2,4), (2,1), (2,2), (3,2), (4,2), (3,3), (4,3), (3,4), (1,2), (1,3), (2,3), (3,3), (2,4), (3,4), (2,5)\} = \{(1,1), (2,1), (1,2), (2,2), (3,2), (4,2), (1,3), (2,3), (3,3), (4,3), (2,4), (3,4), (2,5)\}$. This result is the same as that of Figure A.2(d). In the same way, erosion with vector operations can be represented as $A \ominus B = \{(2,2), (2,3)\}$. Refer to Figure A.3(c) to verify this result here. □

4. Realize dilation and erosion with displacement calculation

Displacement operations are closely related to vector operations, and the sum of vectors is a kind of displacement operation. According to Equation (A.2), the displacement calculation for dilation can be obtained from Equation (A.8):

$$A \oplus B = \bigcup_{b \in B} (A)_b. \tag{A.10}$$

The above equation shows that the result of $A \oplus B$ is the union obtained by shifting A at each $b \in B$. It can also be interpreted as follows: to dilate A with B is to shift A according to each b and OR these results.

According to Equation (A.2), the displacement calculation for erosion can be obtained from Equation (A.9):

$$A \ominus B = \bigcap_{b \in B} (A)_{-b}. \tag{A.11}$$

The above equation shows that the result of $A \ominus B$ is the intersection obtained by negatively shifting A for each $b \in B$. It can also be interpreted as follows: to erode A with B is to negatively shift A according to each b and AND these results.

The union obtained by shifting A according to b is also equal to the union obtained by shifting B according to a, so Equation (A.10) can also be written as

$$A \oplus B = \bigcup_{a \in A} (B)_a. \tag{A.12}$$

The intersection obtained by shifting A by $-b$ is also equal to the intersection obtained by shifting B by $-a$, so Equation (A.11) can also be written as

$$A \ominus B = \bigcap_{a \in A} (B)_{-a}. \tag{A.13}$$

Example A.5 A simple algorithm to eliminate salt-and-pepper noise in binary images

Suppose the original binary image affected by salt-and-pepper noise is $f(x, y)$ and the image after noise elimination is $g(x, y)$. Consider the 8-neighborhood $N(x, y)$ of one pixel, then the simple algorithm to eliminate salt and pepper noise in the binary image is as follows:

(1) Calculation: $s = \displaystyle\sum_{\substack{(p,q) \in N(x,y) \\ (p,q) \neq (x,y)}} f(p, q).$

(2) Judgment: If $s = 0$, $g(x, y) = 0$; if $s = 8$, $g(x, y) = 1$; otherwise, $g(x, y) = f(x, y)$.

The above algorithm can be adjusted to remove the spurs on the boundary of the object region in the binary image:

(1) Calculation: $s = \displaystyle\sum_{\substack{(p,q) \in N(x,y) \\ (p,q) \neq (x,y)}} f(p, q).$

(2) Judgment: If $s \leq 1$, $g(x, y) = 0$; if $s \geq 7$, $g(x, y) = 1$; otherwise, $g(x, y) = f(x, y)$.   □

5. Combination of binary dilation and erosion with set operations

Binary dilation and erosion can be combined with set operations. The combination of set operations with dilation and erosion has the following properties:

(1) The processing order of the dilation operation and union operation of the sets can be exchanged (the dilation of the union is equal to the dilated union):

$$B \oplus (A_1 \cup A_2) = (A_1 \cup A_2) \oplus B = (A_1 \oplus B) \cup (A_2 \oplus B).$$
$$(A.14)$$

(2) The processing order of the erosion operation and the union operation of the sets cannot be exchanged (the erosion of the union includes the eroded union):

$$(A_1 \cup A_2) \ominus B \supseteq (A_1 \ominus B) \cup (A_2 \ominus B),$$
$$B \ominus (A_1 \cup A_2) = (A_1 \ominus B) \cap (A_2 \ominus B).$$
$$(A.15)$$

(3) The processing order of dilation operation and the intersection operation of the sets cannot be exchanged (the dilation of intersection is included in the dilated intersection):

$$B \oplus (A_1 \cap A_2) = (A_1 \cap A_2) \oplus B \subseteq (A_1 \oplus B) \cap (A_2 \oplus B).$$
$$(A.16)$$

(4) The order of the erosion operation and the intersection operation of the sets can be exchanged (the erosion of the intersection is equal to the eroded intersection):

$$(A_1 \cap A_2) \ominus B = (A_1 \ominus B) \cap (A_2 \ominus B). \qquad (A.17)$$

Example A.6 Application of combination of dilation and logic operations

Logic operations can also be combined with dilation operations and erosion operations. Combining logical operations and dilation operations can get a hollowed-out label, which can be used to overlay an all-black or all-white image region for labeling. The specific method is to dilate the label text to be used first and then perform the XOR operation between the result and the original text, so that the obtained label can be seen more clearly when overlapped on regions of all black or all white. Figure A.4 shows an example, where Figure A.4(a) is the original text and Figure A.4(b) is the hollowed label of the original text obtained by the above method. □

(a)   (b)

Figure A.4.   An application example of the combination of dilation and logic operations.

A.2.2   Binary opening and closing

Opening and closing can also be regarded as a pair of basic operations of binary morphology.

1. Definition

Dilation and erosion are not mutually inverse operations, so they can be combined in cascade. For example, one can first erode the image and then dilate the result or dilate the image first and then erode the result (here the same structuring element is used). The former operation is called opening and the latter operation is called closing. They are also important operations in mathematical morphology.

The **opening** operator is ∘, A uses B to open is written as $A \circ B$, which is defined as

$$A \circ B = (A \ominus B) \oplus B. \qquad (A.18)$$

The **closing** operator is •, A uses B to close is written as $A \bullet B$, which is defined as

$$A \bullet B = (A \oplus B) \ominus B. \qquad (A.19)$$

Both opening and closing operations can remove specific image details smaller than the structuring elements while ensuring that no global geometric distortion is generated. The opening operation can filter out the spurs smaller than the structuring elements and cut off the slender lap to play a role of separation. The closing operation can fill gaps or holes smaller than structuring elements and join short breaks to play a role in connectivity.

The ability of opening and closing to extract shapes matching its structuring elements from the image can be obtained by the following opening characteristic theorem and closing characteristic theorem, respectively:

$$A \circ B = \{x \in A \mid \text{for some } t \in A \ominus B, \ x \in (B)_t \text{ and } (B)_t \subseteq A\},$$
$$(A.20)$$

$$A \bullet B = \{x \mid x \in (\hat{B})_t \Rightarrow (\hat{B})_t \cap A \neq \varnothing\}. \qquad (A.21)$$

Equation (A.20) shows that opening A with B is to select some points in A that match B. These points can be obtained by the translation of the structuring element B completely contained in A. Equation (A.21) shows that the result of closing A with B includes all points that meet the following conditions, that is, when the point is covered by the mapped and displaced structuring element, the intersection of A and the mapped and displaced structuring element is not zero.

2. Geometric interpretation

Both opening and closing can be combined with the realization of set theory to give a simple geometric explanation. For opening, the structuring element can be regarded as a sphere (on a plane), and the result of opening is the outer edge of the structuring element rolling in the opened set. According to the filling nature of the opening operation, an implementation method based on set theory can be obtained, that is, opening A with B can be obtained by translating all the results of filling B in A and then taking the union. In other words, the following filling process can be used to describe the opening:

$$A \circ B = \cup\{(B)_x \mid (B)_x \subset A\}. \qquad (A.22)$$

Figure A.5 shows an example, where Figure A.5(a) shows A, Figure A.5(b) shows B, Figure A.5(c) shows several positions of B in A, and Figure A.5(d) shows the final result of opening A with B.

There can be a similar geometric interpretation of closing, but now the structuring elements are considered in the background.

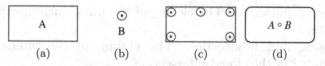

Figure A.5.   Filling characteristics of opening.

Figure A.6.   Geometric interpretation of closing.

Table A.1.   Relationship between set as well as opening and closing.

Operation	Union	Intersection
Opening	$\left(\bigcup\limits_{i=1}^{n} A_i\right) \circ B \supseteq \bigcup\limits_{i=1}^{n} (A_i \circ B)$	$\left(\bigcap\limits_{i=1}^{n} A_i\right) \circ B \subseteq \bigcap\limits_{i=1}^{n} (A_i \circ B)$
Closing	$\left(\bigcup\limits_{i=1}^{n} A_i\right) \bullet B \supseteq \bigcup\limits_{i=1}^{n} (A_i \bullet B)$	$\left(\bigcap\limits_{i=1}^{n} A_i\right) \bullet B \subseteq \bigcap\limits_{i=1}^{n} (A_i \bullet B)$

Figure A.6 gives an example of the geometry interpretation of closing, where Figure A.6(a) gives A, Figure A.6(b) gives B, and Figure A.6(c) is B in several positions of A^c, and Figure A.6(d) shows the final result of closing A with B.

3. Relationship between set as well as binary opening and closing

The relationship between opening and closing as well as the set can be represented by the four interchangeable characteristics listed in Table A.1.

When the operation objects are multiple images, the nature of the set can be used for opening and closing:

(1) Opening and union: The opening of the union includes the opened union.
(2) Opening and intersection: The opening of the intersection is included in the opened intersection.
(3) Closing and union: The closing of the union includes the closed union.
(4) Closing and intersection: The closing of the intersection is included in the closed intersection.

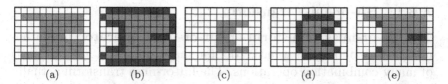

Figure A.7. Comparative example of four basic operations.

Example A.7 Comparative example of four basic operations

Figure A.7 shows the results of four basic operations on the same original set as shown in Figure A.7(a), the structuring elements used here are the origin and its 4-neighborhood. Figures A.7(b) to (e) correspond to the results of using dilation, erosion, opening, and closing operators to act on Figure A.7(a), respectively. Among them, the dark pixels in Figure A.7(b) are dilated pixels, the dark pixels in Figure A.7(d) are pixels dilated after erosion, and the dark pixels in Figure A.7(e) are the pixels that are not removed in the subsequent erosion among the dilated pixels. Obviously, we have $A \ominus B \subset A \subset A \oplus B$. In addition, the opening operation achieves the goal of smoothing the contour and making the object more compact by eliminating the sharp peaks (or narrow bands) on the object, while the closing operation can fill the recesses (or holes) on the object. Both operations reduce the irregularity of the contour. $\square$

A.3 Combined Operations of Binary Morphology

The four basic operations of binary mathematical morphology (dilation, erosion, opening, and closing) were introduced in the previous section. Some people also regard the hit-or-miss transform as a basic operation of binary mathematical morphology. If the hit-or-miss transform is combined with the above four basic operations, it can also form a variety of combined operations and practical algorithms for morphological analysis. This section introduces some combined operations, and Section A.4 introduces several practical algorithms.

A.3.1   Hit-or-miss transform

The **hit-or-miss transform** or **hit-or-miss operator** in mathematical morphology is a basic tool for shape detection and the basis of many combination operations. The hit-or-miss transform actually corresponds to two operations, so two structuring elements are used. Suppose A is the original image and E and F are a pair of sets that do not coincide with each other (they define a pair of structuring elements). The hit-or-miss transform is represented by $\Uparrow$, which is defined as

$$A \Uparrow (E, F) = (A \ominus E) \cap (A^c \ominus F) = (A \ominus E) \cap (A \oplus F)^c. \quad (A.23)$$

Any pixel z in the output result of the hit-or-miss transform meets two conditions: $E + z$ is a subset of A and $F + z$ is a subset of A^c. Conversely, the pixel z that satisfies the above two conditions must be in the result of the hit-or-miss transform. E and F are respectively called hit structuring element and miss structuring element; see Figure A.8. Figure A.8(a) is the hit structuring element, Figure A.8(b) is the miss structuring element, Figure A.8(c) shows four sample original images, and Figure A.8(d) is the result (dark pixels) of hit-or-miss transform on these images. It should be noted that the two structuring elements must satisfy $E \cap F = \varnothing$, otherwise the hit-or-miss transform will give an empty set result.

Example A.8 Effect of different structuring elements

Using different structuring elements in the hit-or-miss transform will produce different results. Figure A.9 shows a comparison example. For the image in Figure A.9(c), if the structuring element in Figure A.9(b) is used, the result obtained is shown by the dark pixels

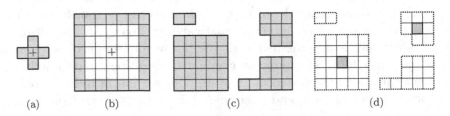

(a)   (b)   (c)   (d)

Figure A.8.   Hit-or-miss transform examples.

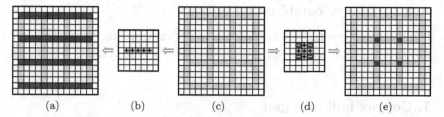

Figure A.9.   Effect of different structuring elements.

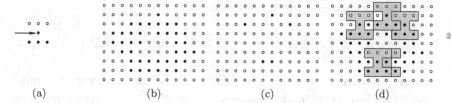

Figure A.10.   Hit-or-miss transform example.

in Figure A.9(a); if the structure element of Figure A.9(d) is used, the result obtained is shown by the dark pixel in Figure A.9(e). For the structuring elements in Figures A.9(b) and (d), "+" means that it belongs to the structuring element that is hit, "−" means that it belongs to the structuring element that is not to be hit, and the unmarked point means that it can be ignored/arbitrary.   □

Example A.9 Hit-or-miss transform example

Refer to Figure A.10, where • and ○ represent the object and background pixels, respectively, and the pixels that are not drawn are pixels that do not need to be considered. Let B be the structuring element shown in Figure A.10(a), and the arrow indicates the pixel corresponding to the center (origin) of the structuring element. If the object A shown in Figure A.10(b) is given, then the result of $A \Uparrow B$ is shown in Figure A.10(c). Figure A.10(d) gives a further explanation. The object pixel remaining in the result of $A \Uparrow B$ corresponds to the pixel in A whose neighborhood corresponds to the structuring element B.   □

A.3.2   Binary combination operation

Combination operations combine basic operations to complete some meaningful operations or realize some specific image operation functions.

1. Convex hull of region

The **convex hull** of the region is a representation of the region (see Section 9.5). Given a set A, a simple morphological algorithm can be used to get its convex hull $H(A)$. Let B_i, $i = 1, 2, 3, 4$, represent four structuring elements; first, construct

$$X_i^k = \left(X_i^{k-1} \Uparrow B_i \right) \cup A \quad i = 1, 2, 3, 4 \quad \text{and} \quad k = 1, 2, \ldots, \quad \text{(A.24)}$$

where $X_0^i = A$. Now, let $D_i = X_i^{\text{conv}}$, where the superscript "conv" means convergence in the sense of $X_i^k = X_i^{k-1}$. According to these definitions, the convex hull of A can be represented as

$$H(A) = \bigcup_{i=1}^{4} D_i. \quad \text{(A.25)}$$

In other words, the process of constructing the convex hull is as follows: first, use B_1 to iteratively perform the hit-or-miss transform on A, and when there is no further change, combine the obtained result with A and record the result as D_1; then, use B_2 to repeat iteration and union and record the result as D_2; if this process is carried out again with B_3 and B_4, then D_3 and D_4 are obtained; finally, the four results D_1, D_2, D_3, D_4 are combined to obtain the convex hull of A.

Example A.10 Convex hull construction example

Figure A.11 shows an example of constructing a convex hull. Figure A.11(a) shows the four structuring elements used. The origin of each structuring element is at its center. "×" means that its value can be arbitrary. Figure A.11(b) shows the set A whose convex hull needs to be constructed. Figure A.11(c) is the result of four iterations using Equation (A.24) starting from $X_1^0 = A$. Figures A.11(d) to (f) are the results obtained from $X_2^0 = A$, $X_3^0 = A$, and $X_4^0 = A$

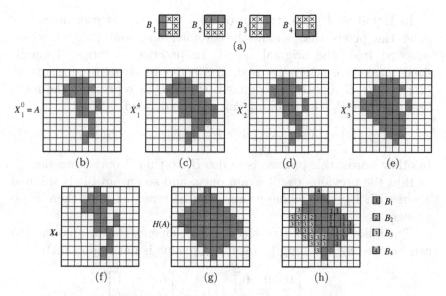

Figure A.11. Convex hull construction example.

by using Equation (A.24) for two, eight, and two iterations, respectively. Finally, according to Equation (A.25), the above four results are combined to obtain the convex hull shown in Figure A.11(g). Figure A.11(h) uses numbers (of structuring elements) to indicate the contribution of each structuring element to the construction of the convex hull. □

2. Thinning

In some applications (such as computing a skeleton), it is desirable to erode the object region but not to split it into multiple sub-regions (that is, the remaining object region is still a connected region). It is necessary to detect some pixels located at the boundary of the object region first, if they are removed without splitting the region into multiple sub-regions, then they can be removed. This work can be done by **thinning** operations. Use the structuring element B to thin the set A and mark it as $A \otimes B$, and $A \otimes B$ can be defined as follows with the help of the hit-or-miss transform:

$$A \otimes B = A - (A \Uparrow B) = A \cap (A \Uparrow B)^c. \qquad (A.26)$$

In Equation (A.26), the hit-or-miss transform is used to determine the pixels that should be thinned out, and then they are removed from the original set A. In practice, a series of small-sized masks are generally used. If a series of structuring elements $\{B\} = \{B_1, B_2, \ldots, B_n\}$ is defined, where B_{i+1} represents the rotation result of B_i, the thinning can also be defined as

$$A \otimes \{B\} = A - ((\cdots((A \otimes B_1) \otimes B_2)\cdots) \otimes B_n). \qquad \text{(A.27)}$$

In other words, this process is to use B_1 to thin A once, then use B_2 to thin the previous result again once, and so on until it is thinned again with B_n. The whole process can be repeated until there is no change.

The following set of four structuring elements (hit-or-miss masks) can be used for thinning (x means the value is not important):

$$B_1 = \begin{bmatrix} 0 & 0 & 0 \\ x & 1 & x \\ 1 & 1 & 1 \end{bmatrix} \quad B_2 = \begin{bmatrix} 0 & x & 1 \\ 0 & 1 & 1 \\ 0 & x & 1 \end{bmatrix}$$

$$B_3 = \begin{bmatrix} 1 & 1 & 1 \\ x & 1 & x \\ 0 & 0 & 0 \end{bmatrix} \quad B_4 = \begin{bmatrix} 1 & x & 0 \\ 1 & 1 & 0 \\ 1 & x & 0 \end{bmatrix}. \qquad \text{(A.28)}$$

Example A.11 Thinning example

Figure A.12 shows a set of structuring elements and a thinning example. Figure A.12(a) is a group of structuring elements commonly used for thinning. The origin of each element is at its center. "$\times$" means that the value of the pixel can be any value. White and gray pixels take value zero and value one, respectively. If the points detected by structuring element B_1 are subtracted from the object, the object will be thinned from the upper part, if the points detected by structuring element B_2 from the object, the object will be thinned from the upper-right corner, and so on. On using the above set of structuring elements, we get symmetrical results. In addition, the odd-numbered four structuring elements have a strong thinning ability, while the even-numbered four structuring elements have a weaker thinning ability.

Figure A.12(b) shows the original set to be thinned, with its origin at the upper-left corner. Figures A.12(c) to (k) show the

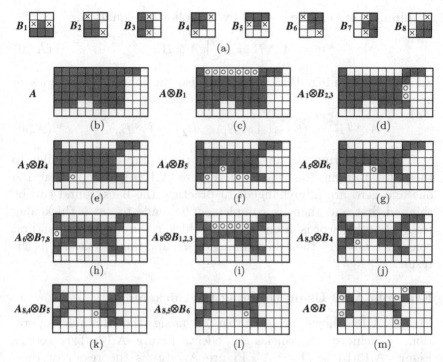

Figure A.12.   Thinning example.

results of using each structuring element for thinning in turn (circles mark the pixels thinned out in the current step). The convergence result obtained after the second thinning round with B_6 is shown in Figure A.12(l), and the result of converting the thinning result into mixed connectivity to eliminate the multi-path connectivity problem in Figure A.12(l) is shown in Figure A.12(m). In many applications (such as obtaining a skeleton), the object needs to be eroded but not broken down into several parts. To this end, it is necessary to first detect some points on the object contour, and after removing these points, the object should not be divided into two parts. Using the hit-or-miss masks above can satisfy this condition. □

3. Thickening

Using the structuring element B to thicken the set A is denoted as $A \otimes B$. From a morphological point of view, **thickening** corresponds to thinning and can be defined by the following equation:

$$A \otimes B = A \bigcup (A \Uparrow B). \tag{A.29}$$

Similar to thinning, thickening can also be defined by a series of operations

$$A \otimes \{B\} = ((\cdots ((A \otimes B_1) \otimes B_2) \cdots) \otimes B_n). \tag{A.30}$$

The structuring elements used for thickening can be similar to those for thinning, as shown in Figure A.12(a), except that the one and zero are interchanged. In practice, the background can be thinned first and then its complement is made to get a thickening result. In other words, if one wants to thicken the set A, one can first construct $D = A^c$, then do thinning on D, and finally take D^c as the result.

Example A.12 Using thinning for thickening

Figure A.13 shows an example of using the thinning operation to achieve the thickening effect. Figure A.13(a) is set A, Figure A.13(b) is $D = A^c$, Figure A.13(c) is the result of thinning D, and Figure A.13(d) is the D^c obtained by making the complement of Figure A.13(c). Finally, after thickening, a simple post-processing is performed to remove the disconnected points to obtain Figure A.13(e).   □

4. Pruning

Pruning is an important supplement to thinning and skeleton extraction operations, or it is often used as a post-processing means for thinning and skeleton extraction. Because thinning and skeleton extraction often leave redundant parasitic components, some post-processing means are needed to remove them. For example, post-processing methods, such as pruning, are needed to eliminate them.

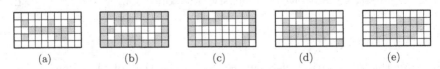

Figure A.13.   Using thinning for thickening.

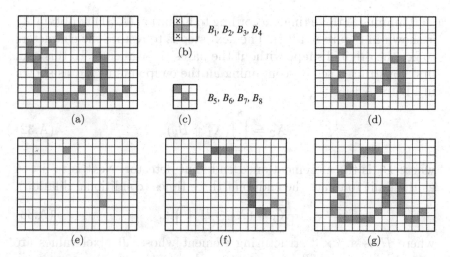

Figure A.14. Pruning example.

Pruning can be achieved by combining the aforementioned methods. In order to explain the pruning process, consider the method used in automatic recognition of handwritten characters, where the shape of the skeleton of the character is generally to be analyzed. The characteristic of these skeletons is that they contain parasitic segments due to the unevenness in the erosion of character strokes.

Figure A.14(a) shows the skeleton of a handwritten character "a". The parasitic segment at the left end of the character is a typical example of parasitic components. To solve this problem, its endpoints can be eliminated continuously. Of course, this process will also shorten or eliminate other segments in the character. It is assumed here that the length of the parasitic segment does not exceed three pixels, so only segments whose length does not exceed three pixels can be eliminated. For a set A, thinning A with a series of structuring elements that can detect endpoints can get the desired result. Let

$$X_1 = A \otimes \{B\}, \tag{A.31}$$

where $\{B\}$ represents the series of structuring elements used for thinning, as shown in Figures A.14(b) and (c). There are two structures in this series, and each series can get four structuring elements by rotation, so there are eight structuring elements in total.

Thinning A three times according to Equation (A.31) to obtain X_1 is shown in Figure A.14(d). The next step is to restore the characters to get the original shape without the parasitic segments. To this end, first construct a set X_2 containing all the endpoints in X_1, as shown in Figure A.14(e):

$$X_2 = \bigcup_{k=1}^{8} (X_1 \Uparrow B_k), \qquad (A.32)$$

where B_k is the aforementioned endpoint detector. Next is to use A as the limit to dilate the endpoint three times (conditional dilation):

$$X_3 = (X_2 \oplus H) \bigcap A, \qquad (A.33)$$

where H is a 3×3 structuring element whose all pixel values are one. As in region filling or connected component extraction, such conditional dilation can prevent the production of elements with a pixel value of one outside the region of interest (as shown in Figure A.14(f)). Finally, the union of X_1 and X_3 can provide the final pruning result, as shown in Figure A.14(g):

$$X_4 = X_1 \bigcup X_3. \qquad (A.34)$$

The above pruning involves iteratively using a group of structuring elements for eliminating noise pixels. The general algorithm only recycles this group of structuring elements once or twice, otherwise it may cause undesired changes to the object region.

A.4   Practical Algorithm of Binary Morphology

Using the various basic operations and combination operations of binary mathematical morphology introduced previously, a series of practical algorithms of binary mathematical morphology can be formed to solve practical image processing and analysis problems. Several algorithms are specifically introduced below.

A.4.1   Noise elimination

There are often some small holes or islands in the binary image after segmentation. These small holes or islands are generally caused by system noise, threshold selection, or preprocessing. Salt-and-pepper noise is a typical type, causing small holes or islands in the binary image. Combining the opening operation and closing operation can form a morphological noise filter to eliminate this type of noise. For example, opening the image with a structuring element composed of a central pixel and its 4-neighbor pixels can eliminate pepper noise and closing the image with a similar structuring element can eliminate salt noise.

Figure A.15 shows an example of noise elimination. Figure A.15(a) includes a rectangular object A. Due to the influence of noise, there are some noise holes inside the object and some noise blocks around the object. Now, the structuring element B shown in Figure A.15(b) is used to filter out noise through morphological operations. Here, the structuring element should be larger in size than all noise holes and noise blocks. First, the structuring element B is used to erode A to obtain Figure A.15(c), and then B is used to dilate the erosion result to obtain Figure A.15(d). The serial combination of these two operations is the opening operation, which eliminates the noise block around the object. Now, B is used to dilate Figure A.15(d) to obtain Figure A.15(e), and then B is used to erode the dilation result to obtain Figure A.15(f). The serial combination of these two operations is the closing operation, which eliminates the noise hole inside the object. The whole process is opening first and then closing, which can be written as

$$\{[(A \ominus B) \oplus B] \oplus B\} \oplus B = (A \circ B) \bullet B. \qquad (A.35)$$

Through the comparison of Figures A.15(a) and (f), it can be seen that the noises inside and outside the object region have been all eliminated and the object itself has not changed much except that the original four right corners have become rounded corners.

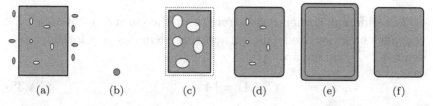

(a)   (b)   (c)   (d)   (e)   (f)

Figure A.15. Example of noise elimination.

A.4.2   Corner detection

A **corner point** on a contour is a pixel with a sudden change in slope, that is, a position with a large absolute **curvature**. The corner points can be extracted with the help of morphological operations. First, select a round structuring element of appropriate size, use this structuring element for opening, and subtract the result from the original image. Choose two more structuring elements: one is smaller than the opened region and the other is larger than the opened region. Use these two structuring elements to erode the remaining opened region and compare the two results obtained. This is equivalent to a band-pass filter for shape. The size of the structuring element needs to be selected according to the angle of the corner point because the area of the opened residual region changes with the angle of the corner point. On decreasing the angle, the area of the opened region increases, and the area covered by the structuring elements also increases. Therefore, first use the structuring element with the largest area for detection. If there is no result, gradually reduce the area of the structuring element until the corner point is detected, and at the same time, the angle information can be obtained.

Corner points can also be detected by asymmetric closing. **Asymmetric closing** involves dilating the image with one structuring element and then eroding the image with another structuring element. The idea is to make dilation and erosion complementary. One way is to use two structuring elements, the cross "+" and the diamond "$\Diamond$". The following equation represents the asymmetric closing operation on image A:

$$A^c_{+\Diamond} = (A \oplus +) \ominus \Diamond. \tag{A.36}$$

The corner strength is

$$C_+(A) = |A - A^c_{+\Diamond}|. \tag{A.37}$$

For different corners, the strength of the corners rotated by 45° can also be calculated (the structuring elements are forked/cross-shaped "$\times$" and square "$\square$"):

$$C_\times(A) = |A - A^c_{\times\square}|. \tag{A.38}$$

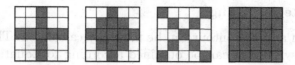

Figure A.16.　Four structuring elements: $+$, $\Diamond$, $\times$ and $\Box$ in turn.

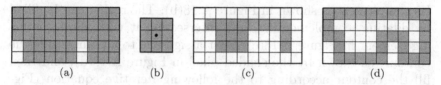

Figure A.17.　Example of contour extraction.

Combining the above four structuring elements, as shown in Figure A.16, the corner detection process can be written as

$$C_{+\times}(A) = |A^c_{+\Diamond} - A^c_{\times\Box}|. \qquad (A.39)$$

A.4.3 Contour extraction

There is a set A, and its contour is denoted as $\beta(A)$. The **contour** can be extracted by first eroding A with a structuring element B, and then the difference between A and the erosion result is obtained, that is:

$$\beta(A) = A - (A \ominus B). \qquad (A.40)$$

Figure A.17 shows an example, where Figure A.17(a) shows a binary object A in an image, Figure A.17(b) shows a structuring element B, Figure A.17(c) shows the result of eroding A with B, that is $A \ominus B$, and Figure A.17(d) shows the final contour $\beta(A)$ obtained by subtracting Figure A.17(c) from Figure A.17(a). Note that when the origin of B is at the boundary of A, a part of B will be outside of A. Here, it is generally set to zero outside of A. Also, note that the structuring elements here are 8-connected and the resulting contour is 4-connected.

A.4.4   Region filling

The region and its contour can be mutually calculated. The contour of the known region can be obtained according to Equation (A.40). Conversely, the region can also be obtained by filling the known contour. Figure A.18 shows an example of **region filling**, where Figure A.18(a) shows a set A of the contour points of the region. Its complement is shown in Figure A.18(b). The region can be filled by dilating, complementing, and intersecting it with the structuring element in Figure A.18(c). First assign one to a point inside the contour, as shown by the shaded pixel in Figure A.18(d), and then fill the contour according to the following iterative equation (Figures A.18(e) and (f) give two of the situations in two intermediate steps):

$$X_k = (X_{k-1} \oplus B) \cap A^c \quad k = 1, 2, 3, \ldots . \qquad (A.41)$$

Stop the iteration when $X_k = X_{k-1}$ ($k = 7$ in this example, see Figure A.18(g)). Here, the intersection of X_k and A includes the interior of the filled region and its contour, see Figure A.18(h). The dilation process in Equation (A.41) will exceed the contour if it is not controlled, but the intersection of each step with A^c restricts it inside the region of interest. This dilation process can be called a conditional dilation process. Note that the structuring element here is 4-connected, while the original contour to be filled is 8-connected.

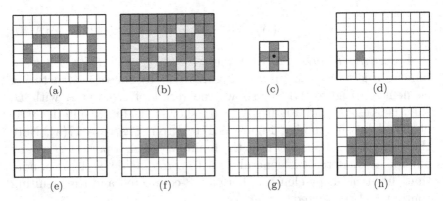

Figure A.18.   Example of region filling.

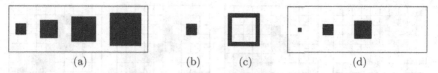

Figure A.19. Using the hit-or-miss transform to detect the square regions.

A.4.5   Object detection and positioning

To explain how to use the hit-or-miss transform to determine the location of a square region of a given size, see Figure A.19, which is an example of **object detection and localization**. Figure A.19(a) shows a set of original images, including four solid squares of 3×3, 5×5, 7×7, and 9×9, respectively. The 3×3 solid square E in Figure A.19(b) and the 9×9 square frame F (the side width of pixel is one) in Figure A.19(c) are combined to form the structuring element $B = (E, F)$. In this example, the hit-or-miss transform is designed to hit the region covering E and missing the region covering F. The final result is shown in Figure A.19(d), which is equivalent to the detection of three eligible objects (determined by the structuring elements of the hit-or-miss transform).

A.4.6   Extraction of connected components

Let Y represent a **connected component** in the set A, and let a point in Y be already known, then the following iterative expression can be used to get all the elements of Y:

$$X_k = (X_{k-1} \oplus B)IA \quad k = 1, 2, 3, \ldots. \tag{A.42}$$

Stop the iteration when $X_k = X_{k-1}$, and then $Y = X_k$ can be taken.

Equation (A.42) is exactly the same as Equation (A.41) except that A is used instead of A^c. Because the element to be extracted here has been marked as one, the intersection with A in each iteration can remove the dilation centered on the element marked with zero. Figure A.20 shows an example of connected component extraction. The structuring elements used here are the same as that in Figure A.17(b). The value of the lightly shaded pixels (that is, the connected component) in Figure A.20(a) are one, but it has not been

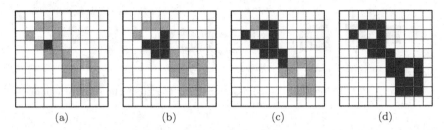

Figure A.20.   Example of extraction of connected components.

discovered by the algorithm at this time. The value of the dark-shaded pixel in Figure A.20(a) is one, and it is considered to be a known point in Y and used as the starting point of the algorithm. Figures A.20(b) and (c) show the results of the first and second iterations, respectively, and Figure A.20(d) shows the final extraction results.

A.4.7   Regional skeleton extraction

In Section 9.6, the skeleton concept and a method of calculating skeletons are introduced. Here is a technique for calculating the **skeleton** using mathematical morphology. Let $S(A)$ represent the skeleton of A, which can be expressed as

$$S(A) = \bigcup_{k=0}^{K} S_k(A). \tag{A.43}$$

$S_k(A)$ in the above equation is generally called the skeleton subset, which can be written as

$$S_k(A) = (A \ominus kB) - [(A \ominus kB) \circ B], \tag{A.44}$$

where B is a structuring element and $(A \ominus kB)$ represents the erosion of A with B for k consecutive times, which can be expressed by T_k, namely

$$T_k = (A \ominus kB) = ((\cdots (A \ominus B) \ominus B) \ominus \cdots) \ominus B. \tag{A.45}$$

K in Equation (A.43) represents the number of the last iteration before A is eroded into an empty set, namely

$$K = \max\{k | (A \ominus kB) \neq \varnothing\}. \tag{A.46}$$

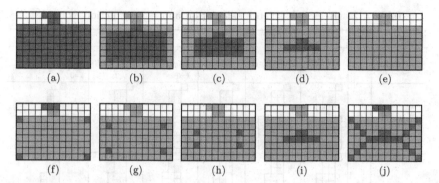

Figure A.21. Example of morphological skeleton.

Example A.13 Morphological skeleton calculation example

In Figure A.21, Figure A.21(a) is the original image (T_0 that has not been eroded), which contains a rectangular object with a small appendage above it. Figures A.21(b) to (e) respectively show the set T_k obtained by successive erosions, namely T_1, T_2, T_3, T_4. Because $T_4 = \varnothing$, $K = 3$. Figures A.21(f) to (i) show the calculated skeleton set S_k, namely S_0, S_1, S_2, S_3. Figure A.21(j) shows the final skeleton S (including two connected parts). □

Equation (A.43) shows that the skeleton of A can be obtained by the union of the skeleton subset $Sk(A)$. Conversely, A can also be reconstructed with $Sk(A)$:

$$A = \bigcup_{k=0}^{K} [S_k(A) \oplus kB], \qquad (A.47)$$

where B is the structuring element and $(S_k(A) \oplus kB)$ represents the dilation of $S_k(A)$ with B for k consecutive times, namely

$$[S_k(A) \oplus kB] = ((\cdots (S_k(A) \oplus B) \oplus B) \oplus \cdots) \oplus B. \qquad (A.48)$$

Table A.2 gives an example of **regional skeleton extraction** and reconstruction, where the structuring element B used is the same as in Figure A.17. The first column in the table gives the number of iterations k. In the second column, the "first row" is the original region set, and the "second row" and "third row" are the results of using B to erode A once and twice, respectively. If A is eroded one more time, an empty set will be produced, so here $K = 2$. The third

Table A.2.   Regional skeleton calculation and reconstruction example.

Column	1	2	3	4	5	6	7
Calculation		$A \ominus kB$	$(A \ominus kB) \circ B$	$S_k(A)$	$\bigcup\limits_{k=0}^{K} S_k(A)$	$S_k(A) \oplus kB$	$\bigcup\limits_{k=0}^{K} [S_k(A) \oplus kB]$
First row	$k=0$						
Second row	$k=1$						
Third row	$k=2$						

column in the table is the result of opening the corresponding set in the second column with B. The fourth column gives the difference set obtained by subtracting the corresponding set in the third column from the set in the second column. The above two sets in the fifth column are both partial skeletons (a subset of skeletons), and the bottom set is the finally obtained regional skeleton. Note that this final skeleton is not only thicker than needed but also disconnected. This is because the previous derivation process only considered the erosion and opening of the set and did not deliberately ensure the connectivity of the skeleton.

Each set in sixth column of Table A.2 gives the result of dilating the corresponding set in fourth column by k times (i.e., $S_0(A)$, $S_1(A) \oplus B$, $[S_2(A) \oplus 2B] = [S_2(A) \oplus B] \oplus B$). Finally, the seventh column gives the results of reconstruction of A. According to Equation (A.43), these results are obtained by the union of the dilated skeleton subsets in the sixth column.

Example A.14 Actual example of morphological skeleton calculation

Figure A.22 shows the actual example results of calculating the skeleton using the above mathematical morphology method.

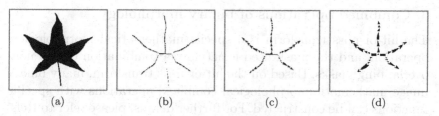

Figure A.22. Actual example of morphological skeleton calculation.

Figure A.22(a) is a binary image; Figure A.22(b) is the skeleton obtained by using the 3 × 3 structuring element in Figure A.17; Figure A.22(c) is the skeleton obtained by using a similar 5 × 5 structuring element; Figure A.22(d) is the skeleton obtained by using a similar 7 × 7 structuring element. Note that in Figures A.22(c) and (d), the petiole is not retained due to the larger mask (can be compared with the skeleton calculated by the binary object region skeleton algorithm in Example 9.11). □

A.5 Key Points and References for Each Section

The following indicates the key points of each section and provides some targeted guidance for further references.

1. Basic set definition

Mathematical morphology is a mathematical tool for processing and analyzing images based on morphology; see Ref. [1]. On the definition and operation of sets, one can see more detailed introductions in related books or various mathematics manuals, such as Ref. [2].

2. Basic operations of binary morphology

The four basic operations of dilation, erosion, opening, and closing are the basis of mathematical morphology. More introductions to basic operations can also be found in Refs. [1,3,4]. The structuring elements used here basically contain the origin. When the origin does not belong to the structuring element, the situation is somewhat special. For further discussion and examples, please refer to Ref. [5].

3. Combined operations of binary morphology

The hit-or-miss transform is a special mathematical morphological operation, and the mask used is actually a combination of two non-overlapping masks. Based on the hit-or-miss transform, many binary image mathematic morphological combined operations with specific functions can be constructed. For further details, please refer to Refs. [3,4,6]. Converting the thinning result into mixed connectivity to eliminate the multi-path connectivity problem in Figure A.12(l) can be found in Ref. [7]. The content of topology thinning in 3D images can be found in Ref. [8].

4. Practical algorithm of binary morphology

This section discusses some practical binary morphological algorithms for specific image applications. Unlike the combined operations introduced in Section A.3, these practical algorithms do not emphasize general functions but focus more on solving specific problems in practice. For example, corner points can be detected with the aid of asymmetric closing; see Ref. [9]. When eliminating salt-and-pepper noise, using a structuring element consisting of a central pixel and its 4-neighbor pixels for opening the image can eliminate pepper noise and the same for closing the image can eliminate salt noise; see Ref. [10]. Figure A.19 explains how to use the hit-or-miss transform to determine the location of a square region of a given size; see also Ref. [10]. With the widespread application of mathematical morphology, many algorithms have been proposed to solve practical image application problems. For example, a method for detecting news headlines based on morphological operations can be found in Ref. [11].

References

[1] Serra, J. *Image Analysis and Mathematical Morphology [M]*. USA, Salt Lake City: Academic Press, 1982.

[2] Compilation Committee of Encyclopedia of Mathematics. *Encyclopedia of Mathematics*. China, Beijing: Science Press, 2000.

[3] Russ, J. C. and Neal, F. B. *The Image Processing Handbook*, 7th Edn. UK, London: CRC Press, 2016.

[4] Gonzalez, R. C. and Woods, R. E. *Digital Image Processing*, 4th Edn. UK, London: Prentice Hall, 2018.

[5] Zhang, Y.-J. *Image Engineering (II) Image Analysis*, 4th Edn. China, Beijing: Tsinghua University Press, 2018.

[6] Mahdavieh, Y. and Gonzalez, R. C. *Advances in Image Analysis*. USA, Bellingham: DPIE Optical Engineering Press, 1992.

[7] Zhang, Y.-J. *Image Engineering (I) Image Processing*, 4th Edn. China, Beijing: Tsinghua University Press, 2018.

[8] Nikolaidis, N. and Pitas, I. *3-D Image Processing Algorithms*. USA, New Jersey: John Wiley & Sons, Inc., 2001.

[9] Shih, F. Y. *Image Processing and Pattern Recognition — Fundamentals and Techniques*. USA, New Jersey: IEEE Press, 2010.

[10] Ritter, G. X. and Wilson. J. N. *Handbook of Computer Vision Algorithms in Image Algebra*. UK, London: CRC Press, 2001.

[11] Jiang, F. and Zhang, Y.-J. A caption detection algorithm based on morphological operation. *Journal of Electronic and Information Technology*, 2003, 25(12): 1647–1652.

Appendix B

Visual Constancy

Visual constancy means that the physical characteristics (size, brightness, color, texture, shape, space, motion) of objective targets may be changed in the environment, but the **human vision system**'s intuitive experience of the properties of these targets maintains (does not change) its inherent characteristics.

In a broader sense, visual constancy is a type of perceptual constancy. Perceptual constancy, also called subjective constancy, means that when objective conditions change within a certain range, our perception impression maintains its stability to a considerable extent. It is an important characteristic of people's perception of objective things, and it has many applications in practice.

B.1   Visual Constancy Theory

Constancy here means that although some characteristics in the objective world have changed, the human cognitive system can still overcome these changes and maintain the original knowledge and understanding of objective things.

B.1.1   Various constancy

People describe objective things from multiple dimensions, so constancy also has multiple dimensions. Taking visual constancy as an example, there can be size constancy, brightness constancy, color constancy, shape constancy, motion constancy, etc.

1. *Size constancy*

Size constancy is very common in daily life. For example, consider that when a person observes two adults from different distances, although the image of the closer person on the retina will be larger than the image of the far person on the retina, the final result of the human perception will be that the heights of the two persons are relatively close to each other. For another example, when a person observes a child who is closer and an adult who is farther away, although the image formed by the child on the retina may be larger than the image formed by the adult on the retina, the final perception is that adults are still taller than children. This is the manifestation of the size constancy of the human visual system.

The following further discusses the sensory relationship between object size and distance during observation. The actual size (physical size) of the objects in the scene and the visual size on the retina (the size calculated by the viewing angle) are often different, and the visual size is often different from the size that people ultimately perceive. The study of the relationship between these three sizes is called the study of the constancy of size perception. The constancy of size perception refers to the fact that people can more accurately perceive the physical size of objects at different distances, and it does not completely change due to changes in the viewing angle. In practice, the perception size is not always exactly the same as the physical size of the object. The general situation is that the perception size is between the visual size and the physical size indicated by the perceptual constancy law and is more biased toward the latter. This is because people generally perceive an object in a relatively familiar environment, and other familiar objects in the scene have a prompting effect on the distance and actual size of the object.

Example B.1 Examples of perception size, viewing angle size, and constancy size

Move a 4-m-long object (physical size) in front of the eyes from 1 m to 4 m, and its length should become 1 m based on the viewing angle calculation at the new distance, but in reality the observer feels that its length is still more than 3 m.

The degree of constancy of size perception can be represented by quantity. The method is to use the ratio to calculate the value of perception size and the deviation from the viewing angle. The following two ratios are commonly used:

(1) R_B, named after the proposer Brunswik: It is often used in size perception and is defined as

$$R_B = \frac{R - S}{C - S},$$ (B.1)

where R is the perception size, S is the size calculated according to the viewing angle, and C is the physical size. If $R_B = 0$, the perception size is equal to the size calculated according to the viewing angle, and there is no constancy. If $R_B = 1$, the perception size is equal to the physical size, which has complete constancy.

(2) R_T, named after the proposer Thouless: It is often used in brightness perception because physical brightness and perceived brightness have a certain logarithmic relationship, which is defined as

$$R_T = \frac{\log R - \log S}{\log C - \log S}.$$ (B.2)

In addition to size constancy, common constancy also includes intensity/brightness constancy (the observed brightness of a scene changes with time is a constant), color constancy (no matter how the light used to illuminate the object changes, people can always recognize the color of the object itself), geometric/shape constancy (for example, an object will have a different appearance when viewed from different angles, but people can still recognize it correctly), motion constancy (observing moving objects at different distances can give its moving speed similar judgment results), and so on. Among them, intensity/brightness constancy and color constancy can also be called spectral constancy. In summary, these constancies indicate that perception remains stable despite changes in an observer's feeling.

2. Color constancy

Among various constancies, **color constancy** has received more attention. First of all, it is very common that the human visual system can maintain color constancy for a wide range of object surfaces and lighting conditions and can correctly perceive the color of the scene in different seasons (such as summer or winter) and time periods (such as dawn or dusk). Second, it has many applications. Obtaining color constancy descriptions from images is not only important for digital photography but also critical for many computer vision, color-based automatic object recognition and color image processing. For example, it can be used to detect and see information from space photography or to show structures that are difficult to see through X-rays in the medical field. Finally, research on it is still in progress. Although there are many color theories (such as three-color theory and opposite theory), they are mostly limited to describing the relationship between color stimulus values and color perception. Since the relationship between the color observed by people and the wavelength and brightness of light is not completely in correspondence, color vision is not only derived from external physical stimuli but not completely determined by the properties of external physical stimuli, so these color theories are still difficult to explain color constancy phenomenon. For this reason, many different color constancy theories/models have been proposed. At present, the more representative ones include retinex (retina + cortex) theory, bilinear model, color gamut mapping theory, color coefficient law, spectrum sharpening theory, and neural network model.

B.1.2   Retinex theory

The retinex is a new, hybrid word composed of two words (retina and cortex). The word has a history of more than half a century. It emphasizes that both eyes and brain play a role in human visual processing. The **retinex theory** is based on the two elements of the retina and the cortex to explain some human visual characteristics. This theory can explain the human visual system's perception of scenes and/or the formation of images. Its basic idea is that the light of a certain point perceived by the human eye not only depends on the absolute light value reflected by the point but also is related to the light value reflected around the point (the simultaneous contrast and Mach band effect introduced in Section 1.1 are two examples). The theory has been put forward for about half a century.

When discussing the perception of the human visual system under ambient light of different brightness, the retinex theory points out that the brightness perception of different scenes of the human visual system here mainly depends on the reflected light of the scene and has nothing to do with the illumination light. According to this theory, the image $f(x, y)$ can be represented as

$$f(x, y) = e(x, y) \bullet r(x, y),$$ (B.3)

where $f(x, y)$ is the brightness value of the pixel at (x, y); $e(x, y)$ is the illuminance value at (x, y), which represents the brightness component of the surrounding environment lighting and has nothing to do with the scene itself; $r(x, y)$ is the value of the reflection function at (x, y), which represents the ability of the scene to reflect light and has nothing to do with lighting. In this way, the theory gives a mathematical model for imaging. If the reflection function can be estimated correctly, it can provide a representation that does not change with the illuminance for any given image.

Take the logarithm of both sides of Equation (B.3):

$$\lg[f(x, y)] = \lg[e(x, y)] + \lg[r(x, y)].$$ (B.4)

If $R(x, y) = \lg[r(x, y)]$, then

$$R(x, y) = \lg[f(x, y)] - \lg[e(x, y)].$$ (B.5)

Because $e(x, y) = f(x, y)/r(x, y)$, Equation (B.5) can also be written as

$$R(x, y) = \lg[f(x, y)] - \lg[C(x, y) \otimes f(x, y)],$$ (B.6)

where $C(x, y)$ represents a function related to the pixel with coordinates (x, y), also called the **center-surround** function.

According to the existing color theory, color is the combined result of the brightness of the three channels. In terms of color perception, the retinex theory says that the surface color that people perceive is closely related to the reflectance of the object surface. The color change effect caused by lighting is normally gentle, often manifested as a smooth lighting gradient, while the color change effect caused by the change of surface shape is usually manifested as a sudden variation. By distinguishing these two forms of change, people can distinguish between the light source change and the surface change, thereby knowing the surface color change caused by the light source change and keeping their perception of the surface color constant.

Considering that color images have three channels, when discussing color images, Equation (B.6) can be written as

$$R_k(x,y) = \lg[f_k(x,y)] - \lg[C_k(x,y) \otimes f_k(x,y)], \qquad (B.7)$$

where $k = 1, 2, 3$ correspond to the red, green, and blue channels, respectively; $R_k(x,y)$ is the output of the kth channel; $f_k(x,y)$ is the intensity value of the kth channel pixel; $C_k(x,y)$ corresponds to the center-surround function of the kth channel. If $C_k(x,y)$ can be determined, then the reflection function can be determined according to the image function. Generally, $C_k(x,y)$ is often taken as a Gaussian function. In logarithmic space, the original image is subtracted from the convolution of the Gaussian function and the original image. The physical essence is to remove the smooth part of the original image (reflecting the color constancy) and highlight the rapidly changing part of the original image. If the Gaussian function is sharper, the details in the image are more prominent; if the Gaussian function is flatter, the image tone is better maintained. In practice, the multiscale retinex algorithm is often used, which combines the advantages of using different scale Gaussian functions to convolve the original image.

Finally, it is pointed out that since the color perception of the middle part and edge part of the retina have some differences in a strict sense, so if the spectral distribution of different illumination sources are different, even if the illuminances on the scene are the same, the color perception will still be different. This also shows that color constancy is not a very strict concept. It is known from psychological experiments that the constancy of color vision will be affected by spatial depth information and scene complexity. In addition, the retinex theory assumes that the brain compares the recorded brightness of each color channel in the same scene. This has nothing to do with the spectral composition of light (and therefore independent of the relative intensity of light). The construction of the surface color of the object in the brain is the result of "comparative comparison" according to the retinex theory. The retinex theory is fundamentally different from other color perception theories because it only includes comparison without mixing or superimposition. Therefore, the retinex theory does not provide a complete description of human color constancy.

B.2 Application to Image Enhancement

The enhancement algorithm based on the retinex theory is an image enhancement method based on the spatial domain. This theory simulates the imaging principle of the human visual cortex and establishes a simplified image formation model. It can extract the color constancy of the image, compress the dynamic range of the image, improve the local contrast in image, and effectively display the details submerged in the shadow region.

There are many retinex algorithms proposed, and some effects on images can be seen at http://dragon.larc.nasa.gov/retinex/servo2/index.html. The following describes the typical basic algorithms in combination with two specific applications.

B.2.1 Foggy day image enhancement

In the images collected in foggy days with low visibility, many scene features are covered or blurred, resulting in reduced image contrast and color degradation. The commonly used contrast enhancement method does not consider the reasons for degradation, so it easily causes color distortion and amplifies noise. Considering that the color contrast is reduced in the mist, but the image details are still richer, the retinex algorithm based on the color constancy theory can be used to enhance the image, which can effectively correct color distortion.

The simplest retinex algorithm is an algorithm based on path comparison. It divides the image into three color channels of red, green, and blue (RGB), and solves the brightness relationship in each channel separately to obtain the relative brightness value. Usually, N random paths are selected and operations such as ratio computing, continuous multiplication, and averaging are used, and finally the pixel value of the processed object pixel is obtained. Suppose here that there are n pixels on the path from pixel (x_1, y_1) to pixel (x_n, y_n) and their pixel values are $f_1, f_2, \ldots, f_n$, then the brightness relationship between the starting point S and the ending point E can be expressed as

$$\frac{E}{S} = T\left(\frac{f_2}{f_1}\right) T\left(\frac{f_3}{f_2}\right) \cdots T\left(\frac{f_n}{f_{n-1}}\right). \tag{B.8}$$

The $T(x)$ in Equation (B.8) is the threshold function:

$$T(x) = \begin{cases} 1 & 1 - T \le x \le 1 + T \\ x & \text{otherwise.} \end{cases} \tag{B.9}$$

The $T(x)$ defined in this way only considers large brightness differences and ignores subtle differences. Because the human eye's perception of brightness conforms to the exponential form, in practice, the logarithm of Equation (B.8) must be taken (at the same time, the calculation is simplified):

$$\lg\left(\frac{E}{S}\right) = \lg\left[T\left(\frac{f_2}{f_1}\right)\right] + \lg\left[T\left(\frac{f_3}{f_2}\right)\right]$$

$$+ \cdots + \lg\left[T\left(\frac{f_n}{f_{n-1}}\right)\right]. \tag{B.10}$$

An improvement to the above basic algorithm is to compare multiple pixels simultaneously in space to improve efficiency. The specific sequence is to first compare the relationship between long-distance pixels, next shorten the pixel interval, then compare the relationship between short-distance pixels, and repeat. The schematic diagram when proceeding in a clockwise direction is shown in Figure B.1. In this way, the relationship between the longer-distance pixels in the last time will be inherited to the next shorter-distance pixel comparison.

Suppose the size of the input image is $M \times N$, and the maximum pixel value is Max. In specific implementation, first find the initial interval $D = 2P$, $P = \log_2[\min(M, N)] - 1$. Construct a comparison image with the same size as the input image and initialize each pixel

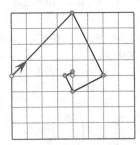

Figure B.1.   Order of distance comparison between pixels.

value to Max. Next, the pixels are compared. The comparison of pixels at the same distance can be called a comparison of the same order (P is the order). The comparison starts from the pixels with the largest distance and iterates n times in each order. First, put the horizontal pixel difference into the comparison image to see if Max needs to be updated, and then put the vertical pixel difference into the comparison image, and see again if Max needs to be updated. If the distance is one, then the final estimate is obtained. For color images, the above process is performed on three channels, and then the results are averaged.

When processing an image with insufficient light, if the three components are adjusted in the RGB space, it is possible that the relative values of the three components or the ratios between them are changed, resulting in a larger color variance between the output image and the original image. One way to solve this problem is to convert the original image from RGB space to HSI space and only enhance the intensity component while keeping the chroma components unchanged, so that both the intensity and the color information of the original image can be retained. After the luminance component is enhanced, it is transformed back to the RGB space together with the chrominance components. For the image after illumination compensation, the previous method can be used to eliminate the fog.

The algorithm based on path comparison is relatively simple, but its effect is strongly dependent on path selection. If the accuracy of brightness estimation is improved by simply increasing the number of paths, the calculation complexity will be greatly increased, and it is also difficult to determine the exact range of path length and number.

B.2.2 Infrared image enhancement

Commonly used infrared thermal images have the following characteristics:

(1) They describe the temperature distribution of the scene, they are gray-scale images, and there is no color or shadow (3D perception), so for the human eye, the resolution is low and the resolution potential is poor.

(2) Due to the thermal balance of the scene, long wavelength, long transmission distance, atmospheric attenuation, etc., they have strong spatial correlation, low contrast, and blurred visual effects.

(3) The detection capability and spatial resolution of the thermal imaging system are lower than that of the visible-light charge-coupled device (CCD) array, making the resolution of infrared images lower than that of the visible-light image.

(4) The random interference of the external environment and the imperfection of the thermal imaging system bring a variety of noises to the infrared image, such as thermal noise, shot noise, 1/f noise, photon electron and fluctuations noise. These noises with complex distribution make the signal-to-noise ratio of infrared images lower than that of ordinary TV images.

(5) The inhomogeneity of infrared images is caused by the inconsistency of the response characteristics of the detection units of the infrared detectors and the defects of the optical and mechanical scanning system. It causes the non-uniformity of the infrared image, which is reflected in the fixed pattern noise, crosstalk, and distortion of the image.

The imaging mechanism of infrared images is different from that of visible-light images. However, the imaging mechanism is analogous to visible-light imaging. The following assumptions can be made: the infrared radiation emitted by the object is the reflection of infrared light by the object under the illumination of the infrared light source, and the infrared image is formed by the infrared light reflected by the object. By analyzing and comparing the signal and histogram characteristics of the infrared image with the low-illumination visible-light image, it can be seen that the characteristics of the two are the same. Therefore, the retinex algorithm can be used to process infrared images as gray-scale images.

The retinex algorithm with the center-surround function is generally used to calculate the reflection component. This is inspired by the homocentric opponent receptive field of concentric circles (consisting of a central mechanism with a strong excitatory effect and an inhibitory peripheral mechanism with a weaker effect but larger area) in the study of human vision. According to the relationships that the intensity of a spherical wave (light wave) propagating in the air is proportional to the square of the amplitude and the amplitude is inversely proportional to the distance between the field point and the source point, the center-surround function $C(x, y) = 1/(x^2 + y^2)$ can be used. Now, the form of Gaussian function is often taken, that is, $C(x, y) = C(x, y, \sigma) = k \bullet \exp[-(x^2 + y^2)/\sigma^2]$, where k is the normalization constant. It indicates that the closer the point to the center pixel, the greater the influence on it, and the weight distribution of the influence degree is Gaussian.

In the center-surround retinex algorithm, the output value of the pixel is only determined by the pixels in the center-surround mask. Here, the mask size is a key parameter. If the mask is too large, the enhancement effect will not be obvious and the efficiency of the entire algorithm will be affected, so the algorithm cannot take into account the entire image. If the mask is too small, the local enhancement effect is better, but the overall effect and the color fidelity are poor, and there will be the phenomenon of "halo artifacts" at the same time. Further research work is still in progress.

B.3 Key Points and References for Each Section

The following indicates the key points of each section and provides some targeted guidance for further references.

1. Visual constancy theory

More discussion on the measurement ratio of size perception constancy can be found in Ref. [1]. For the discussion of the color constancy theory/model, please refer to Ref. [2]. The source of the nouns of retinex and the historical research of retinex theory can be found in Refs. [3,4]. More discussions on the image brightness imaging model of Equation (B.3) can be found in Ref. [5].

2. Application to image enhancement

More detailed discussions on foggy image processing (including enhancement and restoration methods) can be found in Ref. [5]. For the content of color space conversion and color enhancement, please refer to Chapter 6.

References

[1] Hao, B. Y., Zhang, H. C., and Chen, S. Y. *Experimental Psychology.* China, Beijing: Beijing University Press, 1983.

[2] Agarwal, V., Abidi. B. R., Koschan, A., *et al.* An overview of color constancy algorithms. *Journal of Pattern Recognition Research,* 2006, 1(1): 42–54.

[3] Land, E. H. The Retinex. *American Scientist,* 1964, 52(2): 247–264.

[4] Land, E. H. and McCann, J. J. Lightness and the Retinex theory. *Journal of the Optical Society of America,* 1971, 61(3): 1–11.

[5] Zhang, Y.-J. *Image Engineering (I) Image Processing,* 4th Edn. China, Beijing: Tsinghua University Press, 2018.

Answers to Self-Test Questions

Some answers have explanations.

Chapter 1 Computer Vision Fundamentals

1.1 Vision Basis

1.1.1   (A); (C).

1.1.2   (B). Other options are not directly related to different spatial locations in the image.

1.1.3   (C).

1.2 Vision and Image

1.2.1   (D).

1.2.2   (A); (B); (D).

1.2.3   (A); (B); (D).

1.2.4   (B).

1.2.5   (A); (C); (D).

1.2.6   (A), no compression.

1.2.7   (B); (C).

1.2.8   (B).

1.2.9   (C).

1.2.10 (C).

1.3 Vision Systems and Image Techniques

1.3.1 (A); (C). Image segmentation output is the object, and image matching output is the relation.

1.3.2 (B); (D). Image synthesis input is data, and image enhancement output is still image.

1.3.3 (B).

1.4 Overview of the Structure and Content of This Book

1.4.1 (C); (D).

1.4.2 (B).

1.4.3 (A); (C).

Chapter 2 2D Image Acquisition

2.1 Acquisition Device and Performance Index

2.1.1 (B); (C).

2.1.2 (B).

2.1.3 (A); (C).

2.2 Image Brightness Imaging Model

2.2.1 (B); (C).

2.2.2 (A); (D).

2.2.3 (C).

2.3 Image Space Imaging Model

2.3.1 (A).

2.3.2 (C); (D).

2.3.3 (B).

2.3.4 (D).

2.4 Sampling and Quantization

2.4.1 (C).

2.4.2 (C), the gray level in the smooth region should change slowly, but a step will occur when the image has not enough gray levels.

2.4.3 (D).

2.4.4   (B).
2.4.5   (A); (B).

2.5 Relationship between Pixels

2.5.1   (A); (D).
2.5.2   (B).
2.5.3   (B); (D).

Chapter 3 Spatial Domain Image Enhancement

3.1 Operation Between Images

3.1.1   (C), suppose the number of images participating in image averaging is M. After image averaging is used, the mean square error of the new image is $\sqrt{1/M}$ times the mean square error of the noise image; here, $\sqrt{1/M} = 1/10$, that is, $M = 100$, so the acquisition time $= 100/25 = 4\,\mathrm{s}$.
3.1.2   (B); (C).
3.1.3   (D).

3.2 Image Gray-scale Mapping

3.2.1   (B), low gray level will be mapped to higher gray level.
3.2.2   (C), the gray value ranges before and after the transformation are the same, but most of the gray values before the transformation are mapped to a smaller gray value range after the transformation. If only the smaller gray value range after the transformation is used for display, the original large-scale gray values are displayed in the smaller dynamic range.
3.2.3   (B); (D).

3.3 Histogram Equalization

3.3.1   (C), using the envelope curve of cumulative histogram for gray-scale transformation, that is, histogram equalization, will enhance the overall contrast of the image.
3.3.2   (B); (B), the image equalized by the histogram will not change after equalization by the same method.
3.3.3   (B); (C).

3.4 Histogram Specification

3.4.1   (D), it can increase the numbers of low gray-value pixels and high gray-value pixels at the same time, making the image appear more black and white.

3.4.2   (B). Since $I(0) = 0$, then 0 corresponds to 3; $I(1) = 3$, then 1~3 correspond to 5; $I(2) = 7$, then 4~7 correspond to 7.

3.4.3   (C), obtained from the discussion of SML and GML.

3.5 Spatial Domain Convolution Enhancement

3.5.1   (C); (D). Note that the value of the mask coefficient has a great influence on the neighborhood operation and its results.

3.5.2   (B). Using the neighborhood average can eliminate noise but also blur the details. The larger the mask, the more obvious the blur. Using median filtering or adding a thresholding can eliminate isolated noise points and reduce blur.

3.5.3   (C); (D).

3.5.4   (B); (D).

3.5.5   (C). The cross-shaped mask takes into account both directions, and the size is small, so the error is small. Both (A) and (B) have directivity when eliminating noise.

3.5.6   (C); (D), according to the analysis of the principle of action, the effect of histogram equalization is to sharpen the image and is closer to nonlinear filtering.

3.5.7   (A); (B).

3.5.8   (D).

3.5.9   (B). Since only the position of the object contour in the image is of concern, we only need to separate the object from the background.

Chapter 4 Frequency Domain Image Enhancement

4.1 Fourier Transform and Frequency Domain Enhancement

4.1.1   (A); (C).

4.1.2   (B).

4.1.3   (A); (D).

4.1.4   (C).

4.2 Frequency Domain Low-Pass Filter

4.2.1 (B); (C).

4.2.2 (A); (B); (D). These three filters have slow transitions between high and low frequencies, longer tail extensions, and weaker ringing.

4.2.3 (C).

4.3 Frequency Domain High-Pass Filter

4.3.1 (B), cutoff frequency can be different for different filters; (C), high-pass filtering cannot eliminate false contours.

4.3.2 (C). Histogram equalization can restore the dynamic range

4.3.3 (B); (D).

4.4 Band-Pass Filter and Band-Stop Filter

4.4.1 (A); (B), band-pass filter and band-stop filter are complementary to each other.

4.4.2 (C); (D).

4.4.3 (A); (B); (D). Combine filters with different cutoff frequencies.

4.4.4 (B).

4.4.5 (C), $N(u, v) = (-jA/2)[\delta(u - a, v - b) - \delta(u + a, v + b)]$, so these two pulses should be filtered out in the first and third quadrants.

4.4.6 (C), because band-pass filter and band-stop filter are complementary; (D), use low-pass filter and high-pass filter at the same time to remove the intermediate frequency.

4.4.7 (D).

4.5 Homomorphic Filter

4.5.1 (B); (D).

4.5.2 (C).

4.5-3 (D).

4.5.4 (A); (C).

Chapter 5 Image Restoration

5.1 Image Degradation and Model

5.1.1 (A); (B); (D).

5.1.2   (A).
5.1.3   (B).
5.1.4   (C).

5.2 Inverse Filtering

5.2.1   (A); (C).
5.2.2   (A); (B); (C).
5.2.3   (B).

5.3 Wiener Filtering

5.3.1   (A); (B); (D).
5.3.2   (A).
5.3.3   (C).

5.4 Geometric Distortion Correction

5.4.1   (B).
5.4.2   (C).
5.4.3   (A); (B); (D).

5.5 Image Repairing

5.5.1   (A); (B); (C).
5.5.2   (B); (D). Generally, a small area is also a small scale, but a large area does not necessarily have a large scale. For example, many regions with small areas need to be repaired. In this case, the total area is large (the sum of many small areas) but the scale is not large.
5.5.3   (C); (D).

Chapter 6 Color Image Enhancement

6.1 Color Vision

6.1.1   (A); (D).
6.1.2   (C); (D).
6.1.3   (A); (C).
6.1.4   (A); (B).

6.2 Color Model

6.2.1 (B); (D).
6.2.2 (B).
6.2.3 (D).
6.2.4 (A).
6.2.5 (C).
6.2.6 (C).

6.3 Pseudo-Color Enhancement

6.3.1 (C), from the shape of the three transformation functions and the histogram where the gray level is mainly concentrated in the middle, it can be seen that most of the pixels in the original image will pass the green filter, so there will be more green components in the color image.
6.3.2 (C); (D).
6.3.3 (D), only in this case, the input is a gray-scale image.

6.4 True-Color Enhancement

6.4.1 (A); (C); (D).
6.4.2 (B); (C).
6.4.3 (B).
6.4.4 (C), the I component diagram is an average diagram of the R component diagram, the G component diagram, and the B component diagram.
6.4.5 (D).

Chapter 7 Image Segmentation

7.1 Segmentation Definition and Method Classification

7.1.1 (D).
7.1.2 (C); (D).
7.1.3 (B), boundary technology uses discontinuity, regional technology uses similarity.

7.2 Differential Edge Detection

7.2.1 (A); (C).
7.2.2 (B).

7.2.3   (A); (D).

7.2.4   (D).

7.2.5   (B), the distance between the pixels on both sides of the oblique edge is $\sqrt{2}$ times as large as the distance between the pixels on both sides of the horizontal edge or vertical edge. The gray-scale difference of the pixels on both sides of the edge increases with the distance, so the response to the former is greater than that of the latter.

7.3 Active Contour Model

7.3.1   (A); (C).

7.3.2   (D), the large gray-scale transformation of the current contour indicates that there is still a gap from the final contour.

7.3.3   (B).

7.4 Thresholding Segmentation

7.4.1   (B).

7.4.2   (A); (D).

7.4.3   (C), when $P_1 > P_2$, the $p_1(z)$ curve moves up or the $p_2(z)$ curve moves down, and the intersection of the two curves moves to the right.

7.4.4   (B). Note that the transformed histogram can have many shapes, depending on how it is transformed.

7.4.5   (C); (D). Note that median filtering can eliminate noise but cannot increase the peak-to-valley gap.

7.4.6   (C). Note that not only the object but also the background can form clusters. The number of clusters is also related to the selected feature axis. In addition, note that clustering does not use the spatial information of pixels, but the degree of pixel correlation is related to the spatial information.

7.5 Threshold Selection Based on Transition Region

7.5.1   (A); (C); (D).

7.5.2   (B); (C).

7.5.3   (D).

7.6 Region Growing

7.6.1   (C); (D).

7.6.2   (A).

7.6.3   (C), when $T = 1$, the region obtained is the seed pixel itself, when $T = 2$, the region obtained is the letter L, and when $T = 4$, the region obtained is the full image.

Chapter 8 Primitive Detection

8.1 Interest Point Detection

8.1.1   (C).

8.1.2   (B); (C); (D).

8.1.3   (A); (C), the foreground and background are complementary

8.1.4   (C); (D).

8.1.5   (B).

8.2 Elliptical Object Detection

8.2.1   (C).

8.2.2   (A); (C); (D).

8.2.3   (B); (C).

8.3 Hough Transform

8.3.1   (A); (B); (D).

8.3.2   (B).

8.3.3   (C).

8.3.4   (B).

8.4 Generalized Hough Transform

8.4.1   (D).

8.4.2   (A); (C).

8.4.3   (C).

Chapter 9 Object Representation

9.1 Chain Code Representation of Contour

9.1.1   (B).
9.1.2   (A); (C).
9.1.3   (C).
9.1.4   (D).
9.1.5   (C).
9.1.6   (A).

9.2 Contour Signature

9.2.1   (D).
9.2.2   (C).
9.2.3   (B).

9.3 Polygonal Approximation of Contour

9.3.1   (C), the maximum error is the distance between the diagonal points of the pixel.
9.3.2   (A), the merging is carried out in series; (C), the polygon obtained by the split approximation is inscribed with the contour.
9.3.3   (B); (D). Note that for the circular object contour, the splitting method splits in half each time.

9.4 Hierarchical Representation of Objects

9.4.1   (B).
9.4.2   (D).
9.4.3   (A).

9.5 Bounding Region of Objects

9.5.1   (A); (D).
9.5.2   (B).
9.5.3   (C).

9.6 Skeleton Representation of the Object

9.6.1 (C), the skeleton line is the angular bisecting line.
9.6.2 (A).
9.6.3 (B).
9.6.4 (C); (D).

Chapter 10 Object Description

10.1 Basic Contour Description Parameters

10.1.1 (C), contour point has 4-direction connection.
10.1.2 (D).
10.1.3 (B).
10.1.4 (A), there are two diagonal segments on the contour.
10.1.5 (C).

10.2 Basic Region Description Parameters

10.2.1 (C).
10.2.2 (B).
10.2.3 (C).

10.3 Fourier Description of Contour

10.3.1 (D).
10.3.2 (A).
10.3.3 (B); (D).
10.3.4 (C), also called circular conjugate symmetry.

10.4 Wavelet Description of Contour

10.4.1 (C).
10.4.2 (B); (D).
10.4.3 (A); (C).
10.4.4 (B); (C).
10.4.5 (A); (C). Note that the number of coefficients is related to
        the accuracy, but the accuracy is not completely determined
        by the number of coefficients.

10.5 Region Description with Region Invariant Moments

10.5.1   (B); (D).
10.5.2   (D).
10.5.3   (B).

10.6 Object Relationship Description

10.6.1   (D).
10.6.2   (C).
10.6.3   (B).

Chapter 11 Texture Description Methods

11.1 Statistical Description of Texture

11.1.1   (B).
11.1.2   (A).
11.1.3   (D), all of them are some combinations of co-occurrence matrix values.
11.1.4   (B).
11.1.5   (D).

11.2 Structural Description of Texture

11.2.1   (C).
11.2.2   (A); (C). There are two types of vertices in the pattern, and two representations are required.
11.2.3   (D).
11.2.4   (C).

11.3 Spectral Description of Texture

11.3.1   (C); (D).
11.3.2   (B); (D).
11.3.3   (D).

Chapter 12 Shape Description Methods

12.1 Shape Compactness Descriptor

12.1.1   (B).
12.1.2   (A); (C).
12.1.3   (D).
12.1.4   (B), the ratio of the diagonal of the square to the side length.
12.1.5   (C).

12.2 Shape Complexity Descriptor

12.2.1   (C).
12.2.2   (A); (D).
12.2.3   (B).

12.3 Descriptor Based on Discrete Curvature

12.3.1   (B).
12.3.2   (B); (D).
12.3.3   (C).

12.4 Topological Descriptor

12.4.1   (D).
12.4.2   (B).
12.4.3   (B).

Chapter 13 Object classification

13.1 Invariant Cross-Ratio

13.1.1   (C).
13.1.2   (A); (B); (D).
13.1.3   (B); (C); (D).
13.1.4   (A); (C).
13.1.5   (A); (B).

13.2 Statistical Pattern Classification

13.2.1 (B); (D).
13.2.2 (B).
13.2.3 (C).

13.3 Support Vector Machines

13.3.1 (B).
13.3.2 (C); (D).
13.3.3 (D).

Index

Printed in the United States
by Baker & Taylor Publisher Services

Printed in the United States
by Baker & Taylor Publisher Services